COURAGE

COURAGE

The Politics of Life and Limb

RICHARD AVRAMENKO

University of Notre Dame Press

Notre Dame, Indiana

Notre Dame, Indiana 46556
www.undpress.nd.edu

Manufactured in the United States of America

Library of Congress Cataloging-in-Publication Data

Avramenko, Richard.
Courage : the politics of life and limb / Richard Avramenko.
p. cm.
Includes bibliographical references and index.
ISBN-13: 978-0-268-02039-2 (pbk. : alk. paper)
ISBN-10: 0-268-02039-6 (pbk. : alk. paper)
1. Courage—Political aspects. 2. Political ethics. I. Title.
JA79.A89 2011
172—dc23
2011025672

∞ *The paper in this book meets the guidelines for permanence and durability of the Committee on Production Guidelines for Book Longevity of the Council on Library Resources.*

For Julie Ruder

4 August 1984 – 11 July 2010

Contents

Preface

This book was twice born in pain. The original concept came to me as I tried to make sense of the September 11, 2001, attacks. On a bus, stuck in traffic on the Key Bridge in Washington, D.C., I watched the first plumes of smoke rising from the Pentagon. Later, from a rooftop in Georgetown, I listened to the fear expressed by friends and students. Where are the rest of the planes? Where will the next one hit? Is that smoke coming from State Department? We all had friends working at State Department. Later that day, in his first public statement, President Bush stated what many of us were thinking: "Freedom itself was attacked this morning by a faceless coward and freedom will be defended." I had, of course, already been thinking about courage and cowardice, but the political salience of the topic was not yet clear. On September 12, it became clear. Courage becomes a preeminently political category as soon as one abandons the long tradition of regarding it through a moral lens and, instead, examines it through a phenomenological lens. In other words, rather than inquiring into the virtue of a particular man or woman, one can ask about the nature of the community that emerges around varying ideas of courage. The events of September 11 forced me to answer—without sinking in the ugly morass of cultural relativism—how a singular political act can be regarded as heroic courage by one people but faceless cowardice by another.

The start of the production phase of this book coincided with the death of my fiancée, Julie Ruder. A careful reader, a challenging interlocutor, a patient listener, Julie knew every page of the manuscript. I think it is safe to say that no elections specialist in the world knew Tocqueville as well. As the central piece of my academic life, the project permeated our lives together. She was my first line of editorial defense, and, when my courage wavered, it was she who stood resolutely and kept our project together. It was Julie who revealed to me the connection between courage and love. I thus owe much to Julie for marching with me through the toughest parts of this book-writing campaign, and it is with a heavy heart that I write these final words. The bottle of wine we bought together several years ago in anticipation of this book's arrival stands as a steady reminder of all that was left unfinished with her passing. For the first time, I think I understand the depth of Achilles's pain on the beach at Troy when he too was "swallowed up by a black cloud of grief." It is to Julie that I dedicate this book.

Thanks are owed to many other people who have been involved, directly or indirectly, in the writing of this book. First among these are my teachers. Barry Cooper, though much too long ago for him to remember, guided me through my salad days at the University of Calgary. It was with Cooper that I first read Plato's *Laches* and a surprisingly large chunk of the canon. During my first kick at the graduate school can, at Carleton University, Tom Darby and Randy Newell immersed me in a world of Hegel, Nietzsche, and Heidegger. From this world I have not escaped—and I have no desire to do so. At Georgetown University, Joshua Mitchell showed me how to put it all together. To him I owe much, and I am deeply grateful for his continuing guidance and friendship. Much the same can be said of Gerald Mara and Mark Warren, both of whom generously read a grotesquely unpolished version of this book. Without them this book would not exist.

Many friends deserve thanks, not only for enduring my incessant talk of *Courage*, but for shaping the direction of the project itself. Almost every idea in this book has been discussed over fatted ox-thighs and bowls of wine with Mark Mitchell. These Homeric meals continue to fortify argument, body, and soul, and I am grateful for every moment with the Mitchell tribe. John von Heyking has been steadfast in exploring the boundaries of both *andreia* and *philia* with me. Von Heyking's knack for stripping arguments down to their bare bones has made this a better book; I am grateful for his careful reading of several chapters. Much the same can be said about my sisters-in-arms from graduate school. Farah Godrej and Rachel Templer have heard the story of *Courage* too many times to count. Their careful reading of various chapters and their steady friendship are imprinted on the heart of this book. Last, but certainly not least, to Shayne Butcher I owe much. It is from him that I have always learned the practical lessons of manly courage.

Thanks also go to my colleagues at the University of Wisconsin–Madison, especially in the Department of Political Science. From limiting my service work to the trivial, to providing teaching release, to sponsoring a roundtable on an early draft, my colleagues have given much support for the completion of this project. The roundtable was especially fruitful, and I owe a large debt to Andy Sabl for coming from UCLA to chair the event and commenting in detail on the manuscript. Laura McClure, John Zumbrunnen, Jimmy Klausen, Howard Schweber, Helen Kinsella, and Gaelan Murphy were incredibly generous with their time and ideas, and the book is much better for having passed through their hands.

Finally, I am grateful to the University of Notre Dame Press for publishing this book. In times of shortening lists and tightening budgets, they took on a project outside the mainstream of political science and political theory. Rebecca DeBoer has been the consummate professional in steering the project into port. The anonymous reviewers read the manuscript in the spirit it was intended and were incredibly generous in their comments and suggestions. I thank them both wholeheartedly. Elisabeth Magnus's painstaking and meticulous copyediting has made the book much more readable than I could ever make it. It used to be de rigueur to thank someone for typing the manuscript. Modern word processing has eliminated this need. Thus all errors in the book are thanks to me.

ONE

(Re)Introducing Courage

The Retreat of Courage

Man is nothing other than what he makes of himself, and nothing is more difficult to make than a courageous man. It is for precisely this reason that courage, as a topic of serious political and social debate, is not popular. At dinner parties it occasionally has its moments, and as a theme for ethicists and moralists it is afforded some serious consideration now and then. However, scholarly discussion regarding our social and political lives, for the most part, eschews serious discussion of courage. This has not always been so, and in the history of political thought one finds serious attention and praise given to courage by thinkers as diverse as Plato, Aristotle, Aquinas, Mencius, Bacon, Montaigne, and so on. Much the same can be said of the history of literature, poetry, biography, music, and, for that matter, almost every realm of human artistic endeavor. Only in the modern and especially the postmodern age has courage retreated from the forefront of social and political considerations. There are various reasons for this retreat, but central is that to talk about courage, as will become abundantly evident in the following considerations, is also to talk about manliness. Thus to talk about political order and its relationship to courage is to be exclusionary, perhaps even sexist—a charge all prudent thinkers need to fear.

Not only do we risk excluding the feminine when bringing courage into political considerations, we risk excluding those who do not live up to the difficult standard presented by courage. Although many modern thinkers regard it as a right and proper virtue, courage cannot be a requisite of political considerations and participation because making it a requisite would be tantamount to erecting barriers to full civic participation. The rationale here is straightforward: courage is a virtue possessed by few, and if one must possess courage to be a good citizen then there will necessarily be few good citizens. As such, many political theorists reject this virtue rather than hold it up as an integral part of general civic participation and good character.[1] For example, Mark Warren argues that participation in democracy and democratic institutions should not require courage at all. If democratic institutions function as they ought, they are "reducing and containing the risks of political engagement."[2] The task of democracy is to ensure that citizens do "not require heroism" and to "protect spaces for moral persuasion—the most fragile of public spaces—so that moral voice requires something less than heroism."[3] Good citizenship, it seems, ought to be attainable regardless of one's courage. And to push this position perhaps to its logical conclusion, if one demands of one's fellow citizens the virtue of courage by, say, creating anything resembling a confrontational arena of participation, one is a bad citizen.

There is further reason for the retreat of courage from our political and social considerations. To contend that good political order requires courage is to say the coward has no place in political life. We know that not all people are courageous, which means that at least a few people writing about politics will disqualify themselves from political participation. After all, it would be very difficult to hold courage a necessary virtue for political participation yet know oneself to be a coward. In other words, only the courageous will be inclined to say that courage is important, and because thinkers are a notoriously timid lot it stands to reason that scholars not only ignore courage but often reject it altogether. People are hardly inclined to argue that they themselves are inadequate for their own topic.

Much the same can be said of the virtues in general. In the premodern world, especially in the world of the ancient polis, talk about virtue (arête) was de rigueur. Courage was considered part of virtue, and the central task of the polis was to assist in the fullest possible unfolding of the virtues and perfection of its citizens. However, as William Galston points out, two generations in the West have functioned on the assumption that one can, and should, sever the liberal polity from concerns not only of courage but of the virtues themselves.[4] This view of virtue, and of courage in particular, is the progeny of Immanuel Kant's proclamation that the good citizen is not necessarily the same as the virtuous individual. Kant's point is very clear: man, he claims, "even if he is not morally good in himself, is nevertheless compelled to be a good citizen. As hard as it may sound, the problem of setting up a state can be solved even by a nation of devils (so long as they possess understanding)."[5] Put otherwise, the virtues, or the perfection of individuals, are unnecessary so long as we adequately rationalize our institutions and procedures.

John Rawls is central in promulgating this argument against "perfectionism." Rawls posits that the good polity and its institutions cannot aim for the development of "perfected" citizens because such a goal requires an unachievable agreement on how a perfectly virtuous citizen would look. As Rawls says, people "do not have an agreed criterion of perfection that can be used as a principle for choosing between institutions. To acknowledge any such standard would be, in effect, to accept a principle that might lead to a lesser religious or other liberty, if not to a loss of freedom altogether to advance many of one's spiritual ends."[6] As such, through much of the twentieth century—especially the latter half—the push was toward a political order predicated on the basic structures and institutional procedures of the polity rather than on virtuous citizens. Because the virtues are manifold they must also be relative, and if they are relative there can be no requirement in a pluralistic polity of any virtue. To demand one virtue of citizens, such as courage, might very well infringe on another virtue, such as passivity, and because all virtues are relative one cannot assert courage to be better than passivity. In other words, one can neither say that courage is better than cowardice nor that cowardice is better than courage—one can say, however, that our political and social organization should demand neither.

The Charge of Reason

Looking closely at such attacks on courage and the virtues, it is evident that not all virtues are under attack. What remain insulated from attack, or more precisely, what these attacks tacitly promote, are the noetic virtues. For example, discussions of political order reject courage because it privileges physical capacities instead of intellectual virtues—to exclude cowards is to exclude them for failings in action, not failings in the capacity to reason. While the general run of humanity may not be capable of living up to the difficult standards that courage and most of the other virtues demand, the general run of humanity is capable of reasoning, at least to some degree. Accompanying the retreat of courage, then, are the emergence and elevation of an alternative way of regarding human beings. This alternative informs large swaths of modern social and political order. No longer are human beings regarded as most fully developed when they realize, or at least strive to realize, the moral virtues. No longer does the complete human being need to be pious, just, temperate, or courageous. Instead, the fully developed human need only be intellectually virtuous. Courage thus finds itself in constant retreat from the charge of rationality.

We see, then, two divergent ideas of human beings in our discussion of political order. Political science, as a discipline, is an attempt to construct general principles about the way the world of politics works. But when we say the "world of politics," we mean a world shared by a plurality of human beings. So political science, as obvious as this may seem, is concerned with human beings, with how they organize themselves and how they behave together. Because it concerns human beings, it must have at its center an adequate idea of human beings. This idea of human beings—this philosophical anthropology—then guides and grounds the search for good political order and the understanding of disorder. Modern political science, and the social sciences at large, tend toward a certain philosophical anthropology, often called the rational actor model, sometimes the utilitarian model, sometimes the *homo economicus* model. The basic principle of this anthropology is this: human beings are rational creatures employing their rationality instrumentally to further their happiness. There is then a catalog of preferences, interests, or values, each of which contributes to this happiness, each of which is pursued with this capacity to reason instrumentally.

Social scientists, unless they have descended deeply into some second-order reality, recognize that human behavior is often complex, imperfect, limited, self-contradictory, and unpredictable. Therefore, for the most part, they do not wed theories of political order to strict notions of material preferences. Jon Elster, for example, excoriates economics as a discipline for failing to recognize that the end of nearly all human action is to maximize emotional satisfaction. Economists, as he so cuttingly puts it, almost universally ignore emotions and have thus "totally neglected the most important aspect of their subject matter."[7] The assumption that material goods are the end of rational action ignores the fact that quite often people prefer emotional pleasures to material goods and, importantly, that "emotional satisfaction is largely (but not only) derived from encounters with other people rather than from material goods and that, moreover, these are encounters not mediated by the market ('Can't buy me love')."[8] This, compounded with the facts that emotions are very difficult to measure, that people are not often good at rationally managing their emotional lives, that emotions and tastes may even be detrimental to our economic interest, and, finally, that emotions "are only to a small extent under the control of the will," poses some serious problems for the vision of man as a rational actor.[9]

Beyond the emotional objection to the rational actor model is another problem rarely, if ever, discussed with regard to this philosophical anthropology. Supposing that we recognize a manifold catalog of values, tastes, preferences, *and emotions* that an independent rational actor can pursue, we are left with one decisive problem: no matter how diverse this table of preferences is, no matter how it is shuffled, the model proceeds with one preference steadfastly at the top—self-preservation. Self-preservation is *the* presupposition that underwrites this model. To enjoy the material goods we have rationally pursued, to enjoy the emotional satisfaction of a material good or an emotionally satisfying relationship that we have more or less pursued rationally, we must stay alive. Some thinkers, like Thomas Hobbes, describe self-preservation as the right of nature, something so obvious that we can construct the first law of nature around it.[10] Others, like John Finnis, go so far as to call it "a self-evidently basic form of good (or basic human value)."[11] The problem with this presupposition is that human beings (and this can be vividly, empirically verified) do not always behave this way. We can point to many instances where people are willing to risk life and limb for the sake of something other than life and limb. It is for precisely this reason that courage needs to be brought back into our political discourse. Courage discloses a disruption of the hierarchy of human preferences that predicates the rational actor model.

The rational actor model provides that human beings make cost-benefit calculations. We are willing to pay more and more for something, depending on how much we value that thing. To reap the benefit of that for which we have borne the costs, however, we must remain alive. For example, I am *always* willing to pay a dollar for a muffin—if I am feeling peckish, the muffin has a value equivalent to a dollar. I might also be willing to give all my money for that same muffin, were I starving to death. In this case, the value of the muffin increases relative to my hunger. However, and this is of crucial importance, I am never willing to die for the sake of the muffin. If I am not starving, I simply do not care enough to risk life and limb for the sake of a muffin. And even if I were starving, dying for the sake of a muffin would defeat the purpose of the muffin. Much the same can be said with regard to any material good, or even any emotional good.

This said, the rational actor model is a good story. It explains a great deal about how we live together, about the political and social order we create for ourselves, and about how people behave with regard to muffins and other things in our empirical world. Courage, however, picks up where this story leaves off. Courage tells us the part of the story where self-preservation is bumped off the top of the preference hierarchy. Courage obtrudes when, contrary to the usual calculus of the rational actor model, one is willing to die for the sake of, say, a muffin. In other words, courage obtrudes when our average everyday relationship to life and death is suspended. In this sense, then, to inquire into courage is to inquire into a phenomenon that supplements, perhaps even completes, the story of how human beings live together. Courage tells about how we die together.

Cares and Fundamental Cares

To talk about courage in conjunction with politics is thus to throw the conventional way of thinking about human preferences into disarray. It is to say that there are two discrete models for understanding political action. With one model, we can talk about making rational choices regarding ends that we must be alive to enjoy. With the other, we can talk about courageous actions pertaining to things that transcend our physical existence. In short, we have a rational actor model and a courageous actor model. Yet the difference is not simply alternative ways of pursuing an end. It is not merely the rational pursuit of an end versus the courageous pursuit of an end. Instead, revealed is a basic difference in how we care about things. Whereas the rational actor model demonstrates things we *care* about, the courageous actor model discloses that which we care about *fundamentally*. In somewhat prosaic terms, if one acts for the sake of something, one probably cares about it. If, however, one is willing to risk life and limb for it, then one cares about it *fundamentally*.[12] Of course, it is possible to pursue rationally something we care fundamentally about, but it is hardly likely that we would pursue something courageously about which we do not care fundamentally. People are seldom inclined to risk life and limb for things about which they do not care deeply. We put life and limb on the line only when we care fundamentally about something.

This said, a definition of courage can now be offered: courage is risking life and limb *for the sake of something about which we care fundamentally*. With this emphasis, courage emerges as more than a virtue—it is a revelatory phenomenon. What is being suggested here is that courage, like most phenomena, can be regarded through two different lenses. On the one hand, there is the conventional lens magnifying the virtue itself. It magnifies the sort of person who exemplifies courage and, importantly, the boundaries and limits of what can properly be called courage.[13] This is precisely the sort of lens one peers through when engaging in, for example, the debates between liberals and civic republicans. When Galston, for instance, discusses virtue, he is alerting us to certain habits and practices necessary for maintaining the liberal polity. More specifically, virtues, including courage, are needed to buttress "the two key features" of liberal society: "individualism and diversity."[14] For Michael Sandel, similar virtues are brought to bear for republican ends rather than liberal. The debate, as he informs us, circles around two concepts of autonomy, and it is not clear that there is any enmity per se between the two camps.[15] What is clear is that the lens employed in this debate illuminates the virtues that most effectively lend themselves to their fundamental cares. Let us call this the empirical lens.

The second lens, while certainly lending clarity to the nature of the virtues, directs its interpretive power in a slightly different direction. Rather than asking, "What is courage?" or "How can courage be employed for the sake of our fundamental care?" it asks, "What does the invocation of a powerful concept like courage tell us about our collective lives?" or "What does courage tell us about how we exist meaningfully in the world?" In other words, this lens, which we might refer to as existential, magnifies certain truths about the community from which the concept emerges. It reveals, as my italicized definition of courage suggests, basic "for-the-sakes-of" or "cares." If, for example, we peek through the existential lens at the liberal–civic republican debate, it illuminates the various virtues invoked for the sake of a shared care of existing together as autonomous individuals. It reveals that both parties hold autonomy to be integral for a meaningfully shared world. It also reveals what they do not hold to be integral. For example, neither Galston nor Sandel suggests that the virtues be brought to bear for the sake of, say, honor, or the glory of God, which would make for a different debate indeed. The revelation of what we do not care about fundamentally is as important as what this lens reveals.

Courage, however, is more than one virtue amid a catalog of virtues. Because courage is, at bottom, risking life and limb for the sake of something, it is the existential virtue par excellence. In revealing "for-the-sakes-of" for which one is willing to die, it discloses fundamental cares. In disclosing that which supersedes self-preservation, courage reveals something beyond the physical being of our individual lives. It reveals a distinction between physical life and that which is greater than physical life, a distinction constituting the very basis of transcendence. Transcendence is usually invoked to describe a realm of existence higher than the mundane. Transcendence, however, need not pertain to the divine. To transcend literally means "to climb over." Courage reveals the transcendent character of human existence. It discloses human beings looking beyond their empirical existence. Courage is thus the existential virtue par excellence because, in disclosing fundamental cares, it brings into brighter light the distinction between empirical and existential. In bringing fundamental cares to light, courage reveals both the mereness of physical life and the transcendent possibilities of human life. Courage, in toto, reveals meaningfulness in human existence.[16]

The power of this second lens should thus be manifest. The existential lens magnifies the kernel of our very being. Human beings *qua* human beings have the capacity to care fundamentally. It might be argued that other creatures care fundamentally as well, but only human beings care fundamentally about things other than their own empirical lives. Of course human beings can (and ought to) care about their physical lives, but, as will become evident in the following chapters, caring fundamentally about one's physical life is the hallmark of a coward. Other creatures might appear to care about things other than their physical being, but a simple biology of genetic maximization is adequate to explain away these anthropomorphic views of animals. Humans, for example, are the only creatures that can care fundamentally about, say, abstract ideas. While a dog might put itself between a child and an attacker, it does this because said child is positively associated with food and the exigencies of biological life. A dog does not behave courageously because it thinks it would be un-dogly to run away. Alternatively, a man can stand courageously because to do otherwise would be unmanly. Only humans are capable of caring fundamentally about things that add meaning to life. Only humans care fundamentally about things transcending their empirical selves.

To claim that humans are unique in their capacity to care is not altogether new. In a chapter of his *Being and Time* called "Care as the Being of Dasein," Martin Heidegger argues that "Dasein's Being reveals itself as *care*."[17] His meaning is fairly straightforward: because human beings are nothing more than what they make of themselves, their very nature is determined by what they care about in the world in which they live. Their nature, which is to say their existence, is coterminous with their actions in their world. Thus, when human beings act, they do it for the sake of something about which they care. And care, Heidegger says, is not to be understood merely in the sense of "will, wish, addiction, and urge" because these types of phenomena are themselves founded on a human being's cares.[18] If we will something, our will points toward a care. If we wish something to come about, our wish points toward a care. Similarly, we can become addicted to something or have urges for something, both of which speak to a care. Of course, we can be consumed by addictions and urges, but this consumption only further discloses that one's cares lie at the core of one's being. Thus, as Heidegger puts it, "Dasein, in the very basis of its Being, is care."[19]

Because acting courageously puts one's existence at stake, it binds one's fundamental cares to that same stake. As courage reveals "the stuff one is made of," it reveals what one cares about fundamentally. To illustrate this point, Heidegger recounts an ancient fable:

> Once when "Care" was crossing a river, she saw some clay; she thoughtfully took up a piece and began to shape it. While she was meditating on what she had made, Jupiter came by. "Care" asked him to give it spirit, and this he gladly granted. But when she wanted her name to be bestowed upon it, he forbade this, and demanded that it be given his name instead. While "Care" and Jupiter were disputing, Earth arose and desired that her own name be conferred to the crea-

> ture, since she had furnished it with part of her body. They asked Saturn to be their arbiter, and he made the following decision, which seemed a just one: "Since you, Jupiter, have given its spirit, you shall receive that spirit at its death; and since you, Earth, have given its body, you shall receive its body. But since 'Care' first shaped this creature, she shall possess it as long as it lives. And because there is now a dispute among you as to its name, let it be called 'homo,' for it is made out of humus (earth)."[20]

The fable is significant because it speaks of a primordial understanding of the relationship between human beings and Care. First, it demonstrates that human being owes its very shape and existence to Care. Second, it demonstrates that the human belongs to Care "as long as it lives." That is, between birth and death, his basic existential structure is given by Care. Third, it speaks a familiar language; humans are composed of body (earth) and spirit. In other words, humans have their empirical being and a way of being that transcends the empirical. But most importantly the myth demonstrates that it is Care that joins these two ways of being. As Heidegger puts it, "In care this entity has the 'source' of its Being . . . [and] the entity is not released from this source but is held fast, dominated by it through and through as long as this entity 'is in the world.'"[21] Thus, when we will, wish, or have an urge for a care, something about the way we exist in the world is revealed. When, however, one acts courageously—when one risks physical being for the sake of a care—one discloses the care that most accords with one's existential structure. In revealing fundamental cares, courage also reveals the basic structure of existence.

Saying that the basic structure of human existence is care brings to mind an important school of feminist psychology. In *In a Different Voice*, Carol Gilligan argues that human beings per se are not defined by care—rather, this distinction falls to women. It is women, Gilligan argues, who "not only define themselves in a context of human relationship but also judge themselves in terms of their ability to care."[22] Men, on the other hand, tend to "focus on individuation and individual achievement." When this focus "extends into adulthood . . . maturity is equated with personal autonomy,

[and] concern with relationships appears as a weakness of women rather than as a human strength."[23] In short, Gilligan argues that women function in their daily lives by a different ethic—an "ethic of care."[24] This ethic of care—also known as feminist ethics—stands in contrast to the ethic more natural to men, which Gilligan refers to as justice ethics.[25] The capacity to make objective, rational judgments about right and wrong predicates this ethical system. It relies on the actor's ability to extract himself imaginatively from his context before making moral choices. For example, one should not dwell on one's situation when making moral choices; instead, one ought to behave as though wearing "a veil of ignorance," to borrow an expression of John Rawls.[26] Such a "veil" ensures that one's own interests, one's own particular relationships, do not becloud one's rational, universalist, ethical reasoning. In other words, justice ethics is a deontological moral system revolving around universal categories, such as "human being" and "rights." It is a "masculine" ethics that stands in contrast to the feminine ethic of care revolving around the local and the particular, such as "my friends" and "my family." With the ethics of care, then, humans are not viewed as separate, physical beings engaging in endless "conflict over life and property that can be solved by logical deduction."[27] Instead, actors in any moral dilemma are "arrayed not as opponents in a contest of rights but as members of a network of relationships on whose continuation they all depend."[28] To extract oneself from this network is tantamount to denying the very basis of one's existence because to be human in a meaningful way is to exist in a world of relationships. The ethics of care is thus predicated on a "relational ontology,"[29] meaning that our existence is bound up in our relations with others. The contrast, then, is between "a self defined through separation and a self delineated through connection."[30]

How these selves come to light further highlights the distinction between the two ethics. Just as justice ethics insists on reason and logical deductions to resolve conflict, self-understanding comes from the same source. The ethic therefore depends on a certain level of intellectual virtue that develops as people emerge from childhood. Care ethics, on the other hand, is instinctive and intuitive. As Gilligan points out, the good of a life filled with connections and relationships (colloquially known as friends and family) is something women "know" all along. They understand very early on that a life "favoring the separateness of the individual self over connection to others, and leaning toward an autonomous life of work than toward the interdependence of love and care," makes a life "out of balance."[31] Men, she tells us, recognize the importance of intimacy, relationships, and care as well, but not until midlife—"something women have known from the beginning . . . [but] because that knowledge in women has been considered 'intuitive' or 'instinctive,' a function of anatomy coupled with destiny, psychologists have neglected to describe its development."[32]

A certain irony thus comes to light. Courage, when regarded through the traditional empirical lens, tells us who is manly and who is unmanly. It tells us how one man separates himself from other men. Harvey Mansfield, for instance, defines manliness as "confidence in the face of risk."[33] Manliness and courage, it seems, go hand in hand. Courage, he tells us, reveals basic differences between the sexes: how they speak, how they assert themselves as individuals, how they regard territoriality, and how they make distinctions in general. Regarded through the existential lens, however, courage reveals humans, both men and women, as caring creatures. By examining courage through an existential lens, we are not being exclusionary on the basis of sex. In fact, in revealing fundamental cares, courage envelopes both the feminine and masculine. A point of convergence is revealed, where humans in general can be regarded as creatures intuitively and instinctively concerned with things transcending their empirical, rational selves. As the following chapters demonstrate, courage, examined through the existential lens, reveals a close kinship between relational ontologies and meaningful existence. It reveals both men and women as creatures defined by care; it reveals a "manly" world of caring and self-overcoming and, at the same time, a womanly world of courage.

The importance of courage in the study of political order should be coming to light. To construct general principles about the world of politics, we need a decent understanding of human existence. By looking at courage we are able to gain an understanding of how and what actors *are* at bottom because, when people are willing to risk life and limb, they disclose their fundamental cares. Such a disclosure reveals the shape and limits of their very being. It reveals the boundaries of their lived world that cannot be crossed without disruption of that simple and ever-so-rationally organized hierarchy of human goods. It reveals the threshold beyond which self-preservation ceases to be their first law of nature. Courage trumps not only the preference for self-preservation but the preference for other-preservation as well. It is as likely to result in the killing of others as in the destruction of one's own existence. And this holds for men and women alike. The importance of courage in our political life is manifest: courage sheds light on why people are willing to kill or be killed.

Communities of Care

Courage reveals cares, and these cares point beyond the empirical self. As such, they are necessarily bound up with other human beings. To borrow again from the ethics of care, courage is part of a relational ontology. To say this, however, is also to say that a courageous act cannot be performed in isolation. It pertains only to human action because it can neither recognize itself nor be recognized on its own. It cannot exist independent of human beings. There is, for example, no Platonic *eidos* of courage. Though we speak of transcendence, we speak only of finite transcendence. Thus courage exists only as it pertains to human action. It is humans who determine which actions are courageous; therefore, there is actually no such thing as courage—there are only courageous actions and courageous people. Insofar as courageous actions need to be recognized as such by other human beings, and insofar as courage points beyond the courageous actor, it is impossible for an individual to designate himself as courageous. This determination needs to come from without. An individual can be considered courageous only within the context of the community in which he acts. Courage, as part of a relational ontology, depends on a plurality of human beings.

The problem with this understanding of courage is that there is no universal agreement on what constitutes courage. For example, let us invoke—although it is something of a cliché—the image of the modern soldier throwing himself on a grenade to save, say, his buddies or a room full of schoolchildren. Few images better evoke care and the other-directedness of courage. Yet if we imagine the same soldier throwing himself on the same grenade to save, say, a muffin, there will be much less agreement as to whether the action is courageous. Even more vividly, if nobody or nothing at all is in the room (not even the muffin), either to bear witness or to be preserved by the action, the act simply cannot be called courageous. More likely, it will be considered foolish. After all, what kind of person throws himself on a grenade for no reason? Yet the physical act is identical: a man throws his body over an exploding grenade. The difference is not merely that self-preservation ceases to be his fundamental care but that in the latter example the courageous action has no meaning. Throwing oneself on a grenade for the sake of nothing is meaningless. In the former example, broad agreement that the action had some meaning is possible; some general agreement can be found that the end for the sake of which the soldier threw himself on the grenade was meaningful. What this means, then, is that the fundamental care revealed by the soldier's courage coincides with that of the people witnessing the action. Courage reveals the fundamental care of the courageous actor, but for it to be considered courage it must participate in a community of shared fundamental cares. If a consensus on a definition of courage is reached, then courage reveals *communities of care.*

Yet even as it is part of a relational ontology and even as it reveals fundamental cares and communities of care, courage is not something we choose. Take, for example, the soldier throwing himself on the grenade—it is unlikely that the action involved choice. In such situations, one reacts intuitively or instinctually. Choice indicates a decision based on principle, logical deduction, and rationality about acting courageously. One does not *choose* to act courageously in a given situation. Instead, one *musters* courage. Although acting rationally might itself require courage, courageous actions emerge from beneath the liminality of reason. There is, then, no reason to consider communities of care to be chosen, or even open to a rational accounting. Like courage, their source lies beneath the liminality of reason.

Modes of Articulation

These communities of care point to another aspect of political life that courage reveals: the mode by which we establish and maintain these relationships. Normally, human beings are thought to create and to perpetuate their communities around their capacity to speak a shared language. In this case, speech functions as the joints of the relational world. Speaking, or being articulate, is therefore a mode of articulation. Usually when we say someone is articulate we mean one is well-spoken, that one has the capacity to give words to thoughts. *Articulate* also means that one can express thoughts in a succession of coherently connected words expressing a larger idea. To be articulate is to have the capacity to fit things together into a coherent whole. It is to unite by forming a joint or joints. If, however, we regard the basis of community to be shared cares rather than a shared capacity for speech, then a path is opened to exploring alternative ways of envisioning these cares. Community need not depend on words to be articulated. We need not be articulate to be articulated. We need not be logical to be relational.

Thus, whereas most visions of political order resort to reason as the basis of community, courage reveals other modes. For example, social contract theory depends heavily on reason as the mode of articulation. Much the same can be said in modern democratic theory, which is predicated on the principle that rational, discursive association will, or at least ought to, form the bedrock of political communities. Yet if we think carefully about social contract theory, there is a hint of something other than speech in play. When social contract theories suggest that humans can find themselves implicitly, or tacitly, in a contract, there is an admission that we can be jointed together without words, articulated without reason, connected without *logoi.* Jean-Jacques Rousseau, as will become clear in the chapter on moral courage, suggests that communities of care are articulated by emotions and feelings, such as pity and compassion. Feelings, as opposed to reason, are not amenable to rational explication. They are, quite literally, illogical; they are mysterious, discerned by intuition and instinct. Hence, when we look at our political communities through the lens of courage we can more readily observe the contours and nuances of human relations formed by modes of articulation other than the discursive.

Order of Engagement

There are as many kinds of cares as the human imagination permits. If we can imagine something, we can care about it. There are, however, finite fundamental cares. Few of us can imagine a long list of things for the sake of which we would risk life and limb. In fact, as fundamental cares go, it is possible to identify concretely a limited number. For instance, in our own liberal world the U.S. Marine Corps motto, "Death before dishonor," does not sound completely foreign to us. While not a credo for everyone, it expresses an abiding fundamental care: honor. It is not by coincidence that this credo stems from a military culture because honor is usually associated with warriors and martially oriented cultures. As such, honor is closely related to a certain type of courage: *martial courage*. It might be convenient for politicians to believe that their soldiers fight for the sake of liberty or autonomy, for the sake of the king, for the fatherland, or for the sake of some other abstract principle. However, the fact of the matter is that once soldiers are in battle, what keeps them on the line, what prevents them from fleeing, what inspires them to march directly into harm's way, what permits them to act heroically, is a fundamental care for honor. Of course, what exactly is meant by honor needs to be determined, and this is what the next chapter of this book explores.

The next chapter looks at martial courage as the ideal type of courage. It is ideal not in any Platonic sense but because when the idea of courage is invoked one typically envisions warriors in battle. A cursory glance at the literature pertaining to courage bears this out; the most usual and most worshipped type of courage is precisely the sort on display in war and battle. It is *andreia*, as the ancient Greeks called it, "manly courage." It is the courage of the Homeric hero, the courage of David facing Goliath, the heroism of a soldier throwing himself (meaningfully) on a hand grenade, or the courage of the superheroes in our childhood comic books. These descriptions and portrayals of *andreia*, both by commentators and by the warriors themselves, reveal over and over not just a disdain for self-preservation but also an abiding care for honor. One need only think of the Spartan way of life as a paradigmatic example of this community of care.

It may, nevertheless, seem strange to refer to any type of courage as ideal. We have established, after all, that courage is defined by its context—that there is no universal agreement on what constitutes courage, empirically speaking. One is no more correct in holding Gandhi and his nonviolence as the paragon of courage than the infamous Charge of the Light Brigade. Courage, however, has not always been regarded so equivocally. In the Homeric world courage was the exclusive domain of warriors and was easily determined: Did the warrior stay in the fight with his brothers-in-arms, or did he turn and flee dishonorably for the sake of himself? It was a simple standard. The good man had the mettle to forgo his own safety (in battle) for the sake of others. In Sparta there was but one type of courage: martial courage. Only later, and this is the story unveiled in this book, have other types of courage been imagined.

Specifically, this book tells the story of how political courage, moral courage, and economic courage developed either in opposition or in supplement to martial courage. It is a story of how martial courage, with violence as its attendant mode of articulation, became inadequate for the imaginative reality of more differentiated human relations. It tells a story of other types of courage emerging in tandem with the development of different fundamental cares. At the same time, however, it tells the story of the abiding power of martial courage and the central place it holds in our political self-understanding. Though we may reject martiality and reject honor as the pivotal point of our shared meaningful existence, the traditional place of martial courage as the ideal type of courage is not easily jettisoned, culturally, logically, or imaginatively.

This said, the purpose of this book is not to hold martial courage up as the highest type of courage. Instead, this book provides a phenomenological starting point and basic hermeneutical language for recognizing and describing fundamental cares and modes of articulation that range beyond the modern, Western obsession with autonomy and rationally articulated communities. Thus, while the effort here is not to rank these different types of courage, readers themselves may rank the following types of courage, and this is to be expected. Because courage is bound up with fundamental cares, and because these fundamental cares are associated with different modes of articulation, it only stands to reason that one type of courage may be preferred to another.

Should the reader be predisposed to care about honor, she will quite naturally regard martial courage not just as a type but as the highest type. However, just as martial courage reveals a fundamental care for honor, it also uncovers violence as the attendant mode of articulation. In warrior cultures, where honor is the fundamental care, the joints between human beings are established and maintained by violence and the continuous threat of violence. This is a fairly obvious claim when we consider how combatants are connected to combatants on the other side of a battle line—adversaries establish and maintain a relationship through violence. Less obvious is the violence that articulates comrades in arms and the larger community of care. Often, especially in the liberal democratic West, we either ignore this fact or, acknowledging it, reject it out of hand as a decent mode of articulation. Communities revolving around honor are often hierarchical, and hierarchies are necessarily predicated on and maintained by violence or the threat of violence, a relationship Michel Foucault understood well.[34]

Thus one can easily imagine a distaste for martial courage, honor, and violence. It is, however, more difficult to let go of the selflessness and transcendent character of martial courage. As such, one can easily imagine people having a taste for another type of courage explored in this book: political courage, moral courage, or economic courage. In fact, as has already been suggested, one can very easily imagine people with no taste for courage at all—and, accordingly, no taste for this book. In any case, the point in setting down these descriptions of courage is not to rank one as preferable to another. Instead, the task is to invoke courage as a revelatory phenomenon shedding light on radically different ways human beings can organize themselves in pursuit of a meaningful, shared existence.

Courage illuminates the meaningfulness in human action that contradicts our usual, liberal understanding of collective life. If the reader finds one of the types of courage preferable to another, then as much is revealed about the reader's cares and political commitments as about courage. And I will consider the book a success, at least by this measure.

What follows, then, is an analysis of four different manifestations of courage, along with the fundamental cares and modes of articulation attending them. The study begins with a rather sympathetic presentation of martial courage in the ancient world. By invoking the Spartan case, it shows good reason for the enduring appeal of courage throughout human history. The Spartans epitomize both the possibility for unselfish citizenship and human transcendence and the incredible human capacity for violence and destruction. From the story of the Spartans, chapter 2 demonstrates that martial courage and honor are not merely artifacts of the ancient world—they still pertain in the modern world. Martial courage appeals because it can underwrite, if not beget, a type of citizenship and way of being together in the world that provides deep and meaningful relationships.

Chapter 3 begins with an earnest objection to martial courage by asking, If this is courage in its most traditional milieu and appearance, must we then accept that all of our relationships will be predicated on violence? If we esteem martial courage, must we always live under the threat of violent death? This chapter proceeds with the invocation of a moment in classical Athens where precisely these questions are asked. What emerges is a courage I refer to as political courage. In this vision of courage, epitomized by Plato's Socrates, self-preservation is trumped by a fundamental care for justice. The long-standing model of Achillean courage and the Spartan love of honor are transmogrified into a completely new moral system—a moral system that opens the way to a novel form of political life. Associated with the displacement of honor by justice is the kernel of a new mode of articulation. Whereas martial courage joins people together with violence, political courage turns to discourse, which is to say, it turns to human reason. So in the case of *political courage, discourse* is brought to bear for the sake of *justice.*

Chapter 4 turns to the appearance of moral courage and heroism in the work of Jean-Jacques Rousseau. For Rousseau, as for other thinkers both before and after, courage has an enduring appeal. But for Rousseau, unlike the thinkers who developed the concept of political courage, the turn to reason and discourse is as problematic for human community as the reliance on violence in martial courage. Rousseau's thought develops a different type of courage that reveals autonomy as the fundamental care. This is not to say that honor and justice are completely rejected as human goods. But Rousseau's idea of courage points to a way of being in which human beings are not dependent on external forces for their happiness. And because Rousseau is highly suspicious of both reason and violence as acceptable modes of articulation, he turns to sentiment—specifically, to compassion—to connect human beings to one another. For Rousseau, because courage is not a rational capacity, it makes no sense to make it dependent on human reason; moral courage is like martial courage in that it resides on the subrational aspect of our humanity. *Moral courage*, then, brings *compassion* to bear for the sake of *autonomy*.

The appearance of economic courage and heroism in Alexis de Tocqueville's *Democracy in America* is the focus of chapter 5. Whereas others seek to retain all that is good about the martial virtues but reject violence, Tocqueville sees a different possibility emerge in the American democratic milieu. Americans have not rejected martial courage and honor altogether; nor have they simply reformulated martial courage by, say, associating it with an alternative fundamental care and a more domestic mode of articulation. Instead, they have accomplished an amazing feat: they have managed to turn the very definition of courage on its head. Rather than claim that courage—be it martial, political, or moral—is by definition about selfless acts, they hold acts of self-aggrandizement in high esteem. Tocqueville observes that while greed and the love of gain have almost universally been condemned as vices, in America they adopt the color of courageous acts. Thus courage in the economic realm—risking life and limb for the sake of wealth—is an honorable pursuit in the democratic way of life. In *economic courage*, then, *exchange* is brought to bear for the sake of *well-being*.

The final chapter of this book considers how reflections on courage can contribute to a deeper understanding of our own political and social lives. In particular, it asks how this analysis of courage and the concomitant identification of very divergent fundamental cares can help us understand what we might otherwise dismiss as irrational behavior on the part of other human beings. It explores how the recognition of cares and associated behaviors that defy the usual understanding of *homo economicus* might help us understand other people and their willingness to risk life and limb for the sake of things we usually have great difficulty understanding. The reader will also be invited to consider how this interpretive approach can be brought to bear in situations that may not accord with the four manifestations of courage discussed within this book. For example, she will be asked to consider the possibility of kinds of courage and cares not explored in this book, such as existential courage, or caring fundamentally about God, joy, or even authenticity. Finally, should the reader have the heart to read to the end, she will be reminded that despite the usefulness of courage for our social scientific understanding of the political world, it remains a human virtue that can save us when our own reason fails us and our community.

TWO

Martial Courage and Honor

La lessive de l'honneur ne se coule qu'au sang.
[The laundry of honor can be bleached only with blood.]

—French proverb

Good heavens, Mardonius, what kind of men are these that you have brought us to fight against—men who compete with one another for no material reward, but only for honor!

—Xerxes, king of Persia, after learning of Spartan courage (Herodotus *Histories* 8.26)

Thermopylae: Martial Courage Epitomized

Any discussion of courage must begin with a discussion of men in battle—with martial courage. From time immemorial, this is when courage comes most vividly to the fore. It is where men prove their manly worth and cowards cannot escape the bright light of day.

And if we want to talk about courage and its relationship to honor, few cases are as luminous as ancient Sparta and, in particular, the story from Thermopylae, where the famous Spartan Three Hundred met the invading Persian hordes. The battle took place in 480 BC, ten years after the Athenians had routed the Persians at Marathon. This rout, while a setback to Persian imperial designs, was inconsequential for the general measure of Persian military power.[1] More meaningful, however, is the reaction of Darius, the Persian king. He regarded the defeat not in technical and empirical terms but in terms of insult and dishonor. Thus he vowed revenge and began preparations but died before his army marched. The insult was bequeathed to his son and heir, Xerxes, who was determined to get "satisfaction and revenge [τιμωρήσασθαι]" (7.8a) or to "punish the Athenians for the outrage [ἄδικα] they committed upon my father and upon us" (7.8b).

Xerxes assembled a massive force and marched on Greece not only to avenge the loss at Marathon but to redress another "insult" the Persians had suffered at Sardis (5.102). According to Herodotus, when the Persians returned they had marshaled 1,207 triremes manned by 241,000 sailors as well as 1,700,000 infantry and a cavalry of 80,000. With the contingents picked up en route, Xerxes arrived with a fighting force of 2,641,610. Herodotus claims that with the servants, the camp followers, the crews of the provision boats, and so on, "Xerxes, the son of Darius, reached Sepias and Thermopylae at the head of an army consisting, in all, of 5,283,220 men" (7.186). The immensity of the force, even by modern standards, must have been awe-inspiring.[2]

It is thus in the context of insult and revenge (τιμωρήσασθαι) that the battle of Thermopylae must be understood.[3] Herodotus's story goes like this: after Xerxes led his massive force into Greece, the Greeks, contrary to their normal ways, confederated against the foreign invaders. Whereas normally they quarreled constantly among themselves for honor, the invasion brought them together as only the threat of violent destruction can (7.145).[4] The confederacy, known as the Hellenic League, was still vastly outnumbered, so their usual way of fighting, in phalanxes on smooth and open ground, would serve them poorly. Thus, as Herodotus says, "The

Greeks on their return to the Isthmus then discussed, in consideration of the warning they had received from Alexander, where they should make a stand. The proposal which found most favor was to guard the pass of Thermopylae, on the grounds that it was narrower than the pass into Thessaly and at the same time nearer home" (7.175).

Strategically speaking, the decision was sound. The pass at Thermopylae, Herodotus reports, was fifty feet wide and both to the east and the west narrowed to a single wagon track (7.176).[5] The idea was to determine a place of battle eliminating advantage by limiting the number of troops able to be employed at any one time. The pass at Thermopylae was well suited for this, and the Greeks, after careful consideration, came to "the realization that the Persians would be unable, in the narrows of the pass, to use their cavalry or to take advantage of their numbers" (7.177). By fighting in the narrows at Thermopylae, then, the battle would pit the Greek way of war against the Persian. It would eliminate flanking maneuvers and keep the fight equal until one side simply ran out of replacements.

The reason this battle epitomizes martial courage is that, despite the immediate elimination of the Persian numerical advantage, behind the truncated battlefront were three million replacement troops. The Greek force mustered at Thermopylae had hoplite contingents from various cities numbering only about four thousand. Even if the Greek contingent proved superior and repeatedly decimated the Persian front line, seemingly inexhaustible replacements were ready to step forward. The contingent of four thousand, then, was not sent to defeat the Persians per se; the odds were heavily against this notion. It could be argued that the stand had other, practical merits—that it would delay the Persian advance so that the unconquered cities could continue preparing for later battles, the navy could continue to be prepared, and Persian supplies would be depleted. Millions of people, after all, require enormous supplies of food and water. None of these arguments, however, adequately explains the Spartans' courage and their refusal to retreat even when it was evident that fighting on would no longer serve any of these interests.[6]

The Spartans, however, were not throwing themselves meaninglessly on a grenade. The contingent was under the command of King Leonidas and three hundred handpicked Spartiates.[7] Herodotus offers an explanation of the purpose of the stand: "Leonidas and his three hundred were sent by Sparta in advance of the main army, in order that the sight of [the Spartans] might encourage the other confederates to fight and prevent them from going over to the enemy, as they were quite capable of doing if they knew Sparta was hanging back" (7.206). The Spartans' courage was not brought to bear merely for the sake of testing their skill against the Persians. Instead, it aimed at en-couraging, so to speak, the rest of Greece. Without this example of courage, the larger community itself would falter. In the Spartan view of things, it was better for the larger community to see three hundred full Spartiates perish than to see them retreat. The refusal to retreat, then, was not for the sake of doing every last bit of damage possible to Persian force—though in hindsight it did its share of damage—but rather to bring to light a common care that transcended mere physical life.

In describing the stand thus, one is forced to ask: What could possibly inspire three hundred Spartans to muster such courage in the face of such overwhelming odds? About what did they care so fundamentally that they would evince such courage? We could agree with some modern authors, such as William Ian Miller, that it is a mystery, but a better explanation can be offered.[8] Herodotus reports an exchange between Xerxes and Demaratus, an exiled Spartan king, days before the battle at Thermopylae. Xerxes, after inspecting the myriads of his army, says to the Spartan: "Tell me, then—will the Greeks dare to lift a hand against me? My own belief is that all the Greeks and all the other western peoples gathered together would be insufficient to withstand the attack of my army—and still more so if they are not united. But it is your opinion upon this subject that I should like to hear" (7.101).

Demaratus, assured that his honesty will not be punished, says much about Spartan community. The first thing he highlights is that, unlike the Persians, the Spartans are not fighting merely for the sake of wealth. As he puts it, "Poverty [πενίη] is Greece's inheritance from old" (7.102). The Spartans will stand firm in the face of these overwhelming numbers not because they hope to profit from it but because of their virtue (ἀρετή), which was acquired not by chance but by laboring under a certain wisdom (σοφία) and her mighty laws (νόμου ἰσχυροῦ). What Xerxes faces, then, is a people who, because of this virtue, are now able to keep "both poverty and despotism [δεσπόσυνος] at bay" (7.102).

Demaratus appears to be pointing to cares that might inspire such courage: preventing poverty and despotism. The negatives here, however, indicate that these are not *ne plus ultra* cares—that they are not fundamental. In other words, if Spartan courage is exercised for the sake of keeping poverty and despotism at bay, it would seem that a care more fundamental is threatened by abject poverty and despotism. Demaratus's words reveal more. Spartans, he says, "will not under any circumstances accept terms from you which would mean slavery [δουλοσύνην] for Greece; secondly, they will fight you even if the rest of Greece submits. Moreover, there is no use in asking if their numbers are adequate to enable them to do this; suppose a thousand of them take the field—then that thousand will fight you; and so will any number, greater than this or less" (7.102). The Spartans, it appears, are willing to stand courageously in the face of such overwhelming odds for the sake of a positive fundamental care: rather than "no despotism," it might well be freedom. This, however, is not quite what Demaratus is saying. The language he uses—δουλοσύνη—means slavery, but the term is bound up with the idea of labor.[9] Spartan courage can thus be understood as the willingness to risk life of limb for a certain way of life. Demaratus is indeed talking about freedom, but not freedom for its own sake and certainly not freedom as understood in the modern world. Sparta, after all, was no bastion of liberal freedoms.[10] In fact, from a very early age, the laws prescribed every particular of a Spartan's life and his conduct was under extremely close scrutiny. Freedom must therefore be understood as freedom from having to labor as a slave, but not because a laboring slave is unfree. Laboring *qua* laboring is an unbecoming way of life. Laboring is not how a proper man lives, and it is certainly not how a courageous warrior lives. Hence, freedom, as least in our average everyday understanding, is not the fundamental care for which the Spartans evidenced such courage at Thermopylae.

So let us probe a little deeper. The Spartans, we see, were willing to risk life and limb to keep from having to labor as slaves. Yet when it became materially obvious that victory was impossible, they still refused to retreat. When most of the non-Spartans fled the pass, the Spartans remained. As Herodotus tells us, Leonidas "thought it unbecoming [οὐκ εὐπρεπέως] for the Spartans under his command to desert the post which they had originally come to guard" (7.220). The Spartans, then, under the leadership of Leonidas, refuse to appear "unbecoming." In the Spartan world, to be unbecoming or unseemly is a serious violation of important social standards, whether these are explicit or tacit. For the Spartans, there is a close kinship between laboring as a slave and deserting one's post in battle. To do either is not to be a good man (ἀνερ ἀγαθός). To retreat is unbecoming because it is dishonorable and cowardly. For precisely this reason Leonidas dismissed the other cities: "He realized that they had no heart [ἀπροθύμους] for the fight and were unwilling to take their share of the danger" (7.220). "Unwillingness to share in the danger" is, of course, another way of saying the men from the other cities were afraid. One might go so far as to say that they lacked courage, that they were cowards. In Sparta, as we are beginning to understand, nothing is more unbecoming to a man or a community than dishonor and cowardice.

The Fundamental Care: Honor

The story Herodotus gives us of the Spartan Three Hundred begins to throw light on community with honor (τιμή) as the *ne plus ultra* care. The Spartans cannot retreat from Thermopylae because to do so is to abandon that which lies at the heart of their being. To flee or to retreat would be to abandon honor, and the Spartans are, in the final analysis, constituted by what Plato and many ancient writer refer to as φιλοτιμία (*Republic* 545a, 548c).[11] What is interesting is that when the language of φιλοτιμία is raised, it is very often coupled with φιλονικία—literally, the love of victory. The word usually carries with it a pejorative sense, as in the English "contentiousness" or "quarrelsomeness." It is, however, sometimes used to indicate a slightly more positive trait, as in "competitiveness" or "eagerness for rivalry." In either case, when coupled with the love of honor it indicates fierce competitiveness and a deep desire to be recognized as a winner, which is precisely how the Spartans were regarded in the ancient world. In the *Republic*, for instance, when setting down the five types of souls, Plato claims that the first defective type is that of "the man who loves victory and loves honor [φιλόνικόν τε καὶ φιλότιμον], like the Spartan citizen."[12] It is not particularly controversial to point to Sparta and her martial courage as being bound up with honor. As will soon become more evident, this can be said with some confidence about all warrior societies. But Sparta, according to one commentator, is something of a historical anomaly, and this anomaly can in great part be understood "in the relationship between Spartan institutions and those values, between Spartan laws and Spartan honor."[13] The anomaly is not simply that it was an honor culture, because this way of being was de rigueur in the ancient world.[14] Just as Sparta can be called an honor culture, so can Athens, Persia, and many other Mediterranean societies. But the intensity of the sentiments pertaining to honor, and its conceptual partner, shame, in Sparta is unique. In fact, the intensity of this fundamental care—this φιλοτιμία—struck even other Greeks as noteworthy. Xenophon, an Athenian who understood honor and the link between courage and honor well, speaks to this: "In other states when a man proves a coward [κακὸς], the only consequence is that he is called a coward [κακὸς]. He goes to the same market as the brave man, sits beside him, attends the same gymnasium, if he chooses. But in Lacedaemon everyone would be ashamed [ἀισχυνθείη] to have a coward with him at the mess or to be matched with him in a wrestling bout."[15] In Sparta, then, if one lacks courage one loses one's honor at home, and nothing is more important than honor.

How, then, might we understand honor? Even to discuss the concept steers us into some rather murky waters and embarks us on an adventure not often undertaken by political scientists.[16] This is perhaps because the concept itself is so amorphous that it is anathema to objective political science. To be sure, the field is full of studies focusing on preferences and values, but the very idea of honor seems highly resistant to this sort of analysis. Honor is not merely another preference in the catalog accompanying the rational actor model; it does not easily map onto the utility-maximizing model. It is, as one anthropologist puts it, an often unwritten handbook for conduct in a particular society. Of course, "All societies have rules of conduct, indeed the terms 'society' and 'social regulations' are coterminous. All societies sanction their rules of conduct, rewarding those who conform and punishing those who disobey. Honour and shame are social evaluations and thus participate of the nature of social sanctions, the more monolithic the jury, the more trenchant the judgment."[17] Stanley Brandes claims that honor might best be understood as "esteem, respect, prestige, or some combination of these attributes, depending on local usage."[18] Edward Westermark, again speaking from an anthropologist's point of view, offers a slightly more precise definition: "A man's honour may be defined as the moral worth he possesses in the eyes of the society of which he is a member."[19] All these definitions, with all their similarities, are not quite adequate. That honor and shame regulate conduct is not particularly surprising. Plenty of things regulate human conduct, such as laws, the threat of violence, habit, and religion. But there is something different about the way that honor and shame function. Honor and shame are not merely mechanisms regulating behavior; the categories themselves define the individual.

Julian Pitt-Rivers, who has offered one of the most thoughtful commentaries on honor, speaks directly to this issue. Like other anthropologists, he holds that "honour is the value of a person in his own eyes, but also in the eyes of his society. It is his estimation of his own worth, his *claim* to pride, but it is also the acknowledgement of that claim, his excellence recognized by society, his *right* to pride."[20] One's conduct constitutes one's being. Thus to behave according to the prescriptions of honor is one thing, but to be honorable is quite another. The former is an empirical statement, the latter existential. One can act honorably in almost any circumstance, but to be honorable one must be recognized as such by others in one's community. Pitt-Rivers articulates this well; honor, he claims, "provides a nexus between the ideals of a society and their reproduction in the individual through his aspiration to them.

As such, it implies not merely an habitual preference for a given mode of conduct, but the entitlement to a certain treatment in return. . . . The sentiment of honour inspires conduct which is honourable, the conduct receives recognition and establishes reputation, and reputation is finally sanctified by the bestowal of honours. Honour felt becomes honour claimed and honour claimed becomes honour paid."[21] In other words, if one is honorable in one's conduct, one is honored publicly; or in Hegelian terminology, one garners recognition, one is esteemed, or, as is common in modern parlance, one is respected or "recognized."[22]

However, to be recognized, esteemed, or respected requires that one move about in a community where such categories can pertain. Thus the size and the character of the community are extremely important, as is the level of interaction between the participants. This is precisely why Peristiany points to smaller communities as the soil in which φιλοτιμία grows. As he writes, "Honor and shame are the constant preoccupation of individuals in small scale, exclusive societies where face to face personal, as opposed to anonymous, relations are of paramount importance and where the social personality of the actor is as significant as his office."[23] One can hardly imagine issues of honor mattering in large-scale societies where members move in their average everyday lives with little face-to-face interaction. If one need not face one's neighbors, one need not worry about being shamed. In Sparta, however, the community was small and homogeneous, designed specifically to ensure just the sort of interaction that engenders the categories of honor and shame.

Although Sparta had the sort of demographics and civic structure conducive to promoting the love of honor, it also had another tradition that contributed to the love of honor. According to Spartan legend, the city became great because of her laws, which were given by Lycurgus. Lycurgus, Plutarch tells us, and subsequent Spartan kings were descendants of Heracles, the mightiest warrior of all time.[24] There was, then, a sort of congenital system of honor. If, for example, one was a descendant of Heracles—the only human to ever be promoted to the Greek Pantheon—one would be born with a certain degree of honor. At bottom, this meant that the good

Spartan would be like Heracles: courageous and godlike. To be otherwise was to somehow fall short of one's birthright. It was not only to disappoint the citizens who had previously lived up to these divine standards but to dishonor a gift of the gods themselves. But in Sparta, as in much of the ancient world, one's honor was not merely determined by one's birth. That would serve only to predispose people to honoring the wellborn, yet the wellborn were equally susceptible, if not more so, to behaving dishonorably and being dishonored.

What was of more importance, and would certainly trump being wellborn, was an individual's virtues (*aretai*). The catalog of *aretai*—a word that might better be rendered as "qualities" or "excellences"—would be quite long. One's appearance could garner honor, as was the case with Telemachos in Homer's *Odyssey* or Alcibiades in Plato's *Symposium.* Similarly, one could be endowed with great rhetorical skill, speed in running, and skill in singing, dancing, and seamanship, all of which could garner some degree of honor. Much the same could be said about ethical excellences, but, as Hans van Wees puts it, "By far the most prominent male excellence . . . is military prowess. Not only are great warriors honoured and given special privileges, but physical strength and courage are such important qualities that 'the best men' often simply means 'the best fighters,' and 'a bad man' equals 'a coward.'"[25]

Pitt-Rivers acknowledges this relationship between honor and manly courage. In fact, he goes so far as to say that the two are inextricably related: "The equation of honour with valour and cowardice with dishonour, apparent in this, derives directly from the structure of the notion, quite regardless of the historical explanations which have been offered for this fact."[26] For the Spartans, then, who cared fundamentally about honor, to retreat at Thermopylae would be cowardly and therefore dishonorable. To leave the battle would be to leave behind honor and, because honor resided at the pinnacle of their social values, would also disrupt the hierarchical order of their society. In Sparta, as in all cultures where honor is the fundamental care, the designation of honorable and dishonorable is stark: "Cutting across all other social classifications it divides social beings into two fundamental categories, those endowed with honor and those deprived of it."[27] In Sparta, these conceptual categories could be given real substance. One was either courageous or cowardly, Spartiate or Helot, citizen or slave, honorable or dishonorable.[28] And, when push came to shove, in a community like Sparta, "no person is acceptable, whatever his position and achievements, if he lacks the components of honour."[29] Nothing was more important than maintaining one's honor by maintaining one's reputation as a courageous warrior.

The Fate of the Coward: Dishonor

The fate of the coward in Sparta was not to be taken lightly. Xenophon's description is vivid:

> When sides are being picked for a ball game that sort of man is often left out with no position assigned, and in dances he is banished to the insulting places. Moreover in the streets he is required to give way, as well as to give up his seat even to younger men. The girls of his family he has to support at home, and must explain to them that his unmanliness [ἀνανδρία] is to blame. He must endure having a household with no wife, and at the same time has to pay a fine for this. He must not walk around with a cheerful face, nor must he imitate men of impeccable reputation: otherwise he must submit to being beaten by his betters. When disgrace [ἀτιμία] of this kind is imposed on cowards I am certainly not at all surprised that death is preferred there to a life of such dishonor [ἀτιμία] and ignominy [ἐπονείδιστος].[30]

In short, the fate of the coward was exclusion from the community. When his honor was lost, he lost his place in that very context on which his existence as a man depended—the community of warriors. In ancient Sparta, then, it is clear why Xenophon unambiguously states that "the citizens considered an honourable death [τὸν καλὸν θάνατον] preferable to a life of disgrace [τοῦ αἰσχροῦ βίου]."[31]

Such an extreme dictum does not sit well with our modern sensibilities. We do, however, still hear "Death before dishonor" in modern circles. Of course this kind of talk is mostly heard in military circles, but that it still exists is of no small significance. Death before dishonor is not some historical peculiarity of Sparta or the ancient world. Theodore Fontane, a late nineteenth-century German novelist, often wrote of the dictates of honor in the Prussian Junker class. In his *Effi Briest*, for example, he tells of a minor aristocrat named Innstetten who accidentally discovers an infidelity of his wife from six years earlier. Although the affair is long past, and although no one besides his wife and her lover know of the affair, Innstetten finds he must act on the dishonor. He decides to challenge the lover to a duel and enlists his friend, Wüllersdorf, to be his second. Wüllersdorf, of course, sees the irrationality of the plan and tries to dissuade Innstetten. Innstetten's reasoning, if we might call it that, reveals much about honor:

> "I've turned this thing over and over again in my mind. We're not isolated persons, we belong to a whole society, we're completely dependent on it. If it were possible to live in isolation, then I could let it pass. . . .
>
> "I went to your place and wrote you a note and by doing that the game passed out of my hands. From that moment onwards, there was someone else who knew something of my misfortune and, what is more important, of the stain on my honor; and as soon as we had exchanged our first words, there was someone else who knew all about it. And, because there is such a person, I can't go back."
>
> "I'm still not sure," repeated Wüllersdorf. "I don't like using a stale cliché but there's no better way of putting it: 'I'll be as silent as the grave,' Innstetten."
>
> "Yes, Wüllersdorf, that's what people always say. But there is no keeping a secret. And if you do as you say and are discretion itself toward others, even so *you* know about it. . . . The fact of the matter is, that from this moment onwards I'm dependent on your sympathy (in itself not something very pleasant) and every word that you hear me exchange with my wife will be checked by you, whether you want to or not, and if my wife talks about fidelity or, as women do, sits in judg-

ment on another woman, than I shan't know where to look. Or suppose it happens that, in some quite ordinary question of an affront having been given, I suggest that allowance might be made because there was no intention to insult, or some such thing, then a smile will cross your face or at least start to cross it and in your mind you'll be saying to yourself: 'Good old Innstetten, he has a real passion for running chemical analyses on insults in order to discover exactly how much insulting material they contain, and he *never* finds enough choking gas in them. He's never yet been choked by anything. . . .' Am I right, Wüllersdorf, or not?"

Wüllersdorf had risen to his feet. "I think it's terrible that you're right, but you *are* right. I won't torment you any longer with my question as to whether it's necessary. The world simply is as it is and things don't go the way that *we* want but the way that *others* want. All that pompous talk about 'God's judgment' is nonsense, of course, we don't want any of that, yet our cult of honor is idolatry. But we must submit to it, as long as the idol stands."[32]

Honor, then, even in the late nineteenth century, is bound up with a man's manliness. But this manliness is more than just the capacity to act violently; it is also about the informal ways and means that social norms are perpetuated and enforced. It is about standing firm in the face of injustices, even if by our twenty-first-century standards the issues at hand no longer pertain. After all, in our age should a man be cuckolded or be transgressed in some extralegal way, there is little recourse. The duel, it seems, is no longer invoked to settle a difference. Thus when boundaries are crossed for which there is no legal redress, without the prescriptions of a particular honor code all that is left is brute violence—and brute violence is just that—brutish.[33]

The link between honor and manly courage, then, forces us to look at just what exactly is at stake. One way of looking at this is to emphasize this split from brutishness. From this vantage, courage is regarded as an exclusively human capacity. To be sure, animals can be ferocious, but they cannot be courageous because courage, rightly understood, pertains to community, the larger group in which we participate and derive our meaningful existence.

As another anthropologist puts it, "One aspect of honour, then, is a struggle of self-discipline over cowardice and sensuality, flaws of animal nature that continually threaten to limit the natural nobility of man."[34] Unlike animals, human beings have the capacity for self-discipline, which is to say, the capacity for restraining the needs of the individual for the sake of the larger community. Animals, of course, will behave ferociously to protect their offspring, but the difference between this ferocity and human courage is that the former can be explained in terms of genetics. That is to say, animals are programmed to protect their genetic investments. Of course, humans are animals too, and there is no shortage of moving stories about parents who go to incredible lengths to protect or save their children from physical harm. This, however, is not what makes courage distinctly human. Human courage, when it transcends the physical, is for the sake of the community in an existential sense. It aims at maintaining the very order that affords the individual his or her meaningful place in the world. This courage is, as Innstetten says, what moves us to fight duels, because "with people all living together, something has evolved that now exists and we've become accustomed to judge everything, ourselves and other, according to its rules. And it's no good transgressing them, society will despise us and finally we will despise ourselves and not be able to bear it and blow our brains out."[35]

It is this communal and self-overcoming character of courage that helps us understand why honor resides at the center of Spartan society. To be Spartan was to stand with the community. And to do this, at least minimally speaking, was to be worthy of honor. As such, to be Spartan was to be courageous, because to be courageous was to protect the polis, not just from physical destruction but as the locus of collective meaning. This is precisely why honor is bound up with manliness, because "manliness implies not only the condition of being courageous but the ability of a man to do something efficient and effective about the problems and dangers which surround him."[36] To be courageous, one needs to act for the sake of one's comrades.

There is a story from the battle of Thermopylae that illustrates this point, not to mention how Sparta takes all of these categories to the extreme. Herodotus reports that "two of the three hundred Spartans, Eurytus and Aristodemus, are said to have been suffering from acute inflammation of the eyes, on account of which they were dismissed by Leonidas before the battle and went to Alpeni to recuperate" (7.229). Leonidas's decision to release the men from battle service does, of course, make sense. If one's eyes are swollen shut, one will contribute little in the close combat of the phalanx. Now, it must be kept in mind that Eurytus and Aristodemus were full Spartiates, which is to say, they had spent their entire lives, or at least since they were seven years old, training and preparing to hold their place in the battle line. Moreover, the training in Sparta for the previous decade had been with an eye to this particular battle, in anticipation of standing firm against the invading Persians. To be sent home at such a time would, to the Spartan warrior, be like training one's whole life for the Olympics, only to be sent home the day before for a case of pinkeye.[37]

In any case, Eurytus and Aristodemus went to Alpeni, which was very near the Hot Gates. There the two men quarreled about whether they should return to Sparta or rejoin the contingent. Being blind, of course, meant they would indubitably and immediately be killed, which was at that moment the obvious fate of the entire contingent. As Herodotus reports,

> These two men might have agreed together to return in safety to Sparta; or, if they did not wish to do so, they might have shared the fate of their friends. But, unable to agree which course to take, they quarreled, and Eurytus had no sooner heard that the Persians had made their way round by the mountain track than he called for his armour, put it on, and ordered his helot to lead him to the scene of the battle. The helot obeyed, and then took to his heels [φεύγοντα], and Eurytus, plunging into the thick of things, was killed. (Herodotus 7.229)

Aristodemus, on the other hand, chose not to plunge into the fray. By modern, rational standards, this would be the appropriate thing to do—to opt against the battle and fight another day. The distinction here, however, is not between folly and prudence. The distinction is between the actions of the Spartiate and the Helot. Whereas the Spartan warrior falls into the collective and perishes there (τὸν δὲ ἐσπεσόντα ἐς τὸν ὅμιλον διαφθαρῆναι), the slave flees. Or, to be more accurate, the slave at least gets near the fighting before he flees (τὸν μὲν ἀγαγόντα οἴχεσθαι φεύγοντα). Aristodemus, however, got nowhere near the battle and simply stayed at Alpeni.

The language Herodotus uses to describe Aristodemus's staying at Alpeni is revealing. Whereas Eurytus plunged in and died and his slave fled, Aristodemus, "finding that his heart failed him [λιποψυχέοντα] stayed behind [λειφθῆναι]" (7.229). Herodotus uses λιποψυχέοντα—which Sélincourt here renders as "His heart failed him." The word is actually a compound, consisting of λείπω (to leave) and ψυχή (soul, spirit, breath, mind, or heart). Literally, then, Herodotus says that Aristodemus's soul left him. To say, however, that his soul had left would seem to indicate that he had died. Of course Aristodemus did not die, but his heart left him. But "to leave" (λείπω) in this sense has another, more important connotation. It means, according to Liddell and Scott, "to forsake, abandon, desert, leave in the lurch." It means to come up short or to be lacking in something. Thus λιποψυχέοντα is to lack spirit or to fail in courage. By not returning to his place in the line with the rest of the Three Hundred, Aristodemus exhibited cowardice and did, in a sense, die because his spirit failed him. To be a part of the fighting unit, to be a part of the phalanx, to be a part of, and contribute to, the esprit de corps, was precisely what it means to be Spartan. Herodotus's language thus reveals that Aristodemus, his heart leaving him in the lurch, also left his brothers in the lurch. λειφθῆναι, after all, is just the aorist infinitive of λείπω. Like the slave, or perhaps worse than the slave, Aristodemus not only stayed at Alpeni but came up short and forsook the very thing that made his existence meaningful. By fleeing the battle, he fled himself. His behavior was un-becoming, so to speak.

This assessment of Aristodemus seems harsh: to call a man a coward because, blind, he opts against throwing himself in the fray and perishing. However, Aristodemus's actions were judged in comparison with the other man afflicted by the same malady. Herodotus suggests that the dishonor Aristodemus was subject to stemmed directly from the fact that his courage did not measure up to that of his companion: "Now if only Aristodemus had been involved—if he alone had returned sick to Sparta—or if they had both gone back together, I do not think that the Spartans would have been angry; but as one was killed and the other took advantage of the excuse, which was open to both of them, to save his skin, they could hardly help being very angry indeed with Aristodemus" (7.229). So what distinguished the two was that one chose to fight, while the other chose to go home. One emulated the slave who fled, while the other plunged into battle. One action was worthy of honor, while the other was a shameful deed. One man stayed to offer whatever help he could, while the other saved his own skin. The ignobility of Aristodemus's action thus was not merely that he fled but that he prioritized himself over the community.[38]

The dishonor Aristodemus suffered was not insignificant. As Herodotus tells us, "Upon his return Aristodemus was met with censure and dishonor [ἔιχε ὄνειδός τε καὶ ἀτιμίην]; he suffered this sort of dishonor [ἠτίμωτο]—no Spartan would give him a light to kindle his fire, or speak to him, and he was called The Trembler [ὁ τρέσας]" (7.231). So the penalty for cowardice was not death per se but what we have come to know as "ostracism." To be shunned or given the "silent treatment" was, for all intents and purposes, a sort of death itself. As one commentator puts it, this dishonoring should be understood in an active sense: it amounted to "a sentence of 'social death' that rendered the individual *apolis*, 'without a polis,' and therefore politically rightless, landless, and without a share in the cults of his ancestors."[39] In its most extreme form, this dishonoring took the form of driving the transgressor into exile. Notably, the words for fleeing a battle (φεύγω) and going into exile (φεύγω) are identical.[40] This form of dishonor, as one would expect, was not suffered lightly. The ramifications were both physical and existential. As Joseph Bryant puts it: "The cup of exile was a bitter draught indeed, a lament repeatedly sounded in Greek poetry and prose as one of the worst fates that could possibly befall a human being: the loss of property and all civic right; no longer able to honor the tombs of ancestors; old friendships lost and new ones unlikely . . . ; forced into dependency upon others for protection or compelled to turn to piracy or mercenary service; and not least the soul-wrenching homesickness, rendered all the more unbearable by a searing thirst for vengeance."[41] To be dishonored, then, was quite similar to being exiled. Although one was not removed physically from the city, one was excluded from all meaningful relationships. When one was removed from the moral life of the city, when one's fellow citizens refused to recognize that one even existed, there was little reason to remain, either morally or physically. Not only was one shunned in daily life, one was utterly denied that about which one cared fundamentally—honor.

To be a coward, or even to be perceived as a coward (which is analogous in an honor society), is to somehow leave one's fellows in the lurch. It is to flee from the responsibility one has to others. To be dishonored, in return, is to be denied everything salutary that one can gain from participating in a social and political world with one's fellows. To be dishonored, in this active way, is to have one's "social self" revoked. In a society where one's personal identity is wholly dependent on the collective identity, the ramifications of this revocation are extensive. William James, speaking to this point, imagined a case of absolute shunning and describes the psychology of it as follows:

> A man's Social Self is the recognition which he gets from his mates. We are not only gregarious animals, liking to be in sight of our fellows, but we have an innate propensity to get ourselves noticed, and noticed favorably, by our kind. No more fiendish punishment could be devised, were such a thing physically possible, than that one should be turned loose in society and remain absolutely unnoticed by all the members thereof. If no one turned round when we entered, answered when we spoke, or minded what we did, but if every person we met "cut us dead," and acted as if we were nonexisting things, a kind of rage and impotent despair would ere long well up in us, from which the cruelest bodily tortures would be a relief; for these would make us feel that, however bad might be our plight, we had not sunk to such a depth as to be unworthy of attention at all.[42]

This so-called silent treatment, however, is not the only form of dishonoring. Kipling Williams points to "shunning," "cold-shouldering," "being sent to Coventry," "time-outs" for children, school suspensions and expulsions, and even excommunication. He claims that this practice in human culture is so pervasive "that it transcends time and is evident in almost all civilizations and known cultures."[43] Roger Masters defines the practice in general as "denying a voice to those who are deemed morally reprehensible" and claims that it "is a particularly important and revealing phenomenon, because it shows both the strength of social bonds (Hirschman's loyalty) and the mechanisms by which coercion can be used to reinforce social norms."[44]

This method of reinforcing social norms obviously requires smaller face-to-face communities because its efficacy requires participation of almost all members of the community. When the community is too big for this to be efficacious—when one can simply move to another state and reestablish oneself—the exclusionary dishonoring must be enforced through prisons (as the American frontier and Australia are no longer available outlets for social outcasts) or executions. Of course, prisons and capital punishment are ostensibly used to protect society from the physical dangers presented by the offenders, but the same argument is used in other cases. The coward is dishonored because, even though the battle is behind him, he represents a threat to the community. While the threat is not imminent and physical, the failing of the individual can perpetuate itself communally, both genetically and morally. He is left in the lurch because he has left his fellows in the lurch. And Sparta, with its rather limited number of Spartiates, was small enough that the shunning of Aristodemus could be thorough.

The Fate of the Dishonored: Social Death

We have seen already why Aristodemus, and others who suffer dishonoring, bear the load so heavily. To be deprived of honor is to be excluded from the integrated polis. It is to be denied integrity, as it were. Herodotus mentions the story of another survivor from the stand at Thermopylae: "There is also a story that one more of the three hundred—Pantites—survived. He had been sent with a message into Thessaly, and on his return to Sparta found himself in such disgrace [ἠτίμωτο] that he hanged himself" (7.232). What is interesting is that this survivor simply returned to Sparta having no idea what had occurred at Thermopylae and that he did not have a partner by whom his courage could be measured. Nevertheless, he suffered great dishonor, presumably in the same form as Aristodemus. Like a good Spartan, he felt the prick of dishonor so deeply that he killed himself. William Ian Miller suggests that both Aristodemus and Pantites suffered the fate of the "sole survivor." He points to the fate of another sole survivor in Herodotus's *Histories*, this time an Athenian. About twenty years prior to the battle at Thermopylae, in one of the internecine intra-Greek conflicts, the Athenians had sent an army to Aegina. There are conflicting accounts of how it happened, but as it turned out the Athenians were routed and only one of their men returned to Athens alive. But as Herodotus tells us, "Even the sole survivor soon came to a bad end; for when he reached Athens with a report of the disaster, the wives of the other men who had gone with him to Aegina, in grief and in anger that he alone should have escaped, crowded round him and thrust their brooches, which they used for fastening their dresses, into his flesh, each one, as she struck, asking him where her husband was. So he perished" (5.89). Of course, this man perished in actuality, but the prick of dishonor, so to speak, completed the job of the social death before the outcast needed to do it himself. It is not too likely, as Miller suggests, that the man might have been brooched to death simply for being the bearer of bad news, because there is more to it than this.[45] In the eyes of the Athenian women—who were every bit a part of the honor culture—something was askew when a single man returned from the battle. A shadow was cast over the man's quality as a warrior. Doubt was cast on his character.

These doubts, of course, concern courage, and they are doubts that might always afflict a sole survivor. How could one man survive? Did he run away? Did he malinger? Did he do everything he could to prevent the disaster? As Miller puts it, "The sole survivor is in a rather ambiguous position. Surviving raises suspicions about his courage, envy for his luck, and vague nagging doubts that his survival is in some unfathomable way part of the causal mechanism that produced the death of others."[46] If this is difficult for the modern mind to fathom, one need only imagine what we would think if a man returned as the sole survivor from two military debacles. The first time would be unremarkable. The second time, however, would create deep suspicions. Even in more "humane" times such as ours, there would be whispering—perhaps not to his face, but certainly in more discreet quarters there would be talk, precisely the sort of talk that cuts deep in an honor culture.[47]

We have already established that there is good reason to consider Sparta an honor culture, and, in much the same way as the Homeric world. One of the more astute readers of Homer recognizes this and informs us that "in Homer the end is undoubted: the chief good is to be well spoken of, the chief ill to be badly spoken of, by one's society, as a result of the successes and failures which that society values most highly."[48] So whereas a modern speaker might refer to a good or bad conscience, or "inner goodness," what is of preeminent importance in an honor culture is how one is regarded, how one is seen, or how one's contemporaries speak of one. Whether one's mind or intentions are virtuous is, at best, of secondary importance. One's reputation is what matters. As Spartans—which is to say, as men who loved honor to such a degree that it was noteworthy even by ancient standards—Aristodemus and Pantites must have suffered as deeply as any character in Homer from their tainted reputations. Even if they were completely courageous men, even if they demonstrated nary a moment's cowardice, a tainted reputation would have made life unlivable for them. According to Adkins, Aristodemus's and Pantites' stories are merely exemplary of a longstanding tradition in the heroic world:

> If to have a good reputation is more important than anything else, "loss of face" must be as terrible as it was in Homer. Examples abound: Theognis apostrophizes his heart, *thumos*, urging it not to give in, for surrender would delight his enemies; Hesiod, earlier, recommends that one should not marry a wife who will make one the laughingstock of the neighbors; Ajax, on coming to himself, refers to the mockery and insult he has suffered; Electra, apostrophizing the absent

> Orestes, says that he is dead and gone, and their enemies are laughing; and Megara says significantly that death is a terrible thing, but that to die in a manner which would give her enemies the opportunity to mock would be a greater evil than death.[49]

Again, in all these examples, that which is important is what people say. As Adkins recognizes, even "facts are of much less importance than appearances, and hence . . . intentions are of much less importance than results. The Homeric hero cannot fall back upon his own opinion of himself, for his self only has the value which other people put upon it."[50] To be laughed at in public is, in a very distinct way, to have not only one's courage called into question but also one's manliness. To be a good man in Sparta is to be a good warrior. To be a good warrior is to be courageous. Thus to be a good man is to be courageous. It confirms that one measures up to the heroic tradition of one's forefathers—the tradition of manly courage and martial valor. Failing to live up to this standard means that one is left out of the epic story of Herculean martial glory. One is excluded from the community, not just physically and morally, but also temporally because not to measure up to Heracles is not to measure up to the very definition of a Spartan man. So whereas noble deeds garner honor and ignoble deeds dishonor, the dishonored man must suffer the corollary of dishonor: shame (αἰδώς).

The depth of this painful exclusion cannot be overstated. If one is excluded in this way, one must live in constant shame; and in an honor-loving culture, the stain of dishonor is not easily bleached. This, as many commentators point out, is a basic difference between shame cultures and guilt cultures. Ruth Benedict, trying to make sense of Japanese culture after the Second World War, offered one of the earlier distinctions between shame cultures and guilt cultures. As she put it,

> True shame cultures rely on external sanctions for good behaviour, not, as guilt cultures do, on an internalized conviction of sin. Shame is a reaction to other people's criticism. A man is shamed either by being openly ridiculed and rejected or by fantasying to himself that he has been made ridiculous. In either case it is a potent sanction. But it re-

> quires an audience or at least a man's fantasy of an audience. Guilt does not. In a nation where honor means living up to one's own picture of oneself, a man may suffer from guilt though no man knows of his misdeed and a man's feelings of guilt may actually be relieved by confessing sin.[51]

Thus guilt pertains to a state of mind where one's own behavior is not constrained by public scrutiny. Distinctions of right and wrong and prohibition against transgressions, whatever those might be, are much more nuanced because one must be first and foremost concerned with the eye of a judging deity. In the Christian world, God knows a man's thoughts. One can therefore no more hide transgressions of the mind than one can hide transgressions of action from the public eye. In fact, sinful deeds are probably much easier to hide from the public than sinful thoughts are from an omniscient deity. From this vantage, then, what other people think—public shame, ridicule, embarrassment, and so on—is not the basis for right action. What others say is not the primary mechanism checking misdeeds. Moreover, when misdeeds do occur, one need not redeem oneself in the eyes of the public; rather, one must seek forgiveness from God.

This is not to say that guilt is wholly distinct from public opinion. Bernard Williams, for example, argues that

> the differences in the experience of shame and of guilt can be seen as part of a wider set of contrasts between them. What arouses guilt in an agent is an act or omission of a sort that typically elicits from other people anger, resentment, or indignation. What the agent may offer in order to turn this away is reparation; he may also fear punishment or may inflict it on himself. What arouses shame, on the other hand, is something that typically elicits from others contempt or derision or avoidance. This may equally be an act or omission, but it need not be: it may be some failing or defect.[52]

In a shame culture, on the other hand, what other people think is of paramount importance. According to E. R. Dodds, "The strongest moral force which Homeric man knows is not the fear of god, but respect for public opinion, *aidōs*. . . . In such a society, anything which exposes a man to the contempt or ridicule of his fellows, which causes him to 'lose face,' is felt as unbearable."[53] In many ways, the concept of shame as it existed in the ancient world is a paradox to the modern Western mind. It is, on the one hand, an all-too-familiar idea; who among us has not worried what our peers think of our work, has not been embarrassed by some slip of the tongue, has not fretted that our colleagues are whispering behind our backs? Yet on the other hand it is unlikely that we would consider suicide if our reputation were somehow besmirched. Moreover, and this may be the key to understanding our distance from the ancient world in this regard, it is very unlikely that many moderns could understand the terrible shame a Spartan felt at being considered a coward. Perhaps a father, having been too frightened of water to jump into a swimming pool to save his child, might get a sense of this shame afterwards. What is more likely in the modern context is that such a father would be pitied for having to suffer the terrible consequences of a malady, a condition beyond his control. No such quarter would be granted the Spartan. Cowardice is not a malady. It is a failing of one's character. The Spartan would be forced to suffer the full shame of the flaw in his character—indeed, in his very being.[54]

The shame of a Spartan, however, would not just be all consuming *after* some actual or imagined failing. It would also possess him before he violated some normative standard. There are, then, two interrelated ways of understanding shame. This is precisely why Douglas L. Cairns argues that to comprehend this phenomenon fully in the ancient context, we must understand not only *aidōs* but also *aideomai*. *Aidōs* is a noun and, as we have already discovered, is most often translated as "shame." The most general way to understand it is as "an inhibitory emotion based on sensitivity to and protectiveness of one's self-image." It entails a "concentration on the self and one's own status, [and] is prompted by and focuses on consideration of the status of another person in one's own eyes."[55] *Aideomai*, on the other hand, is a verb "that is used in two more or less distinct ways, either to convey inhibition before a generalized group of other people in whose eyes one feels one's self-image to be vulnerable, or to express positive recognition of the status of a significant other person; the two stock English translations, 'I feel shame before' and 'I respect,' thus succeed in isolating distinct senses of the Greek term."[56] In other words, *aidōs* pertains to how one feels about one's self, while *aideomai* pertains to how one feels about others in relation to the self. In modern parlance, for the former we might say, "I feel embarrassed." For the latter, it would be appropriate to think in these terms: "I've really embarrassed myself in front of her." To feel *aidōs* is therefore to feel that one has failed to measure up to one's own expectations. *Aideomai*, on the other hand, is falling short not just of an external party's expectations but also of that person—hence the second understanding of *aideomai*, "to respect."

A few illustrations will be helpful here. *Aidōs* appears in the *Iliad* at least a dozen times.[57] Twice it is used to indicate nudity or exposed parts. For example, early in the book, after taking Achilles' prize, Agamemnon is verbally abused by Thersites. Odysseus comes to Agamemnon's defense and says, "If once more I find you playing the fool, as you are now, nevermore let the head of Odysseus sit on his shoulders. . . . If I do not take you and strip away your personal clothing, your mantle and your tunic that cover your αἰδώς, and send you thus bare and howling back to the fast ships, whipping you out of the assembly place with the strokes of indignity."[58] Later, when Priam is importuning Hektor to fight Achilles, he claims that "for a young man all is decorous when he is cut down in battle and torn with the sharp bronze, and lies there dead, and though dead still all that shows about him is beautiful; but when an old man is dead and down, and the dogs mutilate the grey head and the grey beard and the parts that are αἰδώς, this, for all sad mortality, is the sight most pitiful" (*Iliad* 22.75). In both these instances, the term is used euphemistically for body parts not usually on display. As Bernard Williams points out, "The word *aidoia*, a derivative of *aidōs*, 'shame,' is a standard Greek word for the genitals, and similar terms are found in other languages."[59] In this sense, *aidōs* is the equivalent of *pudendum*—of that which should not been seen. It is important to note here, however, that even though the term is being used corporally, it encompasses a certain publicity. That is, it is not the pudenda themselves that are shameful, but rather being seen in a way one would not want to be seen.

These two instances of the term's use should not fool us into thinking that the Homeric Greeks were some sort of proto-Victorians. The term also pertains to modesty that is not necessarily sexual. For example, when the Trojans are encamped very near the Greeks, Nestor asks for a volunteer to go into the Trojan camp as a spy. Diomedes, roused by his "courageous spirit [θυμὸς ἀγήνωρ]" (*Iliad* 10.220), volunteers, but when it comes time for him to pick a partner his sense of shame makes him hang back. Thus Agamemnon says to him, "Diomedes, pick your man to be your companion, whichever you wish, the best of all who have shown, since many are eager to do it. You must not, for the respect that you feel in your gut [αἰδόμενος σῇσι φρεσὶ], pass over the better man and take the worse, giving way to shame [αἰδοῖ] and looking to his degree—not even if he be kinglier" (10.234–39, translation modified). Here *aideomai* is about both shame (Diomedes' feelings about himself) and the "respect he feels in his gut," what we might call his embarrassment about picking, and subsequently commanding, a warrior who outranked him or who had superior fighting abilities. Agamemnon's exhortation suggests that Diomedes should set these considerations aside and focus on choosing the right man for the job so that the mission will succeed. Further, even though a better fighter and more courageous man might end up eclipsing Diomedes and receiving all the *kudos* and honors afterwards, Diomedes is advised not to let his sense of shame or his love of honor interfere with the success of the larger community.[60] Although the honorable man loves honor and victory, he is courageous only if, when push comes to shove, he subordinates his personal honor and victory to that of the collective.

In this culture, it is especially shameful to be exposed as a coward, not only before one's comrades in arms, but before, and by, those of lower status. Even the Trojans express this sentiment. For example, Hektor, when trying to pluck up the courage to meet Achilles, says this: "Since by my own recklessness I have ruined my people, I feel shame [αἰδέομαι] before the Trojans and the Trojan women with trailing robes, that someone who is less of a man [κακώτερος] than I will say of me: 'Hektor believed in his own strength and ruined his people.' Thus they will speak; and as for me it would be much better at that time, to go against Achilleus, and slay him, and come back, or else be killed by him in glory [ἐϋκλειῶς] in front of the city" (22.110). Here Hektor imagines the ultimate embarrassment of being seen as a coward in front of the whole city, particularly, the women, and of being criticized by a lesser man, which is to say, a less courageous man. *Aidōs* and *aideomai* therefore are both rooted in the warrior's sense of manly courage.

Shame, however, is invoked not only to inhibit unseemly behavior but also to incite certain deeds. Cairns recognizes this dual function of shame and rightly points out that shame is used to "decry cowardice or shirking in battle; to remind the soldiers in the field of that fact. Thus in some passages [of the *Iliad*] the simple cry '*Aidōs!*' can be enough to raise the prospect of the charge of cowardice and [in others] to spur the combatants on."[61] Of course, this incitement is not to just any deeds but rather to courageous action. For example, Hera, when seeing the Argives retreating, yells at them in a stentorian voice: "Αἰδώς, you Argives, poor nonentities splendid to look on. In those days when brilliant Achilleus came into the fighting, never would the Trojans venture beyond the Dardanian gates, so much did they dread the heavy spear of that man. Now they fight by the hollow ships and far from the city" (*Iliad* 5.787–91). A bit later, when Hektor is approaching the ships, Agamemnon exhorts his men: "Αἰδώς, you Argives, poor nonentities splendid to look on. Where are our high words gone, when we said that we were the bravest? Those words you spoke before all in hollow vaunting at Lemnos when you were filled with abundant meat of the high-horned oxen and drank from the great bowls filled to the brim with wine, how each man could stand up against a hundred or even two hundred Trojans in the fighting" (8.228–34).[62] Thus the concept is used not only to point out failings in martial matters but also to prompt warriors to fight more vigorously. In other words, whereas cowardice begets shame, shame encourages.

The Selflessness of Courage

What we have discovered thus far is threefold: first, martial courage is bound up with the fundamental care for honor; second, to fail in martial courage is to find oneself dishonored; and third, to be dishonored is to live with shame. A question that I would like now to address is whether this stain of shame can ever be bleached. Let us address this by returning our analysis to the hapless Aristodemus, the sole survivor of the Spartan Three Hundred at Thermopylae. We know that after that battle the Persians continued into Attica. Eventually they were met in battle by the allied Greek forces at Plataea. Unlike the battle at Thermopylae, here the Greeks routed the Persians. As Herodotus reports, after many terrible setbacks the Persians took refuge behind a wooden wall, "but once the palisade was down, the Persians no longer kept together as an organized force [στῖφος]; soldierly virtues were all forgotten; chaos prevailed and, huddled in thousands within that confined space, all of them were half dead with fright. To the Greeks they were such easy prey that of the 300,000 men (excluding the 40,000 who fled with Artabazus) not 3000 survived. The Spartan losses in the battle amounted to 91 killed; the Tegeans lost 16, the Athenians 52" (9.70). The routing of the Persian force, then, coincides with the abandonment of the soldierly virtues. They fall when chaos prevails, when fear spreads, and, most importantly, when they fail to keep together as an organized force—a phrase to which we will return presently. Herodotus, of course, praises the fighting of all the allies, but all were surpassed by the valor of the Spartans because it was they who undertook the hardest task and were matched against the best of the enemy warriors (9.70).

But of the Spartans, it was Aristodemus who was most distinguished in his fighting. As Herodotus puts it, "The greatest courage [ἄριστος] was shown, in my opinion, by Aristodemus—the one held in disgrace and dishonor [εἶχε ὄνειδος καὶ ἀτιμίην] for being the only one saved of the Three Hundred at Thermopylae" (9.71, my translation). After battles, it was customary for the Spartans to give prizes of valor to those who had distinguished themselves. The practice was not unlike the American practice of awarding the Medal of Honor or the British tradition of awarding the Victoria Cross. The traditions are remarkably similar. According to U.S. Army regulations:

> The Medal of Honor is awarded by the President in the name of Congress to a person who, while a member of the Army, distinguishes himself or herself conspicuously by gallantry and intrepidity at the risk of his life or her life above and beyond the call of duty while engaged in an action against an enemy of the United States; while engaged in military operations involving conflict with an opposing foreign force; or while serving with friendly foreign forces engaged in an armed conflict against an opposing armed force in which the United States is not a belligerent party. The deed performed must have been one of personal bravery or self-sacrifice so conspicuous as to clearly distinguish the individual above his comrades and must have involved risk of life. Incontestable proof of the performance of the service will be exacted and each recommendation for the award of this decoration will be considered on the standard of extraordinary merit.[63]

Since the award's inception in 1861, it has been given only about 3,400 times, and currently there are only about 150 living holders of the award. The Victoria Cross is Britain's highest award for gallantry and has been given just 1,354 times since 1854. The awards themselves are crafted by a London jeweler from the bronze of a Chinese cannon captured from the Russians at the siege of Sebastopol. Qualifications for the Victoria Cross are slightly less bureaucratic than those for the American Medal of Honor: "It is ordained that the Cross shall only be awarded for most conspicuous bravery, or some daring or pre-eminent act of valour or self-sacrifice or extreme devotion to duty in the presence of the enemy."[64] Bureaucratic or not, the description for eligibility resonates precisely with the criteria regarding prizes for valor in Sparta. As one would expect, these modern prizes for valor go to the soldier who distinguishes himself from others in matters of courage. But it must be recognized that it is not courage unadorned that is being revealed here. Just as it was for the Spartans, the prize is reserved for those who are courageous for selfless reasons. Thus the Spartans, the British, and the Americans all explicitly connect courage and self-sacrifice.[65] Martial courage is courage only when it is bound up with selflessness.

This point is made very clear when Herodotus tells us that others besides Aristodemus fought valiantly at Plataea. In particular, Herodotus points to three Spartans, Posidonius, Philocyon, and Amompharetus. What is of particular interest here is how the Spartans treated Aristodemus:

> However, when, after the battle, the question of who had most distinguished himself was discussed, the Spartans present decided that Aristodemus had, indeed, performed great deeds, but that he had done so merely to retrieve his lost honour, rushing forward with the fury of a madman in his desire to be killed before his comrades' eyes; Posidonius, on the contrary, without any such wish to be killed, had fought bravely, and was on that account the better man. It may, of course, have been envy which made them say this; in any case, the men I mentioned all received public honours except Aristodemus—Aristodemus got nothing, because he deliberately courted death for the reason already explained. (9.71)

So Aristodemus was refused the prize. Though he had showed the greatest fighting ability, the honors went to other men. The stain of dishonor and cowardice, it seems, is not easily bleached.

So how is it that the man who demonstrates the greatest fighting skill is denied the honors? Could it be that we need to derive a new definition of courage? On the contrary, our definition of courage—risking life and limb for the sake of something—remains a good one. Aristodemus fought skillfully at Plataea and took more risks than any other Spartan but cannot be considered courageous because the risks he took were for his own benefit, not for the sake of the community. There were thus two errors in Aristodemus's effort to erase the stain of dishonor. First, "he rushed forward with the fury of a madman," and second, he had a "desire to be killed before his comrades' eyes."

In the modern understanding of courage, the first point hardly seems to be an error at all. In fact, this act seems to fit the bill for the highest form of courage. The charge into battle, after all, seems to get all the publicity in our times. One need only think of innumerable chest-beating Hollywood images: those Civil War scenes where men in either blue or gray scream out and charge across the field; the courage displayed at Gallipoli, which has reached Homeric proportions in Australian lore; the storming of the beaches of Normandy on D-Day, one of the most celebrated moments of World War II; and the charge of Teddy Roosevelt and his Roughriders, which is indelibly imprinted in American epic historiography. In fact, in 1998 President Clinton, who himself had no military experience, awarded the Medal of Honor posthumously to Roosevelt for this very charge. In short, the charge into battle has become the epitome of modern martial courage. Yet poor Aristodemus, who rushed forward with the fury of a madman, fought in the most distinguished manner, and survived, was denied the prize.[66]

Aristodemus's first error was therefore not a lack of courage per se but rather the way it was mustered. The Spartans, it must be kept in mind, fought in phalanx formation. The success of any military society can be traced primarily to a certain military innovation; and while modern successes tend to hinge more on technological advances, Sparta's success grew out of the virtue of her warriors and this method of waging war. Phalanx fighting was done close together, shoulder to shoulder, as it were. It was a form of fighting that had been around since Homer but was perfected by the Spartans. Homer describes the phalanx thus: "As a man builds a solid wall with stones set close together for the rampart of a high house keeping out the force of the winds, so close together were the helms and shields massive in the middle. For shield leaned on shield, helmet on helmet, man against man, and the horse-hair crests along the horns of the shining helmets touched as they bent their heads, so dense were they formed on each other" (*Iliad* 16.212–17).[67] The phalanx was composed of columns of heavy infantry, each column typically ten men across the front echelon and ten infantrymen deep. These columns were arrayed with many other such units to be combined into a large and incredibly efficient fighting machine.

The infantryman was armed with a long spear, anywhere from six to twelve feet long, and a sword. At the very least, he wore metal armor on his chest, forearms, and shins, as well as a metal helmet that protected his head and his neck. The heavy infantryman also carried a shield, called an *aspis.* This shield was originally called a *hoplon,* which most likely gave its name to the infantryman, the hoplite. According to Michell, "It is probably true to say that the Spartan heavy-armed hoplite was the most formidable soldier of the ancient world. Indeed, we might go so far as to say that, so far as physique, endurance and training go, he has never been matched in any army at any time. In its prime, the Spartan army was unbeatable, as Pericles and the Athenians very well knew, and never risked a battle with it."[68] In sum, thanks to their lifelong training for war and their mastery of phalanx fighting, the Spartans came to be known as "artists in warfare" (τεχνῖται τῶν πολεμικῶν).[69]

The actual fighting was done in very close quarters and would have been especially intimate, so to speak. John Lazenby describes phalanx fighting as "predominantly hand-to-hand . . . with the opposing phalanxes closing to within a few feet. . . . [T]he men in the front ranks thrust at their opponents with their spears, aiming overarm for the throat and upper part of the body, or underarm for thighs or belly; presumably, too, if a man fell, the man behind him stepped over his body as well as he could and took his place."[70] As Xenophon describes a phalanx encounter: "Crashing their shields together, they shoved, they fought, they slew, they were slain."[71] So one might imagine phalanx fighting as two sides, moving in unison, crashing thunderously together, thrusting their spears either overhand into the enemy's face and throat, or underhand into the groin and belly.

Gore aside, the main point here is that in phalanx fighting success depended on each member in the line doing his duty, and his duty was to hold his place in the line—and this is not meant in any abstract way. In fact, it was eminently practical because the hoplite carried his shield on his left forearm and his spear in his right hand. The shield was held in such a way that it protected not the shield bearer himself but the man to his left. The shields, then, would form an armadillo-like layer of protection for every man in the line. In the intimate fighting space of the phalanx battle, to fail in the line would be to fail the man to the left, whose very specific survival depended on the man to his right. His failure would subsequently imperil the man to his left, and so on. One man's failure would result in a domino effect down the line.[72] To be a good warrior, then, one had to be courageous first and foremost for the sake of another human being—the man fighting immediately to the left.

This is exactly where the hapless Aristodemus fell short of the prize of valor. His first mistake was "to rush forward with the fury of a madman." By rushing forward, by charging the enemy, Aristodemus quite literally put himself in front of his comrades. Whereas such action seems to reveal enormous courage, the fact of the matter is that self-interested courage is not courage—when Aristodemus put himself in front of his comrades, he actually imperiled his comrades. In his thirst to retrieve his personal honor, he left his position in the line and put himself ahead of Sparta and the code that made Sparta great. His lack of self-control in matters of personal glory, for all intents and purposes, negated the possibility of retrieving his lost honor. In fact, it may very well have done the opposite. As Paul Cartledge claims,

> A specifically hoplite value-system and code of honor were necessarily devised to accompany and reinforce the ritualization of hoplite militarism. Self-discipline and self-control (*sôphrosunê, enkrateia*) and all the other qualities that went towards the construction and maintenance of military *taxis* or order (such as rhythmic co-ordination, cohesion, self-sacrifice, collective uniformity and relative egalitarianism) were deliberately fostered. The hoplite's supreme test was to remain "in rank" or "in his proper station" (*en taxei*). This hoplite martial code symbolized the disciplined solidarity of the civic community. Its more narrowly political expression went under the name *eunomia*, that is, orderly obedience to the agreed rules.[73]

By charging forward, Aristodemus violated the norms of martial order, and in so doing he disrupted the symbiotic balance between the civic code and the martial code.

This disruption brings to light Aristodemus's second error: his desire to be killed before his comrades' eyes. In his conversation with Xerxes, Demaratus, the deposed Spartan king, tells the Persian king, "[The Spartans] are free—yes—but not entirely free; for they have a master, and that master is Law, which they fear much more than your subjects fear you. Whatever this master commands, they do; and his command never varies: it is never to retreat in battle, however great the odds, but always to remain in formation, and to conquer or die" (Herodotus 7.104). The civic code, as set down by Lycurgus, aimed at creating a cohesive body politic. This code, which by all reckonings is perhaps the most restrictive and authoritarian civic order ever, was paralleled in the martial code. In the polis, such institutions as the "upbringing" (agoge), the marriage laws, and the common messes all aimed at civic solidarity. Whether these institutions were meant to buttress martial capacity or whether the martial codes were meant to undergird political stability is uncertain. It is certain, however, that the laws of the city were paramount and that these laws put the community before the individual. One must never retreat in battle, one must always remain in formation, and, most important for our discussion, one must conquer or die. The laws of the city did not demand death first and foremost of her warriors. They demanded that he stay in the line, which obviously required that he stay alive, at least as long as possible. Aristodemus's desire to die before the eyes of his compatriots was as egregious a violation of Spartan codes as not staying in the line. In effect, the laws say, "Fight courageously for the meaningful, collective existence we share in Sparta and die if necessary, but do not throw your life away."[74]

In his bid to bleach the stain of dishonor, then, Aristodemus failed. The prize of honor went to Posidonius, and the hapless Aristodemus was further shamed. Miller understands the distinction between these warriors quite well. As he puts it, Aristodemus "wants to die, whereas Posidonius wants to live; he fights to regain lost personal honor, whereas Posidonius fights for the polis, his quest for honor subordinated to and dependent on the success of the group; and thus Aristodemus rushes forward with the fury of a madman, while presumably Posidonius, consistent with his merging of his own interests with the group's, achieves his successes without abandoning his position in the phalanx's shield wall, even though, as it turned out, his actions were of less avail than Aristodemus'."[75] To say, however, that Posidonius's actions were of less avail is to predicate the measure of success on tangible results. In this sense, Miller's analysis is colored by modern sensibilities. Success in the Spartan sense is not primarily based on practical and empirically verifiable results. Miller's argument that the original error, showing too much concern for self-preservation, is balanced in the end by showing too little is misguided because there is no calculus when it comes to honor.[76] Such a calculation could come only from a modern mind.

The Spartan world was a world where selflessness and courage were inextricably wedded, and this was not restricted to the men. The Spartan women were legendary for their poise and self-possession, especially in the face of losing sons and husbands. Steven Pressfield, in his fictional recreation of the battle of Thermopylae, even imagines that Spartan courage in martial affairs is owed to the strength of her women.[77] Plutarch went so far as to compile a collection of pithy sayings attributed to Spartan women that confirmed this over and over. One of the more telling, not to mention well known, sayings is attributed to an unknown Spartan woman. As Plutarch writes: "As she was handing her son his shield and giving him some encouragement, said: 'Son, either with this, or on this.'"[78] Her meaning is clear—she was telling her son to hold his place in the line. To drop the shield in battle was tantamount to running away, the hallmark of cowardice. She was telling her son that he must either hold his shield and cover the man to his left, or die trying. Hence he should either come home with his shield or dead on top of it. And because holding one's place in the line revealed the selflessness of courage, it also revealed that the honor accrued by martial courage pertained not just to the warrior but to his family and to the city as a whole.

Other Spartan women went even further once shamed by their sons' cowardice. A woman named Damatria, Plutarch reports, "hearing her son was a coward [δειλόν] and unworthy of her, killed him when he arrived. This epigram is about her: *Damatrius broke the laws and was killed by his mother—she a Spartan woman and he a Spartan youth.*"[79] Similarly, another unnamed Spartan woman "killed her son for leaving his post [λιποτακτήσαντα] because he was unworthy of his fatherland. She said, 'Not my offspring.'"[80] So not only were these Spartan women vulnerable to the shame brought on by their sons' cowardice, they had in their repertoire remedies for bleaching the stain—they killed their sons and cleansed themselves of the stigma of producing unmanly sons. There is, as far as I can tell, no report of sanctions for these actions and the fact that they are remembered for killing these sons indicates the contrary. Such a position and such capacities by a woman in the ancient world are somewhat surprising not only to our modern prejudices but even to ancient ones. This is probably why Plutarch thought to include a pithy quip from Gorgo, the wife of the same Leonidas who led the Three Hundred at Thermopylae. As Plutarch puts it, after "being asked by an Attic woman: 'Why are Spartan women the only ones who rule over men?' she replied: 'Because we are the only ones who give birth to men.'"[81]

All of these examples of ostracism and disenfranchisement point to a rudimentary aspect of courage. Courage is the glue of the shared public world. It is via courage that ties are created, enforced, and reaffirmed. Moreover, it is important to note that these are political ties. Courage pertains not merely to the private family but to the larger and public "family" of the polis. As such, it is possible to point to the development of hoplite fighting and the Spartan way of life as a turning point in Western political order. Sparta and her phalanx fighting marked a turn from tribal associations to political associations, properly speaking. If, then, we look more closely at the training—the fabled *agoge* endured by Spartan boys—it becomes evident that it was not merely to develop those powerful bodies that so amazed the Persians (Herodotus 7.208).[82] Instead, bound up with this education was a sociopolitical transformation that mirrored effective fighting in the phalanx. As we have seen, in this sort of battle what was of paramount importance was keeping the line intact. Should one warrior fall, the formation itself could quickly fall into complete confusion. It was therefore most necessary that another man fill the void left by the fallen man. However, just as in domestic and political affairs, the natural human tendency in times of crisis is to look for, and to look out for, one's kin. Because this tendency would be perilous in the Spartan way of war, it had to be overcome. In other words, loyalty in Sparta shifted from the family to the polis, and it was precisely at this that Lycurgus's reforms aimed. Xenophon illustrates this nicely. As he writes, following orders in battle is easy enough to grasp, but to understand what it really means to be a Spartan one needs to understand how these men are brought up to learn “the tactic of continuing to fight with whoever is to hand after the line has been thrown into confusion.”[83] In other words, the Spartan warrior trained all his life to act selflessly courageous for the sake of whichever Spartan stood at his side. His training prioritized citizen over kin and the honor of the community over the honor of the individual. In the history of political order, this transition from tribal to political identity is no small accomplishment.[84]

The Enduring Appeal of Courage

From what has been said about martial courage thus far, it would seem that being courageous is a burden we endure to avoid unpleasant consequences. For example, one must be a courageous warrior or be conquered and either enslaved or killed. In less extreme circumstances, one must overcome one’s natural timidity or suffer dishonor, shame, disenfranchisement, or worse, being brooched to death by a gaggle of angry women. Moreover, it appears that to be courageous one must also forgo benefits that accrue directly to the self—one must set aside personal happiness. One must put others first, or put one’s community in general first, to be recognized as courageous. But to view courage entirely in these self-denying terms would exclude the glorification it so often receives. In fact, even though there are steep penalties for failing in courage, it is fair to say that success in times of great risk accrues its own benefits. Of course, discussing courage in terms of costs and benefits seems to undermine the very nature of courage and its precognitive, nonrational character. How can one measure the benefits of something if the subject matter itself is inimical to empirical measure? It is like trying to measure beauty, something that has been attempted but never with great success. But courage, like beauty, has a relationship with human beings. While it may be impossible to say, for example, that a work of art is 87 percent beautiful and that viewers of this work of art will accrue a certain measure of pleasure units, it is still possible to say that the work of art is beautiful. And we can say it is beautiful because we are drawn to its beauty. We are enveloped by it, immersed in it, called to it. Beauty has its appeal, and we find ourselves drawn to it.

Courage functions in much the same way. It has an appeal. While we cannot quantify the strength of its appeal, it nevertheless calls to us. It calls us to be enveloped by it, to be immersed in it, to be involved in it. Courage appeals to us in a precognitive, nonrational way. It simply appeals to us. Its appeal promises nothing, and in it we hear promises of nothing. But we hear the call nevertheless. And that appeal is enduring. Courage is always appealing; cowardice is not. To ignore the appeal of courage is to pass on the opportunity for glory. We might argue that one can be perfectly happy without ever heeding the call of courage, without ever being immersed in it, but we cannot argue that one can live gloriously without heeding it. In fact, there is no reason at all to equate happiness and glory. When we talk about martial courage, we must almost invariably talk about suffering and misery. Even the most decorated warrior must suffer—the training, the march, the incredible tedium that makes up the better part of war. In battle, he must suffer the gore, the stench, the pain, and possibly his own death. E. R. Dodds, speaking in somewhat more general terms, correctly claims that "in the *Iliad* heroism does not bring happiness; its sole, and sufficient, reward is fame."[85] The heroes in the *Iliad* are rarely happy, but they get their glory. The appeal of martial courage, then, is not that it brings happiness in the way we conventionally think of happiness. Heeding the appeal of courage, for example, rarely contributes to commodious living, as Hobbes would have us understand happiness. Yet courage, like beauty, continues to appeal to us.

In terms of glory and fame, we have already seen a central difference between the Homeric world and the Spartan world. For the latter, glory is measured collectively. As is abundantly clear from the case of Aristodemus, personal glory needs to be subordinated to the collective. Yet courageous action can still bring personal glory; after all, we remember the names of Posidonius and Dieneces and warriors who distinguished themselves at Thermopylae and Plataea. But the rest of the men who held their place in the line garnered no fame at all from courageously risking life and limb. Their names are lost, their individual deeds forgotten. What, then, is the appeal of courage? Why do we continue to hold up selfless courage as the pinnacle of human endeavor?

That these questions can be asked at all reveals an important phenomenon. The questions are predicated on the distinction between the individual and the group. It may well be a modern prejudice to think that setting aside the individual for the sake of the collective is a sacrifice at all. In fact, there is a long-standing tradition that holds otherwise. Horace for example, tells us:

> Dulce et decorum est pro patria mori:
> mors et fagacem persequitur virum
> nec parcit inbellis iuventae
> poplitibus timidoque tergo.
>
> Virtus, repulsae nescia sordidae,
> intaminatis fulget honoribus
> nec sumit aut ponit secures
> arbitrio popularis aurae.[86]
>
> [What joy, for fatherland to die!
> Death's darts e'en flying feet o'ertake,
> Nor spare a recreant chivalry,
> A back that cowers, or loins that quake.
>
> True Virtue never knows defeat:
> *Her* robes she keeps unsullied still,
> Nor takes, nor quits, *her* curule seat
> To please a people's veering will.]

For Horace and the Romans, dying courageously in battle is the epitome of virtue. Again however, it is clear that courage points to the group, not the individual. It is sweet and proper not just to die courageously but to die for the sake of the fatherland. That is to say, it is sweet and proper to die for the sake of the common good, a good higher than that of the individual.

This sentiment is echoed in the Christian tradition as well. In John's Gospel we are told by Jesus, "Greater love hath no man than this, that a man lay down his life for his friends" (John 15:13). Here, where love is equated with friendship, one can be no better a friend than by setting one's life down for one's friend. The implications of this are profound because, for both Horace and St. John, the willingness to risk life and limb, whether for the sake of *patria* or friendship, points to a return, if we might call it that, on one's courageous investment. When one sets aside individual glory for the sake of the common glory, one is at the same time insinuating oneself into that collective glory. There is, then, a return on the courageous investment for the individual, and this return is a sense of belonging, or meaningful membership, in the community. Thus one of the enduring appeals of courage lies precisely in subsuming the self into the whole. This subsumption, rather than being regarded as a sacrifice, can be regarded as the creation of a new field of being—a field of being that transcends the finitude of individual existence.

In his *After Virtue*, Alisdair MacIntyre circles around this point. As he puts it: "To be courageous is to be someone on whom reliance can be placed. Hence courage is an important ingredient in friendship. The bonds of friendship in heroic societies are modeled on those of kinship. Sometimes friendship is formally vowed, so that by the vow the duties of brothers are mutually incurred. . . . My friend's courage assures me of his power to aid me and my household; my friend's fidelity assures me of his will."[87] In other words, by participating in a world where courage pertains, one no longer finds oneself in the isolated world of the self. Instead, through courage new possibilities of meaningful friendship are disclosed. The enduring appeal of courage is not merely that one might stand out from the crowd or that one might establish personal heroism and glory. In fact, we might even go so far as to say that such a vision of courage, while lending itself to immortality in the Homeric sense, turns back on itself by isolating the individual from his comrades. The lot of Achilles attests to this: his heroism was as much distinguishing as it was egregious, in the most literal sense of the term. The more run-of-the-mill courage—if there is such a thing as run-of-the-mill courage—is not egregious. On the contrary, courage creates bonds between its participants that are simply not available in times less revealing, and this is precisely what is so appealing about courage.

It is something of a paradox that what is most appealing about courage is at the same time what is least appealing. On the one hand, courage discloses a level of connectedness between individuals that is otherwise not available. Yet on the other hand, friendships created in these times of risk are often the most fleeting. After all, wars end and warriors part ways to go home. Or, as is often the case, people are killed in times of war and friendships are ended suddenly and terribly. This paradox, however, does little to lessen the appeal of courage, and if we listen to what soldiers themselves say about their experience of danger and friendship we might understand the problem a little better. One of the more illuminating accounts of a soldier's experience with courage and danger comes from J. Glenn Gray, an American who served in the intelligence service in the Second World War.[88] For Gray, the experience of battle is inherently appealing because it elevates the emotions, including those that govern and permit friendship. As he puts it, anyone who has experienced firsthand situations of grave danger comes to know "a quality of excitement scarcely experienced before or since. Fear may have been the dominant feature of such excitement; rarely was it the only ingredient. In such an emotional situation there is often a surge of vitality and a glimpse of potentialities, of what we really are or have been or might become, as fleeting as it is genuine. . . . People are reduced to their essence" (14–15). In other words, where death becomes evident and possible, human vitality is elevated to a hitherto inexperienced level.

This understanding of the appeal of courage and battle has been expressed in other quarters as well. Chris Hedges, an American war correspondent, sees moments of courage as providing peaks in the otherwise level, perhaps even boring, field of human existence. As he puts it, "The enduring attraction of war is this: Even with its destruction and carnage it can give us what we long for in life. It can give us purpose, meaning, a reason for living. Only when we are in the midst of conflict does the shallowness and vapidness of much of our lives become apparent. Trivia dominates our conversation and increasingly our airwaves. And war is an enticing elixir. It gives us resolve, a cause. It allows us to be noble."[89] The point made by both Gray and Hedges is clear: when courage pertains, human possibilities, in terms of both cruelty and kindness, are disclosed in a way that is otherwise impossible. Courage appeals because, once experienced in its most poignant form, it reveals the possibility of increased vitality and consequently the possibility of deepened meaning in one's life. For Hedges, this appeal called so loudly to him that he could seriously claim: "There is a part of me that decided at certain moments that I would rather die like this [in a moment of danger] than go back to the routine of life. The chance to exist for an intense and overpowering moment, even if it meant certain oblivion, seemed worth it in the midst of war."[90]

The appeal of courage, however, pertains not only to the disclosure of abstract possibility but to "intense and overpowering moments" between individuals participating together in these experiences. In battle, Gray argues, when one fully realizes that there are other men, just across the way, "who would gladly kill you, if and when they got the chance," one discovers that one cannot survive without depending on others (*Warriors*, 26). While we are easily able to forget this fact in times of peace and safety, in the face of the enemy, when our survival depends not only on our own courage but also on the courage of our comrades in arms, we develop a "cofraternity of danger" (27). By experiencing danger with others, we are alerted to the human need to trust in others and to be trustworthy to others. But not only are we brought face to face with this need, we are alerted to the fact that our very existence depends on this reciprocity of trust. It is thus in times when courage pertains that we are effectively drawn out of our isolated selves in a meaningful way. When we are exposed to this reciprocity of need, a most important aspect of human existence is disclosed—the individual is participating in a field of being that transcends his self. In this, the possibility of friendship is both heightened and deepened.

Moreover, it is when the individual is forced to recognize that he is participating in a field of being that transcends his self that the very idea of transcendence is disclosed. Gray, being a good Heideggerian, steadfastly avoids the language of transcendence. Instead, he refers to battle as providing a "delight in seeing" (29–30). In what is often more pejoratively called "the lust of the eye," or is even reminiscent of Leontius's fascination with the executed in Plato's *Republic* (440a), Gray describes the appeal of battle as bound up with the "desire to escape the monotony of civilian life and the cramping restrictions of an unadventurous existence. . . . War offers the outlandish, the exotic, and the strange" (29). Thus, in situations marked by courage, one finds an aesthetic delight. The visual stimulation of all that surrounds battle provokes the mind to contemplate both the beauty and the ugliness of battle—and yes, Gray argues, battle and destruction can have their beauty. For instance, "There is often a weird but genuine beauty in the sight of massed men and weapons in combat" (31). The rhythmic movements of soldiers marching, variety, proportion and harmony, the smooth lines in weaponry, and the colors and artistry of the machines of war can all contribute to this beauty. As for the ugliness of battle, Gray argues vigorously that, contrary to conventional wisdom, it is "wrong to believe that only beauty can give us aesthetic delight; the ugly can please us too, as every artist knows" (30–31).

This delight in seeing, however, does not stop with the pleasure one takes from looking at things. Gathered together, the moments of delight combine to disclose "the fascination that manifestations of power and magnitude hold for the human spirit" (33). While Gray steadily avoids the language of transcendence in his description of "delight in seeing," we are alerted to how humans are drawn to danger because in its most exaggerated instantiation, battle, man comes face to face with scenes that

> are able to overawe the single individual and hold him in a spell. He is lost in their majesty. His ego temporarily deserts him, and he is absorbed into what he sees. An awareness of power that far surpasses his limited imagination transports him into a state of mind unknown in his everyday experiences. Fleeting as these rapt moments may be, they are, for the majority of men, an escape from themselves that is very different from the escapes induced by sexual love or alcohol. This raptness is a joining and not a losing, a deprivation of self in exchange for a union with objects that were hitherto foreign. Yes, the chief aesthetic appeal of war surely lies in this feeling of the sublime, to which

> we, children of nature, are directed whether we desire it or not. Astonishment and wonder and awe appear to be part of our deepest being, and war offers them an exercise field par excellence. (33–34)

In short, Gray is describing a form of ecstasy—a condition where the individual stands outside himself. This is, of course, the literal meaning of ecstasy. It indicates a detachment of the self from the self and absorption into the world around it, especially into those things for which one's community cares.

In this way, the aesthetic appeal of battle correlates with courage. Just as a work of art may yield an aesthetic ecstasy, participation in battle can yield a "communal ecstasy" (46). Just as the "beauty" of the battle draws us out of ourselves and allows us to connect with the whole of the world, the communal nature of courage does much the same thing. Courage appeals to us because we are drawn to the beauty of dangerous situations. Once enveloped, we perforce undergo a transformation from self-care to other-care. In this example, Gray is showing how care and concern can be transformed from the self and the selfish to the greater whole, to that which transcends the self. As he puts it, "This ecstasy satisfies because we are conscious of a power outside us with which we can merge in the relation of parts to whole" (36). Even more revealing is the emphasis Gray gives the beneficial nature of this transformation. Not only are we transformed, but we are transformed for the better. We become more capable of self-sacrifice, drawn out of depression, and assured that we have a place of belonging in the world. In this sense, courage is not only appealing but also a salvation: "We feel rescued from the emptiness within us. In losing ourselves we gain a relation to something greater than the self, and the foreign character of the surrounding world is drastically reduced" (36–37). In other words, once we are enveloped by courage, we find ourselves no longer in relation to our selves but in relation to that which surrounds. Our existence, because of the threat of danger, finds a locus outside us. I suggest that this locus must not be too far removed from the individual, lest the appeal become faint, inaudible, and abstract. For example, a work of art may, at least for a fleeting moment, appeal to us and draw us out of ourselves, but when the work of art is removed the individual will eventually return to him- or herself. The source of the ecstasy cannot be abstract. It is a thing that calls us out of ourselves. Like the work of art, courage calls out in a nonrational voice, but it must be close enough to be heard, sensed, felt, and even tasted. Courage appeals, but the danger must be proximate and palpable. The transfigurative character of courage requires participation in the dangerous world around us. Thus courage not only allows us to find ourselves *in relation to the world* around us, it appeals to us because it allows us *to find ourselves.*

In battle, as is so evident with the Spartans, success depends on connecting individual capacities to achieve a common goal. In addition, and this is often overlooked in modern conflicts, the connections between individuals that are so necessary for military success depend on a clear knowledge of the mission's goals. So the appeal requires connections, and the connections require a goal. The connection, which Gray calls comradeship, "first develops through the consciousness of an obstacle to be overcome through common effort" (43). What happens, then, is that through this common effort toward a specific goal a bond is created between the individuals. Whether we call it morale, esprit de corps, camaraderie, solidarity, or even friendship, the connection with courage is clear. Individuals, because of this bond, suppress their own interest for the sake of the whole; they step out of their own isolated world into communities of care.

As I have said, Gray calls this connection comradeship and claims that it is one of the enduring appeals of battle (25). When soldiers have a common goal, they can "abandon their desire for self-preservation" (42), and the transfigurative effect has an unmistakable appeal. According to Gray, many soldiers claim that being at risk with their group, in battle with their comrades, "has been the high point of their lives. Despite the horror, the weariness, the grime, and the hatred, participation with others in the chances of battle had its unforgettable side, which they would not want to have missed" (44).[91] Of course, this type of bonding between people is possible in times when courage does not pertain, but "organization for a common and concrete goal in peacetime organizations does not evoke anything like the degree of comradeship commonly known in war. Evidently, the presence of danger is distinctive and important. Men then are organized for a goal whose realization involves the real possibility of death or injury" (43). Self-overcoming, or the deep sort of self-overcoming inherent in martial courage, grows best under the "storm of steel," as Ernst Jünger calls it.[92] The appeal, then, is what Gray describes as something like a "cementing force" between individuals (40), and in battle it is most likely to emerge.

For an act to be courageous in battle, it must demonstrate a sort of self-overcoming, and this self-overcoming lends itself to that unspeakable bond created among fellow combatants. That situations requiring courage often result in the loss of friends, however, is no argument against this point. That men die in battle and suffer horribly may even contribute to this cementing force. Max Weber explores this idea in his *Sociology of Religion*, suggesting that battle, because of the deaths of comrades, contains a religious element that actually deepens the bonds between the warriors. He calls this a "religious brotherhood" (Brüderlichkeitsreligiosität) and characterizes it as a certain "brotherliness of that group of men who are bonded by war." For Weber, this brotherliness emerges from suffering under the strange theodicy that death in battle presents; and, as such, it goes beyond the sort of bonds stemming from the average everyday way of life. He calls it a "battle brotherhood" (Kriegsbruderlichkeit).[93]

What is interesting about this bond is that when a warrior dies it is not broken; in fact, it often takes on an aspect of the sacred. Whether the battle is modern or not, because the shedding of blood is done for the sake of another, dying in battle almost necessarily has the character of sacrifice. Now this sacrifice must not be understood merely in terms of cost, as is the understanding with the economic model of human life. Rather, as Michael Gelven argues, one of the basic aspects of war is that it is about sacrifice, and this concept must be understood as its etymology indicates: "to make holy."[94] To be sure, to sacrifice something is to surrender something valuable, but genuine sacrifice requires more. Gelven invokes the story of Cain and Abel to illustrate how sacrifice in battle differs from other sacrifice. Prior to the murder of Abel, the story we get in Genesis is about sacrifice. Both Cain and Abel make a sacrifice—Cain sacrifices grain, while Abel sacrifices cattle to God. As the story goes, Abel's sacrifice is accepted by God, while Cain's is not. What distinguishes the depth of the sacrifice is not the market value of the thing sacrificed. As Gelven puts it, "on the aesthetic or artistic level" what stands out is that "in Abel's sacrifice blood was spilled, but in Cain's it was not. . . . The suggestion is that only bloody offerings are genuine sacrifices."[95] And in battle, the sacrifice a courageous warrior makes for his battle brothers is most certainly bloody. There is, then, a sacred character to the bond between comrades in arms, and the friendships one makes while risking life and limb in battle are often regarded as pure. They are pure because this is precisely the function of sacrifice—to cleanse the stains of prior wrongdoings. Sacrifice burns away impurity and reaffirms holy connections. Gelven summarizes this point nicely:

> It is this that is provided by sacrifice. Sacrifice makes us holy because the suffering cauterizes the wounds and makes them clean. It is this kind of holiness that is achieved by the warrior in the crucible of battle. War, for all its savagery, is a deeply ritualistic thing, with ceremonies and rites and rituals; but its truest celebrations are not on the parade ground but on the battleground. Dedication is provided by those who battle and only imitated by those who perform ceremonies, as Abraham Lincoln so profoundly teaches us in the Gettysburg Address. It should be seen as a symbol of something else more real. Sacrifice does not show something other than itself; it *establishes* meaning.[96]

Thus risking life and limb for the sake of one's comrades, and seeing the same courage reciprocated by one's comrades, forges the sacred bond of battle-brotherliness—the sort of deep and pure bond people yearn for in their average everyday lives.

This battle brotherhood revealed by martial courage is a phenomenon that has been recognized even in the modern shape of warfare. Chris Hedges, for instance, observes, "Combatants live only for their herd, those hapless soldiers who are bound into their unit to ward off death. There is no world outside the unit. It alone endows worth and meaning. Soldiers will rather die than betray this bond. And there is—as many combat veterans will tell you—a kind of love in this."[97] So whereas modern pacifists would have us believe that war and battle are hatred incarnate, the experience of soldiers reveals something quite different. There is a peculiar and paradoxical relationship between love and death. In battle, amid what appears to be the pinnacle of hate, these deeply satisfying bonds of love between individuals arise directly out of situations where courage is put to the ultimate test. Gray, who testifies to this phenomenon repeatedly, summarizes this appeal of courage: "This kind of love produces a kind of awareness that is lacking in normal life. Our deeper powers lie dormant and undeveloped unless we are pushed to the abyss" (88).[98]

This capacity for self-overcoming, for effacing the individual, and for developing pure and meaningful relationships does not arise *ex nihilo*. Instead, it is deliberately created in the very training the soldier receives. The training of soldiers in boot camp involves little explicit and self-conscious education in courage per se. Instead, courage is derived from the fostering of what Richard Holmes calls the "mysterious fraternity," the tie that binds warriors together. Of course, basic training teaches the important vocation of making war, but its second, and "by no means less important, function is to inculcate the military ethos in recruits, and to ensure that the individual values which prevail in most civilian societies are replaced by the group spirit and group loyalties which underlie all military organizations."[99] Holmes points to oaths of loyalty, which he calls "the first ritual in a ritualistic profession," as the first step in this metamorphosis.[100] Of these oaths, Gray says they have a dual function. First, they link the warrior to the state, regiment, or king; though the particular loyalty is not that important, the point is clear—the warrior first pledges allegiance to a body or figure that represents the community. The oath is therefore the first step out of identity based on the self. Of course, the oath also functions as a symbolic release from personal responsibility. Gray says in *The Warriors* that he frequently heard, not only from Nazis soldiers but from Americans as well, "When I raised my right hand and took that oath, I freed myself of the consequence for what I do. I'll do what they tell me and nobody can blame me" (181). But even while an oath can deflect moral responsibility, this is a peripheral consequence; its first function is to foster the warrior's identity with the group rather than as an isolated individual.[101]

Holmes points as well to a physical metamorphosis that accompanies the creation of the warrior. The Spartans, we know, spent a lifetime perfecting the body for the moment of battle, but in the modern world this must be accomplished much more quickly. The transformation is therefore more superficial: recruits have their long hair shorn and are given uniforms, both of which aim for uniformity. There are, of course, practical reasons for these, such as hygiene, reduced costs for outfitting, the creation of a fearsome appearance, and, in less civilized times, the identification of deserters. But as Holmes correctly observes, the outward transformation also functions symbolically in that it "helps to impress on the recruit his change of status: it is an outward symbol of the inner transformation produced by the oath."[102] The transformation is therefore physical and psychological. In both ways the recruit is being molded to think in terms of "we" rather than "I." Through drill, he is taught new habits and values regarding both obedience and the art of fighting.[103] Drill, Holmes reports, "has an important ritualistic and morale-building role. . . . [It] brings a unit together in a way which even unwilling soldiers may find to be curiously pleasurable."[104] Recruits learn a new language often replete with patriotic images and, perhaps more often, with every imaginable profanity. This new language sets them apart not only from other military units but from the civilian world, where individualism and autonomy remain the hallmarks of the properly lived life. In short, military training aims precisely at fostering a way of being that prioritizes the community over the individual and, at bottom, prepares the warrior for the mysterious fraternity, the *Kriegsbruderlichkeit,* that is part and parcel of the appeal of courage.

Having described this mysterious fraternity, and having made a case that situations calling for courage yield these deep and meaningful connections, one might still posit that the appeal of courage should not be heeded. Despite its appeal for battle brothers, it promotes hatred toward other human beings, the enemy. This objection, however often and eloquently it is raised, overlooks another element of friendship and human connection that occurs in battle. This is the relationship established with the enemy, the very people that the courageous warrior is attempting to kill and is accused of hating. This is not to say that warriors on opposite sides of the line become friends in the way, say, Achilles and Patrokles were friends; rather, the system of honoring and respecting the humanity of the enemy is bound up with courageous and honorable combat. An old but very good example of this can be found in Herodotus. When the Persian fleet first approached Greece, as one would expect, it caused much panic. There were a few skirmishes, and a few Greek ships were taken, but most fled. Herodotus reports, however, that one Greek trireme

> from Aegina, commanded by Asonides, gave the Persians some trouble. One of the soldiers on board—Pytheas, the son of Ischenous—distinguished himself that day; for after the ship was taken, he continued to resist until he was nearly cut to pieces. At last he fell, but, as there was still breath in his body, the Persian troops, anxious to do all the could to save the life of so brave a man, dressed his wounds with myrrh and bound them up with linen bandages. On returning to their base, they exhibited their prisoner admiringly to everybody there, and treated him with much kindness. The other prisoners from this ship they treated merely as slaves. (7.181)

What we see with this example is that the courage of the enemy soldier unites him with his foes. The two sides recognize a common humanity. Respect and honor can therefore apply not only to one's own but to the other as well. The courageous warrior is honorable not only when he is selfless among his own but also when he learns to respect what is virtuous and good in the other. His nobility of soul permits meaningful human connections even across enemy lines.

Another story in Herodotus illustrates this point. We recall that during the fighting at Thermopylae Leonidas was killed and that when he fell the Spartans made great efforts to recover his body. But because all the Spartans ended up dying, the king's body eventually fell into the hands of the Persians. Xerxes, evidently, was so angry at the enormous losses his army suffered that he "went over the battlefield to see the bodies, and having been told that Leonidas was king of Sparta and commander of the Spartan force, ordered his head to be cut off and fixed on a stake" (8.238). Although this contradicts the claim that courage creates bonds among men, even among enemies, Herodotus finds it necessary to report that this action by Xerxes was extremely anomalous and a consequence of him being angrier with Leonidas than he had ever been before. Had he not been so angry, "he would never have committed this outrage upon his body" (8.238) because "normally the Persians, more than any other nation I know of, honour men who distinguish themselves in war" (8.238). Later, after routing the Persian main force at Plataea, a distinguished Aeginetan named Lampon approached Pausanius, the Spartan king, and advised him to repay like with like by impaling the body of Mardonius. Mardonius, after all, was co-responsible for the outrage and was Xerxes' main advisor. The act, it was suggested, not only would increase Pausanius's reputation among Spartans and all the Greeks but would avenge (τετιμωρήσεαι) the dishonor. Pausanius's response was consistent with the Spartan love of honor and respect for the courageous enemy:

> First you exalt me and my country to the skies by your praise of my success; and then you would bring it all to nothing by advising me to insult a dead body, and by saying that my good name would be increased if I were to do an improper thing fitter for barbarians than Greeks—and even then we think it repulsive. . . . As for Leonidas, whom you wish me to avenge, he, I maintain, is abundantly avenged already—surely the countless lives here taken are a sufficient price not for Leonidas only, but for all the others, too, who fell at Thermopylae. (9.79)

So although Mardonius might have behaved dishonorably at Thermopylae, the recognition of courage connected him to Pausanius across enemy lines.[105] The honor the Spartan would bestow on a courageous comrade in arms on his own side was extended to the deserving warrior on the enemy side simply because he had been a worthy adversary.

Such recognition and connection are not only confined to honor cultures of the ancient world or to a noble class. In fact, there is evidence to suggest that this sort of connection is commonplace among warriors of all times. Writing about the experiences of soldiers in the American Civil War, Gerald F. Linderman argues that although soldiers could feel burning antipathy toward the enemy they easily lost it when the enemy displayed great feats of courage. As Linderman puts it, "Courage dissolved antipathy."[106] For example, he cites a Union color sergeant's description of the courage of Pickett's charging men at Gettysburg: "No charge was 'more daring,' and Federal observers felt an 'unbounded sympathy' for those who made it. Shortly, each side began to *express* its admiration of such feats. Indeed, Pickett said that at Fredericksburg 'we forgot they were fighting us, and cheer after cheer at their fearlessness went up all along our lines.'"[107] Some soldiers asserted that the war had forced them to realize "the courage and manliness" of their enemies, which in turn permitted them to speak of the "brotherhood of the enemy."[108]

The bond created by courage across enemy lines is not merely abstract. Linderman gives numerous examples of soldiers of all ranks who, after witnessing the courage of the men they were fighting, not only learned to respect them but actually developed a certain "delicacy in combat." As he writes, "Once soldiers granted the opponent's courage, it seemed necessary to proffer to him general notions of openness and equity, and 'giving the other fellow a fair chance,' as it was put, sometimes meant renouncing a combat advantage. When General John Bell Hood realized that the enemy troops he was about to attack were unaware of the Southerners' presence, he ordered, 'Major, send a shell first over their heads and let them get in their holes before you open with all your guns.'"[109] Recognition of courage in the enemy can foster not only respect in the abstract but also *Kriegsbruderlichkeit* that actually changes the way battles are prosecuted and the way individual soldiers carry out the task of war. Linderman gives another example: "Robert Strong and others of his unit pushed back Confederate skirmishers in a woods, but one Southerner would not withdraw with the others. He stayed to fire and then left with 'some pretty bad words' and a derisive slap at his backside. One of the Federals was angry and shouted, 'Kill him, the Rebel son of a bitch!' but others said, 'No, don't'; it would be a pity to kill so brave a man. Ultimately they cheered the Confederate."[110] Courage closes the gap between soldiers, and not only in the sense of a shared moral transformation: it *literally* closes the gap between individuals. With courage one gets up close and personal, geographically speaking, with the enemy. With courage, the warrior is able to look his enemy in the eye because he is physically close enough to see. Courage removes any abstract idea one might have about one's enemies and permits connections that would otherwise be impossible.

Modern war, Gray argues, removes the need for courage because it keeps belligerents at greater and greater distance. Hand-to-hand combat is practically obsolete, so that the occasions for transfigurative moments provided by courage all but disappear. Having said this, Gray points to a crucial part of even modern warfare: the taking of prisoners. Taking prisoners gives the frontline soldier the opportunity to know the enemy as a human being and thus often functions as a crucial experience for soldiers. In taking prisoners the soldier must close the gap, so to speak. He must come into physical contact with the enemy. Even though the enemy is defeated, the soldier must face the very real possibility that the surrender may be a ruse, the soldier may be a suicide bomber, and so on. But just as the victorious soldier needs to evince courage, so too must the surrendering soldier. As Gray puts it, "The prisoner of war reveals to his opponent that he, too, cherishes life and that he has at least minimal trust in humanity, otherwise he would not be surrendering" (137). Of course, surrendering and being taken prisoner will never garner one honor, but the act is quite different from running away. Not fleeing, not turning around and running away when the battle is lost, but instead putting trust in one's captors is in itself an act of courage. Thus when captor and prisoner meet face to face, a recognition of courage in the enemy can function much like the above-mentioned recognition of courage in actual combat. Gray relates an incident to demonstrate this:

> A certain infantry division, freshly committed to a sector of the front, had transformed its band unit into military police in charge of prisoners of war. I happened to be at the prisoner cage shortly after these music-loving soldiers had received their first batch of prisoners. A group of these youths stood, guns at the ready and very tense, facing the disarmed Germans in a stable of an old farmhouse. They were half expecting the captives at any moment to snarl and spring upon them. As soldiers fresh from the United States, their image of all Germans was that they were treacherous and fanatical storm troopers. For their part, the captured soldiers were apparently glad to be prisoners, though they, too, were apprehensive about the menacing rifles.
>
> We stared at one another with a confused mixture of hostility and fear, all alike victims of ignorance. Suddenly I heard some of the prisoners humming a tune under their breath. Four [who] were a trained quartet and had contrived to be captured together started to sing. Within a few minutes, the transformation in the atmosphere of that stable was complete, and amusing, too, in retrospect. The rifles were put down, some of them within easy reach of the captives. Everybody clustered closer and began to hum the melodies. Cigarettes were offered to the prisoners, snapshots of loved ones were displayed, and fraternization proceeded at a rapid rate. When the commanding officer, just as new to combat as his men, arrived on the scene, he was speechless with fury and amazement. The contrast between abstract image and this glimpse of reality could hardly have been more striking. (137–38)

The significance of Gray's anecdote is clear. Physical proximity of men in combat necessarily transforms the participants. Individuals can hate others in the abstract, but when the gap closes this sort of hatred dissolves. Of course abstract hatred may become personal, but even this speaks volumes about the transfigurative force of courage. Courage creates bonds of both duty and responsibility that transcend the friend-enemy distinction, and these bonds are deep enough to disrupt one of the central conventional wisdoms about war. War is not always conducted in a field of hate; on the contrary, the bonds it creates can dispel unexamined antipathy or even hatred. Courage closes the gap between individuals, be they friend or foe.

The Civic Good of Martial Courage

Before the battle of Thermopylae, Demaratus explains the Spartan way of war to Xerxes. Individually, he claims, the Spartans are as tough as nails, but it is in their capacity to fight together that they surpass other peoples. As he boldly states, "So it is with the Spartans; fighting singly, they are as good as any, but fighting together they are the best soldiers in the world" (Herodotus *Histories* 7.104). If the Spartans epitomize warrior virtues, one wonders how these virtues manifested themselves in Spartan civilian life. In fact, this question need not be restricted to the Spartan case; one might ask whether the good of martial courage and warrior virtues extend to civic life in general. Does the necessary selflessness of the courageous warrior manifest itself as selflessness in civic life? Does the capacity to form meaningful connections with other human beings spill over into peacetime? Are the transfigurative moments of courage present in times of peace? In short, are the virtues of the soldier also the virtues of the citizen?

William James, a self-professed pacifist, understood well the transfigurative effects of martial courage and the virtues of the soldier and was convinced that these virtues were the essential virtues of peace as well. To have a good community, people must be welded together, and no force welds people into cohesive states better than the "dread hammer" of war.[111] Thus for James, the martial virtues "are absolute and permanent human goods" because military discipline and the military experience allow individuals "to get the childishness knocked out of them, and to come back into society with healthier sympathies and soberer ideas."[112] We must subject ourselves to the ordeals of the soldier so that we can rise to difficult occasions that are inescapable in our distinctly human world. James is so sure of this position that he sounds like a good Spartan: "We must make new energies and hardihoods continue the manliness to which the military mind so faithfully clings. Martial virtues must be the enduring cement; intrepidity, contempt of softness, surrender of private interest, obedience to command, must still remain the rock upon which states are built—unless, indeed, we wish for dangerous reactions against commonwealths fit only for contempt, and liable to invite attack whenever a centre of crystallization for military-minded enterprise gets formed in their neighborhood."[113] Put otherwise, civilian life and peacetime require the same virtues as the successful prosecution of war. Civic life needs courage as much as martial life does. For James, however, we need to discover a method other than war that will beget these virtues and a way to transfer them into civic life. If this can be done, he sees the possibility of greatness in what will ultimately be a peaceful world. As he puts it, "It is only a question of blowing on the spark till the whole population gets incandescent, and on the ruins of the old morals of military honor, a stable system of morals of civic honor builds itself up."[114]

James is not alone in this opinion. Tom Brokaw, for instance, in his *Greatest Generation,* praises the millions of men and women who served in the U.S. military during the Second World War. His book is filled with narratives recalling not only their great courage in wartime but also how they comported themselves after the war. As Brokaw puts it, after returning from their wartime vocations, these people "were mature beyond their years, tempered by what they had been through, disciplined by their military training and sacrifices."[115] Many of these returning soldiers partook of the G.I. Bill, which provided America with "a new kind of army now, moving onto the landscapes of industry, science, art, public policy, all the fields of American life, bringing to them the same passions and discipline that had served them so well during the war."[116] Directly from the discipline and experience of war, this generation transformed a war economy into the strongest peacetime economy in the world, made breakthroughs in the sciences and social programs, and turned America into the greatest power in the world. The generation, Brokaw claims, is the greatest America has ever had, and much of their greatness is owed to their experiences of the war and the warrior virtues they brought home.

While Brokaw's claim is largely anecdotal and journalistic, some scholarly studies have yielded similar results. Dave Grossman reports that after World War II ended, veterans maintained the selfless way of life learned during the war experience, in contrast to Vietnam-era veterans, who were far more likely to experience post-traumatic stress disorder (PTSD). He claims that the World War II veterans fared much better after the war precisely because their training and experience aimed specifically at the aforementioned goods of martial courage. This, of course, is not to say that Vietnam veterans were cowardly. On the contrary, trudging through dense jungle foliage littered with antipersonnel mines and unseen enemies took enormous courage. The crucial difference, however, between the two wars is that connections were rarely established between the soldiers who fought in Vietnam as they were between the soldiers who fought in World War II. Soldiers were conscripted for Vietnam and told that they would serve a one-year tour of duty, then be released. As Grossman puts it, they arrived alone and left alone.[117] While they were there, they often had neither the time nor, more importantly, the inclination to make lasting friendships. The very way the war was prosecuted was not conducive to the kind of physical proximity necessary for begetting these deep connections. Many narratives from the war's veterans discuss the detachment they felt from their fellow soldiers. Tim O'Brien, for example, writes of his experience marching through the jungle on an ambush mission:

> One of the most persistent and appalling thoughts that lumbers through your mind as you walk through Vietnam at night is the fear of getting lost, of becoming detached from the others, of spending the night alone in that frightening and haunted countryside. It was dark. We walked in single file, perhaps three yards apart. . . . The man to the front and the man to the rear were the only holds on security and sanity. We followed the man in front like a blind man after his dog; we prayed that the man had not lost *his* way, that he hadn't lost contact with the man to his front. We tensed our eyeballs, peered straight ahead. We hurt ourselves staring. We strained. We dared not look away for fear the man leading us might fade and turn into shadow. Sometimes, when the dark closed in, we reached out to him, touched his shirt.[118]

The scene could not be further from the soldierly connections of the Spartan phalanx fighting. The psychological need to be protected by one's comrade in arms is still there, but the form of fighting is not conducive to it. In fact, this is an understatement. The type of war described is antithetical to these kinds of close connections. As O'Brien later says about the march—the main method of engaging the enemy—because of the land mines "you try to trace the footprints of the man to your front. You give it up when he curses you for following too closely; better one man dead than two."[119] The very nature of the war forced both a symbolic and actual widening of the gap between the soldiers.

In Grossman's understanding, this sort of disconnection between soldiers that resulted from the manner of fighting was paralleled in the sort of social support that returning Vietnam veterans received, and social support is a key factor influencing the degree of PTSD. Just as the soldier went to the battle alone, he returned alone. On leaving Vietnam, veterans would depart "with a mixture of joy at having survived and shame at having left their buddies behind. Instead of returning to parades, they found antiwar marches. Instead of luxury hotels, they were sent to locked and guarded military bases where they were processed back to civilian life in a few days. . . . They were rejected by girlfriends, spit on, and accused by strangers and finally dared not even admit to close friends that they were veterans."[120] In short, because of the shape of the warfare and because of the social and political climate, the transfigurative effects of martial courage were not permitted to take root. The soldiers returning were, in effect, brooched, sometimes to death, by their fellow Americans.

In contrast, when the World War II veterans returned, both the virtues they had acquired as soldiers and the connections they had thereby established among themselves were welcomed and fostered in civic life. As Grossman puts it, when they "came home after the war they returned as a unit together with the same guys they had spent the whole war with, on board a ship, spending weeks joking and laughing, gambling, and telling tall tales as they cooled down and depressurized in what psychologists would call a very supportive group-therapy environment on the long voyage home."[121] Just as armies throughout history had marched home, the World War II veterans underwent a slow transition back into civilian society that permitted the deep connections and the lessons learned in battle to be brought in a healthy way back to the homeland. These veterans, Grossman notes, stayed in touch with their battle brothers and often linked up at reunions and informal gatherings. Moreover, "what was best about being a veteran was being able to hold your head high and knowing just how much your family, friends, community, and nation respected you and were proud of you."[122]

So on the long ocean voyage home the men were able to transition from a group identity revolving around warriors and violence to a group identity revolving around civilian life.[123] Not only was this crucial in reducing the levels of PTSD, there is also evidence that it lent itself to the creation of better citizens. In a recent study, Suzanne Mettler has found that World War II veterans in general were more inclined to participate in public life than nonveterans. But veterans who took advantage of the G.I. Bill were even more public spirited. Mettler's study strongly suggests that it was not the education itself, or the sort of education, that made them more publicly spirited. Instead, it was participating in the shared group experience of the G.I. Bill that spilled over into the selflessness of civic engagement. In other words, participating in the shared training experience of the G.I. Bill mirrored the experience of military training and the war. While according to Mettler such social programs in and of themselves contribute to the well-being of individuals and the communities to which they belong, veterans' greater civic engagement also demonstrates that group identity and selfless courage fostered in the military and made manifest in battle can spill over into civilian life.[124] The transition from individual to group identity that is inculcated in the young warrior and thoroughly internalized under the "storm of steel" can be maintained in times of peace. In sum, the selflessness that is the key to honorable and courageous soldiering becomes selflessness in peacetime and civic honor. Martial courage—the risking of life and limb in war and battle, selflessness, the practice of being drawn out of selfish individualism—is replicated in civilian life. Courage, both on and off the battlefield, is an absolute and permanent human good.

THREE

Political Courage and Justice

Political Courage and the Problem of Violence

Thus far courage has been explored in the context of war and battle. This exploration reveals a deep relationship between a warrior's courage and the love of honor. It also brings to light something deeper: in making himself martially courageous, man creates for himself moments of human possibility—possibilities of self-overcoming, fraternity, and transcendence. Making oneself courageous and sharing danger with one's fellows opens the way to meaningful life in communities of shared cares and responsibilities. In addition, the recreation in civic life of beneficial habits associated with martial courage makes martial courage consistently and deeply appealing in the course of human affairs. The honorable and selfless neighbor, after all, is always more appealing than the dishonorable and selfish. The courageous man is always better than the coward.

There is, however, another way to look at martial courage and the love of honor. Insofar as martial courage is inextricably bound up with warriors and honor, it is also bound up with violence. As Jean G. Peristiany correctly observes, "It is not possible to read about honor and shame . . . without making frequent mental excursions and involuntary comparisons with the *gesta* of chivalry, with school gangs, with street corner societies, etc."[1] In other words, it is easy to imagine noble deeds for the sake of honor and fraternity, or heroes dying gloriously for the sake of friends and family, but it is just as easy to imagine petty thugs violently prosecuting the smallest of insults. One can think of a samurai slicing a peasant in half for making eye contact, men performing honor killings of "besmirched" sisters, and so on. Despite the self-overcoming, transcendence, fraternity, and meaningful community associated with martial courage, one must also recognize that it is bound up with the human capacity for violence and destruction.

The association of martial courage and violence, it must be understood, is not arbitrary or episodic. Honor is, on principle, violent. In honor cultures, offences must be redressed, and redress is almost always violent. Redeeming honor needs violence because the stain of dishonor requires blood for its cleansing. This does not mean the offender needs to be killed—this is but a modern bastardization of an old code—but where dishonor pertains, the appearance of blood is necessary for "satisfaction." According to Johan Huizinga, this blood aspect of revenge and redress is elemental. In the duel, for example, "it is the shedding of blood and not the killing that matters. We can call it a late form of ritual blood-play, the orderly regulation of the death-blow struck unawares in anger. The spot where the duel is fought bears all the marks of a play-ground; the weapons have to be exactly alike as in certain games; there is a signal for the start and the finish, and the number of shots is prescribed. When blood flows, honour is vindicated and restored."[2] Apologies are insufficient in honor cultures. Honor requires blood, and the drawing of blood, of course, requires real, empirical violence.

Julian Pitt-Rivers claims that "satisfaction may be acquired through an apology which is a verbal act of self-humiliation or it may require, and if the apology is not forthcoming does require, avenging. To leave an affront unavenged is to leave one's honour in a state of desecration and this is therefore equivalent to cowardice. Hence the popularity among the mottos of the aristocracy of the theme of *nemo me impune lecessit* (no man may harm me with impunity)."[3] An apology, however, never fully bleaches the stain of dishonor because this form of redress requires the insulted to allow a diminishment of his prestige. It moves the offended in the right direction, but accepting a "mere" apology casts suspicion on one's character. It diminishes one's prestige because one will be suspected as too cowardly to do what *really* needs to be done—to draw blood. Redressing an insult thus goes beyond the particular insult. As Pitt-Rivers puts it, "The satisfaction by which honour was restored was something more than personal satisfaction, for it was accorded by the appeal to the test of courage regardless of the outcome. The duel [for example] finished the matter; the quarrel could not honourably be prosecuted thereafter, either by the contestants or their partisans."[4] In this world, the good man is the courageous man, and the courageous man must be willing and able to draw blood. Thus the good man must also be a violent man, and the relations between individuals, both friends and enemies, is always articulated by violence.

The tradition of courage and honor points to a basic paradox of human existence. While courage opens the way to moments of self-overcoming, transcendence, and fraternity, it also reveals an abiding human attachment to destruction and enmity. And here lies the problem with martial courage. If we must aspire to courage, must we then accept the predication of all our relationships on violence? If we care fundamentally about honor, must we always live under the threat of violent death? Must we be resigned to live in a constant state of war and battle? If we answer these questions affirmatively, it appears courage has an inherent argument against itself. How can courage be praised if it reduces the human condition to a constant state of war and violence? How can manly courage be upheld as a human good if it turns back on itself and destroys human life? We have already discovered that martial courage and honor lie at the heart of the Homeric world—the kidnapping of Helen, after all, was the insult that launched a thousand ships. We have also seen that it later came to be emulated, praised, and pursued obsessively in Sparta. At the same time, however, it can be argued that this vision of manly courage contributed to centuries of incessant warfare. Because the entire ancient world, both within cities and among cities, was articulated by violence, and because the love of honor and victory meant a constant fear of war, slavery, and death, it does not seem surprising if such a way of life fell into disrepute. Or if not into disrepute, it would not be surprising if, at the very least, this form of manly courage came to be questioned by thoughtful people.

This is precisely the argument made by several scholars of classical antiquity. Karen Bassi, for instance, reports that ἀνδρεία does not appear in Homer at all. In the *Iliad*, when rallying the troops, neither Ajax nor Nestor exhorts the troops to "manly courage." Instead they simply say, "Be men" (ἀνέρες ἔστε). As Bassi puts it, "The admonition to 'Be men' is uttered in preparation for armed combat where being a man is proven by physical action, by standing one's ground, and refusing to retreat (i.e. at *Iliad* 15.665–6)."[5] Being a man is strongly associated with bodily activity: "Manliness is modeled on the visible, physical, and martial feats of the heroic *anêr*."[6] To be a man is to perform martial feats, and little ethical distinction is made regarding the form of these actions. It is only with *andreia* that this ethical dimension is introduced, but the actual word *andreia* appears only later, for the first time in Herodotus. It does this precisely because the physical attributes of men and courage, once closely connected, are beginning to be dissociated. According to Sarah Harrell, Herodotus twice in his *Histories* expresses amazement that certain individuals display *andreia*. He is amazed because, whereas traditional "manly" behaviors are naturally associated with men, he comes across examples that contradict this expectation. As Harrell puts it, "The marvelous stories of Artemisia and Telines suggest that, for Herodotus, politics, geography, and ethnicity, in addition to sex and gender—not some single, essential element—all inform his conception of *andreia*."[7] Artemisia, a woman, holds her husband's political position after his death and continues to wage war against Greece; Telines performs an amazing act of political founding, despite being a rather womanly and soft man (θηλυδρίης τε καὶ μαλακώτερος; *Histories* 7.153.4).[8] Whether Herodotus is amazed because these two are women, womanly, Asian, or barbarian, the more important point is that their *andreia*, their manly acts, are not acts of physical prowess but what might more properly be called political acts. As Harrell states, "Telines performed his courageous act when a *stasis*, or factional dispute, had caused part of the population to leave Gela (7.153.2). . . . Herodotus alludes to the fact that this situation could easily have resulted in armed conflict. . . . Telines' *andreia* resides in the ability to prevent, rather than carry out, civil war."[9] Being men and being manly, it appears for the first time, are not necessarily the same. When the idea of manly courage arises in these texts, it reveals a new arena for human endeavor—men can be manly not only on the traditional battlefield but in the political arena. Moreover, though it is still "wondrous," women can also be politically courageous.

Bassi claims that the introduction of *andreia* in the fifth century coincides with a changing political scene. In one of its earliest appearances—in Aeschylus's *Seven against Thebes* (467 BCE)—*andreia* is invoked and maintains the tenor of Homeric martial courage.[10] However, on this occasion *andreia* is used alongside ἀγάνωρ, and both terms are meant to indicate a *surplus* of manly strength.[11] With Aeschylus, raw martial courage is thus presented in a critical light: "From the point of view of the Thebans, the masculinity of the Argives is clearly a negative attribute whether it is called *agênôr* or *andreia*."[12] But this transmogrification is not unique to Aeschylus. Later, in his *Electra*, Sophocles has Electra herself use *andreia* to characterize her manly attributes, and, as Bassi points out, "The use of *andreia* in the *Electra* . . . points to the absence of masculinity in its traditional or normative form and the emergence of a manliness that is no longer *anêr* specific."[13] In short, the very idea of manliness is being called into question as the desirability of community founded on (and maintained by) violence falls into disrepute.

Pericles, Political Courage, and Democratic Leisure

The evolution of courage and manliness is not limited to the tragedians. In Thucydides we also find an evocation of courage reflecting this transformation in Athens. In his *History of the Peloponnesian War*, Thucydides recounts the funeral oration of Pericles after the first year of the war, about 430 BCE. Here Pericles claims that Athenian courage is not necessarily bound up with martiality or the threat of violence under law (νόμος), as is the case with Sparta. Athenian courage, he suggests, does not stem from the compulsion of law but instead reflects a wholly different way of being (τρόπος). To speak of a wholly different way of being, of course, cuts to the core of existence and raises anew the question of fundamental cares. When courage is invoked, we are always well served to make such an inquiry: For the sake of what are a people willing to risk life and limb? We know the Spartan way of being revolves around honor, but for the sake of what is Pericles exhorting his countrymen to further courage?

Pericles is most certainly attempting to keep courage a central part of Athenian virtue (ἀρετη). What is changing, however, is the fundamental care for which courage is invoked. Ryan Balot suggests that it might be reason, or "the reasonable life," that Pericles has in mind as the Athenian fundamental care. As such, Pericles is calling his countrymen to "rational courage." This rational courage, Balot writes, is constituted by "a rational understanding of their duty and by their appropriate behavioural responses to the exigencies of battle—daring and having a sense of shame."[14] Athenians, he argues, are distinct because they make speeches to explain why they should continue to risk life and limb. This is true but says little about a different way of being. There is, for example, no reason to think that Spartan courage was not rational in this way. Spartans, though more laconic, also discussed their duties in battle, and it would be absurd to think that Spartans fell short in the exigencies of battle because they failed to reason strategically beforehand.[15] Moreover, if the previous chapter has revealed anything about their way of being, it is that Spartans knew courage and had an extremely developed sense of shame. The claim, then, that "in Pericles' vision of a rationally based courage, courage is the virtue that inspires individuals to put into practice their underlying values in the appropriate way, at the appropriate time, and for the right reasons" does little to distinguish the Athenian way of being from the Spartan. In fact, it does little to distinguish the Homeric, American, Bushido, or any other way of being, for that matter. Communities exist because fundamental cares are part and parcel of average everyday conversations, speeches, and politics. Thus to distinguish Spartans and

Athenians on the basis of "Athenian rational courage and the Spartans' socially compulsory courage," as Balot does, seems overly complicated.[16] Both Spartans and Athenians were compelled to courage by shame—and the Athenian generals executed after the battle of Arginusae would certainly attest to this.[17]

Clifford Orwin offers another view. He suggests that "Pericles sketches a society in which the fullest development of the citizen is compatible with the greatest devotion to the city."[18] The same, however, can be said regarding Spartans, because Spartan courage in battle is compatible with the greatest devotion to Sparta. The most fully developed Spartan is, after all, he who courageously fights for Spartan honor. Thus claiming that, for Pericles, Athens is special because "she fosters, in freedom rather than through compulsion, an extraordinary blossoming of both public and private life" does not say enough.[19] Even if we were to agree with Orwin that "public life predominates" in Athens and that free participation in it is most important, there is no reason to think that Spartans were not freely participating in their own public life. To participate in the public affairs of Sparta was to fight beside one's battle brothers in the phalanx and subsequently to partake equally of the collective honor garnered from doing so. Insofar as courage aims at a fundamental care, it is necessarily free. This is the existential character of courage.

In pointing to freedom and reason, however, Orwin and Balot are circling the meaning of Periclean courage. What distinguishes Athens from Sparta is the general mode of existence when *not* in battle. As Pericles tells us, to be manly men Spartans live a life of constant straining (μοχθέω). Athenians are superior because, though no less daring (μὴ ἀτολμοτέρους), they live with an "easiness of temper" (ῥᾳθυμία).[20] Now, *rhathumia* is no random quality Pericles throws into the equation. In its typical usage, it indicates a defect, or even a vice. Plato, for instance, uses it to indicate "rashness of speech" in his *Philebus* (μακρὰ ῥᾳθυμία εἴη τοῦ λόγου).[21] Xenophon's Socrates lists it with the vices imperiling Athens: carelessness, slackness, and disobedience (ἀμέλειάν τε καὶ ῥᾳθυμίαν καὶ ἀπείθειαν).[22] Yet for Pericles, strangely, *rhathumia* is not a vice. Instead it has a positive connotation, pointing to a "relaxed" way of being. Spartans, he tells us, "pursue manhood [ἀνδρεῖον] with laborious training [ἐπιπόνῳ ἀσκήσει]." Athenians, on the other hand, with their "more relaxed way of life . . . are no less willing to take on equivalent dangers" (2.39). This more relaxed way of life outside battle is not a means to another end. It does not, for example, aim at inculcating Athenians with martial courage, as does, say, the Spartan *agoge*. It is a *ne plus ultra* good, and it is for this good that Pericles is encouraging his fellow citizens. This relaxed way of being, he is arguing, is that for which Athenians ought to risk life and limb. Thus, in a direct parallel to honor, *rhathumia* becomes a fundamental care. *Rhathumia* is therefore not slackness, laziness, or the rashness of a specific person but a deeply desirable way of living together.[23] It is living together in such a way that, outside battle, the finer things in life can be acquired and appreciated. Pericles' Funeral Oration is thus not merely an exhortation to courage for the sake of freedom or the rational life. Freedom and the rational life are possibilities within a rhathumic way of being but are not constitutive. The meaning of Periclean courage is thus evident: Spartans are courageous but must live a life of constant strain; Athenians are equally courageous but are able to live a rhathumic lifestyle.

In saying this, Pericles appears to be exhorting his countrymen to continue the war and to muster their courage for the sake of *leisure*. What is interesting is that Pericles seems to be deliberately avoiding the actual language of "leisure" (hêsychia). The word appears many times in Thucydides' *History* but not here in the Funeral Oration, precisely when Pericles appears to be describing leisure.[24] According to Helen North, this is a prime example of a great theme in Thucydides: "the contrast between Athens and Sparta."[25] Thucydides, she argues, employs a specialized vocabulary familiar from other sources of the period. Certain words are appropriated by Athens, others by Sparta, and still others are used by both states, or by rival factions within them. *Apragmosynê* and *hêsychia* are distinctive Spartan and oligarchic qualities. *Prothymia* ("enthusiasm"), *synesis* ("intelligence"), *to drastêrion* ("activity"), *tolmê* ("audacity," in a good sense), and *polypragmosynê* ("busybodiness," also, and more surprisingly, in a good sense) belong to the Athenians.[26]

Hêsychia—leisure traditionally understood—is strongly associated with aristocracy and oligarchy. Along with *sophrosyne*, it is descended from the Doric aristocratic tradition and is symbolically antithetical to democracy and the Athenian way of being.[27] This distinction between *rhathumia* and *hêsychia* is corroborated in the Corinthian speech at Sparta. The Corinthians describe the Athenian disdain for "leisure" as follows: "In hardship and danger they toil throughout their lives for such ends, and least enjoy what they have on account of always acquiring and thinking that there is no holiday except in doing what the occasion demands, and that unproductive leisure [ἡσυχίαν ἀπράγμονα] is more of a misfortune than laborious business [ἀσχολίαν ἐπίπονον]. And so, if some were to sum them up by saying that they were born to have no leisure themselves and allow it to no one else [μήτε αὐτοὺς ἔχειν ἡσυχίαν μήτε τοὺς ἄλλους ἀνθρώπους], he would be right" (1.70, translation modified).

It is not leisure per se that does not fit the Athenian way of being, but "unproductive leisure." Thus it appears that Pericles has in mind leisure, but he avoids using the word *hêsychia* because of its aristocratic and unproductive meaning. Leisure and leisure classes, after all, are inimical to democracy, and invoking such language would be politically inexpedient for Pericles as a democratic leader.

What can be interpreted from this distinction is that Pericles uses *rhathumia* to indicate "democratic leisure." The distinction between martial courage and political courage is thus a little clearer. In Sparta, a man's virtue is measured by his capacity for accruing honor in war, and the large part of his life is spent straining toward this end. In Pericles' view, such a way of being is inadequate for the most rewarding human life in the polis among one's fellow citizens. He is thus encouraging Athenians to a courage that aims at democratic leisure, which includes the "love of beauty [φιλοκαλοῦμέν] while practicing economy and [the] love of wisdom [φιλοσοφοῦμεν]" (2.40). It is possible, Pericles is arguing, to care fundamentally about things other than honor and not be soft because of it. One can care about wisdom and beauty "without being enervated [μαλακίας]" (2.40). In Athens one can care about art, one's private affairs, and especially the managerial affairs of the polis and still be as manly as any Spartan.

Pericles' stress on democratic leisure by no means diminishes the importance of reason and speech in this wholly different way of being. What must be understood, however, is that for Pericles reason and speech are instrumental—it is not for their sake that Athenians ought to muster courage. Athenians specifically employ reason and speech, which make up the very substance of political courage, to effectively acquire and apply power in their empire. Though his interpretive lens is colored by a modern and American love of freedom, Josiah Ober recognizes this paradoxical relationship between martial courage and political courage in Pericles' funeral oration: "In the course of Pericles' speech, each praiseworthy ideal eventually points to its opposite. Freedom is proclaimed as the prime good of the polis, but there is a strong hint that, as Thucydides' readers already know, the *dunamis* of Athens deprives the *poleis* within the empire of their freedom."[28] The Athenian way of being derives not merely from physical training (as in Sparta) but from the power of reason and speech. The democratic fora in Athens are therefore part and parcel of the rhathumic way of being. At home, reason and speech are part of a more relaxed mode of acquiring honor and victory. The empire, in turn, provides an arena for martial courage, which then provides the material means required for democratic leisure at home. This is precisely why Pericles argues that

> we are unique in considering the man who takes no part in these [speeches] to be not apolitical [ἀπράγμονα] but useless [ἀχρεῖον], and we ourselves either ratify or even propound successful politics [πράγματα], finding harm not in the effect of speeches [τοὺς λόγους] on action [τοῖς ἔργοις] but in failing to get instruction by speech before proceeding to what must be done. For in that we are both especially daring [τολμᾶν] and especially thorough in calculating [ἐκλογίζομαι] what we attempt, we can truly be distinguished from other men, for whom ignorance is boldness [θράσος] but calculation [λογισμὸς] brings hesitation. Rightly would they be judged strongest [κράτιστοι] in spirit who recognize both dangers [δεινὰ] and

> pleasures [ἡδέα] with utmost clarity and are on neither count deterred from risks [κινδύνων]. (2.40)

Athens is unique, according to Pericles, in that she makes way for pleasure (ἡδέα) while maintaining the older category of manly courage. Athenians, in their external affairs, are very much like Spartans: they love honor and victory, and violence is the prevailing mode of articulation. Among the free citizens of Athens, however, Pericles outright rejects this for a more just way of being—Hesychia (Leisure), after all, is the daughter of Dike.[29]

Thus in Athens courage has its own arena—political life in the democratic government. The politically courageous are not limited to a few godlike warriors. Just as the whole way of being in Athens is more relaxed, so too are the requisites of courageous citizenship. The arena is open to whoever is versed in the weapons of political contests: reasonable speech. This means that physical attributes, such as raw strength, sex, and, especially, hereditary class, cease to be absolute hindrances to partaking of this way of being. As Pericles puts it:

> We have a form of government that does not emulate the practices of our neighbors, setting an example to some rather than imitating others. In name it is called a democracy on account of being administered in the interest not of the few but the many, yet even though there are equal rights for all in private disputes in accordance with the laws, wherever each man has earned recognition he is singled out for public service in accordance with the claims of distinction, not by rotation but by merit, nor when it comes to poverty, if a man has real ability to benefit the city, is he prevented by obscure renown. (2.37)

Whereas in other cities one's merit can be proven only in battle, in Athens good citizenship is also measured by one's proficiency in the prevailing mode of articulation. Whereas with the older generation people were articulated by violence, Pericles finds it praiseworthy that Athenians are articulated in a more relaxed mode. Martial courage—the love of honor and a social order predicated on violence—is thus being directly contrasted to *political courage* and a social order predicated on speech.

It must be stressed, however, that for Pericles political courage and speech are exercised only in the service of rhathumic justice in Athens, between Athenians. With regard to affairs external to Athens, martial courage and violence predominate. Political courage can still be relevant abroad, but martial deeds have priority. Pericles' claim is that Athens' power abroad is a direct result of her internal character (2.41) and that the Athenian empire is a direct result of the exercise of political courage within her walls. But beyond her walls, as Pericles forthrightly says, we need "no Homer to sing our praises nor any other whose verses will charm for the moment and whose claims the factual truth will destroy, since we have compelled [καταναγκάζω] every sea and land to become open to our daring [τολμει] and populated every region with lasting monuments of our acts of harm and good" (2.41). Within Athens, deeds are motivated by the more relaxed things in life. Outside Athens, in pursuit of the different way of being within, deeds that compel are at least equal to speech. In Pericles' view of political order, then, there is a place for both violent and discursive articulation, for both martial and political courage. The daring and courageous deeds of the war dead are eulogized precisely for the sake of their returns within the city—for the sake of a more relaxed way of life where both higher and hedonistic pleasures can be had without enervating effects. In short, democratic leisure is purchased by martial courage in the empire.

Pointing to democratic leisure as a fundamental care leaves unanswered a few questions regarding the rationally articulated community. We know that Pericles eulogizes the war dead because they epitomize manly courage in risking life and limb for the sake of Athens' rhathumic way of life. The virtue of these men, however, lies in their proficiency not only in the art of violence but also in the art of rational articulation. Just as Spartans were esteemed for their martial skills, Athenians are praised for their discursive skills. The heroism of the war dead, for Pericles at least, is that they heard the arguments, were "instructed by speech," then made their deeds equal to the speech. They demonstrated in deed that which was determined by argument: that Athens and her more relaxed way of being transcended their own well-being and, for that matter, their being; "None of these men turned coward [προτιμήσας ἐμαλακίσθη] from preferring the further enjoyment of wealth nor did any, from the poor man's hope that he might still escape poverty and grow rich, contrive to postpone the danger" (2.42). The dead, it seems, were the best Athens had to offer because, from hearing the speeches there, they became her lover (ἐραστὰς) (2.43). But even in becoming her lover, which is to say, in loving a way of life marked by democratic leisure, they were able to "take to the battle a manly courage [ἀνδραγαθίαν] beyond even their forefathers" (2.42, my translation). Through this intermingling of political and martial courage, the dead Athenians proffered their own bodies, which had not become "soft" (ἐμαλακίσθη) from the more refined Athenian habits.[30]

In the case of martial courage, then, the heroic deeds of the warrior find their greatest expression on the battlefield alone. Athenian warriors, however, create a second canvas on which their memories can be recorded. As Pericles puts it, "For in giving their lives in common cause, they individually gained imperishable praise and the most distinctive tomb, not the one where they are buried but the one where on every occasion for word and deed their glory is left after them eternally. The whole earth is the tomb of famous men, and not only inscriptions set up in their own country mark it but even in foreign lands an unwritten memorial, present not in monument but in mind, abides within each man" (2.43). The heroic deeds of the war dead result not in mere physical monuments—though this may also be the case—but in possible future speeches. The speeches enabled by their deeds are not just encomia for those deeds; they are not speeches that merely sing of this or that feat, as, say, Homer's *Iliad* does. The real heroism of these warriors is that they fight and die to ensure a more relaxed home where speech itself can dwell, where "factual truth" (2.41) can be heard, and where citizens are conjoined by the more pleasurable things in life, whether speech, art, the life of the mind, or even more hedonistic pursuits. In other words, through their heroic martial courage, they ensure a space for political courage and the freedom to pursue democratic leisure. The dead were heroic because they recognized that cowardice would put "the most important things at stake" and thus that "cowardice [μαλακισθῆναι] is more painful than death" (2.43).

But as we have said, despite Pericles' evident care for democratic leisure, he occupies a place between martial courage and political courage, strictly speaking. Pericles admits, for example, that honor is still important. As he says, "For a love of honor [φιλότιμον] is the only thing that has no age, and it is not profit [κερδαίνειν], as some claim, but honor [τιμᾶσθαι] that brings delight in the period of uselessness" (2.44). Dramatically speaking, this concern and reminder of the benefits of honor is spoken to the parents of the dead. He invokes honor to comfort the older generation—the generation that fought at Marathon. To the younger generation, to the sons and brothers, he offers a rather different comfort. He tells them that "with regard to honor they will likely be judged slightly inferior" but that they really ought not to be too concerned with it. After all, "the living incur the envy for a rival, but those who no longer offer opposition receive honor with a good will lacking in competitiveness [ἀνανταγωνίστῳ]" (2.45). In short, with this one statement Pericles is proclaiming the inadequacy of honor as the only standard by which the Athenians should live. Honor is not, and cannot be thrown out completely because it has an enduring appeal, especially for the older generation. For the younger generation honor alone no longer suffices, not only because it might well be impossible to live up to the martial courage demonstrated at Marathon, Salamis, and Plataea, but because the demands of honor are antithetical to democratic leisure. To put it bluntly, it is unreasonable to compete with those who cannot be defeated—the dead. The dead cannot be judged fairly, they cannot be outstripped, because they do not participate in the new modes and orders of the rhathumic Athenian community. What the younger generation can live up to, however, is the truth and this is attained through the force of political courage.[31]

As such, Pericles' comfort to the sons and brothers of the dead is this: "From this time the city will rear [θρέψει] their sons at public expense until they are of age" (2.46). What is most important about this pledge, however, is that Athens will bear the costs and burdens of nourishing (θρέψις) the orphans, not into Homeric warriors, but into democratic citizens. The proposal, after all, is not to pay for some sort of Spartan *agoge* but for training in various modes of the proper enjoyment of democratic leisure, like participation in useful contests and the delivery of useful funeral orations.[32] It will be an education first in the habits (τρόποι) underwriting the democratic way of life, which will in turn enable Athens to acquire her external greatness. As Pericles puts it in the conclusion to his oration, "It is among those who establish the greatest prize for courage [ἀρετῆς μέγιστα] that men are the best citizens" (2.46). And for Pericles, the prize for courage is twofold: first, as with the Spartans, it is honor and victory; second, it is living a more relaxed way of life in accordance with the truth of Athenian power.[33]

Pericles, then, regards this political courage as the source of Athenian exceptionalism, but his optimistic view of manly political courage and democratic leisure is not universal. Objection is made, not to his claim that political courage is an essential and desirable element of Athenian culture, but rather to his claim that this way of being can prepare Athenians for martial courage outside Athens. One of the sharpest critiques of this view is found elsewhere in Thucydides' *History*. After Pericles' funeral oration, Thucydides immediately recounts the hellish incursion of the plague in Athens. As one Thucydides scholar claims, this is not by accident: "It could of course be said that the plague flowed from the war in a direct sense (because the crowding of the city and Piraeus was a consequence of the war), but that is not, I think, uppermost in Thucydides' mind at the time." Instead, the evocation of the plague immediately on the heels of Pericles' funeral oration can aptly be compared to Camus' symbolic use of bubonic plague in *The Plague*, "where it serves as a 'symbol of the German occupation of France in the Second World War, and indeed the horrors of war in general.'"[34] Whereas Pericles envisions political courage as the source of a more humane, peaceful, discursive mode of articulation within Athens, Thucydides likens it to the most gruesome internal fractiousness. During the plague, the city was coming apart at the seams. The Attic refugees, Thucydides says, were forced to occupy "the uninhabited parts of the city and the sanctuaries and the shrines of heroes." Even the Pelargikon, "which was under a curse against occupation, . . . was occupied nevertheless under the pressure of the emergency" (3.17). Most poignantly, "Many even made their homes in the towers of the city walls, and wherever each could manage. For the city was inadequate for them when they were all there, but later they divided up the long walls and most of the Piraeus and settled there" (3.17). The image of people living in the walls is very startling—they are neither inside the city nor outside. They dwell in-between. If the walls divide one way of being within the city from another without, the presence of the dead and dying festering in the very walls suggests a collapse of the very boundary that defines the integrity of the city. Thucydides portrays the sick and dislocated as almost an infection in the joints of the city, one that arises as a direct consequence of Pericles' vision of manly courage—indeed, Athens is not much of an education for all Hellas, as Pericles would have his listeners believe. For Thucydides, the physical degeneration of Athens and Athenian human bodies is closely connected with the moral degeneration described in the last few chapters of the plague account. In the end, this means that democratic leisure, while a step in the right direction, provides only a partial account of justice. Hesychia is still only the bastard daughter of Dike.

Aristophanes' Derision of Martial Courage

By the end of the Peloponnesian War, martial courage, honor, and violence became grist for the comedy mill. In fact, Ineke Sluiter and Ralph Mark Rosen go so far as to say that many comic poets were "*obsessed* with *andreia*" and that it was "the most essential and defining characteristic claimed or projected by any comic poet whose literary thrust is satire and mockery."[35] Comic poets such as Aristophanes saw the direction Athens had taken after Pericles' leadership as disastrous and therefore directly attacked his political progeny. For Aristophanes, there simply was no place in late fifth-century Hellas for the Homeric vision of courage. Although it made for wondrous tales to tell children, it was a perilous tradition to follow. In the Homeric accounts, martial courage had brought the Greek cities together for a common cause, and this version of courage had culminated in the united Greek stand against Persian enslavement. Martial courage emerged for the common Greek cause. In the Periclean version, courage no longer afforded the Greeks a moral basis for acting in concert against a unified foreign threat. Instead, the courage Pericles described created a situation where the common glory (κλέος) of the Greek cause was subordinated to the glory of individual cities. Moreover, the glory of individual cities—especially Athens—became subordinated to the glory of the individuals. For Aristophanes, this disintegration of a common Greek cause was directly responsible for the disintegration of the cities into civil war (στάσις) and constant conflict between the Greek cities themselves.

This is precisely why Aristophanes was so mercilessly critical of manly martial courage in general, and of men like Cleon in particular. One of his more hilarious attacks on martial courage is found in his *Frogs* (404 BCE). In this comedy Aristophanes tells a story of the god Dionysus's effort to satisfy his intense desire (πόθος) for Euripides. Because Euripides is dead, he needs to descend to Hades, and to do this he needs instruction from the hero who has made this journey—Heracles. After learning the way down, Dionysus and his slave Xanthias make the journey. Once there they approach the palace of Pluto, where Dionysus, wearing his Heraclean lion skin and carrying a club, knocks. The knock is answered by Aeacus, who launches into a litany of invectives and horrible threats against Dionysus, whom he mistakes for Heracles. After his tirade he departs, and the divine Dionysus, like the quintessential coward, collapses and actually loses control of his bowels:

Xanthias: What have you done?
Dionysus: I am horribly frightened! Call god!
Xanthias: Don't be absurd. Get up quickly! Do you want someone to see you like that?
Dionysus: But I'm faint. Get me a sponge and put it on my heart!
Xanthias: Here, take it. Put it on.
Dionysus: Where is it? (Applies sponge to his posterior)
Xanthias: God of Gold! That's where you keep your heart?
Dionysus: I got so frightened I dropped a bowel-full!
Xanthias: O coward [δειλότατε] of gods or men![36]

For Aristophanes then, emulating the mythical heroic deeds whose stories are passed down from generation to generation is impossible even for a god, and the courageous deeds of Heracles—the slaying of Cerberus, for example—were more acts of deception than acts of heroic courage. Thus the heroics of Heracles, even for the gods, are, here quite literally, a load of excrement. Much the same can be said about mimicking the martial heroics recounted in Homer.

After being called a coward by his slave, Dionysus objects. His actions are, he argues, in fact courageous. As he puts it:

> Dionysus: Me? How can I be a coward when I asked you for a sponge? Another man [ἀνήρ] would have done differently.
> Xanthias: Done what?
> Dionysus: A real coward would have lain there stinking. Me, I stood up and wiped myself!
> Xanthias: O Poseidon! You are courageous [ἀνδρεῖά]!
> Dionysus: By god, so it seems. Weren't you frightened by that rumble of words and threats?
> Xanthias: By god, I didn't even notice.
> Dionysus: Okay now, if you're such a high-spirited courageous man [λημματίας κἀνδρεῖος], grab this club and lion skin and become me—be the superfearless one [ἀφοβόσπλαγχνος]. I'll be you and carry the luggage.[37]

In Aristophanes' critique of martial courage, it doesn't matter whether Dionysus stays on the ground stinking or gets up and wipes himself—the very idea of *andreia* in the old sense is being ridiculed. The courage of the lion, the courage of Heraclean club wielding and violence, is fit only for mockery and derision. Martial courage is a cloak that not only can be transferred easily but can be worn to disguise the cowardly failings of gods, men, and slaves alike. Martial courage—courage of the gut—is a pernicious form of courage not suitable for proper human relations.[38] Gut courage, it seems, almost invariably requires a sponge to clean up the mess, whether excrement or blood.

After setting down this harsh critique of manly, Heraclean courage, Aristophanes provides an exemplary alternative of manly competition. In the *Frogs*, we find a contest between Aeschylus and Euripides that would rival any "hip-hop battle" of our own times. In this competition, Euripides and Aeschylus compete in their poetic skill for a seat at Pluto's dinner table. Aristophanes has his chorus sing praises for this sort of competition:

> And verily do we desire,
> To hear from these two wise men [σοφοῖν ἀνδροῖν],
> Their warring reason dances [λόγων ἐμμέλειαν].
> For their tongues are savage,
> Both resolving not to be cowardly [οὐκ ἄτολμον],
> Nor without intestinal [φρένες] energy.[39]

The competition has a martial and courageous tone, but the poets are engaging in a battle of wits, and their weapon is not Heracles' club but dancing war-words. Aristophanes is clearly raising the possibility of settling differences with reason instead of violence. The two poets, despite marked differences in the substance and style of their poetry, engage in a serious battle but do so discursively rather than violently. In a competition—which is to say, in a situation where something is at stake—they have the courage to proceed, but they rely on their tongues rather than their "guts." Their courage is underwritten by *logos*. They exercise political courage for the sake of a reasonable and discursive resolution to their conflict. Unlike Pericles, who invokes public reasoning to stimulate and fortify citizens to achieve violent martial victories abroad, Euripides and Aeschylus are in this portrayal politically courageous because their goal is to reveal the truth of who is the better man. This agonistic exercise of reason, this political courage, joins together two men who care fundamentally about the superiority of their own discursive capacity.

In the battle itself, the novel nature of this fundamental care becomes clear. Euripides claims that his work is superior because, in choosing themes pertaining to everyday reality, he provided a useful education for his democratic Athenian audience. The exchange between Euripides and Aeschylus is telling:

> Euripides: From the very first word I let no one stay idle,
> My women and my slaves spoke, and neither was less courageous [ἧττον],
> Likewise with master, young girls, and old women.
> Aeschylus: After this, of course, should not you have been put to death for this daring [τολμῶντα]?
> Euripides: Why, by Apollo? I acted for the sake of democracy itself!
> . . . I taught them how to talk.
> . . . By introducing practical affairs,
> Which are useful to us, to which we can make connections,
> I opened the way for people to refute me.
> These are knowledgeable folks,
> Who could shame [ἤλεγχον] my skill [τέχνην].
> . . . By introducing this I taught them to be prudent in these things,
> I taught them to put logic [λογισμὸν] into their skills,
> And scrutiny [σκέψιν] so as to know [νοεὶν] things thoroughly,
> And to be discerning in their practical affairs.[40]

Euripides' lessons clearly pertain to a reasonable and discursive mode of articulation and a further differentiation of the limited account of justice that Pericles provides. Through his skill—his *techne*—with words Euripides claims to be providing the wherewithal for a peaceful and practical way of life, a deeper foundation for a democratic education, and not just for Athenian citizens. He is providing a means for connecting men and women, masters and slaves, old and young, that does not depend on violence. It is especially interesting that Aristophanes has Aeschylus recognize that in providing this education, Euripides is acting courageously (τόλμα). He is taking the privilege of heroism out of the violent deeds of the Homeric hero and putting it squarely in the rational and discursive capacity of every person living in the polis. What is required for meaningful relationships is not the club and lion skin but speech, logic, scrutiny, and the ability to make distinctions. In short, Aristophanes' hero is a citizen capable of making critical evaluations in the average everyday management of the polis, both internally and abroad. This, in Aristophanes' understanding, is political courage, and it is as manly as the courage of a Homeric hero, if not more so.

The Frogs is not the only place Aristophanes is critical of violence as the prevailing mode of articulation. His *Lysistrata* (412 BCE) was written not long after the debacle at Sicily, after seventeen years of nearly nonstop war. In this play the Athenian women attempt to end the war by going on a sex strike. The argument, it seems, is that if the Athenian men cannot restrain their excessive manliness in the martial realm, they will most certainly learn to do it in the private realm. In another play, *The Assemblywomen* (392 BCE), Aristophanes proposes another solution to the problem of war and violence. Here the Athenian women grow out their armpit hair, let their faces get suntanned, don fake beards, and take over the Assembly. A bit later, they vote themselves rulers of the entire city. The scheme, one that echoes Artemisia's assumption of her husband's political position, reveals that unreasonable "gut" politics is not the exclusive domain of men. While the excessive manliness of Athenian men contributed to the long suffering of the Peloponnesian War and the subsequent battered condition of Athens in 392, Aristophanes does not suppose that the city would have fared much better under the rule of women. The play thus becomes a hilarious look at political affairs freed not just from excessive manly courage but from manliness altogether.

In *The Assemblywomen*, the objection to manly courage is stated by the ringleader of the Athenian women, Praxagora: "We women are embarking on this great venture of ours today . . . in the hope that *we* can take over the management of affairs and do a bit of good for the City. Because, as things are at present, the ship's adrift: we're not getting anywhere."[41] However, the women prove to be no better at ruling than the men. The first thing they do is enact a law declaring all property public. The ensuing hilarity is intended to show that gut politics is not a problem exclusive to men. Moreover, the bodily nature of martial courage is not lost once the women take over. Not only do they decree all property to be held in common, they also pass laws ensuring the sexual freedom of women. Praxagora makes girls common property so that "any man who wants to can sleep with them and have children by them."[42] But because men will all make for the pretty girls and ignore the unattractive ones, Praxagora also decrees that "anyone who wants a pretty girl will have to lay one of the plain ones first."[43] Her husband points out that this rule will be unfair to the older men: "Bit hard on some of us older men, isn't it? If we've got to screw an ugly one first, how are we going to make it with the posie?"[44] Praxagora then decrees that the younger girls will be obliged to sleep with an ugly old man before the tall and handsome ones. In general, women's control of the city does not automatically lead to a robust, nonviolent form of political courage in the affairs of the city; instead, it gives rise to another form of somatic politics. When the men ruled, the city was derailed by the demands of martial courage and a violently articulated community. But when the women rule, citizens are no more likely to act reasonable for the sake of a more differentiated justice. Violence is simply replaced by sex; poor political decisions are made not only from the gut but also from an even baser body part. The elimination of men and martial courage from politics does not leave the city ruled by reason and the politically courageous. Even when violence is replaced as the dominant mode of articulation, a certain degree of manliness is still needed. Eliminating manly men from the political arena is not the way to ensure a discursive mode of articulation. Robust reason-battles do not arise *ex nihilo.* The city still needs her men.

Hence, despite his critique of martial courage, Aristophanes is not rejecting manliness altogether. As he suggested in the reason-battle of *The Frogs*, he claims that his public critique is itself a form of manly courage. Indeed, in *The Knights* Aristophanes explicitly calls critique courageous. As Sluiter and Rosen put it, "Real-life battlefields, of course, are commonly invoked as ideal sites of *andreia,* as we say above, because here is where feats of bravery and courage, so often hailed as peculiarly 'manly' virtues, are played out. So it makes perfect sense that polemical poets would claim for themselves some measure of *andreia* in their own metaphorical military campaigns."[45] What makes the comic poets' appropriation of *andreia* so striking is that, despite the irony, they claim to be even more courageous than the single warrior. The political courage of the poet is, after all, the courage of a single man against an entire city. We could go even further and claim that the poet is making a stand against an entire way of being (τρόπος). In the case of *The Knights*, because he is deriding the conventional view of manly courage—the view carrying the authority of Homer—he is taking a courageous and daring stance against the tradition handed down by his poetic forefathers. The declaration of Aristophanes' manly political courage comes from the chorus:

> Had one of the old authors asked me to mount this stage to recite his verses
> He would not have found it hard to persuade me.
> But our poet of today is likewise worthy of this favour;
> He shares our hatred, he dares [τολμα] to tell the truth,
> He boldly braves both waterspouts and hurricanes.[46]

The Chorus, it must be kept is in mind, is composed of knights. The knights, or cavalry, were invariably part of the Athenian aristocracy and would naturally have been opposed to the ascendance of the commoner Cleon. Cleon, Aristophanes' target in *The Knights*, is the general who undeservedly took credit for the victory at Sphacteria and the capture of several hundred Spartiates.[47] In this comedy, Cleon appears as a Paphlagonian leather tanner who is a great flatterer of the Demos. At the time this play was produced, Cleon was, in actuality, the leading politician in Athens, and Aristophanes' attacks on him could have had some actual ramifications. Earlier (in 426 BCE) Cleon had become outraged at Aristophanes for his *Babylonians* and had brought charges against him. Yet Aristophanes threatened to renew his attacks on Cleon in *The Acharnians* and actually did so in *The Knights*.

The critique of Cleon is emphatic. In *The Knights*, Demosthenes says of Cleon, "A greater swine of a stool-pigeon never walked this earth. This tanner-fellow soon got to know master's ways, and then he fell at his feet, licked his boots, wheedled, flattered, sucked up, everything to take him in, with all the trimmings—in real leather."[48] Elsewhere, the Chorus accuses Cleon of being soft (μαλάξης) and cowardly (δειλὸν).[49] Clearly, despite the legal threats, Aristophanes was holding fast to his intention of publicly criticizing Athens' leading politician. In this sense, we can also regard the knights' praise of Aristophanes' courage as tantamount to elevating political courage above martial courage. Adriaan Rademaker echoes this opinion: "Aristophanic comedy tells us much about what it meant to be a man in fifth-century Athens. Many of its protagonists claim for themselves some kind of *andreia*, whether real or feigned, usually when boasting of fearlessness in difficult undertakings, and the poet himself will often assert his own *andreia* when describing his attacks on the monstrous politicians that threaten the city."[50] This is most likely why the women in *The Assemblywomen* are praised for their manly courage (ἀνδρειόταται) after they have discursively addressed their grievances against the current rulers in the Assembly.[51] They are praised when they pursue their grievances against poor political management; they become ridiculous only later, when they abandon discourse as the means of their critique. In Aristophanes' oeuvre, the form of *andreia* that is portrayed as commendable reveals a fundamental care for the discursive resolution of difference, an effort to articulate people with *logos* rather than with bodily force and violence. For Aristophanes, this is in itself a more just way of being.

Having determined this, we must ask why Aristophanes attacks Cleon with such vitriol. What is wrong with Cleon? Does he not take over the city discursively? In Thucydides' *History*, does Cleon not make eloquent speeches? We have already seen that although Aristophanes' fundamental care is nonviolence, he is at the same time trying to retain the manly element of courage. In other words, he is extolling not just political courage but manly political courage. Simply making speeches is not enough; cowardice and courage are determined not merely by individual actions but by the motives underlying them. Joseph Roisman, in a study of courage in the Athenian rhetoricians, observes this very thing: "Both in war and peace, in public or private, courage often translated into prioritizing public over private interests. It proved a man's readiness to share danger with other men and allowed him both to display, and benefit from, his male solidarity."[52] If this is so, then Aristophanes' distinction becomes clear. Political courage is *andreia* only if it is for the sake of the public interest. Privately motivated political courage is somehow base and unmanly and becomes a target for his comic derision—it is not even courage at all, properly speaking. It is like the deeds of Aristodemus at Plataea, which, though they may have been the most daring, were unworthy of the prize of honor because they were for his own sake and were not selfless. Aristophanes is suggesting that political courage, like martial courage, requires selflessness and that this is precisely what is missing from the Periclean vision of justice and democratic leisure.

The Knights supports this point in its depiction of Cleon's defeat by a sausage seller. As Rademaker puts it, "Among the characters in Aristophanic plays, the one who most conspicuously fails to live up to the standards of approved male behavior, is the Sausage-seller."[53] Besides being well versed in theft and lying, he readily admits to engaging in *bineskomên*, or male prostitution (i.e., sausage selling) along with the prostitutes at the city gates.[54] This word, *bineskomên*, especially highlights the (un)manliness of the sausage seller. To translate it as "engage in male prostitution," as Alan Sommerstein does, may be somewhat euphemistic. Earlier in his translation he renders it as "buggery" (878), and others use "pederasty," but Rademaker thinks a more accurate rendering would be "occasionally 'getting fucked' himself."[55] The point is not just to be crude (though this may be Aristophanes' goal) but to emphasize the effeminacy of assuming a subordinate sexual position. At the time, selling one's own body in this manner was considered unmanly because it supposedly indicated a readiness to sell the common interest of the city as well.[56] The sausage seller, then, typifies all that is traditionally unmanly by Athenian normative assessments. Yet despite being a liar and a thief, a pederast, and a great flatterer, Aristophanes has him triumph over Cleon and miraculously transform the people at the end of the play. The point here is clear: while the sausage seller violates every traditional characteristic of manly courage, while his depravity exceeds Cleon's, his unmanly deeds lose their stain of unmanliness by being performed for the common interest. His *andreia* resides in his motive to aid and improve the lot of the whole city, not just himself. Cleon's self-interest, his employment of *logos*, simply cannot be considered manly political courage by Aristophanes' reckoning. Instead, it is the "effeminate" sausage seller who shows manly courage in political life, if for no other reason than his exercise of self-discipline, intelligence, and hard work for the common good. He employs his unpolished *logos* in critical service of the polis, transforming the people by inuring them against flatterers like Cleon who, out of a self-interested motive, pull the wool over their eyes and convince them to adopt disastrous political programs. Cleon, Aristophanes is saying, epitomizes the type of too-manly citizen that is plaguing Athens. The manliness Aristophanes extols instead has little to do with traditional manly qualities, which means that women can also be manlier (in the true sense) than Cleon himself.

Aristotle and *Philokalia*

The questioning of manly courage finds expression not only in tragedy, history, and comedy but—perhaps most profoundly—in the philosophical voices of Athens. In his *Nicomachean Ethics*, for example, Aristotle offers a sustained criticism of the traditional understanding of courage. For Aristotle, courage is not the sine qua non of human virtue; instead, it is merely part of his larger taxonomy of the moral virtues. As part of the moral virtues, courage is not some godlike trait bestowed on some and not on others. Instead, it is like the other virtues, all of which are available to anyone properly trained. As Aristotle puts it, the moral virtues are not given to man by nature but "come about as a result of habit."[57] Neither passions nor faculties, they prepare people to choose the mean between excess and defect, depending on the situation. Moral virtue in general (and courage in particular) "is a state of character concerned with choice, lying in a mean, i.e. the mean relative to us, this being determined by a rational principle, and by that principle by which the man of practical wisdom would determine it" (*NE* 116b39). The courageous man chooses actions somewhere between rashness and cowardice. Insofar as courage involves choice and reason for Aristotle, it can have different magnitudes. Thus Aristotle distinguishes a true courage from five things improperly called courage.[58] The truly courageous man is fearless, not in the face of just any danger, but in the face of the highest. For example, one cannot exhibit true courage when facing death by disease or drowning, for one has no choice in these circumstances—one cannot choose to flee a disease or a sinking ship. Instead, one manifests the highest type of courage when facing the "greatest and noblest dangers" (μεγίστοι κὰι καλλίστοι κινδύνῳ) (*NE* 1115a35), which are often "in battle" (ἐν ταῖς πόλεσι) (*NE* 1115a29).

In saying this, however, Aristotle is not cleaving to the Homeric tradition of martial courage and the love of honor. In fact, Aristotle's invocations of the love of honor usually carry a pejorative tone. For example, explicitly referring to Sparta, he calls φιλοτιμία (along with avarice) the central motive for voluntary injustice (ἀδικημάτων).[59] Moreover, he invokes the love of honor to indicate selfish motivations—a characteristic that violates the selfless character of manly courage and the principles of *Kriegsbruderlichkeit.* Tyrannicides, for example, are more often than not motivated by φιλοτιμία, or the fame one might acquire from such an act (*Politics* 1312a25). The love of honor is similarly associated with weakness, with the limited expectations of democratic farmers, or even with plain, unmanly foppery (περιττότερος) (*Politics* 1318b22, 1267b25).

At bottom, Aristotle rejects the Homeric tradition because, in his reckoning, true courage is informed by reason and ultimately points in a different direction. It is about risking life and limb not for the sake of honor (τιμή) but for the sake of "the noble" (ἡ καλός). As Aristotle puts it, true courage is facing danger, "as the rule dictates, for the sake of what is noble [τοῦ καλοῦ ἕνεκα]" (*NE* 1115b7). Defining "the noble" in Aristotle's thought is never easy. Indeed, the multiplicity of its definitions—as the beautiful, the fine, the fair, the good, the auspicious, and so on—shows how ambiguous the idea is.[60] But clearly Aristotle is pointing to the noble as a fundamental care, for he says of the activity of the courageous man: "His courage is noble [ἀνδρεία καλόν]; therefore its end is nobility, for a thing is defined by its end [ἕκαστον τῷ τέλει]; there the courageous man endures the terrors and dares the deeds that manifest courage, for the sake of that which is noble [καλοῦ ἕνεκα]" (*NE* 1115b22).[61] Aristotle's departure from the Homeric/Spartan way of being can be encapsulated thus: the lover of honor (φιλότιμος) gives way to the lover of the noble (φιλόκαλος).[62] Gut courage gives way to a calmer, more rational courage.

This said, there is a kinship between *philotimia* and *philokalia.* Martial courage, we know, appeals to us because it is bound up with selflessness and solidarity. For Aristotle, as for any political thinker, it would be foolish to jettison this deeply good aspect of martial courage. Hence, in the *Nicomachean Ethics* he tenaciously holds on to this abiding good. Just as martial courage and *philotimia* are bound up with sacrifice and selflessness, so too is his vision of courage and the noble. As Susan Collins puts it, for Aristotle "the noble in the case of courage points first to sacrifice and self-forgetting as the essential part of good action."[63] Aristotle thus continues the tradition of invoking courage as the bedrock of selfless community, yet steadfastly avoids the traditional language of honor. Like Aristophanes, he is taking issue with the brutality and persistent violence associated with this way of being—which is a Spartan way of being through and through. And his disdain for the Spartans is well known. The Spartans, he says, "brutalize their children by laborious exercises which they think will make them courageous" (*Politics* 1338b13). The result of education devoted exclusively to martial courage is that their boys become little beasts "and in reality [they] make them mechanics [βαναύσους]" (*Politics* 1338b34). In fact, they become little mechanics of violence, and for Aristotle there is little noble in this way of being. Thus in education, "what is noble [τὸ καλλὸν], not what is beastly [τὸ θηριῶδες]," should come first (*Politics* 1338b29). *Philokalia,* then, ought to be instilled so that it inspires courageous and selfless acts.

For precisely this reason Aristotle taxonomizes the moral virtues. Whereas Collins, for example, argues that Aristotle is "demoting courage," it is helpful to regard the transformation as a reflection of a more differentiated view of human virtue.[64] Rather than holding courage as the sine qua non of virtue, Aristotle elevates the other virtues, putting them on a par with courage—especially justice.[65] The noble way of being is therefore not merely the way of the warrior but also the way of the citizen who reasons rightly concerning courageous and just action. In this sense, the love of the noble is not altogether unlike the rhathumic way of being that emerges from Pericles' funeral oration, or the dancing war-words of Aristophanes. The brutishness of a community articulated by violence—which is to say, a community predicated on the body—is tempered by the inclusion of reason and, concomitantly, choice. However, a considerable difference between the visions offered by Pericles and Aristotle is that Pericles' rhathumic way of being is colored by hedonism, a corporeal metric of happiness. Likewise, the bawdy alternative offered by Aristophanes falls short of Aristotle's vision of the finer, nobler life. While in each of these examples the hardness of the hypermasculine view of good citizenship is softened by the inclusion of reason, Aristotle's taxonomy of the virtues pushes his vision of the good man toward a more singular vision of the noble way of being. As a part of virtue equal to courage, justice becomes central to the vision rather than merely a fortuitous consequence.

It might thus be argued that Aristotle is merely putting the aristocratic man of leisure in the place of Achilles. However, by taxonomizing the virtues and infusing courage with reason and choice, Aristotle takes it further from the Homeric tradition than either Thucydides or Aristophanes. His vision of courage and the noble is much more noetic and universal than Pericles' vision of rhathumic justice for Athenians (which is likely to be hedonistic and corporeal) or Aristophanes' espousal of Dionysian, dancing war-words. From this vision, a way is opened for participation in the good of political life not just for the hero but for anyone endowed with enough sense to make good choices in whatever situation he or she finds him- or herself. And if this is so, then the good citizen and the good life necessarily include things traditionally relegated to the darkness of the private world. As Stephen Salkever suggests, a central element of Aristotle's discontent with the prevailing political culture "is especially noticeable in [his] according women and womanly activities a greater dignity than does [his] tradition (or its modern adherents)—a revaluation that stems from a deep opposition to the view that the virtues of the best human life are most clearly displayed in the practice of war and the pursuit of undying glory."[66]

Collins echoes this sentiment, suggesting that of "the virtues discussed in the *Ethics*, there is clearly a movement away from the kinds . . . that would be associated with the heroic tradition of Homer, and it could be argued that Aristotle is ultimately concerned with specifically human as opposed to male or female virtue."[67] In his taxonomizing of the virtues, then, the metric for good citizenship is not whether one's actions are heroic but whether they fit in a niche proper to the taxonomy itself.

In sum, for Aristotle, the good citizen courageously and unselfishly purses the noble and good life. The courageous citizen, then, is obviously no Achilles. Achilles, after all, operates on gut courage for the sake of honor. More importantly, his actions are rarely predictable enough to be taxonomized. Like Spartans, he is a brute and nothing more than a master mechanic of violence. He lacks all the characteristics of Aristotle's good citizen: his actions are guided by his love of honor, he is neither great-souled (μεγαλοψῡχία) (1123b1–25b1) nor gentlemanly (καλὸς κἀγαθός), and the choices he makes never find the mean.[68] This is not to say that Aristotle's courageous man is incapable on the battlefield. On the contrary, the courage of the warrior, which Aristotle says also belongs to the "citizen" (πολιτική), comes closest to the true courage he is advocating (1116a21) save for the fact that it is guided by honor. On the battlefield, the courageous man is guided by honor (τιμή)—but what really matters for Aristotle is how the virtuous man lives the bulk of his life. After all, war and battle occupy but a tiny fragment of our lives. What matters is how we comport ourselves during times of peace, when we must live among our friends, our families, and our fellow citizens. During these times the courageous man must exercise the greater part of virtue in pursuit of the good and noble life.

Socrates and Achilles

It has been argued that in positing the great-souled man—the *megalopsychos*—as the model of the new "manly man," Aristotle has in mind Socrates. Jacob Howland, for instance, argues that "the great-souled man is characterized by heroic, superhuman, or godlike virtue, which finds its fullest expression in a deed whereby the whole community is saved. . . . Aristotle names five great-souled men in the *Posterior Analytics*. Of these five, Socrates stands in a class by himself, for he alone is genuinely indifferent to honor and dishonor."[69] That Aristotle regards him in this light is not surprising given his teacher's treatment of Socrates. It is in Plato's dialogues, after all, that Socrates is regularly presented as the heroic savior of the city. His heroism, however, is not Achillean. Instead, it is most manifest in his courageous stand against the excessive manliness and injustice bound up with the Homeric worldview. In the *Gorgias*, for example, Socrates battles against Callicles and what Angela Hobbs describes as his "thumoeidic tendencies gone astray."[70]

In the *Apology*, Plato is explicit in his presentation of Socrates as a new kind of hero. After being sentenced to death for corrupting the youth, being impious, and making the weaker argument stronger, Socrates suggests his punishment ought to be free meals for life in the Prytaneum.[71] The Prytaneum was the home of the central hearth and sacred fire of the city. It stood as the central symbol of vitality and unity for the city and was often the locus of religious and political life. Thucydides reports that in the time of Theseus the Prytaneum at Athens served as the political nexus for all Attica.[72] Additionally, when citizens of that city set out to found colonies, they would take a brand from the Prytaneum to spark the fire in the new Prytaneum. Moreover, the Prytaneum is essentially a feminine symbol because of its association with the hearth. Even in Rome this fire was kept in the Temple of Vesta, goddess of the hearth. In any case, being bestowed free meals in the Prytaneum was an honor reserved for only the greatest of heroes, such as Olympic victors and great war heroes. Socrates' recommendation is so outlandish that the jury cannot retreat from the original death sentence. The point, however, is clear: for Plato, Socrates' discursive examinations of the leading figures in Athens are a service to the city equivalent to any deed of a great athlete or warrior.

Other commentators have compared Socrates' philosophic activities to the deeds of the warrior. Eric Voegelin, for example, writes that "'war and battle,' are the opening words of the *Gorgias*, and the declaration of war against the corrupt society is its content. . . . The battle is engaged in as a struggle for the soul of the younger generation. Who will be the future leaders of the polity: the rhetor who teaches the tricks of political success, or the philosopher who creates the substance in soul and society?"[73] Of course Plato is not pointing to the sword as the weapon of choice in this war and battle against *philotimia* but to the dialogue. Socrates functions as the discursive thrust and parry against the excessively manly elements of Athenian society.

Allan Bloom also recognizes that Socrates is given the character of a warrior. In his interpretive essay on *The Republic*, Bloom highlights the seven passages from Homer that Plato invokes in books 2 and 3. All but one of these passages, Bloom points out, pertain to Achilles, and the relevance of this should not be overlooked: "Socrates brings Achilles to the foreground to analyze his character and ultimately to do away with him as *the* model for the young."[74] Like Aristophanes, Plato is repudiating the Homeric and traditional model of manly courage by calling into question martial courage, the ubiquitous love of honor and victory, and community articulated by violence. Whereas Homer presents Achilles as an ideal hero, Plato casts Socrates in this role and "engag[es] in a contest with Homer for the title of teacher of the Greeks—or of mankind. One of his principal goals is to put [Socrates] in the place of Achilles as the authentic representation of the best human type."[75] The irony is that, in Bloom's interpretation at least, books 2 and 3 of the *Republic* should be understood as Socrates' endorsement of the highest virtue—moderation. As he puts it, "At the end of the warriors' education—an education intended to make them good guardians of a peaceful people—it becomes evident that *the* virtue which has been encouraged is moderation."[76] The irony lies in the fact that moderation is the virtue least demonstrated by Achilles; many of the problems in the *Iliad* arise precisely from Achilles' immoderate love of honor.[77]

So while Bloom is correct in pointing out that for Plato Socrates is the new Achilles, he misses the larger point of invoking the great hero. For Plato, the central virtue for the warrior remains courage; Socrates is portrayed as a new Achilles not to teach moderation but to continue the tradition of manly courage. The difference however, between Achilles and Socrates is that for the latter courage and spiritedness (θυμός) are not simply in the service of the warrior's capacity for violence but also in the service of the warrior's capacity for reason. Moderation, it turns out, is a propitious by-product of courageous reasoning. This is why Socrates provides the example of Odysseus from Homer's *Iliad.* Odysseus, while sitting on the threshold of his palace disguised as a beggar, watching his servants cavorting with the suitors and the suitors despoiling his home, suffered great dishonor and insult. Achilles or any other traditional heroic warrior in this situation would fly into a rage, redress the insult, and reestablish the appropriate order in his community through furious acts of violence. But in this case, and this is why Socrates invokes the example, Odysseus restrains himself. He does so by employing the joined efforts of both his reason and his manly spiritedness. As Plato reminds us, Odysseus "smote his breast" and "reproached his heart with word."[78] The passage is intended to demonstrate that the first virtue is manliness, which he must summon to buttress his reason. The result appears to be a sort of moderation. Because his courage cooperates with his reason, he is able to moderate his desire to burst forth and slaughter the suitors when it would be inappropriate. Not only does Bloom ignore this ordering of courage and reason, but he fails to mention this passage from Homer at all.

The further irony here is that Socrates, though invoking Homer several times as a source of authority, objects vociferously to the poets in general. It would appear that Aristophanes and Socrates are fighting the same battle. After all, both reject the Homeric vision of manly courage and violently articulated community, and both portray themselves as the courageous hero in Athens because of their effort to supplant violence with *logos.* Yet Socrates' rejection of poetry is thorough; he rejects comedic poets like Aristophanes as emphatically as the epic poets. Aristophanes' comedic poetry is, according to Socrates, as corrosive and damaging as Homer's praise of the violent world of Achilles and Agamemnon. In fact, Socrates bans most poems, comedic and epic, because they tell malevolent lies regarding the true nature of the gods and heroes (Plato *Republic*

379e). As is abundantly evident in Aristophanes' *Frogs*, they have a propensity to portray the gods as ridiculous figures. Socrates rejects epic poetry because it portrays the gods as the cause of evil and as changing shape to deceive humans (379c, 381e). For Socrates, such things, true or not, should not be told to children because it will frighten them and make them unduly fear death. It will make cowards of the children; thus, contrary to Aristophanes' self-portrayal, these poets are not heroic benefactors of the city.[79]

So even though poets employ *logos*, the appearance of courage in Plato's work reveals a different concern. According to Bloom, it is not just the substance of the poetry that Socrates finds inimical to the good polity, but poetry as a literary form. As he puts it: "The Socratic critique of poetry is not only that the epic, tragic, and comic poets have not chosen as heroes the most admirable human types, but that their forms make it impossible for them to do so. What is needed is a form of poetry which is not compelled to make what is not truly highest appear to be the highest. Ultimately the Platonic dialogue with its hero, Socrates, is that form."[80]

Put otherwise, poetry, no matter how courageously presented, cannot produce the sort of courage Socrates has in mind because it is, in the final analysis, mimetic. Because it constantly holds up both gods and heroes as liars, cheaters, and cowards and, importantly, extols figures who know only violent community, poetry provokes men to be worse human beings than they were before they heard the poetry. Even more damaging is that the poet himself cannot be the heroic model Aristophanes thinks himself to be. To have the desired effect on the audience, the poet must present an artificial world behind which he himself hides. To draw his audience into this world, the poet must make it more enticing than the real world. In creating this improved world, the poet will most likely have an elevated opinion of himself as, say, a creator of better worlds. The poet, however, "is much less powerful than he thinks he is. Precisely because he must make his audience join in the world he wishes to present to them, he must make appeal to its dominant passions. He cannot force the spectators to listen to him or like and enter into the lives of men who are repulsive to them. He must appeal to and flatter the dominant passions of the spectators. Those passions are fear, pity, and contempt."[81] In other words, the poet, despite thinking himself a heroic citizen, is actually in thrall to the crowd. He is as subservient as any other politician, or slave for that matter, whose power depends on flattery. In this understanding, Aristophanes' critique of Cleon is turned right back on himself. The poet, like a demagogue, is an inherent flatterer and not in control of himself. And since he is not in control of himself, he simply cannot be likened to a courageous warrior. After all, the basic mark of the courageous warrior is self-control. To be courageous, to be an effective warrior, one must have control of his passions. According to Socrates, the poet, simply by favoring *logos* rather than violence, is not necessarily politically courageous or necessarily a beneficent citizen. He may be conspicuous, but the conspicuous display of speech (or violence) does not make one a courageous man.

Politicians and Generals in the *Laches*

For Plato, Achilles with his sword and Aristophanes and Gorgias with their speech are not paragons of manly virtue. As is evident in the *Apology* and many other dialogues, this designation falls to Socrates. In both his speech and deed, Socrates is presented as the courageous savior of the city. This combination of speech (regarding courage) and deeds typical of Socrates' life in Athens comes brilliantly to the fore in an early dialogue—the *Laches.*[82] Despite being famously aporetic, the *Laches* brings together a very appropriate admixture of citizens to discuss the nature of courage. While most commentators are quick to point out that the main characters in the dialogue are Laches and Nicias (who plays a central part in Aristophanes' *Frogs*), the other characters play equally important parts.[83] Of course, they may not be presenting arguments, but their presence and actions are crucial components of the dramatic argument overall. For example, in the characters of Lysimachus and Melesias, Plato presents what might be called average everyday citizenship. These two old men are inconspicuous Athenians and, as most commentators quickly point out, are the undistinguished sons of some very distinguished Athenians.[84] They have proven themselves neither as courageous warriors in battle nor as conspicuous poets, rhetoricians, or politicians. Neither has famous deeds of which to boast, and, as Lysimachus says, "These things make us rather ashamed [ὑπαισχύνομαι] before [our sons], and we blame our fathers for letting us live a soft life [τρυφάω], when we became lads, while they were busy with the affairs of others."[85] Despite this paternal neglect, they are decent characters in an everyday way. They are friendly and clearly care for the well-being of their children. It was they, after all, who paid Stesilaus to demonstrate the art of fighting in heavy armor (ὁπλομαχία) to discover whether such lessons would give their sons the requisite courage for becoming conspicuous citizens.

As for the more conspicuous characters, Plato gives us four: Stesilaus, Nicias, Laches, and Socrates. The most conspicuous citizen—the most active in the affairs of the polis—is the politician Nicias. As Walter Schmid points out, at the time of this dialogue Nicias "is the head of government or the unofficial president in Athens . . . who will soon conclude, with Laches as his ally, the famous Peace of Nicias, which brought to a close the first half of the war that Thucydides recounts in his Peloponnesian War."[86] Thucydides calls him Nicias "the Lucky" and characterizes him as predominantly cautious and pious. With regard to his caution, two interpretations can be set forth: that he was either extraordinarily prudent or self-interested and cowardly. Certainly, both of these descriptions are somewhat extreme, but considering Thucydides' account of Nicias both may be accurate to some degree. In book 6 of his *History of the Peloponnesian War*, when the Athenians are debating the prospects of the Sicilian invasion, Thucydides portrays Nicias as arguing in favor of caution and prudence. Nicias argues that the invasion is dangerous and untimely. Listening to his *logoi* against sailing to Sicily, one is tempted to consider Nicias the embodiment of manly political courage—he does, after all, courageously speak against his fellow citizen's violent propositions. He appears to be the good citizen courageously choosing words over violence, yet he is prepared to go to war if necessary. Closer examination, however, reveals a different motivation. According to Thucydides, what motivates him to speak against violence is not courage and a fundamental care for nonviolent discourse but something quite different:

> Nikias, son of Nikeratos, more successful in his commands than anyone else at the time, expended a great deal more effort toward the peace: Nikias because he wished to safeguard his good fortune where he had been undamaged and held in honor, and to end his own labors and put an end to those of his fellow-citizens immediately and leave to posterity the claim that throughout his life he had never brought harm to the state, thinking that this is what resulted from avoiding risk, every time a man relies on luck as little as possible, and that peace was the way to avoid risk. (*PW* 5.16)[87]

In short, Thucydides considers Nicias a self-interested coward. He appears to stand courageously against naked violence, but he is actually motivated by an abiding desire to avoid risk, not only to his physical person, but also to his reputation. In other words, in his desire to avoid what he considers an even graver risk—the risk *to his name*—Nicias appears cautious and prudent. Thus, even though he does not always appear cowardly with regard to his physical safety, he fears damaging his reputation and posterity—his personal glory. And though he appears to be politically courageous, this fear regarding his reputation proves to be even more corrosive to the community than the basest cowardice in battle. But given that Nicias is a central character in a dialogue on courage, why would Plato include him?[88]

One reason may have been his second defining characteristic—piety. According to Schmid, Nicias "made daily sacrifices, kept a diviner in his own home, and constantly sought out omens for guidance on matters of public and private affairs."[89] Although these traits probably endeared him to many Athenians originally, they brought about his ruin at Syracuse. According to Thucydides, Nicias took the helm of the Athenian expeditionary force after the death of Lamachos and, on account of his piety, brought about the annihilation of the fleet. With the Athenians in rather bad shape after various setbacks in the fighting, Nicias had the opportunity to withdraw the fleet but held back. He feared the response his unsuccessful return would elicit from the Athenians, and, as Thucydides says, he "had no wish to die unjustly, on a shameful charge, at the hands of the Athenians, rather than taking his chances as an individual and meeting his end, if he must, at the hands of the enemy" (*PW* 7.48). On the surface it would seem that Nicias was demonstrating a good amount of manly courage. He did, after all, prefer to stay in the battle rather than return to Athens. But insofar as courage is bound up with putting the common cause ahead of one's personal good, Nicias must be considered less than manly. Because his actions were overwhelmingly guided by his care for personal glory, he failed in his task as a citizen, namely, being a good general, and because as both a politician and general his actions revealed a fundamental care for his own interest—for his personal honor and his love of victory—his courage simply cannot be considered manly political courage.

Nicias's mettle was further revealed when he determined that it was in fact less risky to return home than to stay and fight. Again, it was not entirely cowardly to return to Athens after failing a mission; at the very least his reputation would be destroyed, but there was always a chance he would be executed as well. However, as Thucydides writes, "When they were about to sail away . . . there was an eclipse of the moon; for the moon happened to be full. Most of the Athenians, deeply impressed, urged the generals to stop, and besides Nikias *(who was indeed some what over-credulous about divination and everything of the sort)* said that until he had waited thrice nine days, as the seers dictated, he would not even deliberate about moving first" (*PW* 7.50). The result of this act of piety is well known—the Athenians were slaughtered and Nicias suffered a shameful and unbecoming death. The loss at Sicily marked the beginning of the end for the Athenian empire.

We can thus say that the piety of Nicias was not so different from his fabled caution and prudence. Both were inspired by unmanliness of one sort or another. With his caution he tried to avoid endeavors that put either his person or his reputation at risk. With his piety he attempted to avoid risks that would otherwise be unpredictable. In other words, his fear of the unknown (i.e., of death and the afterlife) was what made him a pious man.[90] This level of superstition, however, runs contrary to modern reason, and, as Schmid indicates, this was about "the same way it was viewed by most rationalists in ancient times—namely, as a fine thing for old women, but not for grown men."[91] In the *Laches*, then, Plato begins with a character who is not courageous either politically or martially. Nicias's political judgment, influenced by his piety, reveals him to be something of an old woman. Piety is simply not compatible with manly political courage and can lead the ship of state into dangerous waters.

Like Nicias, Laches had a significant role in Thucydides' *History of the Peloponnesian War*. Thucydides reports that Laches and Charoiades were co-commanders of the first Athenian expedition to Sicily around 426. After Charoiades was killed, Laches assumed complete command of the fleet, and he was successful in taking Mylai and convincing the Messenians to come over to the Athenians (*PW* 3.90). In addition, Laches was a general at Delion,[92] where he fought beside Socrates. Later, in 423, he was instrumental in finalizing a one-year truce when he "moved, to the good fortune of the Athenians, to accept the armistice according to the terms agreed on by the Lacedaemonians and their allies" (*PW* 4.118). In 421, acting as Nicias's second, Laches was instrumental in negotiating the so-called peace of Nicias, which was to last for fifty years, and finally, in the battle of Mantinea three years later, Laches was killed in combat (*PW* 5.74). His death, however, is hardly mentioned by Thucydides. In sum, Laches is much less conspicuous than Nicias; he was certainly not known for his eloquent speeches, and his martial actions garnered much less recognition than those of Nicias.[93] Despite this, however, Plato has named the dialogue after him rather than the more conspicuous Nicias. Laches is clearly a warrior and represents a brand of citizenship in which discipline, underwritten by martial courage, trumps the unpredictability and spontaneity of speech. In some ways, as will soon be demonstrated, his willingness to participate in the Socratic discourse evidences more courage and consequently more manly political courage, than we ever see from Nicias. It is likely a mistake to do what a few commentators have attempted and hold up Laches as inherently superior to Nicias in terms of manly courage.[94] Plato includes them because they both somehow fall short of the political courage Socrates embodies. To the degree that Laches leans toward martial courage and distrusts a discursively articulated community, Nicias leans in the direction of unmanliness, cowardice, and self-interest. When Laches is willing to be politically courageous, he reveals himself as akin to Pericles in his belief that speech is the precursor and servant to efficacious martial endeavors. When Nicias is willing to be politically courageous he reveals himself as akin to Aristophanes—speech is for the sake of nonviolence and personal glory. The conspicuous political figures in this dialogue therefore provide insight into what Plato has in mind with political courage, but their failings in this regard speak just as loudly.

Sophists and Warriors in the *Laches*

Just as Plato examines Laches and Nicias as representative politicians, he also examines representative warriors. Ostensibly, Plato introduces Stesilaus as the paradigmatic warrior. What is interesting is that although the dialogue picks up immediately after Stesilaus's demonstration, Plato does not present an actual account of the art. Instead, the discussion begins with Socrates' examination of both the spectacle and the interlocutors. Two types of warriors are presented; the warrior on display is not just Stesilaus but Socrates too. It is thus no coincidence that as the dialogue gets under way Socrates is first held up as martially courageous. When Laches introduces Socrates to Lysimachus and Melesias, he begins by recounting Socrates' own exploits as a hoplite. He says that Socrates "exalted not only his father but also the fatherland, for in the flight [φυγη] from Delium he withdrew with me, and I tell you that if the others had been willing to be such as he, the city would have been upright and would not then have suffered such a fall" (181b).[95] For those familiar with this battle, it will be recalled that Socrates' so-called courageous deeds in armor were performed in retreat after the army's rout. Moreover, the retreat itself followed an act of great impiety—the desecration of a sanctuary. That Socrates ignores this point demonstrates that he finds merit in learning the warrior's courage. After all, nowhere in the *Laches* does Socrates indicate that the endeavor taught by Stesilaus should not be pursued. From the very beginning, it appears that two models of martial courage are being presented.

It is when the debate over the merits of learning the art of the warrior gets under way that the real battle begins. Nicias fires the first volley. He argues that the young men ought to learn the hoplitic art. First, the practice will keep the young men busy. It will keep them from idling away their lives "in places where the young love to spend their time when they have leisure" (181e). Apparently Nicias does not consider nonserious recreation beneficial or realize that young men—or at least the young men in the *Laches*—like to spend their leisure time talking to Socrates.[96] Nicias evidently has little regard for the benefits of open and friendly dialogue. Second, the practice of fighting in armor will make the body stronger. Nicias claims that the practice, like gymnastics and horsemanship, offers the requisite drill for producing good, sturdy hoplites. This, for Nicias at least, is important because "only they who exercise themselves in the implements relating to war exercise themselves in that contest in which we are competitors and in those things for which the contest lies before us" (182a). Nicias is conflating the physical skill of the hoplite—his technical skill—with the courage of the warrior and thus, by extension, with political courage. His view of courage is therefore agonistic through and through. The point of learning to fight in heavy armor is for the sake of victory in battle. This is the usual and expected understanding of learning the martial arts. We teach our sons to fight so that they will not be vanquished in a fight. We teach them martial courage so they will be good warriors. The problem, however, is that Nicias is unqualifiedly tying the task and skill of the hoplite in battle to the task and skill of the politically active citizen in the city. He is arguing that if the young are taught martial courage they will learn to apply their lessons, which are indubitably agonistic, to the political realm. In this sense, Nicias's attitude differs little from Lysimachus's earlier confusion of unqualified political conspicuousness and political conspicuousness stemming from political courage. That is, he fails to discriminate between conspicuousness without virtue, which very well may be based on deception or violence, and conspicuousness garnered through prudence, wisdom, moderation, intelligence, or courage. He is more concerned to maintain his reputation as undefeated and lucky than to prevent the slaughter of his navy. He is, in short, advocating the lessons because he regards himself, above all, to be in competition with his fellow Athenians. He is agonistic but entirely incapable of properly distinguishing his enemy. For him, the courage learned as a hoplite can thus be applied in the political world for the sake of personal victory and personal aggrandizement.

Thus Nicias's third point in favor of learning to fight in armor—that it is good for the battle itself—is couched in these same terms. He thinks that if one became an expert hoplite one "would not have to suffer anything from one man, at any rate, nor perhaps from several, but in this way he would gain the advantage everywhere" (182b). Certainly if one becomes an expert fighter as an individual, one has the advantage in all sorts of situations. These situations, however, are not political situations, and an expert fighter is merely that—a fighter. While success in these endeavors may make one conspicuous, it is not the same as political courage. At best, one garners the reputation of being lucky; at worst, one earns the reputation of savagery. This distinction escapes Nicias. He even goes so far as to characterize the benefit of learning to fight in armor as an *apolitical* good. He says that the "study will be of some benefit in the battle itself, when one must fight in the ranks with many others," but that it will be even more beneficial "when the ranks are broken" (182a). In other words, the sort of benefit Nicias sees in learning to fight in armor is not that it will inculcate the young with political courage per se but that it will endow one with great advantage precisely when one is not working in concert with one's fellow citizens. Thus the courage Nicias has in mind is not the sort that begets the type of community Socrates is advocating.

Socrates understands that, just as success in phalanx fighting requires selfless courage, a just community requires a plurality of human beings working selflessly together. Where people are not working toward a common goal, there is no community; where there is no community, there are no citizens and, obviously, there is no political courage. Thus the lesson of courage Nicias supposes

Stesilaus will teach may even hinder good community because it erases the demarcation between fellow citizen and enemy. Nicias goes so far as to ignore the differentiation between fighting expertly against the enemy and fighting expertly against one's supposed friends. For him, it is just as important to outstrip one's countrymen as it is to defeat the enemy in battle. This way of thinking led to the disaster at Syracuse and is obviously predicated on Nicias's own desire for personal glory.

This point, however, only serves to highlight the irony of his final argument in favor of learning the martial art. He claims, "This knowledge would make every man in war not a little more confident and more courageous [θαρραλεώτερον καὶ ανδρειότερον] than himself" (182c). In other words, the art itself, not the courage that comes with it, will make one appear more courageous than one actually is. Learning the art will thus not improve the student, as the old men would like. Instead, the "man will appear more graceful where he must appear more graceful and where at the same time he will appear more terrible to the enemies [δεινότεροσ τοῖς ἐχθροῖς] through his gracefulness" (182d). Again, Nicias's argument betrays that courage—let alone political courage—is not his concern. His concern is with the appearance of virtue, not virtue itself. Moreover, and this is central to understanding Plato's criticism of Nicias, what concerns him is not only appearance but appearance to one's own instead of an external foe. This is precisely why Nicias uses ἐχθρός rather than "enemy" (πολέμιος) in this passage. Whereas πολέμιος clearly indicates an enemy from without—a public enemy—ἐχθρός connotes an enemy within. An ἐχθρός is a private enemy, more akin to a rival in the affairs of a private citizen than a hoplite in enemy ranks on the battlefield. If we hearken back to Nicias's second argument in favor of learning to fight in armor, this becomes clearer. Victory against one's own countrymen, who cannot rightly be called πολέμιοι, is more important than victory abroad. Nicias is consistently more concerned with his reputation, the δόξα, than the greater good of the polis. Open and friendly discourse, the substance and end of political courage, is subordinated to φιλονικία—the love of victory (194a).[97] The courageous warrior—the man of action—especially as he is understood and represented by Nicias, thus proves to be an inadequate model for emulation. But what of the warrior represented by Stesilaus?

In his argument against learning Stesilaus's art, Laches levels a serious charge: "Those who profess it are deceivers" (182e). The Lacedaemonians, he says, who devote their whole lives to the preparation of gaining advantage over others in war, care nothing about this art, and the fact that its teachers will "not so much as set foot on tiptoe" (183a) in Lacedaemon and instead wander to other states where the skills of war are less developed and understood suggests that it is not actually valuable. In this they differ from the poet who has written a tragedy and, rather than wandering around neighboring states, goes straight to Athens, the seat of tragic poetry, to win renown there. Tacitly, Laches is likening Stesilaus to other itinerant teachers of the era, particularly the Sophists, like Gorgias, who come into Athens to ply their trade and put on a spectacle for the people. Like this teacher of hoplitic fighting, they claim to teach virtue, but, as Socrates reveals repeatedly, they impart none to their students. Instead, they teach young men how to gain the advantage over private enemies. In other words, they teach deception, foster ἐχθρός, and extol φιλονικία—hardly the hallmarks of political courage. Both the Sophists and the teachers of hoplitic fighting earn their living by deceiving people who cannot distinguish between courage (or virtue in general) and empty flattery. Laches, who speaks more like a Spartan than an Athenian, penetrates the deception and sees Stesilaus for what he is—not a warrior like Socrates, but a Sophist-warrior.[98]

Laches' penetration of the deception, however, is not attributable to any particular philosophical insight into the education of youth. Instead, it is based on his practical, martial experiences. For example, he tells Lysimachus that he has seen the Sophist-warriors in action and that "of those who have practiced this business of armor no man has ever yet become highly esteemed in war" (183c). Stesilaus, it seems, who has just performed "the display amid so great a crowd, saying great things about himself," once fought alongside Laches in a naval battle, arming himself with an ostentatious and ridiculous scythe-spear. The weapon, Laches says mockingly, was "as distinguished as he himself is distinguished from others" (183d). During the fighting, "the wise business of the scythe attached to the lance" (183d) quickly became entangled in the other ship's tackle and, amid laughter from both the enemy fighters and his comrades, was ripped from his hands. The teacher of manly courage, it appears, was quite unmanned. The weapon was too big and cumbersome for coordinated warfare against external enemies (πολέμιος).

This point is crucial. If the weapon and the technique are ill-suited for the competition against the public enemy, they must have been crafted with a different enemy in mind. The courage represented by Sophist-warriors proves to be just like that of Nicias and the sophists. The enemy is the ἐχθρόι—the personal rivals—on board his ship. In attempting to outstrip his comrades in arms, Stesilaus demonstrates that his art teaches young men neither martial courage, the ability to engage in courageous, sometimes violent, action, nor political courage, the capacity to engage in open and friendly discourse with friends. However, because Laches couches his argument against Stesilaus in terms of martial efficacy, this point is still not clear. The old men are still unable to envision a model of citizenship other than the violent warrior or the shamelessly self-interested and vacuous sophist—each trying to get the better of his rival for the sake of personal aggrandizement.

By rejecting both the martial and sophistic models of courage, the dialogue seemingly arrives at an impasse. The problem is that Lysimachus and Melesias have lost track of the real matter—they still think the issue at hand is learning to fight in armor. As the dialogue progresses, it becomes more and more clear that what is at stake is how the youth are to be educated in political courage. It is Socrates who reminds all the parties present that in discussing ὁπλομαχία one is actually "examining a study for the sake of the souls of the young men" (187d). What is needed is neither an expert in fighting nor an expert in speechifying but an expert (τεχνικός) in soul care, someone practiced in the art of examining those who profess both to have and to teach virtues worthy of emulation. In the *Laches*, and in Athens at large, this role falls to Socrates. Thus in Socrates Plato presents a model of courage that sharply departs from the violence of the warrior and the self-serving, flattering speeches of the Sophist.

Socrates, however, as he is wont to do, denies having any expertise in such matters. He rather ironically says the Athenians should turn to those who profess to teach this virtue—the Sophists. Like Laches, he draws a parallel between the itinerant teachers of rhetoric and the itinerant teachers of fighting in armor. Socrates makes the comparison even more explicit than Laches; after his somewhat ironic lament that he has never had a teacher in the matter of soul care, he says that from his youth up he has desired one but has never had "the wages to pay Sophists, the only ones who proclaim themselves able to make [him] noble and good [καλόν τε κἀγαθόν]" (186c).[99] The irony is this: Socrates, despite his poverty, appears more educated than his much wealthier interlocutors. What is at issue here, however, is not whether one can afford the services of the Sophists. Instead, it lies with the question that begot the dialogue in the first place—What kind of courage shall we teach our children so as to foster good community?

Stesilaus, the Sophist-warrior, has already proven inadequate. Thus the interlocutors turn to Socrates both to answer this question and to serve as a model. What is remarkable at this point in the dialogue is that it is Lysimachus who steps forward. This average everyday citizen who has never been conspicuously courageous orders both Nicias and Laches to "speak and examine in common with Socrates, giving and receiving an account from each other" (187d). The command aims precisely at the sort of courage Socrates is advocating, and the importance of this transformation should not be underestimated. Lysimachus, who at the outset had not even thought to invite Socrates to the discussion of courage, now orders the politicians to participate in the Socratic discourse. Whereas he began with the notion that good citizenship—understood as individual distinction earned through glorious martial deeds—might be acquired through learning martial courage, he is now willing to entertain the prospect that it might also be learned through critical self-examination. Although in a rather unselfconscious way, Lysimachus has discovered that he may already be politically courageous.

What he does not recognize is that critical self-examination is impossible without courage. Nicias, however, knows this well and therefore warns Lysimachus that forsaking the way of the Sophist-warrior with his scythe-spear in favor of the *logos* of Socrates may turn out to be more arduous than the most rigorous martial regimen. He begins by describing the perils of engaging in conversation with Socrates: "You do not seem to know that whoever is very close to Socrates in speech—as if in kinship—and keeps him company in discussion, even if he has earlier begun a discussion about something else, must of necessity not stop but be led around in speech by this man until he falls into giving an account of himself, the way he now lives, and the way he has lived his past life; and that, when one falls into this, Socrates will not let him go before he puts all these things well and nobly to the test" (187e–88a).

In short, Nicias recognizes that engaging in such discourse poses a risk to his reputation. At the same time, however, he recognizes that refusing is equally risky. Thus his concern for appearance forces him into the dialogue, but only disingenuously. He attempts to participate without actually participating. He pays lip service to the good of the Socratic discourse—going so far as to say that he rejoices at being reminded of his ignoble deeds and at being put to the test by the words of Socrates—but only because he thinks he can skillfully predict, and therefore parry, Socrates' word thrusts. In doing so, he will be able to circumvent the examination while at the same time maintaining the facade of courage; he does not care whether his deeds and speech are in harmony, so long as they appear so.

Laches' position on speeches contains no such caveat. He says that he is one who both hates and loves speeches. As if in response to Nicias's disingenuousness, he claims that he "rejoices extraordinarily upon seeing that the speaker and the things said are suitable and harmonious with each other" (188d). That is, he is a lover of speeches (φιλόλογος) when the speaker's deeds match his words. When a man's speech, especially concerning virtue, manifests itself in virtuous action—when he lives his "own life as a concord of speeches in relation to deeds"—Laches considers that man worthy of honor (188d). On the other hand, when Laches sees that someone does not walk the talk, so to speak, he becomes a hater of speech. He even says that he is pained to see discrepancy between a man's actions and his speech and that the better such a man speaks, the more Laches becomes a hater of speech (μὶσόλογος).

After laying out his position on speech and deeds, Laches claims that despite being unfamiliar with Socrates' speech, he will listen to him because he is familiar with his deeds. Socrates did, after all, share the danger with him at Delium, thereby proving his worthiness of "noble speech and of complete frankness" (189a). Thus we see that for Laches, virtuous deeds are not just prerequisite for speech, they are more important than speech because without virtuous deeds one's speech, regardless of its aesthetic quality, is not worth hearing. At least on the surface, this is more appealing than Nicias's assent to the Socratic examination because it does not contain the formulaic caveat. However, Laches' willingness to be taught because of Socrates' virtuous behavior at Delium brings to mind two problems. First, there is no reason to believe that virtuous speech will naturally follow the virtuous behavior on the battlefield. Second, the dialogue participants have yet to determine the precise nature of virtue. Is courage in battle the whole of courage, let alone the whole of virtue? And even if this were virtue, why would one necessarily then be politically courageous as well? And just as problematic, are noble speeches equivalent to political courage? There is no reason to believe that someone who exhibits manly courage in battle will not be inclined to other sorts of vice or have a predilection for brute violence in political or family matters.

In short, Laches does not regard speech as dangerous. He simply cannot fathom a man who can have the discipline of a warrior in battle but can also be highly critical of conformity and discipline when off the battlefield. Whereas Nicias sees danger and assents to the examination only with reservations, Laches is willing to participate without reservation. For him, danger can be shared only in physical battle; critical self-examination—exposing one's soul—in the midst of friends, he thinks, is not dangerous if one has behaved honorably and virtuously. The problem, of course, is that honor and virtue can be recognized as such only through speech. The virtuousness and honorableness of a deed must be established through some sort of discursive cooperation. Subsequent recognition of these deeds must also be disseminated through speech. Where Nicias is concerned with his reputation, that is, how people will speak of him, to the neglect of his deeds, Laches is quite the opposite. Not only does Laches fail to recognize fully the indispensability of courageous speech, he dismisses it or relegates it to the status of, say, elaborate armor—an appropriate accessory for battle but ridiculous if one is a coward or poor fighter. He fails to see the inappropriateness of martial courage in other milieus; he does not see that the general, for example, might be able to avoid violence by learning the political courage advocated by Socrates.[100]

Hunter-Philosopher Courage

The difference between the approaches of the discussants emerges more fully when Socrates finally steers the conversation to the nature of courage and, by eliciting a definition of courage from Nicias and Laches, brings to light the nature of Socratic political courage.[101] The model is arrived at through Laches' effort to define courage. When pressed for a definition, Nicias claims that "if someone should be willing to remain in the ranks and defend himself against the enemies [πολεμίους] and should not flee, know well that he would be courageous [ἀνδρεῖος]" (190e). Socrates agrees but then asks if the man who fights the enemy while fleeing is not also brave. Laches must concede this or risk having his speech be out of harmony with his deeds. After all, he and Socrates were caught up in the flight from Delium. If he denies courage to the man who fights while fleeing, he will in effect be calling both himself and Socrates cowards and, as Socrates points out, impugning the Lacedaemonians because they fought while fleeing the Persians at Plataea and by doing so were even able to win the battle.

Laches, however, is not completely willing to concede this point, so Socrates asks him for a broader definition of courage. He asks Laches to define courage, not only as it pertains strictly to men at arms (τῷ ὁπλιτικῷ ἀνδρείους), but also as it pertains to cavalrymen, members of the navy, and everyone involved in the business of war. Moreover, he would like to hear what Laches has to say about "those who are courageous in dangers at sea, and those who are courageous toward sickness and poverty or even toward politics, and still further not only those who are courageous toward pains of fears but also those who are terribly clever at fighting against desires or pleasures, whether remaining or turning around in retreat—for there are presumably some courageous people, Laches, in such things too" (191d–e). In other words, he would like to hear not just about martial courage but also about economic, moral, and political courage (πολιτικὰ ἀνδρεῖοί).[102] Laches, the steadfast general, is at a loss for words; it appears he has never considered courage away from the battlefield. Thus Socrates' questioning, like the rigging that stripped Stesilaus of his scythe-spear, strips Laches of his manly understanding of courage. His limited definition of courage is, so to speak, as unmanned by Socrates as was the Sophist-Warrior and his scythe-spear.

Socrates, however, gives no quarter and presses him to show the armaments of peacetime courage, to show the weapons used to hunt for community not articulated on violence alone. He wants Laches "to speak of courage in this way: what power is it that is the same in pleasure and in pain and in all those things in which we were just now saying it exists, and that is therefore called courage?" (192b). Laches can find only one response; he calls it steadfastness of the soul attended by noble and good prudence (192c). Socrates contests this by pointing out that it is not necessarily courageous to make prudent decisions regarding, for example, money. Likewise, and Nicias would have done well to heed this point, it is not necessarily courageous to make a prudent decision to fight if and only if one has great advantage over the enemies. In this sense, courage is no more than stubbornness or calculated stubbornness for the sake of advantage. In fact, Socrates takes this argument one step further and suggests that courage so defined would have to include foolish stubbornness or even plain stubbornness (193c). When Laches agrees, it becomes clear that his own definition of courage is synonymous with foolish daring, which has been "revealed to us in what has passed to be shameful and harmful" (193d). The first example of foolish daring was, of course, Stesilaus's impotent stab at the enemy ship with his sophistic weapon and sophistic courage.

The point is not necessarily the precise definitions proffered. Rather, the nature of political courage begins to emerge more fully in this very act of pursuing understanding. As Socrates says to Laches, they ought not to be discouraged by their lack of discoveries; instead, they ought to obey their speech—to persist in the search and to be "steadfast in the hunt" (194a). A bit later, he says, "The good hunter [τὸν ἀγαθὸν κυνηγέτην] must pursue and not give over" (194b).[103] Political courage, it seems, is something like hunting. In hunting, partners agree on a common goal, muster the requisite courage to confront the wild beast (θηρίον), and, from the serious nonseriousness of the endeavor, emerge better friends after sharing in the risks and gains of a common goal. So, although Laches' martial definition of courage fails to account for political courage, it gets them on their way. It takes them from a form of courage that produces a community articulated by untempered violence to the more bounded violence of the hunt, and from courage for the sake of raw self-interest to the coordinated discourse of the hunt. In short, with the metaphor of the hunt, Socrates manages to collapse the twin problems of violence and sophistry into the mediative model of political courage. Political courage is a combination of the violent capacity of the warrior and the discursive knack of the Sophist. Just as this understanding of courage does not subordinate speech in service of martial violence, neither does it entirely reject violence in favor of just any kind of speech, as it appears to do for Aristophanes. In manly political courage there remains a capacity, but not a penchant, for violence.[104] Contrary to the Aristophanic understanding of political courage, in Platonic political courage there is a penchant for speech, but not just speech for the sake of speech. Without courage, self-critical citizenship is impossible. Without courage, the hunt is impossible. Plato is not merely shying away from violence and outrightly rejecting Homeric martial courage. He is no fool and knows that without this courage war is impossible. And, as the Greeks learned at Marathon, war is sometimes unavoidable. However, without political courage, self-critical speech is impossible—without which peaceful, discursively articulated community is impossible. Without political courage, one cannot live justly.

Courageous Citizenship

The remaining question, then, is whether leading citizens—those who act in our stead—can be willing and able hunters. In the *Laches*, the leading citizen is Nicias. To begin, when Socrates bids Nicias to join the hunt, his language is very interesting: "Come then, Nicias, if you have some power, come to the aid of your friends, men who are storm-tossed in speech and at a loss. For you see how our affairs are at a loss. By saying what you consider courage to be, deliver us from perplexity and securely establish in speech what you yourself perceive in your mind" (194c). Socrates is suggesting that the speech (*logos*) of the discussants has led them into a dangerous maelstrom. One must be careful, however, not to confuse this particular *logos* with *logos* in general, for it is the use of speech itself that puts one into the dangers of the storm at sea. Socrates makes a crucial point here. The consequences of speech are much less tangible than the consequences of deeds. When a warrior swings his sword, for example, he knows where his action will focus, what the results are likely to be, and most likely, what the repercussions will be. When he has finished his task the results can be seen, smelled, felt. If, however, one relies on speech to accomplish political ends, the results will indubitably be less tactile. In fact, when the *logos* sets sail politically, one rarely knows where it will ultimately alight. The importance of courage in political affairs, then, becomes even plainer because one needs to muster more courage to act politically with *logos* than with Stesilaus's scythe-spear. The scythe-spear, after all, is designed to create distance between combatants, so that one need not get as close to the dangerous enemy as one would with conventional close-in phalanx fighting. Political courage, however, closes the gap between individuals. As a result, more courage is needed to participate discursively than to employ either sophistry or violence.

Thus when Socrates bids Nicias to define courage by establishing in speech that which resides in his mind, he is challenging him to show the rest of the interlocutors the courage in his own soul by engaging publicly in critical self-examination regarding the justness of his actions. Nicias, we will recall, is well aware of the danger in taking this stormy voyage with Socrates (188a). He knows that speech, and especially the sort of speech that goes on between Socrates and his interlocutors, forces one to expose and concretize one's most unjust thoughts. He knows that if one plays this serious game, one will have to meet the demands of political courage and lay one's soul on the table, as it were, for examination. Consenting to such an examination takes more than a little courage; and if one is concealing anything, one will have to either amend one's ways or not participate. Nicias, it appears, opts for the latter.

Like many leading citizens, both in Athens and in our own time, Nicias, when asked to engage courageously in critical self-reflection, resorts to sloganeering. He says that because Socrates often says a man is good insofar as he is wise, and bad insofar as he is ignorant, the courageous man must therefore be wise. Nicias's use of rehearsed phrases (μάθηματα) indicates his unwillingness or inability to render his *psyche* into speech.[105] Again, the fundamental shortcoming of his character comes to the fore. Armed with stock phrases—which are as ill-suited for this sort of discourse as the Sophist-warrior's scythe-spear in the naval battle—Nicias manages to circumvent a critical examination of the justice of his actions and of the polis he leads. He engages Socrates and Laches as competitors (ἐχθρόι) rather than companions (φίλος) hunting for a form of courage appropriate to teach to both the youth and themselves.[106]

Invoking stock phrases is not the only way Nicias avoids joining the hunt. His very definition of courage allows him to substitute risk prediction for critical self-examination. Though he first says that courage is a sort of wisdom (σοφία), he quickly changes his term and calls it a sort of knowledge (ἐπιστήμη). Specifically, he says it is the "knowledge of terrible and of confidence-inspiring things, both in war and in all other things" (195a). By defining courage as knowledge, then qualifying ἐπιστήμη as knowledge of future goods and evils, it is not surprising that Nicias moves Laches to exclaim: "He is calling diviners [μάντις] courageous. For who else will know whether it is better for someone to live or to die?" (195e). And Laches is correct—for Nicias, courage is merely part of the ability to distinguish between dangerous and safe things, not between better and worse things, and certainly not between just and unjust things.

By Nicias's definition, the courageous man is one who knows what to do with the knowledge he has obtained from an augur—the knowledge of dreadful and confidence-inspiring things. Thus for Nicias, as for Socrates and Laches, good community appears to be rooted in a sort of courage. There is, however, a major difference. If, as he asserts, courage arises from some foreknowledge of goods and evils, then it cannot be the exclusive domain of human beings. Any wild animal (θηρίον) could be called courageous because beasts often demonstrate an uncanny ability to sense impending evil. Moreover, if Nicias's definition of courage is accepted, we must conclude that beasts can possess the very virtues the interlocutors are trying to inculcate into the young—indeed, that a jackass could command a fleet as well as he (196e).

Nicias, of course, is not willing to concede this. Instead, he draws a distinction between courage (ἀνδρεῖα) and fearlessness (ἄφοβος). Wild animals that are unafraid in the face of fearsome things are not courageous on account of forethought (προμηθίας).[107] Instead, they are fearless and stupid (ἄφοβον καὶ μῶρον) (197b). One cannot be called courageous, he thinks, unless one is also knowledgeable. Therefore in Nicias's formula good community depends on courage stemming from some sort of foreknowledge. The good lawgiver, then, can act with certain insights pertaining to the future. The question that must be asked of Nicias, then, is whether one is actually courageous if one is armed with the knowledge of a seer. Are risk prediction and risk management the hallmarks of courage—political or otherwise? For Nicias, risk prediction would allow one to act so as to appear courageous without actually being courageous. If, for example, one knew that foreboding storm clouds would bring only a short and mild storm, one would appear extraordinarily courageous if one sailed fearlessly into it. Yet this decision to sail, despite any political or strategic merits it might have, would be neither fearless nor courageous. Consultation with diviners, seers, haruspices, pollsters, game theorists, or other sundry practitioners of probability theory is therefore not courage, as Nicias believes, and if courage underwrites a community not articulated by violence, then Nicias cannot be held up as a model of courage.

Although Nicias's distinction between courage and fearlessness is useful, his reliance on foreknowledge as the source of courage raises more problems than it resolves. Besides depriving many deserving men the distinction of being courageous (197b) and being predicated on a rather truncated understanding of knowledge, it means that the knack of the seer would be superior, not just to knowledge in its full sense but to the rest of the virtues of a good citizen, a good general, a good philosopher, and so on. That is, ersatz courage (i.e., risk prediction) would render justice irrelevant—if not eliminating it altogether. The seer would be more important than the general, and this would violate a fundamental Socratic precept: "not that the diviner rule the general, but that the general rule the diviner" (199a).

Plato's intention here is clear: if one reduces courage to foreknowledge, there is no need to engage in the hunt with one's fellows—no need to engage in critical self-examination. Instead, one must cleave to the augurs and diviners, close oneself to the arguments of one's fellow citizens, and wait thrice nine days for Promethean gifts—quite the contrary to spending time with Socrates. The *Laches* is situated prior to the disaster at Sicily; therefore, it is clear that Nicias failed to learn this lesson. Just as he is "unwilling nobly" (196b) to participate in a dialogue free of platitudes with Laches and Socrates, Nicias maintains his trust in foreknowledge as the foundation of political courage. His lack of courage prevents him from properly participating in the Socratic examination and at Sicily forces him to trust in diviners and superstition for his actions as a general. Put succinctly, his deficient political courage eliminates the possibility of employing not only the whole of *episteme* but also the fundamental requisite for good citizenship. Because Nicias makes his decisions with only partial courage, he makes them with even less moderation, justice, and prudence (199e).

When Socrates makes this clear to Nicias, the latter's response is rather predictable. He says that although he may have failed to provide a definition and example of courage, he believes he has nevertheless "spoken suitably on the things that we were talking about" (200b). If anyone thinks otherwise, Nicias will return after consulting with Damon—his peacetime seer—to deliver even better μάθηματα. Nicias, in denying the possibility of his own ignorance, remains steadfast in his refusal to participate openly in the discourse and, as he demonstrates later at Sicily, remains steadfast in his resistance to political courage. Laches, on the other hand, recognizes that because he and Nicias have been unable to define courage, they should not be teaching it to the young men. He therefore advises Lysimachus to turn the boys over to Socrates for their education. Yet this advice, prudent as it may seem, reveals that Laches too has missed an important point in the experience. He fails to see that participation in Socratic discourse, and in discourse in general, must be voluntary to be effective. One can neither force Socrates to teach nor force young men to learn. Political courage can be meaningful only if it is freely chosen.

This is exactly why Socrates, when enjoined by Lysimachus to "pay some heed and join in our zeal for the lads to become as good as possible," refuses (200d). Of course, he says, he will join in the zeal, for it would be terrible to do otherwise, but because he has not defined courage he has nothing to teach. Unlike Nicias, who has offered to return the next day with better knowledge, Socrates knows that it would be detrimental for him to return the next day in the capacity of a teacher. The young men would be forced into a submissive role in the teacher-student relationship and would not have to engage in the hunt voluntarily, that is, on the merit of their courage. The essential nature of the hunt—that it be among friends with a common goal—would be preempted. Socrates is aware of this and therefore refuses to come in any other capacity than friend and fellow hunter. He is well aware that if one has the courage at an early age to join the hunt, the lessons learned will not be lost in one's later years. The boys, it appears, have all along had the wherewithal and disposition to earnestly enjoy Socrates' company. Their courage, which may be the result of nothing more than being treated as equals in the discourse, will enable them to participate in the hunt for the right teacher, the right weapon, the right battle, and, importantly, the hunt for justice. It will endow them with political courage, which is an absolute and permanent human good.

FOUR

Moral Courage and Autonomy

Up to now you were only apparently free. You had only the precarious freedom of a slave to whom nothing has been commanded. Now be really free. Learn to become your own master. Command your heart, Emile, and you will be virtuous.

—Rousseau, *Emile*

Suffering Rousseau

After the battle at Thermopylae an inscription was left for the fallen: "Go, stranger, and tell the Spartans that we lay here in obedience to their orders."[1] The inscription is both awe-inspiring and revolting. That the Three Hundred were able to accomplish what they did, that they never wavered in their courage, and that they set the historical standard for martial courage and honor is indeed awe-inspiring. One must ask, however, What kind of city's laws and orders demand this action of her people? Moreover, what kind of people would obey the orders of the city so fanatically? In the previous chapter we discussed the Athenian objection to this Spartan sort of courage and consequent Spartan way of life. Martial courage and the love of honor fell under serious scrutiny because of their inextricable connection with violence. Instead, we discovered a recurring effort to infuse courage with reason, to redirect the good of courage to softer, more relaxed, more just ends. The distinctions were clear: justice rather than honor, and reason rather than violence.

What is not evident in the Socratic objection is a questioning of this sort of unbridled obedience to laws, as epitomized in the inscription on Leonidas's tomb. In fact, quite the contrary is evident in Platonic thought. In the *Crito*, for instance, Plato portrays Socrates in his jail cell awaiting his execution. Crito has bribed the jailor so that Socrates may escape and go into exile or "flee" (φεύγειν).[2] As Crito tells him, he should choose "just what the good and manly man [ἀνὴρ ἀγαθὸς καὶ ἀνδρεῖος] would choose" and accept the offer to flee into exile (45d). Socrates, like the good warrior Plato makes him out to be, refuses Crito's offer to flee and stays in jail. To justify this decision, Socrates invokes the laws of Athens: first, they have afforded him a legitimate birth, educated him, and nurtured him; second, he could have left anytime previously; and finally, it would not be courageous for Socrates to defy the laws because it would undermine the order of the city (51a). For Socrates, running away, just like running away in war and battle, is the epitome of cowardice because it leaves one's battle brothers in the lurch. To ignore the laws would be to act for one's own interest to the detriment of the whole—and such selfish acts are never courageous acts. Instead, running away "would be doing just what the paltriest slave would do" (52d). In short, Socrates stays in the line; he "stands his ground" (παραμένοντας) and refuses to abandon his orders.[3] He selflessly accepts the laws, even though they are unjust, and accepts his cup of hemlock.[4] To the bitter end he is obedient to the laws, and the inscription on his tomb might well read, "Go, stranger, and tell the Athenians that I lay here in obedience to their orders." It is a fitting memorial for the new Achilles—a fitting memorial for the courageous hunter-philosopher fighting discursively for his erotic love of justice.

Yet an objection can be voiced with regard to this image of the courageous citizen. How can one be a courageous citizen if one is slavishly beholden to externally imposed laws? Is not the dictum "Obey or die" the very definition of a slavish existence? How can we possibly admire visions of courageous citizenship that result in the ostracizing of Aristodemus for his blindness or the execution of Socrates for his philosophizing? Is courage necessarily wedded to this sort of absurd heteronomy? If not, can one be courageous for the sake of something other than honor and justice? These are precisely the sort of questions that arise in the thought of Jean-Jacques Rousseau. Like other thinkers, Rousseau is enamored with courage and heroism, but his fundamental care is not honor or justice but autonomy, or, literally, self-rule. Rousseau does care for honor and justice, but these are not *ne plus ultra* cares. For Rousseau, a moral and political order that forces an honorable and courageous man out of his city, or a moral and political order that forces a just and courageous man out of his city, is not good order. And blind obedience to these sorts of laws cannot be understood as courage; on the contrary, it may be a failing akin to cowardice.

For Rousseau, then, courage takes on a moral color, pertaining more to its psychological than to its physical or tangible effects. Courage in this sense can thus be understood as "moral courage," just as we might refer to a moral victory or to moral support. In Rousseau's understanding, moral courage exhibits a teaching of goodness—or correctness—of character and behavior that arises from the conscience. Thus the courage discussed in this chapter is bound up with a sense of right and wrong, with moral obligations stemming directly from the acquisition and practice of this type of courage. Through his invocation of the idea of courage, Rousseau illuminates a moral order where one can maintain one's autonomy, especially in the face of unjust laws, yet at the same time live in a community of other autonomous individuals. Just as Aristophanes and Socrates attempt to jettison the love of honor but salvage all that is good about courage, Rousseau attempts to jettison absolute selflessness and obedience as necessary components of courage, yet salvage courage and heroism. At first glance, the project appears to be an attempt to violate the law of noncontraction because, from what has thus far been revealed about courage, selflessness appears to be nearly synonymous with courage. To remove selflessness from courage seems illogical and unreasonable.

Yet this seeming illogicality and unreasonableness pushes Rousseau toward a new mode of articulation. With the Socratic formulation, justice requires reason and discursive articulation. However, people cannot be articulated discursively and be autonomous at the same time. The very nature of discourse requires a plurality of participants, which makes one dependent on others. In saying this, however, one might be tempted to suggest the alternative, nondiscursive, nonrational mode of articulation with which we are familiar: violence. Violence, however, is simply another form of heteronomy, or rule imposed from without. Hence, Rousseau needs to find a way for human beings to associate that depends on neither reason nor violence. This is precisely why he arrives at the idea of *compassion*, which is neither violent nor dependent on reason.

Compassion, as several scholars have argued, is a central concept in Rousseau's thought that has been underemphasized in favor of more common themes, such as justice, freedom, and the general will.[5] It is my contention, however, that courage, autonomy, and compassion are not discrete categories in Rousseau's thought. Instead, they can be understood only in their mutual relationship of fundamental care and mode of articulation. As will become clear presently, from early on Rousseau focused his attention on his fundamental care—autonomy. The virtuous man, he argues, is he who is willing to risk life and limb for the sake of his autonomy. Courage, autonomy, and compassion all appear in rather undifferentiated forms in the *Discourses* but develop concurrently as Rousseau matures as a thinker. Finally in his *Emile* courage emerges as the foundational virtue of the autonomous human being in a fully articulated community of compassionate citizens.

Natural Courage and the Autonomy of Peoples

In his *First Discourse*, his earliest thoughts concerning courage and heroic virtue, Rousseau addresses a question posed by the Academy at Dijon: Has the restoration of the sciences and arts tended to purify morals (moeurs)? He begins, although in what amounts to a rather unselfconscious manner, with a statement echoing a love of honor usually bound up with martial courage. In the preface to this short essay he claims that he writes, not merely for the approval of the general public, but for an even larger audience. As he says, "I do not care to please either the witty or the fashionable."[6] Instead, he fancies himself to be writing for those who live beyond his own century, for posterity. As we have seen with Achilles and the Homeric world, to do anything for posterity is to do it for the sake of honor. To be recognized and honored by one's contemporaries is one thing, but to extend one's being through history takes the love of honor to another level. So from the very beginning Rousseau situates himself in the tradition of those concerned with honor and appears to be enveloped in a world similar to Achilles'.[7]

This claim can be taken even further. When Rousseau addresses the Academy's question concerning the moral state of contemporary man, he begins with an ironic statement: although it is a beautiful sight to see mankind emerging from darkness—that is, to be enlightened—something has gone terribly amiss. While the arts and sciences have provided for "the safety and well-being of assembled men," they have at the same time made men "love their slavery" and have turned them into "civilized people" (*FD*, 36).[8] In other words, whereas the arts and sciences are thought to have created a more civilized, tamer, and safer world, Rousseau regards this very moralization of the world as a loss. Specifically, this civilized man, this so-called moral man, has been sapped of the very virility that enabled him to achieve the greatness mankind is now experiencing. As Rousseau puts it, the man civilized by the rebirth of the arts and sciences has "the semblance of all the virtues without the possession of any" (*FD*, 36). Though he may be clever and a *bonhomme*, he is not very manly.

In addition, Rousseau contends that while government and laws are meant to protect the body, the sciences and the arts do two other things: they enslave man and make him forget his enslavement. The needs of the body are more and more being met through scientific advances, but the needs of the soul remain unsated. Simply, the arts and sciences make man forget his real needs. And what does Rousseau envision as man's real need? Early in his thought, autonomy appears as the real need because the arts are the very thing reconciling man to his slavery. The arts make him docile on the outside, but in so doing they create a disjuncture with what actually dwells within him—in his gut, so to speak. The arts and sciences are thus merely a veneer. Man has the "virtue" of civility but no real virtue because decency and civility fail to reflect what is inside—what and how a man really is. He is, in his heart of hearts, insincere.[9]

Thus Rousseau laments, "How pleasant it would be to live among us if exterior appearance were always a reflection of the heart's disposition" (*FD*, 37). For Rousseau, what is engraved on the heart is the uncorrupted core, the essence of the individual. External appearance—one's clothing, one's title, one's manners—is but a veneer concealing the real person. In the *First Discourse*, Rousseau says that if we strip away the ornamentation of civility, the "strength and vigor of the body will be found" (*FD*, 37). Rousseau seems to be invoking language redolent of martial courage in the ancient world. He claims, "Ornamentation is no less foreign to virtue, which is the strength and vigor of the soul. The good man is an athlete who likes to compete in the nude. He disdains all those vile ornaments that would hamper the use of his strength, most of which were invented only to hide some deformity" (*FD*, 37). What is interesting is that virtue is not understood in terms of one man acting upon, or in concert with, another. Instead, the relationship emerging from Rousseau's nascent thought pertains to the sort of courage one might invoke in battle: it pertains to strength of body and soul, but it is moral only insofar as the display of manly courage is sincere. In other words, the virtuous man, the courageous man, is one who does not dissemble. Though rustic, he permits his natural vigor and strength to shine forth. Human articulation is thus predicated on the mutual transparency of strength pure and simple. Just as was revealed in the discussion of martial courage, people when stripped of their civility are necessarily joined together through a corporeal strength, which is to say, through a capacity other than reason.

For Rousseau, this particular mode of articulation disappears with the advent of the arts and sciences. Previously people were free to appear to each other as they actually were, but in the modern world, "one no longer dares to appear as he is; and in this perpetual constraint, the men who form this herd called society, placed in the same circumstances, will all do the same things unless stronger motives deter them" (*FD*, 38). The transformation from the natural man, the honest and frank man, to the civilized man has eliminated a particular way the individual relates to other individuals. Instead of being in control of himself—that is, instead of being an autonomous, vigorous individual—he is beholden to the masses; he is part of a herd where all semblance of autonomy and individuality is effaced by the imposition of reason. In the average everyday run of life, society kills the natural man—the man who can courageously guard his autonomy and is free to associate unambiguously and unabashedly his autonomous self with other autonomous individuals. And this unambiguous and unabashed association of the self is precisely what Rousseau calls friendship.

Friendship, as we have seen in our discussions of both martial and political courage, is a deep good that emerges from acting courageously with our battle brothers, whether these are found literally on the battlefield or in the battle for the souls of Athenian youth. However, since the arts and sciences have unmanned man with regard to that which he ought to love—his autonomy—they have also endangered the possibility of true friendship. When a man is too cowardly to put himself on the line for the sake of another, it becomes more and more difficult to get a true sense of his mettle. Friendship, after all, is about risk. As Joseph Reisert puts it, Rousseau regards friendship as a sacred trust: "By becoming someone's close friend, by taking that friend into our confidence, by making our own happiness dependent on our friend's, we give our friend a degree of responsibility for our welfare. We can think of a close friend as a trustee of our welfare and well-being, with a responsibility to look out for our welfare, just as we have responsibility to look out for the welfare of our friend."[10] In friendship we risk not only our empirical selves but the existential. Thus Rousseau claims that in the herdlike existence of the age of arts and sciences, "one will never know one's friends thoroughly, [and thus] it would be necessary to wait for emergencies—that is, to wait until it is too late, as it is for these very emergencies that it would have been essential to know him" (*FD*, 38). The close bonds that emerge with martial courage are precisely the sort of deep and meaningful friendships that Rousseau has in mind. In emergencies, when we risk life and limb, our true friends are disclosed because in such circumstances the possibility for disingenuousness is greatly diminished.[11] One can be uncertain about the person with whom one is dealing, but in an emergency the courage and cares of one's companions will be most plainly on display.

But in average everyday circumstances, Rousseau envisions uncertainty, confusion, and a general diminishing sense of situatedness. As he puts it, without situations that can give rise to courage, "What a procession of vices must accompany this uncertainty! No more friendships; no more real esteem; no more well-based confidence. Suspicions, offenses, fears, coldness, reserve, hate, betrayal will hide constantly under that uniform and false veil of politeness, under that much vaunted urbanity which we owe to the enlightenment of our century" (*FD*, 38). Without the occasional necessary mustering of courage, there is only dissimulation. One cannot know whom one can trust, and without trust one can have no real friends. All that remains are individuals disparaging other individuals. Captiousness will be de rigueur, love of country will die out, and even sober men will be disingenuous and unworthy of praise. In short, decency and morals, as spawned by and expressed in the arts and sciences, are a sham for Rousseau: "Virtue has fled as their light dawned on our horizon, and the same phenomenon has been observed in all times and places" (*FD*, 39–40).

Rousseau again makes this claim when describing the atrophy of courage. As he puts it, "While living conveniences multiply, arts are erected and luxury spreads, true courage is enervated, military virtues disappear, and this too is the work of the sciences and of all those arts which are exercised in the shade of the study" (*FD*, 54). In other words, the arts and sciences sap the manly courage requisite for collective autonomy. Studying the arts and sciences is tranquil and sedentary, and though it enlightens the mind it corrupts the body and saps the vigor of the soul. It is, according to Rousseau, antithetical to the pursuit of military prowess and acumen, for "where will soldiers find the courage to bear excessive work to which they are totally unaccustomed?" (*FD*, 55). Without courage, not only are honor and justice left undefended, but so too is autonomy.

To illustrate this, Rousseau first points to Egypt. Egypt, he states, was once a civilization that, thanks to her virtue, or at least the virtue of her leader Sesostris, aimed to conquer the whole world. However, once she became home to philosophy and the fine arts, "she was conquered by Cambyses, then by the Greeks, the Romans, the Arabs, and finally the Turks" (*FD*, 40). Whereas once Egypt was the home to heroic courage and a bodily vigor that ensured her autonomy, a sort of courage that permitted her to conquer other peoples well beyond her own small corner of the world, the advent of the arts and sciences made her conquerable. In other words, with courage as envisioned by Rousseau, a tightly articulated people is unconquerable; with courage, it not only maintains its autonomy but is free to expand the realm in which it can exercise its freedom.

Similarly, Greece was "formerly populated by heroes who twice conquered Asia, once at Troy and once in the homeland" (*FD*, 40).[12] Learning, however, also reduced this people from free and unconquerable to enervated and corrupt. Here Rousseau may well be referring more to Athens than to Greece as a whole, but in any case with the arts and sciences came the dissolution of the vibrant structure of the society, which was founded on manly courage, and the Greeks were soon enslaved to the simpler yet more virtuous Macedonians. "Greece," Rousseau says, "always learned, always voluptuous, and always enslaved, no longer experienced anything in her revolutions but a change of masters" (*FD*, 40). Without manly courage, Greece could only experience the rule of others, not self-rule. Rome is described in similar terms. It was made great by the simpler virtues of the early founders, but with the rise to fame of "obscene authors" like Ovid, Catullus, and Martial it lost its capacity to maintain its autonomy: "Rome, formerly the temple of virtue, becomes the theater of crime, the shame of nations, and the plaything of barbarians. That world capital finally falls under the yoke she had imposed on so many peoples, and the day of her fall was the eve of the day one of her citizens was given the title Arbiter of Good Taste" (*FD*, 40).

Finally, Rousseau holds up a modern example of learning undermining courage as the primary virtue for establishing and maintaining the autonomy of a people. In China, he claims, one finds an enormous country where learning is held in high esteem. "If the sciences purified morals, if they taught men to shed their blood for their country, if they aroused courage, the peoples of China would be wise, free, and invincible" (*FD*, 41). But insofar as Rousseau holds "moral" to mean free and unconquerable, the arts and sciences have failed in China as well. There, he claims, one finds every sort of vice and crime, and all the erudition of the civil servants and the rationality of the laws could not save that country from the "yoke of the ignorant and coarse Tartar" (*FD*, 41). To be moral, then, is first, to have the wherewithal to resist the yoke of servitude and, second, to be able to put the yoke of servitude on others. It is to preserve the vigor and strength of the body—which Rousseau sums up in the idea of manly courage—in order to resist enslavement of whatever kind.

For this very reason, in contrast to the examples of degenerate Egypt, Athens, and Rome, Rousseau holds up other peoples who have resisted the corruption and loss of autonomy that he claims accompany the arts and sciences. This manly courage is clearly demonstrated, Rousseau holds, in nations that have "by their own virtues created their own happiness and an example for other nations" (*FD*, 41). The Persians, the Scythians, and the Germans, for example, scorned the "vain knowledge" of the so-called civilized nations and did not care that they were thought to be barbarian. But most importantly, Rousseau holds up the Spartans as the paragon of a moral people. It is with Sparta, Judith Shklar argues, that Rousseau found "an image of the perfectly socialized man, the citizen whose entire life is absorbed by his social role." This social role was, of course, the perfection of manly courage for the sake of Spartan freedom, and "it mattered far less to Rousseau whether the heroes of Sparta and Rome had ever really existed, than that such men could *not* be found at all in modern times."[13] Hence, in Sparta Rousseau sees a "republic of demi-gods rather then men, so superior did their virtues seem to human nature" (*FD*, 43). Through their obsession with manly courage and their disdain for vain knowledge, the Spartans maintained their autonomy. Not only were they able to resist the yoke of the Persians and then the Athenian empire, they defeated Athens—"the abode of civility and good taste, the country of orators and philosophers"—on the battlefield (*FD*, 43). With this, Rousseau's praise for Sparta reaches a feverish pitch: "O Sparta! you eternally put to shame a vain doctrine! While the vices which accompany the fine arts entered Athens together with them, while a tyrant there so carefully collected the works of the prince of poets, you chased the arts and artists, the sciences and the scientists away from your walls" (*FD*, 43). Sparta, then, though she left no elegant buildings or stately monuments, left what Rousseau regards as the real testament of a morally courageous people: "Of its inhabitants nothing is left to us except the memory of their heroic actions" (*FD*, 43). And her heroic actions were none other than the preservation of her autonomy.

Rousseau also praises Socrates and Socratic wisdom as the single beacon attempting to steer Athens clear of the degeneracy and enslavement that naturally followed the introduction of vain knowledge. It was Socrates—and in Rome, Cato the Elder—who inveighed against "those cunning and subtle Greeks who seduced the virtue and enervated the courage of his fellow citizens" (*FD*, 45).[14] For Rousseau, if a nation is not to fall prey to effeminate customs, such as are embodied by the fine arts and the study of virtue (rather than the practice), it must preserve its autonomy through military discipline and love of the fatherland: "the sacred names of liberty, disinterestedness, obedience to laws" must prevail (*FD*, 45). Rousseau goes so far as to imagine Fabricius exhorting his fellow Romans:

> What disastrous splendor has succeeded Roman simplicity? What is this strange language? What are these effeminate customs? What is the meaning of these statues, these paintings, these buildings? Madmen, what have you done? Have you, the masters of nations, made yourselves slaves of the frivolous men you conquered? Are these rhetoricians who govern you? Is it to enrich architects, painters, sculptors, and comedians that you watered Greece and Asia with your blood? Are the spoils of Carthage the booty of a flute player? Romans, hasten to tear down these amphitheatres, break these marble statues,

> burn these paintings, chase out these slaves who subjugate you and whose fatal arts corrupt you. Let other hands win fame by vain talents; the only talent worth of Rome is that of conquering the world and making virtue reign in it. (*FD*, 45–46)

The goal is not mere rustic simplicity but the maintenance of autonomy through the expression of power. It is about conquering and not being conquered as a people.

The courage Rousseau extols shares many of the characteristics of martial courage. The difference, however, lies precisely in the fundamental care revealed in his evocation of courage—autonomy. What is most important to recognize about Rousseau's early understanding of autonomy, however, is that this self-rule pertains to peoples rather than individuals. He is talking about the sort of courage a people needs to keep from being enslaved by another people. He derides the arts and sciences because they diminish the sort of courage that lends itself to the autonomy of the nation. While the study of the arts and sciences appears to endow man with a certain kind of power, it is actually prosthetic courage. Focus on the body and tangible strength is replaced and forgotten thanks to the focus on the mind. Rousseau recognizes that such a vocation can certainly lend itself to a certain form of courage but argues that it is more likely to be *pseudoandreia*, false courage, than real courage. It may be effectual on the short haul, but it lacks the corporeal and embodied depth needed for the long run. For just this reason Rousseau says: "Let no one raise as an objection the renowned valor of all those modern warriors who are so scientifically disciplined. I hear their bravery on a single day of battle highly praised, but I am told how they bear overwork, how they endure the rigor of the seasons and the bad weather. Only a little sun or snow, or the lack of a few superfluities is necessary to dissolve and destroy the best of our armies in a few days" (*FD*, 55). In other words, the modern army, with its "scientific courage," can fight fiercely but cannot march. Wars must be decided quickly because prosthetic courage is a veneer that cannot protect the autonomy of a people.[15] Real courage is deeply embodied in peoples who vigorously defend their autonomy over the long haul.

On the Virtue of the Hero

When Rousseau leaves the *First Discourse* behind, he is left with a nagging question. How shall we understand this courage that protects the autonomy of a people? What are we looking for when we talk about the courage of a people, and what exactly is the strength of a people? It is clear even in this cursory evaluation of courage and heroism in the *First Discourse* that Rousseau has not yet worked through the problem. A certain prosthetic courage allows democratic—that is, scientific—peoples to fight fiercely. Yet this same courage does not go deep enough to guard fully against attacks on the autonomy of a people. It is not deeply "embodied courage." Hence, Rousseau is forced to turn his attention to courage that manifests itself in the individual. He asks, What is it about the constitution of an individual that allows him to safeguard the autonomy of his people? In other words, what constitutes individual heroism? In a lesser-known discourse, Rousseau takes up this very theme. The essay is called "Discourse on This Question: Which Is the Virtue Most Necessary for a Hero and Which Are the Heroes Who Lacked This Virtue?"[16]

The "Discourse on Heroism" begins with a shift in Rousseau's language. Rousseau writes that the wise man is certainly concerned with his own felicity but that "the views of the true Hero extend further. The happiness of men is his object, and it is to this sublime labor that he devotes the great soul he received from Heaven" (*DH*, 2). So whereas in the *First Discourse* courage and heroism point to a concern for the autonomy of a people, here courage reveals a fundamental concern with happiness. How this happiness is construed is, of course, of utmost importance. Stephen Salkever offers a broad and, one might say, rather Aristotelian interpretation of what happiness means for Rousseau. "Happiness," he writes, "is not a philosophic or theoretical dream or aspiration, but a phenomenon which exists in varying ways of life which needs to be understood, not invented."[17] For Rousseau, however, talk of happiness rarely departs from talk of autonomy. Insofar as one cares fundamentally about something, one cannot be happy without partaking of and experiencing that something. In other words, because for Rousseau the "fundamental problem of political philosophy" is autonomy, it is possible to say that his first care is also autonomy—that autonomy is the basic requisite for human happiness.[18] This is really not a stretch—if we do not rule ourselves, we cannot be happy; if we are enslaved, we cannot be happy. There is, in Rousseau's corpus, ample evidence for this. For example, Rousseau claims that strong, martially valorous nations have "by their own virtues created their own happiness and an example for other nations" (*DH*, 2). These are the nations that, through martial courage, not only have been able to maintain rule over themselves but have extended their rule to others. The happy nation is, above all, the autonomous nation.

For Rousseau, the hero is concerned with the happiness of his nation, which means his cares are bound up with others. In this sense, as Melissa A. Butler is quite correct to argue, Rousseau fits well into a "care ethics" understanding of human relations. "Issues of care and connection," she argues, "were important in Rousseau's thought," and "quite possibly more than any other writer in 'the canon' of political theory, Rousseau *cared* about *care*."[19] This, however, is not to say that the hero is some sort of *eudaimonistic* philosopher. In fact, in the "Discourse on Heroism," Rousseau goes to lengths to argue that the hero is not a philosopher at all. On the contrary, his role is quite different: "The Philosopher can give the Universe some salutary instructions, but his lessons will never correct either the nobles who scorn them or the People which does not hear them at all. Men are not governed in that way by abstract views; one makes them happy only by constraining them to be so, and one must make them experience happiness in order to make them love it. Those are the occupation and talents of the Hero" (*DH*, 2). While in the *First Discourse* courage and heroism are collective characteristics ensuring the autonomy of the nation, in this discourse courage and heroism are individual virtues that lend themselves to the autonomy and happiness of the collective. Put otherwise, in its first instance heroism was an amorphous virtue of the collective that allowed the pursuit of the autonomy of the nation. Here, heroism is described as a quality of a singular person that begets and maintains collective autonomy. Rousseau is unambiguous on this count: "The heroism which they constitute, detached from all personal interest, has only the felicity of others as its object and only their admiration as its reward" (*DH*, 2). And a bit later he claims that in heroism there is only one "incontestable principle: that among men it is the person who makes himself most useful to others who should be the first of them all" (*DH*, 2–3).

Rousseau does not regard this type of courage conventionally. More often than not, courage, as a virtue, is lumped together with justice, piety, wisdom, and so on. But for Rousseau, the hero is not necessarily a virtuous soul deliberately acting selflessly for the sake of the autonomy of his peoples. Instead, the happiness of the people is residual; it is a collective benefit that accrues from the courageous character of the hero. As Rousseau puts it, heroes are working toward the felicity of all men, but they are not doing this deliberately. Instead, "public felicity is far less the end of the Hero's actions than it is a means to reach the one he sets for himself, and that end is almost always his personal glory" (*DH*, 3). Just as in the *First Discourse*, Rousseau's understanding of courage continues to depart from the categories we discovered in discussions of martial or political courage. It does maintain one central feature: Rousseau still regards the courageous act as one done with honor and glory in mind. However, and this is the crucial departure, in Rousseau's construal of courage and heroism, the goal of the hero is not necessarily the happiness and well-being of the greater community. These are merely fortuitous, perhaps peripheral consequences and happenstances. The hero's heroism does not lie in his "goodness." Instead, as Christopher Kelly puts it, it "is more closely related with effectiveness than with morality."[20] In Rousseau's understanding, the main thing the hero reveals is the desire and capacity to preserve that which he cares most about: his autonomy. That this trickles down to collective autonomy is but a fortuitous consequence.

In this sense, then, the hero is not a pure man, pure philosopher, or pure warrior. He is no Christ-figure, no Socrates, and no Achilles. As Rousseau puts it, "The virtues of the Hero rarely have their source in purity of soul" but instead "need the cooperation of some vices to make them active" (*DH*, 3). Moreover, the hero does not make a people happy or autonomous by dominating them physically. He does so by "subjugating the hearts and gaining the admiration of Peoples" (*DH*, 3).[21] This is a rather sharp departure from the traditional view of the hero, and Rousseau is well aware of this. He writes that "the warrior's valor has long been accepted by most men as the prime virtue of the Hero" but that it is thoughtless to confer esteem and praise on mere "martial valor" because "it is a very odious inconsistency . . . to believe that the benefactors of the human race announce their character by the destruction of men" (*DH*, 4). Rousseau even goes so far as to say that if we ever want lasting peace we ought to banish such heroism from the earth. One simply cannot be considered morally courageous for deeds that inflict bodily pain or death on one's subjects. A dead subject, after all, is rarely a happy subject.

Thus in the *Discourse on Heroism*, as in the *First Discourse*, which was written only a year or two earlier, courage holds an important place. The difference from the earlier work, however, lies in Rousseau's insistence that although courage is of utmost importance, the courage of an Achilles is inadequate and a more robust, inclusive form of courage is needed. Hence, Rousseau declares that "among the qualities that must form the great man, courage is something, but away from battle valor is nothing. The brave man shows his worth only in battle; the true hero shows his every day" (*DH*, 4). Rousseau goes so far as to suggest that courage, which here he calls "valor," should not be considered a virtue at all. It is improper to honor a quality that enables so many scoundrels, like Cataline and Cromwell, to commit their crimes. It is simply impossible, he thinks, to honor a quality that can be used to destroy the fatherland and to murder one's own people. The same can be said about the infamously bloodthirsty figures of history, such as Marius, Totila, and Tamarlane (*DH*, 4). In Rousseau's words: "Let us no longer be told that the palm of Heroism belongs only to valor and military talents" (*DH*, 5). He wants to be clear that heroism is not confined to this sort of virtue because many men have become great without staining their hands with blood. In particular, Rousseau points to "the Legislator of Sparta" who, after ruling the city, "had the courage to return the crown to its legitimate owner who did not even ask him for it" (*DH*, 4). Whereas in the *First Discourse* he holds up the Spartans as the paragon of martial courage we ought to emulate, a few years later he invokes the Spartans to give an instance of heroism without blood. The courageous man, the morally courageous man, declines the opportunity to be a tyrant. He declines the clear opportunity to wrest the autonomy of his own people from them. The courageous hero is the Cincinnatus type who declines a community of relationships predicated on violent compulsion and instead works for the autonomy of his countrymen.

This is indeed a curious turn and points directly to a radically different understanding of courage. In discussing the Spartan Legislator, Rousseau is wrestling to depict a type of courage that enables one to be a "gentle and peaceful citizen" who avenges insult and injury not by killing his enemy but by making him, by example, a decent man (*DH*, 5). Rousseau once again invokes Socrates. In the *First Discourse* Socrates is praised for his contempt for the arts and sciences and the pseudoheroism that follows from them. Here again Socrates is construed as a true hero because, though the oracle endowed him with what amounted to divine honors, he had the courage to recognize this as pseudoheroism. He refused to hold himself above his fellow Athenians, and certainly he made no claims—despite his divine coronation as the best man in the city—to rule in Athens. Instead, Socrates was known for passing his praise to others, such as Alcibiades. He is, in fact, best known for disdaining political positions altogether. This, Rousseau claims, is true courage, and as such, we cannot "refuse Heroism to the person who made heroes of his compatriots" (*DH*, 5).

Rousseau also gives the title of hero to several other character types: the kind of man, for example, who could "preserve his freedom and virtue even at the Court of tyrants, and who dared to assert to the face of an opulent Monarch that power and riches do not make a man happy" (*DH*, 5), or the kind of man who could write against an oppressor in his fatherland, even if the result was his own death. Rousseau also invokes Cato of Utica, who "did not distinguish himself in battles and did not fill the world with talk of his exploits" but instead "from a body of warriors . . . formed a society of wise, equitable, and modest men" (*DH*, 6). Even Augustus,

Rousseau claims, exhibited true heroism in his equitable laws and his pardon of Cinna rather than in his conquest of the known world.

Rousseau's point is clear: courage need not be strictly martial. This is not to say that he repudiates martial courage altogether. Instead, he is attempting to amalgamate the principles of martial courage with what we here call moral courage. If he privileges one of these sorts of courage, it is definitely the latter, for, as Rousseau says, "The social virtues are preferable to courage even in heroes!" (*DH*, 6). But in any case, Rousseau clearly attempts to formulate a vision of courage that is not bound up with the capacity for efficient violence. Heroism belongs to the "philosophical and beneficent warrior who, with a hand accustomed to brandishing arms, removes from your midst the calamities of a long and deadly war, and makes the sciences and fine arts shine among you with Royal splendor" (*DH*, 6). So whereas in the *First Discourse* Rousseau completely repudiates the arts and sciences in favor of raw Spartan martial courage, in the "Discourse on Heroism" he softens his stance. He seeks a union between Apollo and Mars, between the purely noetic and the purely somatic. In making this move, he does not oppose the warrior who defends the wise man who works for our happiness; rather, he portrays the hero as someone who embodies both these traits. In other words—and Rousseau's language betrays this very distinction—he is differentiating between courage (Fr., courage) and bravery (bravoure). To be courageous is to be heroic with *feeling*, or, as the etymology of the word indicates, with the *heart*. It is to be valorous without losing sight of the relationships of care between man and man. It is to be constant, to act with generosity, to be enlightened, and even to be tranquil.

To be brave, on the other hand, may well involve acting brutally, stupidly, and furiously. Though Rousseau himself never raises this point, it would not be unreasonable to assume he had this etymological distinction in mind. Bravery, after all, is derived in both French and English from the Greek *barbaros*—barbarian. In the ancient Greek world the barbarian, by definition, did not speak Greek, and the distinction was not merely linguistic. The non-Greek-speaking peoples were incapable of entering the moral world of the polis. They did not speak Greek and were therefore apolitical.

To use Rousseau's language, the barbarian lacked the virtues that "arise from the different relationships that Society has established between men" (*DH*, 7). With bravery one inserts oneself into relationships predicated on violence for the sake of fame, individual honor, or possibly even wealth. Rousseau's point is clear: one can be a hero "without being brave" (*DH*, 7). Thus bravery, valor, or martial courage—whichever Rousseau chooses to call it—"is not the virtue most necessary for a Hero" (*DH*, 7). Heroism is not just spilling one's blood for country; it is "ardent love for the fatherland" and "invincible constancy in adversity" (*DH*, 7). This heroism, it would seem, is not entirely dependent on courage; it may well be derived from any of the virtues.

Rousseau recognizes this and briefly addresses virtues other than courage. With regard to justice, he says, there is really no correlation, because many men have achieved immortality (Rousseau's definition of the hero) through the most egregious acts of injustice. Heroism certainly does not depend on justice. Much the same can be said for temperance or moderation. In fact, "it is for the lack of [temperance] that the most famous men have made themselves immortal" (*DH*, 8). Temperance is often a hindrance to heroism, and even the most dissolute persons, like Caesar, were not deprived of any of their heroic status for their lack of moderation. Rousseau says much the same about the other virtues too. Prudence, although it prevents great faults, is also "the mortal enemy of high performances and all genuinely heroic acts" (*DH*, 8). It is simply antithetical to grand enterprises. In sum, the virtuous man is the just, prudent, and moderate man; but this in no way implies heroism. On the contrary, "too frequently the Hero is none of those things . . . for glory is the reward of Heroism, but there must be some other reward for virtue" (*DH*, 9).

What is interesting with this assessment of the virtues is that after Rousseau rejects justice, prudence, and moderation as the source of heroism he does not return to the language of courage. Rousseau is wrestling with the concept because, although he wants to talk about courage, he does not want to commit himself to courage as understood in the simple terms of martial courage. Thus, in this little essay, he introduces entirely different language for courage. Whereas prudence is for the statesman, justice is for the citizen, and moderation is for the philosopher, Rousseau assigns "strength of soul" (force de l'âme) to the hero (*DH*, 9). When Rousseau begins to characterize this, he no longer says "strength of soul," but just "strength." This strength (Fr., force) gives cohesion to the virtues by bringing them together to act in concert. As he puts it, "If you do not add strength to animate them, they all languish and Heroism disappears" (*DH*, 9). From this, it seems Rousseau has in mind some kind of increase in amplitude of the other virtues, but this is not necessarily so. Strength here is more qualitative than quantitative, and the quality he has in mind resembles a sort of endurance:

> The Hero does not always perform great actions; but he is always ready to do so if needed and show himself to be great in all the circumstances of his life. That is what distinguishes him from the ordinary man. An invalid can take up a spade and cultivate the soil for a few moments, but he soon becomes exhausted and grows weary. A robust farmer does not endure hard labor without respite, but he could do so without harming himself, and owes this ability to his bodily strength. Strength of soul is the same thing. It consists in always being able to act forcefully. (*DH*, 9–10)

So it is a matter not just of being able to act forcefully but of *always* being able to act with this strength. On this note, one might recall Rousseau's contrast between a modern, scientific army and the Spartan army. The scientific, or democratic, army can fight furiously, but it falters on the long march. It has strength of body but not strength of soul—the strength that would allow it to persevere over the long haul and contribute to the collective felicity over an extended time. It lacks the force that ensures the permanent autonomy of the people: the *force*, soon to be discussed in detail, called "compassion."

Thus whereas in the *First Discourse* bodily strength was almost wholly bound up with courage—a trait that translates into victory on the battlefield—here courage is only partially physical. Rousseau does maintain some of the physicality of courage but adds more qualities: "Everything is great and generous in a strong soul, because it knows how to distinguish the beautiful from the specious, reality from appearance, and to fasten on its object with that firmness that removes illusions and surmounts the greatest obstacles" (*DH*, 10). In other words, paralleling the martial endurance that protects the autonomy of the body politic is a moral endurance that maintains individual autonomy. The heroic characteristic Rousseau calls strength of soul is that which guards "uncertain judgment and an easily seduced heart [that] make men weak and small. To be great, it is necessary only to become master of oneself" (*DH*, 10). The transition from the collective autonomy to individual autonomy, from the body to the soul, is quite clear. In both cases, we need only look to courage and heroism to see Rousseau's fundamental care.

Time, Radical Autonomy, and Friendlessness

The study of courage in Rousseau's thought has thus far revealed a trend. The *First Discourse* concerns the autonomy of a people and how their heroism lends itself to the preservation of their autonomy. In the *Discourse on Heroism*, Rousseau is concerned with the autonomy of a people and how courageous individuals preserve that autonomy. If we extrapolate this trend, Rousseau will next be concerned with the autonomy of an individual and how the courage of that individual protects his own autonomy. In other words, the retreat from the collective world to the individual will be complete. This retreat is precisely how the *Second Discourse* can be understood—as Rousseau's effort to cope with a deep and troubling assault on the autonomy of each and every individual, not by external, martially constituted forces, but by time.

Let me begin by recurring to the second part of the *First Discourse*, where Rousseau turns his attention to the arts and sciences. In particular, he examines the arts and sciences to see what results from the progress of "the vanity and emptiness of those proud titles that dazzle us, and that we so freely give to human learning" (*FD*, 47). He emphasizes that the pursuit of knowledge (arts and sciences) is dangerous because from it arise "many errors, a thousand times more dangerous than the truth is useful" (*DH*, 49). Moreover—and note well the language here—the pursuit of the sciences necessarily causes an "irreparable loss of time" (*FD*, 49) and, for reasons to which I will return presently, Rousseau regards the "misuse of time . . . a great evil" (*FD*, 50).

Thus for Rousseau the result of the spread of the arts and sciences is "the disastrous inequality introduced among men by the distinction of talents and the debasement of virtues" (*FD*, 58). In this distinction we find the crux of his argument. In differentiating talent and virtue, Rousseau reveals his mistrust of reason as the sole basis of human relations. He says that with the rise of the principles of the Enlightenment, "one no longer asks if a man is upright, but rather if he is talented. . . . Rewards are showered on the witty, and virtue is left without honors. There are a thousand prizes for noble discourses, none for noble actions" (*FD*, 58).[22] Wit, we see, is contrasted with virtue, and discourse with action. Wit and discourse, for Rousseau, are closely related to the mind. This is not surprising because they are a product of reason, which, in the Enlightenment tradition, is considered atemporal. Virtue and action, on the other hand, are most closely related to the body—to the temporal. As such, we see things temporal standing in direct contrast to things atemporal. The eternal is directly contrasted with the temporal.

What, then, about the arts and sciences so disgusts Rousseau? Why will a happy people necessarily become unhappy when ignorance is ostracized? The answer to these questions lies in Rousseau's understanding of virtue and corruption. In the *Second Discourse*, Rousseau imagines a hypothetical state of nature where man is truly virtuous, subject only to natural infirmities—infancy and old age—and lives side by side with the other beasts (*SD*, 108). This natural man, Rousseau envisions, would be "an animal less strong than some, less agile than others, but all things considered, the most advantageously organized of all . . . satisfying his hunger under an oak, quenching his thirst at the first stream, finding his bed at the foot of the same tree that furnished his meal; and therewith his needs are satisfied" (*SD*, 105). In short, natural man, full of the strength Rousseau extols, exists in unity with his immediate and physical world. He need not plan for the future, for he cannot even imagine want. "He can have neither foresight nor curiosity," and he is undisturbed by anything; and in what would be the greatest bliss for Rousseau, his soul can "be given over to the sole sentiment of its present existence without any idea of the future" (*DH*, 117). Natural man is aware of neither temporality nor atemporality. He lives outside time—without foresight—and therefore outside the fear of enslavement and death. He is free to live in his space without being ruled by the constant oppression that the awareness of time, and therefore his mortality, imposes.

Thus for Rousseau the purest state of virtue is existence in and with the raw experience of the palpable or corporeal sensations. This existence is a state of unity between man and his physical world. The truly virtuous man is happy because he is aware of neither world nor man; such awareness would require that a rift exist between the two—that temporal man be aware not only of the temporality of his humanity and the atemporality of the cosmos, but also of their direct contrast to each other. However, because natural man's physical passions are compatible with his world, his imagination is not sparked and he can remain ignorant of this fact. In this state, "Everyone peaceably waits for the impulsion of nature, yields to it without choice with more pleasure than frenzy; and the need satisfied, all desire is extinguished" (*SD*, 135). Natural man remains blissfully unaware of his temporality simply because he has no need for reflection. In this unity between man and world, neither the temporality of the body nor the atemporality of the world is suffered. "This period of the development of human facilities," Rousseau claims, "maintaining a golden mean between the indolence of the primitive state and the petulant activity of our vanity, must have been the happiest and most durable epoch" (*SD*, 150–51). Man's happiest existence, he argues, is when he is not ruled by, beholden to, or oppressed by his timely nature. He is happiest when he lives in the present without being aware of the present. And because man's nature is determined by this timeliness, man is most happy when is not oppressed by himself. Man is most happy when he is individually autonomous.

From where, then, does unhappiness come? If the happy man is the autonomous man, then the unhappy man is ruled by forces outside himself. For Rousseau, unhappiness lies in the fact that man cannot live outside time, which means that man cannot live outside the fear of death. Simply, man lives in the world and then passes out of it; yet the world remains. The world is atemporal, and man inevitably comes to know this fact, which is as certain as the passing seasons. As much as it chagrins Rousseau, he nevertheless realizes it, and this is why he must "begin by setting all facts aside" (*SD*, 103). Even in his imagined world of the solitary and noble man, the leaves will change colors, the air will get cooler, and man, despite maintaining the solitude of the self, will be forced to reflect on his situation. Thus we must concede that even in the "facts-set-aside" state of nature man would be reflective and that it is erroneous for Rousseau to "dare affirm that the state of reflection is a state contrary to nature and that the man who meditates is a depraved animal" (*SD*, 110).

Let us pretend for a moment, however, that Rousseau's imaginary world could exist. If we do this, we must agree that man's "desires do not exceed his physical needs, the only goods he knows in the universe are nourishment, a female, and repose; the only evils he fears are pain and hunger. I say pain and not death because an animal will never know what it is to die; and knowledge of death and its terrors is one of the first acquisitions that man has made in moving away from the animal condition" (*SD*, 116). In other words, moving away from the Edenic state is becoming aware of the evils of time and timelessness. It is, so to speak, a fall into time. Reflection, which is a mental comparison of the past to the present so as to predict the future, is the activity that causes man to be unhappy because it forces man both to be aware of time and to participate in it. Reflection begets foresight and agitates the imagination. For Rousseau, this is the genesis of human unhappiness; when man becomes aware of time, he becomes aware of the certainty of his own death.[23]

The awareness and fear of one's certain death is not a new theme. For St. Augustine, much as for Rousseau, the fall into this awareness of time occurred in an Edenic past. The difference however, lies in Augustine's response. Augustine does not bemoan lost ignorance, for it is irretrievable; postlapsarian man must bridge the chasm between the temporal and the atemporal with wisdom. Once man becomes aware of the temporal (of himself), he must seek knowledge of the atemporal (of God) lest he be paralyzed by the fear of death. Wisdom is the knowledge of God, the atemporal other. For Augustine, "'to be happy' means nothing else than 'not to be in want,' that is, 'to be wise.'"[24] Not to be in want means simply not to be afraid—not to be afraid of having temporal things, like bananas or one's life, taken against one's will by a tyrant, for instance. Knowledge, or wisdom, of the atemporal also cannot be taken against one's will, and for Augustine, wisdom is virtue and ensures everlasting life.[25] Thus, despite being aware of both the atemporal and the temporal, man can maintain his autonomy.[26]

Rousseau also accepts that the fall into this awareness of time occurred in the past, but for him it did not happen when man ate the forbidden fruit. Instead, the fall occurred when man started planting his own apple trees. More precisely, it occurred when "men began to look to the future" (*SD*, 154) by planting wheat and manufacturing the tools of harvest. In other words, man was turned from his ignorance of both temporality and atemporality. He came to live completely within the fetters of time and, consequently, in fear. Man is always planning for the future and always planning to defend his wheat from others. "Metallurgy and agriculture," Rousseau contends, "were the two arts whose invention produced this great revolution" (*SD*, 152). This great revolution—from a happy existence in the present (though without awareness of a thing called the present) to a general awareness of time—presents the central paradox of Rousseau's thought. One must be engulfed by the present to be a whole person, but human community is historical, and history includes the past, present, and future. As Mark Temmer argues, "Of the three aspects of time none tempted and repelled Jean-Jacques Rousseau more than the present. In this realm he discovered an ecstasy as real as his agony was deep, a divine plentitude and self-sufficiency opposed by an experience of emptiness which denied him the pleasure of love and friendship."[27] Thus the introduction of a future orientation wrests man from his happy existence in the present by making him aware not only of the future but of the present and past as well. In short, man begins to suffer time. He is distended in time.[28]

It is not difficult to agree with Rousseau on several points. Yes, man perforce finds himself in the temporal world but alienated from the atemporal. And indeed, so long as one remains aware of the chasm between one's self and atemporality, one will necessarily be unhappy. The problem, however, is that Rousseau addresses his unhappiness—his enslavement to mortality—by attempting to unify temporality and atemporality internally. He attempts to transform man's consciousness of time from an objective reality to a subjective and instinctual part of the individual personality. In a sense, Rousseau is trying to derationalize time. He rejects reason as a means for bridging the chasm and instead thinks that man can reconcile himself to the fact of his mortality by looking within, by looking "at the bottom of [his] heart" (*FD*, 54). In other words, he thinks that if one looks outwardly into the world, one will only receive confirmation of one's enslavement. The self, then, "is torn between two opposing attempts at self-unification. This first takes place in the pure present and manifests itself in oscillation between a wish for self-deification and a desire for paradisiac languor, the other in an almost Platonic aspiration for spiritual oneness before, after, and beyond experienced reality, with its pleasures and responsibilities."[29] In Rousseau's words, the "savage lives within himself" and alone. The social man lives in history, among other human beings. He is "always outside of himself, [and thus] knows how to live only in the opinion of others" (*SD*, 179).

But so what, one may ask? How is it a problem if Rousseau believes we should not "seek our happiness in the opinion of another if we can find it within ourselves" (*FD*, 64)? The problem is that this approach is premised on a dubious, if not fallacious, understanding of time. The belief that man reached the apex of happiness when he was completely within himself means that man must withdraw from the temporal world to regain that happiness. This internalization does not release man from his enslavement to the fear of his mortality; the chasm between the finite life of the body and the infinite life outside the body, which foresight forces man to recognize, remains. The only difference is either that one will, for a while at least, forget about the unfortunate situation into which one has been thrown, which will result in a further existential impasse, or that the internalized unity of temporality and atemporality will transform, nay, deform, one's understanding of limitations naturally imposed by human temporality. In other words, when one affirms one's autonomy by stepping out of time, one rejects the boundaries formerly delineated by the distinction between temporal and atemporal. Although the inward-directedness of the temporal may remind one of the temporal unity one's primordial ancestors once felt in the natural world, the inward-directedness of the atemporal may delude one into feeling oneself atemporal. Simply, withdrawing into oneself because one is afraid is not courage.

The fact remains, however, that Rousseau's state of nature exists only when we set all facts aside. Man lives in the world with other men. Rousseau's antidote to the fear all men experience may work in his ersatz state of nature, but it is problematic for people who live in a community with other people. Putting man in the state of nature does not eliminate the need for courage because man still lives in time. Putting man in the state of nature to remove him from time does not put him in a state of radical autonomy. Rejecting all reason and all violence in favor of heartfelt sentiments toward the body and the world will result in either *rêverie*—obsessive thoughts of the temporal—or obsession with inward atemporality. The former produces a friendless and reclusive hermit, the latter a megalomaniac. Either way, Rousseau's solution produces poor neighbors, for nobody wants to live next door to a lunatic or a tyrant. Rousseau eventually recognized that the elimination of fear, which is the elimination of the need for courage, ultimately results in the sort of friendlessness that makes life unlivable. He came to see that without courage there can be no community and that without community there can be no friendship. This is precisely the problem Rousseau attempts to remedy in his *Emile.*

Emile: First Lessons in Courage

Rousseau's *Emile* is concerned with many things. For example, according to Alan Bloom it is Rousseau's attempt to provide "a healing education" so as "to reconcile nature with history, man's selfish nature with the demands of civil society." It is "an experiment in restoring harmony to that world by reordering the emergence of man's acquisitions in such a way as to avoid the imbalances created by them while allowing the full actualization of man's potential" (*E*, 3).[30] Laurence Cooper suggests that while most read *Emile* as a prescription for nonphilosophic education, "Rousseau takes his place alongside Plato and others who, by proffering the philosopher as the highest human type, propound an aristocratic view of the life of the mind and therewith of human possibilities as such."[31] While these interpretations are helpful, I argue that *Emile*, at bottom, is concerned with what Rousseau calls "first lessons in courage" (*E*, 77–78). Here Rousseau goes to great length to illustrate the difference between natural man, civil man, and the citizen. The meaning of Rousseau's portrayal becomes more luminous when put in terms of courage.

Rousseau's vision is as follows: natural man has a good and ample amount of manly courage. He is a good hunter and an efficient warrior—the perfect defender of communal autonomy. Civil man, whom we have seen in detail in the *First Discourse*, is hopelessly trepid. He is the bourgeois man who threatens to debase all that is good about man. He is the man dominated by his appetites, acquisitive impulses, fear of death, and fear of public opinion. Not surprisingly then, Rousseau's plan of education in *Emile* does not aim at turning the child into the courageous, yet solitary, natural man described in the *Discourses*. Nor does it aim to produce civil man, such as the Frenchmen or Genevans of his time, who are seemingly free but everywhere in chains. Rather, Rousseau envisions the creation of a new type of man with a new type of courage. Rousseau calls this new type of man "the citizen." He is a hybrid of the natural and civil man who embodies what is right and proper about each of these types. This hybridization is necessary because, as demonstrated in the first part of this chapter, natural man, despite his abundance of manly courage, cannot live within any articulated human community. He lacks the basic tools for living in society. If, for example, natural man found himself in Paris, because of his manliness and consequent radical autonomy, he would find himself friendless among men, alone in the crowds of society. But civilized man, though he can and does live in community, is enervated and weak and is not living happily, as Rousseau understands happiness: "Natural man is entirely for himself. He is numerical unity, the absolute whole which is relative only to itself or its kind. Civil man is only a fractional unity dependent on the denominator; his value is determined by his relation to the whole, which is the social body" (*E*, 39–40). Civil man—if he can be called a "man" when he is so denuded of his natural vigor and courage—is wholly dependent on others for the meaningfulness of his existence; he is in no way autonomous and thus in no way happy.

Rousseau's "citizen," then, is a synthesis of the manliness of the natural man with both the gentleness of the civil man and the selflessness of the hero. The aim of the educative effort in *Emile* is "to denature man, to take his absolute existence from him in order to give him a relative one and transport the I into the common unity" (*E*, 40). A new type of courage—not martial courage, not political courage, but moral courage—is instilled that can both foster a law-abiding, well-ordered, solidaristic community like Sparta and carve out a space for one's autonomy.[32] This moral courage is not exercised fundamentally for the sake of honor, as martial courage is, or fundamentally for the sake of justice, as political courage is. The mode of articulation is neither violence nor reason, but what Rousseau refers to as pity or compassion. By this, Rousseau means that individuals are joined together via reciprocal sentiment, the recognition of one's self in another. This, according to Rousseau, is true living. "To live is not to breathe; it is to act; it is to make use of our organs, our senses, our faculties, of all the parts of ourselves which give us the sentiment of our existence. The man who has lived the most is not he who has lived the most years but he who has most felt life" (*E*, 42). Living is not merely the preservation and extension of our empirical being through, say, violence. Nor is it merely employing our reason. Instead, it must be understood as "feeling" life, which is to say, experiencing the sentiments that arise from both the good and the bad. To feel life, to live, is therefore not to be sheltered from the harsher realities of living, be they social or spiritual, individual or collective. It is to feel both joy and sadness, both pleasure and anger. In the educative project outlined in *Emile*, the child is not to be sheltered from the harsh realities of living in the early years because one who has felt life "best knows how to bear the goods and the ills of this life" (*E*, 42). This is Rousseau's earliest lesson in moral courage. The pupil is inculcated with the courage that prepares him for all of life, not just war or discussion, and that enables him to seize, to maintain, and to enjoy his autonomy. He is taught bodily courage infused with the sentiment of our existential selves. Rousseau thinks these lessons will enable the "man," when he is grown, to "no longer have need of any guide other than himself" (*E*, 50).

Yet despite his concern for the education of "the soul," Rousseau does not abandon concern for the body. On the contrary, he maintains that "the body must be vigorous in order to obey the soul" (*E*, 54). Like the courageous Spartan, or the hero in the *Discourse on Heroism*, the truly living individual must have a certain amount of physical strength. Indeed, Rousseau doubts that a person lacking bodily strength can have moral strength.

Though Rousseau envisions a community articulated by reciprocal sentiment, he clearly does not have in mind a community of weaklings. The pity that joins individuals is not the enfeebled pity that he finds problematic in Christianity.[33] There is more than a residue of the manliness in the martially articulated communities that he praises in his earlier work. This is especially evident in his attacks on medicine as a morally enervating influence: "I do not know of what illness the doctors cure us; but I do know that they give us quite fatal ones: cowardice, pusillanimity, credulousness, terror of death. If they cure the body, they kill courage. What difference does it make to us that they make cadavers walk? It is men we need, and none is seen leaving their hands" (*E*, 54).[34] In another passage, philosophers and priests are included in this indictment: "Do you want to find men of true courage? Look for them in the places where there are no doctors, where they are ignorant of the consequences of illnesses, where they hardly think death. Naturally man knows how to suffer with constancy and dies in peace. It is doctors with their prescriptions, philosophers with their precepts, priests with their exhortations, who debase his heart and make him unlearn how to die" (*E*, 55). Like the martially courageous individual, the morally courageous individual is unafraid of death. But whereas the martially courageous individual is, in a sense, inoculated against his fear of death by practicing arts that prevent violent death in combat, the morally courageous individual is inoculated against inordinate fear of any kind of death, whether by violence, accident, or sickness. Because his imagination is not agitated by doctors' accounts of illness or priests' threats of eternal perdition and divine retribution, he can face death with tranquility.

For this reason Rousseau advocates the so-called "natural education" of Emile, an education reminiscent of the pastoral scenes of Longus's *Daphnis and Chloe*, and the tutor in *Emile* chooses his pupil first on the basis of his physical hardiness. The invalid is no student for Rousseau and is certainly no promising material from which to develop the autonomous citizen.[35] Rousseau's education is for the hale and hearty, and the only thing medicine is good for is hygiene (*E*, 55). This education should be carried out in the country, far from the philosophers and doctors, because the cities are too crowded. As Rousseau puts it, "Men crammed together like sheep would all perish in a very short time. Man's breath is deadly to his kind. This is no less true in the literal sense than the figurative" (*E*, 59). Further, the cities are full of the sort of people who will insist on telling the pupil enfeebling religious stories. In the country, the pupil will be able "to renew [himself], as it were, and to regain in the midst of the fields the vigor that is lost in the unhealthy air of the overpopulated places" (*E*, 59).

To encourage this vigor, this necessary precondition for moral courage, Rousseau suggests that newborns be washed, and washed often, in water that is a natural temperature. The child should be able to bathe in both very hot water and very cold water. By becoming accustomed to water of various temperatures, he will become accustomed to air at different temperatures. As we recall, good warriors must be able not only to fight fiercely in battle but also to march. If they are to win not just battles but wars, they need the sort of vigor that will allow them to endure difficulties more trying than the rare collision with the enemy in pitched battle. Precisely the same applies to moral warriors battling against moral enslavement. For Rousseau, moral courage requires a hardiness of mind as much as body. The bizarre regimen Rousseau prescribes for the infant is thus created so "that our children can be led back to their primitive vigor" (*E*, 59), a vigor that sustains both strength of body and strength of soul.

The courage fostered by this kind of education is not merely for the sake of martial victory or discursive engagements—it is for the sake of autonomy. As Rousseau puts it, the goal is to "prepare from afar the reign of [the pupil's] freedom and the use of his forces by leaving natural habit to his body, by putting him in the condition always to be master of himself and in all things to do his will, as soon as he has one" (*E*, 63). The child is born fearful and timid. He is weak and ignorant and "fears everything he does not know" (*E*, 63). Thus Rousseau suggests that we determine what the child will be exposed to by deciding whether the exposure will "make him timid or courageous" (*E*, 63). The child should be "habituated to seeing new objects, ugly, disgusting, peculiar animals . . . until he is accustomed to them, and, by dint of seeing them handled by others, he finally handles them himself. If during his childhood he has without fright seen toads, snakes, crayfish, he will, when grown, without disgust see any animal whatsoever. There are no longer frightful objects for whoever sees such things every day" (*E*, 63). Similarly, Emile must be accustomed to and unafraid of masks, whether these are cute or ugly, and of gunfire.

Rousseau also links hardiness to education in the development of speech. When a child is not always being coddled by his mother or nurse, he is "forced to learn to say very clearly and loudly what he needs to make [his mother] understand" (*E*, 71). Here again, a rural setting is helpful: when children are out in the fields, they have to learn to make themselves heard from a distance. Moreover, they are more concerned with being heard than with the ornamental niceties of unaccented speech. These niceties of speech, Rousseau claims, can later be corrected, but the outcome of stifled and oppressed speech cannot. As he puts it, "Those [problems] that one causes children to contract by making their speech dull, obscure, and timid, by incessantly criticizing their tone, by picking all their words to pieces, are never corrected" (*E*, 72). At first glance, Rousseau's emphasis on loud and forceful speaking seems rather absurd, but a later passage shows just why it is necessary: "A man who learns to speak only in his bedroom will fail to make himself understood at the head of a battalion and will hardly impress the people in a riot" (72–73). Education in speech can be regarded as one of the most rudimentary foundations of moral courage: one can never be autonomous if one can never be heard. The vigor and courage to be heard by others is the most basic capacity one must possess to rule oneself. The capacity to shout "No!" at moral enslavement is as important as having the martial skill to avoid physical enslavement.[36]

In the second book of *Emile* Rousseau invokes the language of "first lessons in courage" (77–78). The lessons are directed at the child who is just out of infancy and learning to walk and talk—the child at the age when he is prone to falling and bumping and bruising himself. They consist mostly of little experiences of pain. It is important that the child be accustomed to these minor pains because, as Rousseau puts it, in "bearing slight pains without terror, one gradually learns to bear great pains." A bit later he reiterates, "Without courage and without experience, [one] believes he is dead at the first prick, and faints on seeing the first drop of his blood" (*E*, 78).[37]

Rousseau's point here is not entirely clear. For instance, what exactly are the great pains for which the child is being prepared? Why is it important that the child become accustomed to the sight of his own blood? At first glance, it would appear that such lessons are most conducive to the training of a warrior. In fact, one is tempted to point to the Spartan *agoge* for a similar sort of training. For Rousseau, however, the child should be permitted to run and to fall a hundred times a day, not because this will train the child for success in a Spartan phalanx, but because it will develop his autonomy. As Rousseau puts it, "The well-being of freedom makes up for many wounds. My pupil will often have bruises. But in compensation, he will always be gay. If your pupils have fewer bruises, they are always hindered, always enchained, always sad" (*E*, 78). The child that is allowed to fall—the child learning his first lesson in courage—is also training in happiness. To be autonomous, after all, is to be happy.

With this first lesson in courage Rousseau's more differentiated understanding of courage begins to emerge. In language echoing that of the *Discourse on Heroism*, Rousseau claims that the lesson regarding falling and enduring minor pains will contribute to the child's "strength." Although in *Emile* he does not specifically use the language of "strength of soul," the idea remains the same.[38] By becoming accustomed to falling, which is to say, not being propped up by another human being, children learn to be self-supporting. As Rousseau puts it, they will be "able to do more themselves, they need to have recourse to others less frequently. With their strength develops the knowledge which puts them in a condition to direct it. It is at this second stage that, strictly speaking, the life of the individual begins. It is then that he gains consciousness of himself. Memory extends the sentiment of identity to all the moments of his existence; he becomes capable of happiness or unhappiness. It is therefore, to begin to consider him here as a moral being" (*E*, 78). Clearly, first lessons in courage will make the child neither happy nor unhappy, but from them he will learn to rely on himself—to be a morally free being. For Rousseau, then, the first real lesson in courage is a lesson in moral courage, which prepares the way for the individual to become autonomous and happy.[39]

We have already established that for Rousseau one must be autonomous to be happy. Moreover, Rousseau consistently associates autonomy with courage, specifically moral courage. This moral courage is not merely corporeal; it also pertains to the soul. In *Emile*, Rousseau makes the connections between courage, happiness, and autonomy explicit. Happiness, according to Rousseau, is not some absolute measure. One cannot define precisely what it means to be happy because both our desires and the condition of our bodies are continually in flux. As such, our happiness cannot be absolute. Instead, happiness pertains only to the experience of pain and pleasure. To the extent that we suffer pain, we are unhappy. To the extent that we feel pleasure, we are happy. Thus, when we desire something but are deprived of it, we experience pain and are unhappy. "Every feeling of pain is inseparable from the desire to be delivered from it; every idea of pleasure is inseparable from the desire to enjoy it; every desire supposes privation, and all sensed privations are painful" (*E*, 80). Consequently, if we desire something and we are not deprived of it, we are happy. Of course, Rousseau, whose first love is autonomy, emphasizes that one who is absolutely happy can satisfy all his desires *by his own faculties:* "A being endowed with senses whose faculties equaled his desires would be an absolutely happy being" (*E*, 80).

If being happy consists of equilibrium between one's faculties and desires, then one may find happiness simply by increasing one's faculties, or power, to satisfy one's desires, or by reducing one's desires to the degree of one's power to satisfy them. These formulas may be true, but they are not necessarily what Rousseau prescribes. Instead, he claims that happiness is found "in diminishing the excess of the desires over the faculties and putting power and will in perfect equality. It is only then that, with all the powers in action, the soul will nevertheless remain peaceful and that man will be well ordered" (*E*, 80). In language reminiscent of *The Discourse on Equality*, Rousseau calls this equilibrium the "original state" or "natural condition." He characterizes the original state as one where the imagination does not disrupt the balance between power and will. Unhappiness in the *Second Discourse* also pertained to the imagination. Rousseau argued there that when man becomes cognizant of time, and therefore his own mortality, his imagination begins to conjure images of his own death. Since one's desire to live forever is beyond one's power, and since having desires beyond one's power makes one unhappy, the imagination is the prime source of unhappiness, especially when one's imagination ventures into metaphysics, or, as Rousseau calls it in *Emile*, "the imaginary world" (*E*, 81).

This designation is crucial and demands elaboration. Rousseau's claim is that we need moral courage to be autonomous and happy. But to be happy we cannot be dragged into "the imaginary world." But what exactly is this imaginary world? Rousseau states that "the real world has limits; the imaginary world is infinite" (*E*, 81). Matthew Maguire goes so far as to suggest that, for Rousseau, "the imagination no longer finds a limit in the infinite or in the alterity of God; it is itself infinite."[40] In other words, the real world is the immanent world, the world where beings live, eat, and breathe, where things come into being and pass away, where things have finite life expectancies, and where things are limited, whether natural resources or the time we have to live. The real world is, in short, the human world—the world of human dwelling.

The imaginary world is therefore the world where these restrictions do not pertain. It is the world not only of the infinite but of our imaginary needs. As Maguire puts it, "The imagination is . . . the infinite space in which the finite self can identify and extend its desires."[41] It is the world in which we dwell when our imagination creates needs unnatural to our existence in the real world. It is the world we create imaginatively when we conjure desires that outstrip our strength. It is the world of unhappiness. As Rousseau describes: "Unable to enlarge the one, let us restrict the other, for it is from the difference between the two alone that are born all the pains which make us truly unhappy. Take away strength, health, and good witness of oneself, all the goods of this life are in opinion; take away the pains of the body and the remorse of conscience, all our ills are imaginary" (*E*, 81). Thus the real world must be opposed to the imaginary world because the latter makes us weak. Strength, health, and courage are nearly synonymous with autonomy. Weakness and strength are relative not only to the creature being discussed but also more specifically to a state of mind in that creature. The strong, healthy, autonomous, happy creature is one whose needs are in equilibrium with its capacities. To be strong, healthy and happy, one needs only the courage to avoid any unnecessary sojourn into the imaginary world. To be morally courageous, then, is to have the strength to resist, not only physical enslavement (though this is needed too), but enslavement of the soul.

This brings us back to our discussion of the hero. For Rousseau, "He whose strength surpasses his needs, be he an insect or a worm, is a strong being. He whose needs surpass his strength, be he an elephant or a lion, be he a conqueror or a hero, be he a god, is a weak being" (*E*, 81). Heroism, then, is not merely the Homeric warrior's intrepid advance into battle. Instead, it is open to anyone morally courageous enough to keep himself from being dragged into the imaginary world. The hero is, in the first place, someone who does not allow his pride to delude him into thinking that he exists above and outside of the real world, someone whose imagination does not displace him from that world. Happiness requires the courage to accept one's finite nature and to live according to it. Insofar as we can live this way, we will not be dependent on external forces, whether real or imaginary, for our happiness. If we can be heroic in this manner—if we can be morally courageous—we shall be happy because "we shall always be sufficient unto ourselves" (*E*, 81).

Foresight, the Promethean Myth

From what has been said, it would seem that Rousseau is encouraging his reader to oppose reason to the irrational world of religious dogma and metaphysical fantasies. This, however, is not necessarily so. Instead, his claim is that disembodied reason can unsettle the equilibrium between desire and capacity. Reason is the faculty that agitates us, and "it is by dint of agitating ourselves to increase our happiness that we convert it into unhappiness" (*E*, 81). Reason, for Rousseau, is bound up with the imagination and prompts us to look to the future, alerts us to what we do not have in the present, and suggests what we might have in the future. Thus understood, it is foresight (prévoyance), and Rousseau is forthrightly negative in his assessment of this Promethean capacity: "Foresight! Foresight, which takes us ceaselessly beyond ourselves and often places us where we shall arrive. This is the true source of our miseries" (*E*, 82, but see also 34, 77, 78, 108, 226). Foresight drags us beyond our natural strengths, out of the equilibrium necessary for our happiness.

Rousseau implies that fear is somehow unnatural and can arise only when reason is present. For example, he claims that a child will be afraid of thunder and lightning only after he has been told that sometimes they can kill. A child's natural inclination will be curiosity, but when the demands of curiosity are met with suggestions that incite imaginings of future harm, the child will be afraid. Hence, Rousseau says regarding children, "When reason begins to frighten them, make habit reassure them" (*E*, 64). The habits that inoculate the child against these "reasonable" fears are predicated not on reason but on something prior to reason. However, Rousseau is not suggesting that reason stand in opposition to imaginative fears. Reason is not the cure for or inoculation against fantastical desires and the imaginary world—it is the cause.

So if reason will not deliver us from enslavement, what will? Once again, Rousseau invokes the language first used in the *Discourse on Heroism.* What must be opposed to these fantasies is natural strength: "O man, draw your existence up within yourself, and you will no longer be miserable. Remain in the place which nature assigns to you in the chain of being. . . . Your freedom [ta liberté] and your power [ton pouvoir] extend only as far as your natural strength [tes forces naturelles], and not beyond. All the rest is only slavery, illusion, and deception" (*E*, 83). The character of this natural strength, however, remains somewhat undisclosed. It is not reason, yet it is not the unabated barbarism of the warrior. Rousseau is not championing martial courage. What he has in mind is the courage that liberates the individual from dependence on forces both internal and external while still enabling him to remain part of his community. It is an entirely new sort of heroism.

This new heroism—this moral courage—guards against both the infectious social malady of reason and foresight and the very real problem of social relations predicated on unmitigated and unabashed violence. It is a "real" faculty, a natural faculty, rather than one that comes to us through the authority of society. If we avoid dependence on this artificial faculty, Rousseau claims, there will be but one result: "You can do what you like: never will your real authority go farther than your real faculties" (*E*, 84). The problem, of course, it that "society has made man weaker not only in taking from him the right he had over his own strength but, above all, in making his strength insufficient for him" (*E*, 84). By increasing his desires, society makes man insufficient unto himself. Society creates in adults the sort of "whims" (fantaisies) more proper in a child. It enkindles "desires which are not true needs and which can only be satisfied with another's help" (*E*, 84).

It is for these reasons, then, that Rousseau prescribes these first lessons in courage. Moral courage prevents us from being carried away by the fantasies arising from foresight run amok. It prevents us from being seized by the imaginary fears that our capricious faculty of reason conjures up and prepares us to cope with risk in the real world. To foster this courage, Rousseau suggests that children must not be sheltered from risk. For example, we should not keep a child from learning to swim simply because it is risky. Instead the child should be taught to swim because learning to cope with the risk of drowning will both enable him to experience the joys of swimming and prevent him from taking serious risks in water when he is older. When he is grown and in the company of friends, he will be less inclined either to avoid water altogether or to act rashly in the water because of his vanity. Emile, Rousseau thinks, "would not be rash even if the whole universe were watching" (*E*, 132). Accustomed to risk, he would not be disturbed by it. Nor would he be swayed by the opinion of others to demonstrate that he was not afraid of water. By extension, this kind of education would produce an autonomous man who felt no need to throw himself recklessly into battle, as Aristodemus did after Thermopylae, to garner the praises and recognition of his comrades.

In a similar vein, Rousseau suggests that many night games should be played with the student because in the dark this new sort of courage is most needed. Fear of the dark is a natural failing of both man and animals, and, as Rousseau puts it, "reason, knowledge, wit, and courage deliver few men from the exaction of the tribute. I have seen reasoners, strong-minded men, philosophers, soldiers intrepid by daylight tremble like women at the sound of a leaf at night" (*E*, 134). Notwithstanding the gendered language Rousseau employs, his point is clear.[42] Moral courage is most necessary in the dark because there our foresight suffers its greatest shortcomings. In the dark we become ignorant of the things that surround us. Rousseau's mistrust of reason and foresight, let alone community articulated by foresight, runs deep. In the daylight, when foresight incites the imagination, our reliance on it is not as incapacitating as at night. In the dark, however, when foresight cannot operate, we must turn elsewhere to maintain ourselves and to prevent the imagination from carrying us away. When courage based on foresight fails, that is, when political courage fails, we are, for all intents and purposes, blinded. The faculties we have come to rely on for finding our way and connecting to our fellows are rendered useless.

To illuminate this point, Rousseau recounts a story from his own youth. As a child, he says, he was terribly afraid of the dark. Once he was challenged by his cousin to go into the dark night, through a cemetery, and into the church to retrieve the Bible. Because the challenge involved his honor he found himself unable to decline it (*E*, 136). As the story goes, the cemetery and the darkness of the night did not frighten him, but entering the church did. On opening the door of the temple, "in perceiving the profound darkness which reigned in this vast place, I was seized by a terror which made my hair stand on end. I moved back; I went out; I took flight, trembling all over" (*E*, 136). According to Rousseau, a special type of courage is needed to overcome the darkness of the church. What makes the church spooky is its assault on our autonomy. The darkness of the church is like a certain type of enslavement.[43]

The rest of the anecdote brings out exactly this point. After darting out of the dark church, the boy is ashamed at his cowardice and determines to return. Once he is back in the church, the fright comes back so powerfully that he loses his head (*E*, 136). He stumbles around among the pews, confused and disoriented; though he is familiar with the church's layout in the daylight, at night he can no longer find either pulpit or door. When at last he finds the door he bolts from the church, resolving "never to go in there alone again except by daylight" (*E*, 136). In other words, he resolves never to return to the church without being able to see the things before him—without his foresight. In that moment of fear he forgets his concern over his honor.

But the story does not end there. Little Rousseau returns to the house and hears his patron laughing, presumably at his cowardice. Even worse, he hears the lady of the house giving orders to the serving girl to prepare a lantern for his rescue. Not only is he about to lose the honor accrued from even undertaking such an expedition, he is going to receive help from outside parties, and feminine help at that. Upon realizing this, Rousseau is transformed: "Instantly all my frights ceased, leaving me only the fright of being encountered in my flight. I ran—I flew—to the temple without losing my way; without groping around, I got to the pulpit, mounted it, took the

Bible, jumped down, in three bounds was out of the temple, whose door I even forgot to close. I entered the room, out of breath, threw the Bible on the table, flustered but *palpitating with joy at having been ahead of the help intended for me*" (*E*, 136, emphasis added). Three conclusions come immediately to mind from this anecdote. First, the church is portrayed as a threat to autonomy. On this point Rousseau is a right and proper participant in the Enlightenment. But second, in pointing to the shortcomings of foresight for maintaining autonomy, Rousseau reveals his apostasy from Enlightenment values. Foresight is insufficient in the daytime and utterly useless in the darkness. Autonomy cannot be maintained by reason alone. What we need resides beneath the liminality of reason. Third, and finally, moral courage is what enables one to forgo others' help. It ensures one's autonomy from the church, which was the creation of human reason. In short, for times when foresight invariably fails, a child should be inoculated against creating or imagining things that threaten his autonomy, like religions and gods.

Reading and the New Mode of Articulation

Emile is educated so that his well-being will be "independent of either the will or the judgments of others" (*E*, 103). The effort is to inure him against bugaboos and fantasies resulting from the unbridled exercise of reason. However, Rousseau is not so foolish as to think that simply by placing Emile in the countryside and concentrating on educating him physically he will protect Emile from the assaults reason can wage against his autonomy. Emile is human, after all, and to be human is to have this faculty of reason. It simply cannot be ignored. The task of *Emile*, then, is not to prevent or extinguish reason but to put it in its proper place, which is in line with the other human capacities. For this reason Rousseau advises against exercising a child's reason at too early an age. Most tutors, he thinks, embark far too early on the development of their pupils' reason by forcing children to read. As he puts it, "Reading is the plague of childhood and almost the only occupation we know how to give. At twelve Emile will hardly know what a book is" (*E*, 116).

Janie Vanpée argues that Rousseau's proscription against books relates to his opposition to Diderot's *Encyclopédie* and the *philosophes'* "unquestioned assumption of reading as a basic means to acquire and transmit knowledge."[44] Reading, she argues, "is first and foremost an activity that informs and transforms the acquisition of knowledge. It is a practice that affects the practitioner. Far from giving direct access to knowledge, reading can just as easily block its dissemination. For from guaranteeing instant knowledge and wisdom, reading can corrupt, mislead, or turn the reader into a foolish pedant."[45] Hence children should not be *forced* to read. Instead, Rousseau advises that if one makes it to the child's advantage to read he will learn to do it on his own, when he needs it. The child must be robust and healthy first: then reading—which is reason manifest—will serve the man, not vice versa. The child, when grown, will have the capacity, the bodily vigor, and the courage to restrain his reason and stand firm in his autonomy, so that he will not be forced to employ his reason instrumentally for the sake of another rather than for the sake of himself. He will have the qualities that are "united in almost all great men: strength of body and strength of soul; a wise man's reason and an athlete's vigor" (*E*, 118).

So Rousseau wants to ensure that when Emile does exercise his reason, that reason will be embodied so that it is safeguarded by bodily vigor. And the order of the education is clear: first the body, then reason. As Rousseau puts it, "This was the education of the Spartans: instead of being glued to books, they began by being taught how to steal their dinner" (*E*, 119). Stealing is, of course, neither merely a bodily exercise nor merely an exercise of reason. It combines corporal dexterity and mental cunning. Even better, it was carried out for the sake of autonomy. It taught the Spartan youth how reason ought to serve the body, and in so doing it freed them from their dependence on others for their dinner.

In general terms, Rousseau is against using books in the early education of his pupil because they create a barrier between the child and his embodied experience of the world.[46] Books, by presenting stories of heroes, enkindle the imagination. They incite the child to imagine himself to be other than himself—a recipe certain to bring about unhappiness. Rousseau, however, makes exceptions for the stories of two heroes: Alexander the Great and Robinson Crusoe. With regard to Alexander, Rousseau relates a story of a governor who loved to use a story of Alexander to educate his pupil. As Rousseau puts it, "He admired Alexander's much-vaunted courage. But do you know in what he found this courage to consist? Solely in having swallowed at a single gulp a bad-tasting potion, without hesitation, without the least sign of repugnance" (*E*, 111). Rousseau says that although he initially did not regard this act as courageous in and of itself (but instead as foolhardy), he came to see its importance for the education of youth: not so much because Alexander had firmness to drink the potion in a gulp as because "Alexander believed in virtue; it is that he staked his head, his own life on that belief; it is that his great soul was made for believing in it. Oh what a far profession of faith was the swallowing of that medicine!" (*E*, 111, but cf. 241). Alexander's imagination did not paralyze him in the present by conjuring up fantasies of the future.

Rousseau, despite his general opposition to book learning, does recommend one book, and, not surprisingly, it is not the Bible. Instead, it is Defoe's *Robinson Crusoe.*[47] There Rousseau finds described "a situation where all man's natural needs are shown in a way a child's mind can sense, and where the means of providing for these needs emerge in order with equal ease," and he argues that "it is by the lively and naïve depiction of this state that the first exercise must be given to his imagination" (*E*, 184). *Robinson Crusoe,* like most books, stimulates the imagination, but unlike most other books this one also restrains it by keeping his imagination focused on the real world. The child, first and foremost, will not wish himself to *be* Robinson Crusoe but rather will imagine what he would *do* in Crusoe's place. The book trains the imagination on things pertaining to the maintenance of his autonomous self in a world where all social relations are severed or, as Rousseau more likely has in mind, where social relations become inimical to autonomy.

It is then perhaps a bit of an overstatement to claim, as Allan Bloom does, that the purpose of *Robinson Crusoe* is "to provide [Emile] with a vision of the whole and a standard for the judgment of both things and men" (*E*, 7). Rousseau's general goal is to rein in Emile's faculty of reason. At the age when Emile is beginning to inquire into more profound questions of human existence, he is given *Robinson Crusoe* to prevent his imagination from launching him from the mundane to the imaginary world. This particular book will train him to concentrate on what he would do for himself in Crusoe's concrete time and place and then only to "worry about the measures to take if this or that were lacking to him" (*E*, 184). In other words, Emile's imagination turns to practical preparations for autonomy: "He will want to know all that is useful, and he will want to know only that" (*E*, 184). He will not be moved to visions of the Whole and a universal standard of judgment that detract from his autonomy.

Denise Schaeffer is right to argue "that Defoe's novel is central to the formation of Emile as a self-conscious individual and thus that Crusoe's function in Emile's education is not the forestalling of sociality but rather the gradual introduction of sociality."[48] Unlike other scholars, Schaeffer does not think that Rousseau makes a special exception of this one novel because it trains Emile in how to live like the natural man of the *Second Discourse.* Before Crusoe alighted on his island he was already a self-conscious, civilized man. Landing on the island did not divest him of his relationship with Christianity, his dependence on the arts and sciences, or his awareness of time. What it did do, however, was deprive him of his false sense of happiness derived from his interdependence with other civilized human beings. As Rousseau puts it: "Robinson Crusoe on his island, alone, deprived of the assistance of his kind and the instruments of all the arts, providing nevertheless for his subsistence, for his preservation, and even procuring for himself a kind of well-being—this is an object interesting for every age and one which can be made agreeable to children in countless ways" (*E*, 184). The novel offers Emile an example of how civilized man must live when the "rigmarole" of society collapses. Where Schaeffer's argument falls short is in the far too general claim that *Robinson Crusoe* gradually introduces Emile to sociality. Rather, for Rousseau, the novel prepares Emile for a self-conscious existence after the social articulation predicated on foresight and reason breaks down. It introduces Emile not to sociality in general but specifically to sociality based on compassion. The isolated island state depicted in the book removes the hero from the worlds of justice, honor, transcendence, and money and prepares him for a completely new mode of articulation. In Rousseau's words: "This state, I agree, is not that of social man; very likely it is not going to be that of Emile. But it is on this very state that he ought to appraise all the others. The surest means of raising oneself above prejudices and ordering one's judgments about the true relations of things is to put oneself in the place of an isolated man and to judge everything as this man himself ought to judge of it with respect to his own utility" (*E*, 184–85). In other words, the isolated island world of Crusoe prepares Emile for social relations that are not inimical to his autonomy: relations based not on mutual dependence but on the practice of putting oneself in the place of others. The novel is introduced exactly when Emile's faculty of reason begins to assert itself in questioning how he will live with other human beings. It comes precisely when the pupil's reason and imagination can draw him into dark edifices. Rousseau's imperative to all tutors at this point is quite clear: "When the chain of knowledge forces you to show him the mutual dependence of men, instead of showing it to him from the moral side, turn all his attention at first toward industry and mechanical arts which make men useful to one another" (*E*, 185–86). And the novel does precisely this. It directs Emile's attention to the fundamental question Rousseau imposes on him: "What is this good for?" (*E*, 179). If the lesson is taught well, the student's reason will not lead him astray. The exercise of reason will be restricted to—or one might even say focused on—the pursuit of human relations that mutually encourage autonomy. The faculty of reason, or foresight, is restricted to what Rousseau calls "man's most universal instrument, which is good sense" (*E*, 178). This good sense is an amalgamation of action and thinking, of body and mind. As he puts it, "We have made an active and thinking being. It remains for us, in order to complete the man, only to make a loving and feeling being—that is to say, to perfect reason by sentiment" (*E*, 203).

The Art of Compassion

This is an interesting departure from the traditional understanding of reason. Normally, reason stands in contrast to sentiment. Bound up with sentiment are the passions, which are often considered catalysts for conflict and violence. But for Rousseau, reason does not necessarily stand in contradistinction to the passions; it is not so simple as to say that one is either passionate or reasonable. Whereas Plato envisions a political courage that is bound up with the public exercise of reason, Rousseau is skeptical regarding the power of human reason: "Reason alone is not active. It sometimes restrains, it arouses rarely, and it has never done anything great. Always to reason is the mania of small minds. Strong souls have quite another language" (*E*, 321). Rather than trumping the passions, reason is repaired by the language of the passions. In essence, Rousseau is envisioning a mode of articulation based not on reason but on, as he variously calls it, sentiment, feeling, sense, or instinct. In other words, the hero—the man with strength of soul (force de l'âme)—speaks another, nonreasonable language, to invoke a rather oxymoronic idiom.

In this oxymoronic idiom we find the binding structure of this mode of articulation. Rousseau endeavors to inculcate Emile with moral courage, and this courage is a nonreasonable language that fosters autonomy. Emile's education aims to enable him to live autonomously while engaging in "the moral relations of man to man" (*E*, 207).[49] The goal of these first lessons in courage is to prepare the child for an autonomous adulthood, but not the life of natural, solitary man—for this is a state he will never experience, nor should he desire to. Rousseau is endeavoring to create the autonomous man who can both live in and contribute to decent society.

This decent society, however, remains somewhat mysterious because, for Rousseau, "there is no decency without utility" (*E*, 197). The utility of which Rousseau speaks is not the typical understanding of utility. The utilitarian thinking of, say, Raskolnikov in Dostoevsky's *Crime and Punishment* stands in direct contrast to what Rousseau has in mind. Raskolnikov, it will be recalled, murdered an old moneylending woman because with her money he could help hundreds of destitute people. Raskolnikov makes the "reasonable" decision that killing one person for the happiness of hundreds is justified in terms of utility. For Rousseau, this sort of reasoning is to be avoided. Reason, divested of sentiment, permits the violation of his first rule of morality: "The only lesson of morality appropriate to childhood, and the most important for any age, is never to harm anyone" (*E*, 104). But because utility can easily become nothing more than the instrumental application of reason, it needs something else to keep it moral. Therefore, in Rousseau's understanding, reason is remedied by sentiment—utility is completed by compassion. Compassion is the weapon of the morally courageous citizen. The good man is the courageous man, the autonomous man, the man with the vigorous character who does no harm. And he does no harm precisely because the first lessons in courage are inextricably bound up with what Martha Nussbaum calls the basic social emotion—compassion.[50] In short, the nonreasonable "language" of sentiment perfects reason.

So whereas the Spartan boy learns the art of fighting and Socrates teaches dialectics, Emile is armed with compassion. One might be tempted to say that Emile "relearns" compassion, because we know that for Rousseau pity is a natural virtue. In the *Second Discourse* we are told that man has "an innate repugnance to see his fellow man suffer. I do not believe I have any contradiction to fear in granting man the sole natural virtue that the most excessive detractor of human virtue was forced to recognize. I speak of pity [la pitié], a disposition that is appropriate to being as weak and subject to as many ills as we are; a virtue all the more universal and useful to man because it precedes in him the use of all reflection; and so natural that even beasts sometimes give perceptible signs of it" (*SD*, 130). Pity, then, is "the pure movement of nature prior to all reflection [refléxion]" (131). In this sense, reflection must be understood as part and parcel of reason. When we reflect we turn our minds back in time. We are, quite literally, turning our attention away from the present and into the past. Pity, however, requires no such turning. It allows one to connect and identify with others without losing one's self. For Rousseau, "it is evident that this identification must have been infinitely closer in the state of nature than in the state of reasoning. Reason engenders vanity and reflection fortifies it; reason turns man back upon himself, it separates him from all that bothers and afflicts him" (132). Thus whereas pity establishes heartfelt bonds between man and man, reason, ironically, dissolves those bonds.

The problem is that the natural virtue called pity atrophies as man moves into society. For Rousseau, as Clifford Orwin puts it, "As reason and amour propre wax, compassion must inevitably wane," so "today's compassion [is] a faded relic of its resplendent self."[51] Emile must consequently relearn this natural virtue. Indeed, pity in its pure form is perhaps beyond the reach of both Emile and the tutor. It is thus helpful to distinguish between the natural virtue called pity and the learned (or relearned) virtue of compassion. In the state of nature both humans and animals experience pity. In society, however, pity is gone, and humans must learn the moral equivalent—compassion. Whether we call this moral equivalent sympathy or, as Rousseau often does, commiseration, it refers to the art of suffering what another being suffers.

Rousseau tells us, "A young man raised in a happy simplicity is drawn by the first movements of nature toward the tender and affectionate passions. His compassionate heart is moved by the sufferings of his fellows" (*E*, 220). The first lessons in courage are meant to prepare Emile for an autonomous adulthood that is nevertheless enriched by meaningful human relationships. Strenuous training that permits the child to suffer the bumps and bruises of his falls gives a certain form to the heart, the locus of sentiment. The child is taught to feel before he is taught to think, and "thus is born pity, the first relative sentiment which touches the human heart according to the order of nature. To become sensitive and pitying, the child must know that there are beings like him who suffer what he has suffered, who feel the pains he has felt, and that there are others whom he ought to conceive of as able to feel them too" (*E*, 222). In other words, the education prescribed by Rousseau aims at stimulating the imagination of the pupil such that he can suffer what others suffer. In so doing, Rousseau is quite certain that "the first sentiment of which a carefully raised young man is capable is not love; it is friendship. The first act of his nascent imagination is to teach him that he has fellows" (*E*, 220).

In saying this, however, we face something of a contradiction. It is imagination—which we have referred to as reason running dangerously amok—that Rousseau is trying to quell with his educative project. But as several scholars point out, compassion is bound up with the imagination.[52] As Rousseau puts it, "We let ourselves be moved by pity . . . by transporting ourselves outside of ourselves and identifying with the suffering animal, by leaving, as it were, our own being to take on its being. We suffer only so much as we judge that it suffers. It is not in ourselves, it is in him that we suffer. Thus, no one becomes sensitive until his imagination is animated and begins to transport him out of himself" (*E*, 223). But how are we to understand this praise of imagination if, as we have seen, the imagination also drags us into inordinate and fantastical fears? The imagination, after all, is what causes the boy's fear in the church; it is what conjures up images of death and the afterlife that attack our autonomy and therefore our happiness. The difference is that whereas the unhealthy type of imagination distends our existential selves in time, imagination strengthened with compassion promotes a spatial extension. This distinction warrants further consideration.[53]

In the *Second Discourse*, Rousseau claims that the first corruption of man stems from the emergence of metallurgy and agriculture. Both are corrupting in their temporal aspect. When Rousseau invokes metallurgy, he has in mind two things: the manufacture of swords and of plowshares. The manufacture of weapons is for the sake of future battles, real or imagined. To craft swords is to imagine oneself outside one's present. It is to transport oneself to the future, for the sake of either protection or victory, honor, and immortality. Similarly, crafting plowshares for the sake of agriculture is a plan for the future. Whereas hunting and gathering serve the immediate needs of the body, plowing and planting serve the body in the future. Agriculture (like warfare) is a temporally imaginative project that creates habits of mind inimical to the happy life. With regard to time in *Emile*, Rousseau says that his pupil "does not treat even clock making very seriously. The happy child enjoys time without being its slave. He profits from it and does not know its value. The calm of the passions, which makes the passage of time always uniform, takes the place for him of an instrument for measuring it at need" (*E*, 187). The well-educated man, then, is not beholden to the temporal aspect of his imaginative projects. His imagination, though not inert, remains incorporated, both trained and restrained by the physicality and spatiality of the body. As Rousseau puts it, "Time loses its measure for us when our passions want to adjust its course according to their taste. The wise man's watch is evenness of temper and peace of soul. He is always on time for himself, and he always knows what that time is" (*E*, 187).

To be trained and restrained by one's own physicality also means to be tempered by the first possibility of the body—suffering. To be compassionate is to feel, or imagine, oneself in the physical place of another person. It is a spatially imaginative project. To suffer with another physical body is to have compassion or, quite literally, "to suffer with" the weakness of another body. This, according to Rousseau, is precisely what is required for decent moral relations between human beings. As Rousseau puts it: "It is man's weakness which makes him sociable; it is our common miseries which turn our hearts to humanity; we would owe humanity nothing if we were not men. Every attachment is a sign of insufficiency. If each of us had no need of others, he would hardly think of uniting himself with them. Thus from our very infirmity is born our frail happiness" (*E*, 221).[54] Decent moral relations require an expansion of our spatial horizons, not our temporal horizons; and the expansion of spatial horizons directly lends itself to human happiness. Hitherto Rousseau has led us to believe that to be happy one needs to be autonomous. Yet in *Emile* it also becomes evident that one cannot be happy in complete isolation. Happiness also requires decent moral relations, which is another way of saying that human beings need to discover the deeply rewarding relationships that emerge under the "storm of steel."

So, for Rousseau, to be autonomous is to be happy. But he does not advocate a solitary existence. On the contrary, he too is convinced that it is not good for man to be alone.[55] As he puts it, if given a choice, "I would want a society around me, not a court; friends, and not protégés. I would not be the patron of my guests; I would be their host. The independence and equality would permit my relationships to have all the candor of benevolence; and where neither duty nor interest entered in any way, pleasure and friendship alone would make the law" (*E*, 348–49). The aim is community based on a reciprocal respect for the autonomy of others. And since to be autonomous is to be happy, it follows that to be heteronomous is to be unhappy. Moreover, to experience the suffering of another is to experience oneself in his heteronomous place. The man capable of decent moral relations will sympathize with the autonomous aim of others. As Rousseau puts it, a man capable of decent moral relations "suffers when he sees suffering. It is a natural sentiment" (*E*, 251). And who is the man capable of decent moral relations? Who is capable of this compassion? The pupil who has received the first lessons in courage as outlined in *Emile*.

In sum, for Rousseau the enduring appeal of courage remains. Moral courage enables the pupil to resist both physical enslavement and the moral enslavement that one experiences in the darkness of the church. It endows him with the capacity for happiness because it goes hand in hand with compassion. "Pity," Rousseau claims, "is sweet because, in putting ourselves in the place of the one who suffers, we nevertheless feel the pleasure of not suffering as he does" (*E*, 221).[56] Moral courage enables Emile to "become capable of attachment" without relinquishing his autonomy. It allows him to be sensitive to others without being unmanly. In short, it ensures Emile the happiness of autonomy and, at the same time, the enjoyment of the sacred attachment of friendship.[57] Emile unforgets the natural sentiment of compassion and is taught to recognize and avoid attachments to others who would not extend the same compassion to him or would not suffer should Emile lose his autonomy. Properly educated, Emile

> is laborious, temperate, patient, firm, and full of courage. His imagination is in no way inflamed and never enlarges dangers. He is sensitive to few ills, and he knows constancy in endurance because he has not learned to quarrel with destiny. With respect to death, he does not yet know well what it is; but since he is accustomed to submitting to the law of necessity without resistance, when he has to die, he will die without moaning and without struggling. This is all that nature permits at this most abhorred of all moments. To live free and to depend little on human things is the best means of learning how to die. (*E*, 208)

FIVE

Economic Courage and Wealth

There is something wonderful in his resourcefulness and a sort of heroism in his greed for gain.

—Tocqueville, *Democracy in America*

The Effeminacy of Moral Courage

Thus far we have discussed two general alternatives to the excessive manliness of the Homeric tradition—and of honor cultures more broadly. In the Athenian context we found courage invoked not merely for the sake of honor, but for the sake of democratic leisure, the noble, or justice. Manliness itself was softened by drawing on reason as the primary weapon of the virtuous human being. In Rousseau's work courage is invoked for the sake of autonomy. Like Plato, Aristophanes, and Aristotle, Rousseau rejects violence as the primary source of political and existential order, yet at the same time he harbors a deep-seated distrust of reason. Thus he softens excessive manliness by drawing on compassion as the preferred weapon for both the virtuous citizen and community building. In essence, Rousseau melds Spartan virtue with an ethic of care.[1]

A dispassionate evaluation of this position may at first glance lead one to think that there is nothing manly at all in Rousseau's vision of courage—that it is merely wet-eyed sentiment unfit for manly, heroic types. For example, Clifford Orwin accuses Rousseau of initiating a "discourse of compassion" in which compassion serves as "a substitute for virtue."[2] In Rousseau's thought, he argues, compassion simply secularizes Christian mercy and opposes sappy sentimentalism to rational self-interest. "This sentimentalism," Orwin argues, "implied a new and (it seems fair to say) more feminine notion of masculinity. More than any earlier understanding of human perfection, it tends toward the androgynous, for it characterizes even male excellence in terms of sensitivity to others, which means ultimately to their suffering."[3] Thus for Orwin, Rousseau's educative aim is to increase pity in men—to make men less masculine by disentangling manliness from cold rationality. One needs compassionate sentiment to be manly, not reason. Self-restraint is not necessary, so long as adequate tears follow. Thus "compassion is anything but a reliable basis for public policy."[4]

Isaiah Berlin is even more critical of Rousseau. Whereas Orwin targets Rousseau's notion of compassion as the basis of community, Berlin targets Rousseau's thinking regarding his fundamental care, autonomy (though Berlin prefers the term *liberty*), and the means of achieving it. He says that for Rousseau, "liberty is identical with the human individual himself. To say that a man is a man, and to say that he is free, are almost the same."[5] The problem Berlin identifies, not only in Rousseau but in a host of other thinkers, is how an individual can be completely self-ruling yet live in human community. For Rousseau, he says, the solution to this seeming paradox is to argue that "liberty and authority cannot conflict for they are *one;* they coincide; they are the reverse and obverse of the same medal."[6] According to Berlin, this "lunatic vision" spawned Rousseau's idea of the Social Contract and the General Will, two concepts that permit this sort of reasoning:

> To force a man to be free is to force him to behave in a rational manner. A man is free who gets what he wants; what he truly wants is a rational end. If he does not want a rational end, he does not truly want;

> if he does not want a rational end, what he wants is not true freedom but false freedom. I force him to do certain things which make him happy. He will be grateful to me for it if he ever discovers what his own true self is: that is the heart of this famous doctrine, and there is not a dictator in the West who in the years after Rousseau did not use this monstrous paradox in order to justify his behaviour.[7]

Berlin is, of course, overstating the role of reason in Rousseau's thought, but his point is clear. Whereas Rousseau's fundamental care is autonomy, he advocates the abnegation of autonomy to achieve it. And because he was so influential, Berlin concludes that "Rousseau . . . was one of the most sinister and most formidable enemies of liberty in the whole history of modern thought."[8]

Rousseau has also been criticized for advocating an unmanly form of courage. One of the most famous instances of this argument is C. S. Lewis's *The Abolition of Man* (1944). Here Lewis observes that in the rightly ordered human being, "the head rules the belly through the chest."[9] The claim is a restatement of Plato's description of the tripartite soul, which has a reasonable part (logistikon) that is supposed to rule the appetitive part (alogistikon) in confederacy with the spirited part (thumos). In Lewis's terminology, the head is the home of reason, and the chest is the home of the spirited element of man—his drive, dynamism, self-sacrifice, and creativity. In the chest resides the heart, the home of courage; courage, after all, shares the Latin root for heart, *cor*. Lewis, as such, is speaking directly to the object of our analysis—*andreia*, or manly courage. To have chest is to have heart. To have chest is to be courageous, to be manly. Finally, the belly is the home of the appetites. So reason (the head), in confederacy with courage (the chest), restrains and rules the appetites (belly). For Lewis, the problem with the modern educational project, which directly descends from Rousseau's *Emile*, is that its goal is the breeding of "men without chests." As he writes, "In a sort of ghastly simplicity we remove the organ and demand the function. We make men without chests and expect of them virtue and enterprise. We laugh at honour and are shocked to find traitors in our midst. We castrate and bid the geldings be fruitful."[10]

To argue that we live in an age of chestless men is thus to say that men no longer have manly courage, or that men are no longer manly. In claiming this, however, Lewis reveals his definition of courage to be specifically martial courage. If courage and one's mettle as a man are determined only "in the third hour of bombardment," as he would have us think, then he is right that the age of courage is over.[11] If the categories of the knightly-aristocratic framework of human relations are the measure of manliness, then in modern times we are most certainly seeing the abolition of man. If Rousseau's project of replacing martial courage with moral courage has indeed succeeded, it has also vitiated the tradition of linking courage with the male sex and of basing the bonds of community on violence. This, of course, was precisely Rousseau's intention.

Lewis, however, is a little off the mark. It is not courage per se that has atrophied but martial courage as the quintessential manifestation of courage. And it is not moral courage that Lewis (or Orwin or Berlin, for that matter) finds objectionable but the mode of articulation bound up with Rousseau's moral courage. Compassion requires "fellow feeling." It requires that every person recognize in the other that which is the same in him—namely, the capacity for suffering. It requires him to intuit a shared weakness and a common sensitivity. In other words, moral courage both needs and fosters the sense of equality. The objection to moral courage thus comes not from thinkers who prefer violence to compassion but from those who reject the egalitarianism that necessarily stems from compassion. Nietzsche, for instance, loathes what he calls the "leveling of mankind" and accuses the proponents of egalitarianism of being bitter and resentful Last Men.[12] Similar objections come from José Ortega y Gasset, Carl Schmidt, Martin Heidegger, and those who, in general, are doing battle against what Alexandre Kojève calls the Universal Homogeneous State.[13] Their arguments are usually replete with martial metaphors and fierce invective against Rousseau, the democratic age, and the new vision of courage and its corollaries: egalitarianism and compassion. In short, they claim that moral courage and compassion denude us of honor, strip us of "true" courage, eliminate heroes, and vitiate all that is elevated in human community.

In Alexis de Tocqueville we also find a thinker who sees the age of equality as colored by unmanly courage, so to speak. Because of his family's experience with the French Revolution—his father imprisoned and his grandfather-in-law guillotined—one would think Tocqueville would follow the path of Nietzsche and others more disposed to martial courage and its attendant mode of articulation.[14] One would think he too would reject the new age for its lack of honor, its unmanliness, and the absence of beautiful self-sacrifice that makes martial courage so appealing. This, however, is not Tocqueville's position. Instead, Tocqueville presents a conflicted view of the modern age and courage—a view that attempts to reconcile the aristocratic and democratic worldviews and to see the good in both. His natural understanding of aristocratic feelings and ideas gives him a unique perspective on objections to the egalitarian and "effeminate" age ushered in by Rousseau's championing of moral courage. He recognizes the untenability of community begotten of martial courage, yet simultaneously recognizes the inadequacy of moral courage for satisfying the masculine, adventurous, and aesthetic demands of the human soul. Thus in Tocqueville we find a thinker who understands intuitively the tradition of courage but also recognizes that if we are to continue enjoying its salutary effects it must be integrated into the age of equality. Tocqueville understands well that courage is essential for both the creation of our communities and the safeguarding of our souls but claims that it can no longer remain the exclusive domain of men. Hence, in what follows it will be demonstrated that Tocqueville is telling a story about a type of courage amenable to the age of equality. He is presenting a courage that is neither too manly nor too effeminate. In *Democracy in America* we find Tocqueville's gift to his honor-loving, inegalitarian aristocratic brethren: an unmanned courage that is not unmanly.

Tocqueville on Honor and Equality

The gift begins with Tocqueville's thoughts on equality. Unlike many aristocrats, Tocqueville does not reject the modern age for its egalitarianism and all its accompaniments. Instead, he addresses equality in a matter-of-fact way, as the book's opening sentence illustrates: "No novelty in the United States struck me more vividly during my stay there than the equality of conditions."[15] He observes the phenomenon without condemnation but also without praise, simply asserting it as the primary characteristic of the modern, democratic age. It is a historical movement that is not the result of a particular political event and cannot be stopped. "The gradual progress of equality," he says, "is something fated. The main features of this progress are the following: it is universal and permanent, it is daily passing beyond human control, and every event and every man helps it along" (*DA*, 12). The factual character of this claim, which is no small claim, does little to alert the reader to Tocqueville's opinion regarding the ubiquitous spread of equality. What it does do, however, is separate him from the likes of Nietzsche and Ortega y Gasset, who condemn the coming age *in toto.*

Marvin Zetterbaum refers to this view as Tocqueville's "inevitability thesis." He argues that Tocqueville's "understanding of history . . . and his neutrality *vis-à-vis* democracy and aristocracy are very closely related."[16] In other words, there is a logic to Tocqueville's neutrality. If the spread of equality is inevitable, then it is not only illogical but also futile to praise or to condemn it, and this is not the sort of political science to which Tocqueville aspires.[17] Whether Tocqueville views equality positively is debatable. More germane to this discussion, however, is the reason Tocqueville posits its inevitability. Zetterbaum is probably right in claiming that the inevitability thesis serves as "the shield behind which [Tocqueville] can maintain his neutrality, a neutrality that is not only compatible with the cause of democracy, but actively promotes it. Whatever undermines the inevitability thesis undermines his neutrality and the cause of democracy as well."[18] In other words, Tocqueville is offering his European brethren a twofold lesson. First, the spread of equality is neither a new phenomenon nor a passing fad. It is a permanent tendency in history.[19] Second, nothing can be done to halt this historical movement. Thus there is little sense in pining away for the days of yore when manly courage and honor were the ordering principles of social and political life. Those times are gone and they are not coming back—like it or not. Thus the lesson: get on board with the coming equality or get swept away by it.[20]

The argument that his aristocratic brethren should either go along with the new age of democracy or get swept away by it is hardly a persuasive sales pitch. For some, like Nietzsche, asking the martially courageous man to behave according to a different code is like "telling the bird of prey not to hunt."[21] For these thinkers, the love of honor and agonistic competition is not a social construction to be rejected or embraced according to the spirit of the day but a disposition inscribed on one's very being. For the aristocrat, suggesting that martial courage and honor be replaced with moral courage and pity, or with political courage and discourse, is tantamount to asking a man not to be a man. It destroys the ground from which community has sprung from time immemorial. After all, to honor is to elevate in rank; it is to set one man above another. Heroism and honor are, by definition, hieratic and hierarchical. They distinguish one man from another. They are an aristocracy's basic tools of social order.

Tocqueville thus sees honor as incompatible with the American democratic milieu. As Sharon Krause puts it, he is keenly aware that "it is the inequalities of recognition entailed by honor that make it objectionable from the standpoint of modern democracy."[22] One cannot be dogmatically committed to equality, yet regard another person as one's natural and moral superior simply because he is a virtuoso of violence and martial courage, or because his ancestor was. Hence Tocqueville found that in the America he visited, honor, as traditionally understood, was almost absent,[23] not because Americans were striving to eradicate it but because its absence is a natural outcome of the equality of conditions. In an egalitarian world, honor cannot be the measure of good citizenship because it is incompatible with both the prevailing dogma of equality and the social consequences of equality.[24]

Tocqueville's Sociology of Violence

There are, of course, many practical reasons that a democratic, trading people will repudiate violence, but theoretically speaking, violence, like honor, fails to fit the logic of equality. The close tie between honor and violence means that as honor diminishes, violence will diminish with it. Martial courage then loses its authoritative place in the maintenance of community. So to maintain the social goods and the existential appeal of courage, Tocqueville must reconfigure the vision of human nature that dominates the inegalitarian world and the prevailing understanding of man as a natural mechanic of violence and as naturally concerned with honor.

This is no small task: it requires an argument that cuts to the very core of human existence. Rousseau, as we have seen, recognizes this problem and attempts to construct human beings not as naturally violent but as naturally compassionate. He is offering an alternative philosophical anthropology that turns the traditional, martial view of human beings upside down. Tocqueville shares several of Rousseau's views in this regard. For example, like Rousseau, he sees human beings as quite rigid in their habits and ways of thinking. These rigid habits and ideas, however, are not universal truths for Tocqueville. Instead, they are a consequence of the time and place from which they emerge. Thus in the nature-nurture debate Tocqueville leans heavily toward nurture—man is not much more than what he makes of himself. Hence, the love of honor is no more deeply inscribed on the heart than, say, the love of liberty. Rather than deny that humans are violent and honor loving by nature, Tocqueville says that the things about which we care fundamentally, and the ways we articulate our relationships, are socially constructed. We are no more naturally mechanics of violence or naturally honor loving than we are naturally compassionate. Violence, honor, and compassion are learned in the world into which we are thrown at birth.

However, for Tocqueville one aspect of human nature transcends particular times and places. He offers it not to produce a new and improved theory of human nature (or a more pessimistic account, à la Hobbes) but to demonstrate the possibility of shifting fundamental cares. This constant should be familiar: human beings tend to be self-interested creatures.[25] Courage, as we have seen in the preceding chapters, is traditionally invoked as a means for overcoming this abiding problem. For Tocqueville, self-interest is a constant, but, at least prima facie, he does not present it as an evil. Instead, he discusses it as a fact from which we must proceed as social scientists. As he puts it, "Personal interest [l'intérêt personnel] . . . provides the only stable point in the human heart" (*DA*, 239).[26] Although self-interest may manifest itself as the love of honor, this is but one possibility among many. How this self-interest expresses itself is contingent on social and historical circumstances. Like honor, it is bound up, not with universal categories, but with things "particular and momentary" (*DA*, 617). For example, we have already seen that for Tocqueville man exists in a world progressing toward universal equality. The result of this historical march is the democratic regime and, at least in America, a certain type of democratic man. This democratic man is therefore a particular manifestation of the self-interested character. Divorced from the old aristocratic and hierarchical principles of Europe, the Puritan arriving on the shores of America carried in his heart the basic principles of democracy and, once there, found fertile ground "where it could grow in freedom and, progressing in conformity with mores, develop peacefully within the law" (*DA*, 18). He found an unprecedented equality of social conditions in which a variety of new cares and concerns could come to the fore.

And how does Tocqueville describe these cares? They are "reputation, power, and above all, wealth [la richesse]" (*DA*, 655). At first glance they seem not so different from the cares described by, say, Thucydides, Machiavelli, or Hobbes, but there is a crucial difference in Tocqueville's thought. While all human beings care about reputation and power, the democratic soul cares fundamentally about wealth (richesse), or, as Tocqueville frequently puts it, the love of well-being: "The love of comfort [l'amour du bien-être] has become the dominant national taste [le goût national et dominant]. The main current of human passions running in that direction sweeps everything along with it" (*DA*, 532).[27] In this "love of wealth [amour des richesses]" Tocqueville says one can see the sort of "energetic passion [passion énergique]" that one normally associates with martial courage (*DA*, 621). This fundamental care clearly trumps the love of honor: "Love of wealth [l'amour des richesses]," Tocqueville writes, "takes the place of ambition, and prosperity [le bien-être] quenches the fires of faction" (*DA*, 306).[28] Thus, while in an aristocracy men vigorously pursue reputation and power in the form of honor, in a democracy they vigorously pursue wealth. The Achillean adventurer is replaced by the intrepid entrepreneur.

With one sweeping statement, then, Tocqueville dismisses the view that honor, honor codes, manly courage, and the traditional virtues are eternal verities. Instead, he reconstructs them as socially contingent. This is not to say they are random—on the contrary, there is a strong sense of path dependence in Tocqueville's thought. For example, if the "cradle" into which we are first thrown is replete with lovers of honor, we will most likely find ourselves caring fundamentally about honor. This, however, is not a given. The first European immigrants to America found the "empty cradle of a great nation" and were thus able to free themselves of the age-old tradition of martial courage (*DA*, 30). In this empty cradle they were free to nurse a gentler form of community. Freed from the strictures of aristocratic hierarchy, they could live in an equality of conditions and "have enough property to want order and not enough to excite envy" (*DA*, 636). In other words, a completely new community of care could emerge—one where people could care fundamentally for wealth and consequently where they could "love peace, which favors industry and gives every man a chance to bring his little undertaking quietly to a conclusion" (*DA*, 648).

Equally important is that by untethering man from the tradition of honor, Tocqueville is able to leave behind violence as a natural human propensity. Democratic man is not predisposed to violence; violence is simply not an intrinsic part of his character. In fact, Tocqueville says the opposite: "Violent political passions have little hold on men whose whole thoughts are bent on the pursuit of well-being. Their excitement about small matters makes them calm about great ones" (*DA*, 638). Thus for Tocqueville violence is not part of the inherent nature of the individual—if he even has one. This means violence need not be understood as an anthropological problem. It can be reconstrued as a sociological problem.

Even if human beings are not violent by nature, Tocqueville must admit that violence remains a political reality, even in democratic societies.[29] Rather than suggesting, as Hobbes does, that it be controlled through the establishment of a monarchic form of government, or, as Nietzsche does, that it be allowed to run free as artistic impulse, Tocqueville describes it as a residual social problem that will diminish on its own, becoming more and more marginal and peripheral as the new order of equality takes hold. Indeed, he claims that "one can accept it as a general and constant rule that among civilized nations warlike passions become rarer and less active as social conditions get nearer to equality" (*DA*, 646).

Thus whereas in Hobbes's state of nature every man is enemy to every man and there is no place for industry or invention, no culture, no commodious buildings, "no Arts; no Letters; no Society; and which is worst of all, continuall feare, and danger or violent death; And the life of man, solitary, poore, nasty, brutish, and short,"[30] Tocqueville imagines, in early America, a state of nature that was just the opposite. He claims that when the first Europeans arrived in the Americas, violence as described by Hobbes or Nietzsche was practically nonexistent among them.[31] If violence had been a natural part of the human constitution, it should have been shipped over on the *Mayflower* with the rest of the European baggage, but for Tocqueville violence as the predominant mode of articulation was simply not present in American society. He can therefore reject the philosophical anthropology of man as violent by nature and thus open the way to a more rational, less violent mode of social articulation that is more amenable to democratic community.

The Relativization of Honor

To argue, as Tocqueville has, that resisting the age of equality is futile, and that violence is not carved into man's very nature, does little to assuage the concerns of those who esteem martial courage and care fundamentally about honor. To dismiss this type of courage is, after all, to dismiss the tradition of *manly* courage. Tocqueville recognizes this and therefore goes to great lengths to include the language of manly courage and honor in his description of the democratic world. Thus whereas, for example, Lewis sees the modern age as one where honor and manliness in general have been displaced by syrupy sentiment, Tocqueville argues that honor is still a vital part of the communal configuration. Honor is not obsolete; rather, the matrix of human relations that determines the form honor takes is different. For Tocqueville there is no set definition of honor. Instead, "Every time men come together to form a particular society, a conception of honor is immediately established among them, that is to say, a collection of opinions peculiar to themselves about what should be praised or blamed" (*DA*, 620).[32] Universal categories for praise and blame simply do not apply. Honor is relative to the time and place of the particular human community. For example, Tocqueville points to the Romans, an eminently aristocratic society, who "held certain peculiar notions about glory and disgrace which were not solely derived from general notions of right and wrong" (*DA*, 620). Among them "courage was more honored and valued . . . than any other virtue. And that is proved by the fact that it was called '*virtus*,' using a generic term for one particular quality" (*DA*, 620). So in Rome virtue and courage were synonymous, but courage was narrowly defined as martial courage. To be virtuous in Rome, one had to demonstrate courage in battle. One's standing, vis-à-vis other Romans, was measured by how one carried oneself on the battlefield. The fabric of Roman society was woven from the warp and woof of martial relationships.

According to Tocqueville, a residual of this martially articulated society was European feudalism. Here too, community was largely articulated by violence, and martial courage was held in great honor. As Tocqueville writes: "The feudal aristocracy was born of war and for war; it won its power by force of arms and maintained it thereby. So nothing was more important to it than military courage. It was therefore natural to glorify courage above all other virtues. Every manifestation thereof, even at the expense of common sense and humanity, was therefore approved and often even ordained by the manners of the time" (*DA*, 618). In the aristocracy, then, through occasional outbursts of violence, the bonds between individuals were forged, affirmed, and reinforced. Interestingly, although the hierarchy determined by these occasional outbursts of violence was for the most part arbitrary, this mode of community formation intrinsically set bounds on the expression of violence. In other words, whereas community was foregrounded by the courage mustered on the battlefield or the dueling ground, these events were, by and large, rare. But more important than their frequency were their scope and purpose. Although the aristocracy was born of war and for war, for Tocqueville this way of life was more tranquil and thus happier. When hierarchical relations were called into question—when matters of honor were contested—violent outbursts reestablishing the order of social and political articulation were quite likely. The battles, however, were most often limited in scope and were fought for the sake of honor and recognition, not necessarily for material aggrandizement or the mere annihilation of the enemy. So whereas tranquility was the prevailing characteristic of the feudal aristocracy, it was clear that "a noble should not tranquilly suffer an insult, and was dishonored if he let himself be struck without fighting—that was a result of the basic principles and needs of a military aristocracy" (*DA*, 619).

Tocqueville, then, is well aware of the inherent arbitrariness of the aristocratic hierarchy, but at the same time he lets it be known that the system has some redeeming features. In a community where martial courage prevails, and the articulation of the community is bound up with honor, there is no need to utterly destroy one's enemy in war. In fact, such actions might well be dishonorable in themselves.[33] The fundamental care for honor requires that one recognize and honor the courage and prowess of one's opponent. Killing the opponent, theoretically speaking, defeats the purpose of fighting for honor. Thus the occasional outbursts of violence are followed by an abiding desire to return to the more usual tranquil state of affairs.[34]

In the democratic age, when concern for honor diminishes before the onslaught of equality, the possibility that a community will wage war for limited political objectives is seriously curtailed. As Eliot Cohen puts it, "Tocqueville, therefore, describes escalation in democratic warfare as a quantum leap, a radical transformation of popular attitudes towards warfare that requires some time and effort to achieve, but which produces an extraordinary explosion of violence."[35] Citing the case of World War I, Cohen points out that in the absence of a motivation of honor bound up with martial courage Americans were at first enormously reluctant to enter the war but that when they did so they were committed not to a narrow political aim such as maintaining the balance of power in Europe but to "the most extreme objectives."[36] Such extreme objectives may be ideological, economic, or some combination of the two, but in any case America, as the remaining great power, finds itself in a situation where entering these sorts of wars is becoming commonplace. Without at least a modicum of honor, limited wars with limited objectives become more and more rare.[37]

For Tocqueville, the eclipse of martial courage and honor, and concomitantly the disappearance of limited wars, weakens the bonds of associational life in the democratic community. Tocqueville claims that "feeling and ideas [les sentiments et les idées] are renewed, the heart enlarged, and the understanding developed only by the reciprocal actions of men one upon another" (*DA*, 515) and that limited outbursts of communal violence are an instance of such actions: "When a violent revolution occurs among a highly civilized people, it cannot fail to give a sudden impulse to their feelings and thoughts [aux sentiments et aux idées]" (*DA*, 460). The exercise of martial courage and honor is salutary in that it pushes individuals to transcend their narrow self-interest, strengthens the bonds between individuals, and reinvigorates community.

Democratic Honor and Economic Courage

Despite his praise for the order of things in the aristocratic world, Tocqueville has mixed feelings about honor as it manifests itself in a democracy. Americans, he says, have a keen sense of honor, but they direct their "praise and blame" elsewhere. Martial courage is not praised as the measure of good citizenship, and given that wealth is the fundamental care, all the virtues, including courage, must lend themselves to its satisfaction. Hence, in America, Tocqueville discovers what can only be called *economic courage.* American honor is based not on valorous deeds on the battlefield but on courage in trade and industry.

To say that the virtues that lend themselves to the acquisition of wealth are honored in America presents some problems because such a claim is, in effect, a clever rhetorical sleight of hand. Honor in aristocratic cultures is the fundamental care—the *ne plus ultra* good—and martial courage is the means to acquiring it. Thus we can say that martial courage is revered, appreciated, or even loved because it is useful for acquiring honor. In Tocqueville's language, an action is "praised or blamed" for gaining or losing honor. Thus, to say that martial courage is honored because it accrues honor is tautological. Martial courage is indeed "honored" but only in the sense that it is praised, or revered, or appreciated. This "honoring" is not the same as "honor." The verb has a different meaning from the noun.

Hence, this related formulation is also problematic: (1) economic courage yields wealth; therefore, (2) economic courage is honored, which means (3) honor still exists in the democratic milieu. This, however, is how Tocqueville asks us to think about honor in a democracy. He knows well that honor, as a *ne plus ultra* good, is moribund in the democratic world; he knows well that it has been supplanted by wealth. At the same time, however, he wants to maintain the category, at least as a rhetorical trope. In other words, Tocqueville deliberately substitutes the verb for the noun: honor (noun) still exists in America, because Americans honor (verb) certain actions. Specifically "all those quiet virtues which tend to regularity in the body social and which favor trade are sure to be held in special honor by this people, and to neglect them will bring one into public contempt. But all those turbulent virtues which sometimes bring glory but more often trouble to society will rank lower in the public opinion of this same people. One could disregard them without forfeiting the esteem of one's fellow citizens, and perhaps by acquiring them one might run a risk of losing it" (*DA*, 621). In other words, the virtues *useful* for successful trade—which yields wealth—are honored. Blamed (called vice) are those things antithetical to it. Martial courage—which yields honor or, as Tocqueville puts it here, glory—hinders trade and is therefore dishonored. There is, then, a certain point of agreement between aristocrats and democrats. "Both," Tocqueville claims, "rank courage first of virtues and count it the greatest moral necessity for a man" (*DA*, 622). But the sorts of courage that are praised are radically different because each is inextricably bound up with its own fundamental care. Economic courage is honored because it is ideal for the efficacious pursuit of trade and industry.[38]

Sharon Krause sees this point in Tocqueville's thought as well. As she puts it, "Tocqueville shows the consequences of democracy that generate its resistance to honor, but also shows why democracy needs honor and where in American society honor might be found."[39] The problem with Krause's interpretation, however, stems precisely from Tocqueville's rhetorical sleight of hand. Democrats do not need honor (noun). In fact, the logic of the egalitarian mind rejects it. Democrats love wealth. Tocqueville would prefer they love liberty, but because one cannot force sudden shifts in fundamental cares the best one can hope for is to attenuate the problems that attend the excessive love of wealth. This point is not lost on Krause: "To support individual liberty against the twin danger of majority tyranny and 'mild' despotism, Tocqueville seeks to inspire in the democratic character qualities associated with aristocratic mores and tied to old-regime honor."[40] In other words, Tocqueville's effort is not to find where honor remains hidden in American society, as Krause first suggests, but to mitigate rhetorically the ugliness of the love of the wealth by imbuing it with that age-old partner of honor—namely, courage. Consequently, the aforementioned formulation would be better understood as follows: (1) economic courage yields wealth; therefore, (2) economic courage is honored; therefore, (3) we can use the language of honor; consequently, (4) manliness must still exist in the democratic milieu.

And this is precisely what Tocqueville is attempting to argue. While his language suggests that a liberalism with honor (noun) is possible, reality suggests something quite different. All that is left is the language of honoring (verb) that can whitewash cupidity, a vice regarded with disgust by honor lovers the world over. And though resistance to the spread of equality is futile it could seriously hinder the prospects for Tocqueville's own fundamental care—liberty. Hence, Tocqueville's strategy is to make democracy more palatable for those who adhere to a code of honor. And he does this by carving out a small place in the democratic world for a remaining trace of honor in the form of economic courage. In short, Tocqueville is attempting to construct a liberalism begotten by useful honoring (verb) rather than beautiful honor (noun), and predicated on useful courage (economic) rather than beautiful courage (martial).

Useful Courage and Useful Passions

Just how different these configurations of manly courage are should not be understated. In aristocratic societies based on martial courage, Tocqueville sees a universal condemnation of the love of money and pursuit of gain as a vice called greed. But "no stigma attaches to love of money in America, and provided it does not exceed the bounds imposed by public order, it is held in honor. The American will describe as noble and estimable ambition that which our medieval ancestors would have called base cupidity. He would consider as blind and barbarous frenzy that ardor for conquest and warlike spirit which led the latter every day into new battles" (*DA*, 620). In America the characteristics that are shunned or considered dishonorable are those that do not lend themselves to industry—sloth, apathy, and disorder—and the most honored characteristic is courage in industrial undertakings. What one culture would consider unfettered greed is a virtue in the other, and what one culture would consider unfettered barbarism is a virtue in the other.[41]

The transformation of avarice from vice to virtue may have gone furthest in America, but it was not unique to America or to the time of Tocqueville's account. In what is becoming something of a classic text, Albert Hirschman describes the long history of this conceptual shift. For example, even though the pursuit of glory and honor was a dominant ideology as late as the Renaissance, that period also spelled the beginning of that ideology's downfall.[42] Though the waning power of the church allowed for a revival and invocation of Greek and Roman texts extolling the pursuit of glory, at the same time other thinkers in western Europe, and especially in France, were collectively contributing to the "demolition of the hero." As Hirschman puts it, "All the heroic virtues were shown to be forms of mere self-preservation by Hobbes, of self-love by La Rochefoucauld, of vanity and of frantic escape from real self-knowledge by Pascal. The heroic passions were portrayed as demeaning by Racine after having been denounced as foolish, if not demented, by Cervantes" (*PI*, 11). And less than a century later, the "acquisitive drive and the activities connected with it, such as commerce, banking, and eventually industry, came to be widely hailed" (*PI*, 12).

They were not necessarily hailed because acquisitiveness was considered virtuous and reasonable. The passion for gain was still regarded as a passion, but it came to be regarded as useful in restraining other passions, in what Hirschman refers to as "the principle of the countervailing passion" (*PI*, 20). The idea was that rather than seeing all the passions as merely reprehensible vices that should be struggled against, one could "fight fire with fire," utilizing "one set of comparatively innocuous passions to countervail another more dangerous and destructive set or, perhaps, to weaken and tame the passions by such internecine fights in *divide et impera* fashion" (*PI*, 21). Traditionally speaking, passions could not be separated to fight each other because "the basic passions were believed to feed on each other" (*PI*, 21), but now they could be given the positive role of countervailing other passions.

In Hirschman's reckoning, Francis Bacon was the first to voice this idea in his *Advancement of Learning*, where he proposes "to set affection against affection and to master one by another: even as we use to hunt beast with the beast and fly bird with bird. . . . For as in the government of states it is sometimes necessary to bridle one faction with another, so it is in the government within" (*PI*, 22). Hamilton adopts similar language in *Federalist* 72 where he says that if a president is avaricious, the lust for power (i.e., a second term in office) may trump his lust for money. *Federalist* 51, which makes the argument for division of powers, also uses the idea of a countervailing passion: "ambition must be made to counteract ambition" (*PI*, 30). Very similar claims are attributed to Spinoza, Hume, and, in the eighteenth century, d'Holbach and Helvétius (*PI*, 24–27). It is with Helvétius, however, that Hirschman introduces a key change: the passion that serves the countervailing function is given the name of "interest." As Helvétius puts it, "The moralists might succeed in having their maxims observed if they replace in this manner their injurious discourse by the language of interest" (*PI*, 28).

Interest, then, becomes the "new paradigm" (*PI*, 42) and through various invocations comes to have a positive and even a curative connotation—not because interest is in any way noble but because it is predictable. For Tocqueville, predictability appeals to the democratic American mind in that it supports economic activity, but it is not just in capitalist America that predictability is so appealing. Interest is a concept that fits well with Western rationality in general because it is amenable to calculation—by the empirical method of making calculations based on carefully recorded experience (i.e., data), one can, at least to some degree, predict human behavior.

So employing the principle of interest—especially as it pertains to money—creates a constancy from which an empirical social organization can emerge. Prior to the ascendance of interest, the mind could jump from one desire to another. But Hirschman says of avarice that "the perceived characteristics of this passion, which set it apart from others, were precisely constancy, doggedness, and sameness from one day to the next and from one person to another" (*PI*, 54). Though avarice may be base and ugly, it can be counted on as the same baseness and the same ugliness directing the actions of every person, every day. Its predictability trumps its ignobility. The doctrine is simple and straightforward: "Man loves money and this love is constant" (*PI*, 56).

Predictability and constancy, however, are not the only reasons that the passion for gain, out of all the passions, came to be viewed most favorably. Were these the only tests, then any other passion that was constant and predictable could be substituted. One could, for instance, argue that the passion for destruction and war is also a human constant. What distinguished material interest—the obstinate desire for gain—was that it came to be thought of as harmless. As Hirschman puts it, "The passions were wild and dangerous, whereas looking after one's material interests was innocent or, as one would say today, innocuous" (*PI*, 58). Interest was thus welcomed as a "calm passion" that was at the same time innocent or *doux* (*PI*, 59). To be *doux* is to be well-mannered and polished. It is to be easygoing, polite, safe; we might even go so far as to say effeminate. Interest, then is a soft and peaceful passion, a gentle and calm pursuit that stands in direct contradistinction to the heroism of the warrior that so dominated the aristocratic world. In fact, it is quite possible that interest acquired such positive connotations *because* it stood in direct opposition to the violence of the aristocratic world:

> The image of the trader as a *doux*, peaceful, inoffensive fellow may have drawn some strength from comparing him with the looting armies and murderous pirates of the time. But in France more than in England it may also have had much to do with the lenses with which people looked at different social groups: anyone who did not belong to the nobility could not, *by definition*, share in heroic virtues or violent passions. After all, such a person had only interests and not glory to pursue, and everybody *knew* that this pursuit was bound to be *doux* in comparison to the passionate pastimes of savage exploits of the aristocracy. (*PI*, 63)

So just as Socrates and Plato invoke politics as an alternative to human articulation predicated on violence, these new theorists offer interest as an alternative. Economics becomes an antidote to the poison of violence; a calm and weak passion is elevated and given standing over a strong and violent desire. One is safe, the other is dangerous. One is *doux*, the other is hard.

Prima facie, it would seem that this is a deeply good thing. To replace a dangerous fundamental care with one that is safe and soft makes good sense. The problem with this principle, however, is that anyone who still subscribes to the knightly-aristocratic worldview can see nothing noble about this way of life. For the many it becomes acceptable, but for those who care fundamentally about manly courage and honor it remains low, ignominious, and unmanly. As Hirschman puts it, it is the *doux* way of being, but this is precisely the argument against it. The economic way—though no longer a sin, though a safe way of being—remains a soft and effeminate way of being; for those who admire martial courage and love honor, it is no more appealing than the sausage-selling Athenian political model or Rousseau's wet-eyed, sentimental moral alternative.

Ennobling Economic Courage

Tocqueville recognizes this problem. Thus he spends very little time trying to remove from economics the negative stigma it might have once had in the Christian world—that boat has sailed. Instead, his larger challenge is to infuse the American care for wealth, and contract and exchange as the concomitant mode of articulation, with the sort of nobility that will appeal to those still embedded in the aristocratic way of life. In short, he attempts to imbue economics with the manliness of martial courage and honor. In this way, Tocqueville can present the democratic way of being not merely as a safe alternative to the traditional aristocratic way but as a syncretic improvement. He does this by showing that the most important traits observed in martial courage are transposed into the economic sphere. Rather than portraying the American way of economics as soft, "safe," and womanly, Tocqueville portrays it as manly and courageous. Of course it is not martial courage that he observes but rather

> the type of courage . . . which makes a man brave the fury of the ocean to reach port more quickly, and face without complaint the privations of life in the wilds and that solitude which is harder to bear than any privations, the courage which makes a man almost insensible to the loss of a fortune laboriously acquired and prompts him instantly to fresh exertions to gain another. It is courage of this sort which is needed to maintain the American community and make it prosper, and it is held by them in particular esteem and honor. To betray a lack of it brings certain shame. (*DA*, 622–23)

This type of courage, it seems, both amazes and appalls Tocqueville. In the American configuration, rashness, which in the old aristocratic web of social relations was regarded as womanly and blameworthy, loses its negative stigma and becomes an enviable trait, at least insofar as it pertains to the pursuit of "honor" in the economic sphere.

For Tocqueville, then, there is a distinct kinship between martial courage in the old world and economic courage in the new: "What the French did for the sake of victory, [the Americans] are doing for the sake of economy" (*DA*, 402). For the aristocratic European, this appearance of courage is amazing. Where glory and martial victory are honored, one will go to great lengths to acquire them. But when there is general disdain toward love of gain, there is something both repulsive and intriguing about great displays of courage in economic endeavors. For example, Tocqueville remarks that whereas "the European navigator is prudent about venturing out to sea . . . the American, neglecting such precautions, braves these dangers; he sets sail while the storm is still rumbling; by night as well as by day he spreads his sails to the wind; he repairs storm damage as he goes; and when at last he draws near the end of his voyage, he flies toward the coast as if he could already see the port" (*DA*, 402–3). The American will amazingly scoff at danger and throw caution to the wind when success at trade and industry are at stake. He proves his mettle as a man not in war but in commerce. His courage serves his interest, not his honor.

In the American democratic milieu, then, Tocqueville shows that manliness is defined in relation to the rather unmanly realm of economics. Because of this, Tocqueville says, "such a people is bound to look with favor on boldness in industry and to honor it. . . . Americans have turned rash speculation into a sort of virtue, [and] can in no case stigmatize those who are thus rash" (*DA*, 662). Manliness thus comes to be measured in terms of accumulated wealth rather than martial heroics. In this way, honor itself becomes a commodity that can be transferred readily from one man to another. And one can afford to be rash because a misstep in this economic battle is fatal neither to the body nor to one's reputation as a man. Obviously one can go bankrupt, but in the democratic society bankruptcy leaves no stain on one's character. Just as fortunes can be lost and regained quickly, so too can this economic variant of honor. There is little time to ruminate on the honor of one man's character. As Tocqueville eloquently puts it, "The law of honor exists, but it is often left without interpreters" (*DA*, 624).

Tocqueville is amazed by the boldness that Americans demonstrate in the business of economics. In the democratic man of America, he sees a figure living in a world where, because his stature as a man is determined by his material well-being, he must demonstrate an "eagerness to possess things [that] goes beyond the ordinary limits of human cupidity." He sees a man who is "tormented by a longing for wealth, [and who therefore] boldly follows every path to fortune that is open to him; he is equally prepared to turn into a sailor, pioneer, artisan, or cultivator, facing the labors of dangers of these various ways of life with even constancy; there is something wonderful in his resourcefulness and *a sort of heroism in his greed for gain*" (*DA*, 347, emphasis added).[43] From the aristocratic perspective, nothing could be more oxymoronic. Greed and heroism simply do not fit together. One is either greedy or heroic. Though in a society predicated on martial courage the same man may be both heroic and greedy, he cannot be both at the same time. In America, however, he can, and this is what amazed, appalled, and confounded Tocqueville. In trying to describe this new phenomenon of manly courage, he could only say: "I cannot express my thoughts better than by saying that the Americans put something heroic into their way of trading" (*DA*, 403). In some ways, Tocqueville sounds like Leontius in Plato's *Republic*—he sees a shameful sight and knows he should turn away but cannot bring himself to do so.[44]

Yet Tocqueville does manage to subdue his awe regarding this strange new phenomenon enough to level three general criticisms against it. First, he regards the world predicated on economic courage to be petty. For example, in August 1840, reflecting on an imminent war in Europe, Tocqueville wrote to his old friend and traveling companion Gustave de Beaumont: "These wise reflections do not prevent me, at the bottom of my heart, from seeing all this crisis with a certain satisfaction. You know what a taste I have for great events and how tired I am of our little democratic and bourgeois pot of soup."[45] Like a good aristocrat, Tocqueville could not help feeling disdain for the new configuration of manly courage. In comparison with the eighteenth-century French, modern man is a mere shadow. His merely economic aspirations are utterly base and vulgar from the aristocratic perspective. Thus, when reflecting on his forefathers and prerevolutionary France, Tocqueville comments, "One is amazed at the tremendous opinion that Frenchmen of all ranks had at that time of their country and of their race, at their superb self-confidence."[46] Democratic man, so uncertain of himself and his place in the world, is constantly throwing himself into the project of self-determination. In a world where trade and industry are the first concern, Tocqueville cannot help seeing this new era in France as tedious, stunted, and, in many ways, repugnant.

Tocqueville's second objection to economic courage pertains to his description of tranquility in the aristocratic world. We have already stated that one of the key points separating the world defined by martial courage and the world defined by economic courage is the character of violence. When war or violence breaks out in an aristocratic society, it is an anomaly in an otherwise tranquil world. It is relatively rare and limited. Outside these moments of turbulence, man finds himself in a stable environment, where his position in the world is secure. The moments of violence function as safety valves releasing the pent-up pressures of society in a controlled and one might almost say safe manner. But in America, given the universal involvement in commerce, one finds "a sort of feverish agitation which wonderfully disposes [the mind] toward every type of exertion and keeps it, so to say, above the common level of humanity. For an American the whole of life is treated like a game of chance, a time of revolution, or the day of a battle" (*DA*, 404). In other words, in a world where one's mettle as a man and one's place in society are determined in the economic arena, there is no respite from agitation. One is constantly caught up in a merry-go-round struggle for one's place in society, and, to borrow loosely from Hobbes, the general inclination of all mankind is a perpetual and restless desire for wealth after wealth that ceases only in death.

Tocqueville's third objection to economic courage concerns the isolation of individuals. With the dissolution of the old social order, Tocqueville considered individuals to be more and more cut off from one another—the bonds that had once linked people had dissolved, and thus the habits of acting in concert for the glory of the people had atrophied. In short, individuals felt an oppressive sense of impotency.[47] Rather than acting in concert in a manly enterprise for the glory of the nation, they found themselves acting alone for the sake of private economic interests. We have seen that moral courage, political courage, and especially martial courage are by definition bound up with acts that transcend the self. Traditionally, to be considered courageous, actions must be oriented toward others. Courage is self-overcoming. One cannot live an isolated and self-interested life and still be thought courageous. This said, if courage is bound up with actions that are other-interested, and if in America martial courage is a phenomenon of the past, one would expect America to be populated by the most self-interested human beings the world ever witnessed. Tocqueville, however, does not portray it in this way. For him, tendencies of isolation and individualism in the new order are modulated by other forces. American society is not driven by pure selfishness; instead, bound up with Americans' economic courage is a tradition of selflessness that mirrors that of martial courage. Tocqueville calls this self-overcoming "self-interest properly understood."

Self-Interest Properly Understood

At first glance it may seem rather strange to point to Tocqueville's doctrine of self-interest properly understood as an integral part of manly courage. We must, however, keep in mind that a basic character of courage is that it points to things beyond itself—courage provides a lens through which we can observe how we exist beyond the narrow world of our personal being. If acting courageously, economically speaking, were to take risks merely for the sake of one's own material interest, then this sort of courage would reveal nothing about our collective being. Instead it would reveal only people feverishly exploiting one another in the marketplace, then withdrawing to the quiet of their homes to enjoy their spoils. Tocqueville certainly recognizes this possibility; he calls it "individualism." Individualism, he says, is a new idea that has come to replace the old-world idea of egoism. The difference between the two is stark: "Egoism is a passionate and exaggerated love of self which leads a man to think of all things in terms of himself and to prefer himself to all" (*DA*, 506). When measured by the code of martial courage and the aristocratic way of life, the egoistic man is the coward. He is the man who is either unwilling or unable to place the well-being of his collective world before himself. He is willing to abandon the line and leave his comrades in the lurch to save himself. Or, as we have also seen, he may leave the line to rush headlong into battle, but only for his personal glory. In this case, he may be brave, but he is certainly not courageous. The barbarian, we will recall, is not part of the community—and leaving the line in, say, phalanx fighting is no sign of courage. It may be awe-inspiring, it may be maniacal, but it is not courageous because it reveals one's preference for oneself rather than the solidarity of one's brothers in arms.[48]

For Tocqueville, individualism is similar to egoism, but with an important difference. As he puts it, "Individualism is a calm and considered feeling which disposes each citizen to isolate himself from the mass of his fellows and withdraw into the circle of family and friends; with this little society formed to his taste, he gladly leaves the greater society to look after itself" (*DA*, 506). So, while egoism is in some ways a spurning of one's community, individualism is more of a nonchalant apathy. As one commentator puts it, "By individualism, Tocqueville meant something very different from Emersonian self-reliance or Darwinian rugged individualism. He meant something close to the modern concept of 'privatization.'"[49] One may have commercial interests in the public realm, but no matter how feverishly these affairs are conducted, the tendency is to afterwards close oneself up in the household and shut out the deeply rewarding relations one might have with one's fellows.

This characterization of individualism in democracy is what Joshua Mitchell calls the Augustinian self. By this he means "the kind of self that is prone to move in two opposite directions: either *inward*, in which case it tends to get wholly shut up within itself and abandon the world; or *outward*, in which case it tends to be restive, overly active, and lost amid the world, searching at a frenzied pace for a satisfaction it can never wholly find there."[50] For Tocqueville this was very unlikely to be a problem in the aristocratic world because this type of isolation was simply not possible given the structure of the social conditions. First of all, in aristocracy there is a historical connectedness that naturally makes men feel linked to the past. Families are rooted in the same station and very often the same place for centuries and "so there is a sense in which all the generations are contemporaneous" (*DA*, 507). This generational connectedness, it must be kept in mind, is not merely with past generations, although "a man almost always knows about his ancestors and respects them. . . . His imagination extends to his great-grandchildren, and he loves them. He freely does his duty to both ancestors and descendants and often sacrifices personal pleasures for the sake of beings who are no longer alive or are not yet born" (*DA*, 507). The aristocrat, one might say, has an expansive temporal horizon that encompasses both the past and the future. He feels himself connected with people well beyond the immediate present, and, importantly, he feels duties toward them. A sense of connectedness that is bred in the aristocratic world serves as a natural antidote to individualism.[51]

But in an aristocratic society, human connections extend not only across time but also, at any given time, within and across the society's institutions. As Tocqueville puts it, "Aristocratic institutions have the effect of linking each man closely with several of his fellows" on the basis of their ascribed ranks. His point is not to praise the inequalities in a feudal order but rather to demonstrate that practically speaking "people living in an aristocratic age are almost always closely involved with something outside themselves, and they are often inclined to forget about themselves. It is true that in these ages the general conception of *human fellowship* is dim and that men hardly ever think of devoting themselves to the cause of humanity, but men do often make sacrifices for the sake of certain other men" (*DA*, 507). Because community is predicated on a framework of reciprocal duties and obligations, men are constantly reminded of things outside themselves. By the very nature of the practical relations—both political and economic—between human beings in aristocratic societies, the threat of individualism is mitigated.

The same, however, cannot be said about society where equality has come to hold sway. In egalitarian societies, like democracies, "the duties of each to all are much clearer but devoted service to any individual much rarer. The bonds of human affection are wider but more relaxed" (*DA*, 507). The bonds between people are much weaker because they are much more ephemeral. There are no mystical links between man and man—no congenital relationships of duty and obligation—that naturally draw one's thoughts from oneself to other human beings. Moreover, when positions are not prescribed, when families can rise and fall at almost any time, the link to previous generations is almost nonexistent. Thus the temporal bonds across generations in an aristocracy hardly exist at all in a democracy. This type of bond, we know, is instrumental in drawing the aristocratic man out of his self-contained world; it extends his affections beyond his immediate present. But, as Tocqueville says of democratic peoples, "The woof of time is ever being broken and the track of past generations lost. Those who have gone before are easily forgotten, and no one gives a thought to those who will follow. All a man's interests are limited to those near himself" (*DA*, 507). His meaning is simple: the temporal horizon of democratic man is extremely narrow, and this is mirrored by his truncated social horizon. Social equality destroys the structures that formerly bound people to others and broadened their affections and commitments beyond narrow self-interest. According to Tocqueville, a people dwelling within such narrow horizons feel they

> owe no man anything and hardly expect anything from anybody. They form the habit of thinking of themselves in isolation and imagine that their whole destiny is in their hands.
>
> Thus, not only does democracy make men forget their ancestors, but [it] also clouds their view of their descendants and isolates them from their contemporaries. Each man is forever thrown back on himself alone, and there is danger that he may be shut up in the solitude of his own heart. (*DA*, 508)

In the egalitarian democratic fold, as individualism becomes the norm, broader connections become difficult, if not impossible. In isolation, one can have no sense of the feelings and ideas of other citizens, so the prospects for exercising manly courage and heroism are severely curtailed.

Perhaps more important, unchecked individualism opens the door to despotism. As Tocqueville puts it, "Despotism, by its very nature suspicious, sees the isolation of men as the best guarantee of its own permanence" (*DA*, 509). In plain terms, isolation disempowers people. The Soviet despotic machine was notorious for its practice of isolating citizens by fostering suspicion among them. One need only think of the vivid accounts of this in Solzhenitsyn's *A Day in the Life of Ivan Denisovich.* Even better, one might recall the lives of Rubashov in Koestler's *Darkness at Noon* and Winston Smith in Orwell's *1984* as examples of how isolation both supports and is created by despotic power. Despotism is thus a special threat to democracies for two reasons. First, "Equality puts men side by side without a common link to hold them firm." Second, "Despotism raises barriers to keep them apart. It disposes them not to think of their fellows and turns indifference into a sort of public virtue" (*DA*, 510). In short, there is no such thing as a natural democratic phalanx.

Although Tocqueville sees individualism as seriously undermining his attempt to ennoble democracy with manly courage, he also sees several antidotes. One is American democratic institutions. These maintain freedom indirectly, through the beneficial effects they have on the individuals who participate in them. As Tocqueville puts it, "Citizens who are bound to take part in public affairs must turn from the private interests and occasionally take a look at something other than themselves. As soon as common affairs are treated in common, each man notices that he is not as independent of his fellows as he used to suppose and that to get their help he must often offer his aid to them" (*DA*, 510). So, just as Hirschman argues in terms of economic interest, Tocqueville makes this point in terms of political life. Those who aspire to political power, because they must attain it through free institutions, must turn to other people for support: "It thus happens that ambition makes a man care for his fellows, and, in a sense, he often finds his self-interest in forgetting about himself. . . . The electoral system forges permanent links between a great number of citizens who might otherwise have remained forever strangers to one another" (*DA*, 510).[52]

This use of free institutions to combat individualism, Tocqueville argues, is no accident. The American founders recognized that a political system resting on multiple layers of government—township, state, and federal—would engender broader and deeper bonds by forcing people to be constantly meeting and adapting themselves to the needs and affections of their fellow citizens.[53] For Tocqueville, this applies especially at the local level of politics, because participants in its face-to-face interactions can see close up that their neighbor is not so different from themselves. Thus divides between people can be bridged, or at least prevented from becoming deep and intractable. Individuals may even form the bonds of friendship that can so easily spur them to courageous deeds for the sake of others. Even the deep divide between the rich and poor can be lessened through free institutions. In sum,

> The free institutions of the United States and the political rights enjoyed there provide a thousand continual reminders to every citizen that he lives in society. At every moment they bring his mind back to this idea, that it is the duty as well as the interest of men to be useful to their fellows. Having no particular reason to hate others, since he is neither their slave nor their master, the American's heart easily inclines toward benevolence. At first it is of necessity that men attend to the public interest, afterward by choice. What had been calculation becomes instinct. (*DA*, 512)

What had been the rational calculation of self-interest, through participation in free institutions, descends to the level of instinct—the very level where other-interested courage resides.

A second antidote to unfettered individualism is civil associations, "those associations in civil life which have no political object. . . . There are not only commercial and industrial associations in which all take part, but others of a thousand different types—religious, moral, serious, futile, very general and very limited, immensely large and very minute. Americans combine to give fêtes, found seminaries, build churches, distribute books, and send missionaries to the antipodes" (*DA*, 512). By associations, then, Tocqueville has in mind those nodes where people gather—where people voluntarily emerge from their isolated individualism—to confederate for a particular undertaking. In the aristocratic world associations are not necessary because a few people, through their power and wealth, can simply make such undertakings happen. In democracy, however, individuals on their own cannot accomplish such momentous deeds and thus need associations. Individualism, which is inimical to manly courage, is countered by associational life. Citizens are drawn out of pure self-interest because of their inherent weakness in an egalitarian world.

Tocqueville is very clear on this point: "Among democratic peoples all the citizens are independent and weak. They can do hardly anything for themselves, and none of them is in a position to force his fellows to help him. They would all therefore find themselves helpless if they did not learn to help each other" (*DA*, 514).[54] In other words, in democracies people have the freedom to be individuals and the freedom to embrace individualism. Gone are those mysterious links between man and man that draw them together naturally and permit collaboration in glorious endeavors. Thus their civilization offers them freedom and the possibility of withdrawing into isolated individualism, but at the same time this withdrawal is the very thing that threatens their civilization. In America, where material self-interest is the underlying motivating force for human action, civil associations can, by mitigating self-interest, protect the world that enabled the pursuit of this self-interest in the first place. Citizens in a democracy must learn the art of associating because "if they did not learn some habits of acting together in the affairs of daily life, civilization itself would be in peril" (*DA*, 514).

Tocqueville's point here, however, is that Americans have acquired this habit of association. They are self-interested, but they see that self-interest, in and of itself, is corrosive. They see that their interest—their fundamental care for wealth—can best be served if it is a mitigated self-interest. Individualism in America is therefore combated, in Tocqueville's words, by the doctrine of self-interest properly understood. In the aristocratic world, this sort of self-love was combated by a different sort of morality. At the heart of this morality one finds the "sublime conception of the duties of man," and from these duties "it gratified [the aristocratic man] to make out that it is a glorious thing to forget oneself and that one should do good without self-interest, as God himself does" (*DA*, 525). Such a morality, however, no longer holds sway because to speak of the "beauties" of virtue one must invoke mysteries. These mysteries are for the most part inaccessible to the democratic mind, which perforce rejects the "supernatural" (*DA*, 403). After the democratic world has been disenchanted, all that is left is a general doctrine holding that "by serving his fellows man serves himself and that doing good is to his private advantage" (*DA*, 525). Put otherwise, one forgoes one's raw self-interest not for the sake of virtue but for the sake of a higher self-interest—self-interest properly understood: "American moralists do not pretend that one must sacrifice himself for his fellows because it is a fine thing to do so. But they boldly assert that such a sacrifice is as necessary for the man who makes it as for the beneficiaries" (*DA*, 525).[55]

Tocqueville admits that the doctrine is not new. It has gained a foothold in Europe, but it does not yet reign there. In Europe, virtue talk is still the predominant method for countering self-interest. But because talking about virtue no longer makes sense in America, self-interest properly understood lies at the heart of the moral framework. For Tocqueville this is hardly surprising because such a doctrine fits perfectly well with the pragmatic American mind. As he puts it, "Self-interest properly understood is not at all a sublime doctrine, but it is clear and definite. It does not attempt to reach great aims, but it does, without too much trouble, achieve all it sets out to do. Being within the scope of everybody's understanding, everyone grasps it and has no trouble in bearing it in mind. It is wonderfully agreeable to human weakness, and so easily wins great sway. It has no difficulty in keeping its power, for it turns private interest against itself and uses the same goad which excites them to direct passions" (*DA*, 527). It may not be sublime, but for Tocqueville it is the best theory available for a world in which ideas of equality are taking hold everywhere. So in America he sees a people who feverishly pursue their material interest but at the same time adhere to the doctrine of self-interest properly understood. That doctrine, which in and of itself is a rather subtle piece of rationality, stimulates the way of being that lies beneath the liminality of reason. The doctrine of self-interest properly understood turns the feverish pursuit of material interest into a courageous pursuit. By definition, daring endeavors that transcend personal interest are courageous. Economic avarice becomes economic courage because it is coupled with the doctrine of self-interest rightly understood.

So in both America and France Tocqueville saw an endemic love of material wealth. There was, however, a fundamental difference between the two: in France economic courage had not yet appeared. Whereas the American had partnered an instinct for economic courage with his rational pursuit of wealth, the Frenchman either remained entirely immersed in the enchanted and intuitive aristocratic world or migrated entirely into the rational. Thus Tocqueville saw greed but not heroism in France. Consequently he concluded that "it will always be very difficult for a European merchant to imitate his American counterpart. . . . In acting [heroically in industry], the American is not just working by calculation but rather is obeying an impulse of his nature" (*DA*, 403).

The Feminine Character of Economic Courage

Why can a European, which is to say, a person with one foot still in the world of martial courage and honor, not imitate American heroism in industry? To say, as we have just seen, that the American is "obeying an impulse of his nature" is not especially helpful. Is there something fundamentally different in the natures of the American and honor cultures? What is it about the America milieu that Tocqueville finds naturally different? To begin, one must be cautious about gleaning any proclamation regarding the nature of man from Tocqueville because, as already discussed, he thinks that only one fact can be stated about human nature: "The only stable point in the human heart . . . is self-interest" (*DA*, 239). But even here, he refers to the human heart, not specifically to the European or American heart. At bottom, humans are sociologically rather than biologically constituted.

For Tocqueville, three factors determine the structure of social relations: law, habits, and religion (*DA*, 286–87). Of these, the most superficial factor, the most easily changed, is law. To be sure, law influences human behavior. Often people do obey the law. Laws are more easily obeyed if they comport with habits, but even if they do not, people may be persuaded to change their behavior to comport with laws. Moreover, as any legislator, democratic or otherwise, could tell us, nothing is easier to change than a law. Changing the everyday habits, or, as Tocqueville is wont to call it, the mores (moeurs) of a people, is much more difficult. By *mores* Tocqueville means "the sum of the moral and intellectual dispositions of men in society" (*DA*, 305 n. 8).[56] Mores are an expression of the practical experiences, the habits, and the opinions of a people (*DA*, 308).[57] For example, enacting a compulsory seatbelt law is entirely different from actually getting people to buckle up. Mores run deeper than laws and are thus changed with much more difficulty.

According to Tocqueville, political mores and social customs have hidden causes. The hidden cause for the prevailing configuration of the laws and mores of America is the third factor—*religion*, which is deeper than either laws or mores. This is why he can state with confidence that "the great severity of mores which one notices in the United States has its primary origin in beliefs" (*DA*, 291). The question is the character of this belief. Many readers of *Democracy in America* assume that when Tocqueville uses the language of religion, he has in mind Christianity, whether Catholic or Protestant.[58] While this may be so, it is a mistake to think religion is coterminous with Christianity for Tocqueville. When he says "religion," he has a rather broad notion in mind. For example, when discussing what would best motivate a people to fight to protect their country, he claims that religion is "the main motive force" (*DA*, 94). In the next breath, however, he drops the language of religion and invokes the language of dogma: "For them the permanence, glory, and prosperity of the nation had become sacred dogmas" (*DA*, 94). Then he uses the example of Turkish people and the religion of Muhammad. The form of the religion, let alone the truth of the religion, is, at best, secondary for Tocqueville: "Though it is very important for man as an individual that his religion should be true, that is not the case for society. Society has nothing to fear or hope from another life; what is most important for it is not that all citizens should profess the true religion but that they should profess religion" (*DA*, 290). Later, when he is describing religion and democratic instincts, this becomes even more evident. Here he speaks in terms of "the usefulness of religions" and religious ceremonies in democratic countries (*DA*, 444).[59] Ceremonies, he says, ought to be limited in democracies "to such as are absolutely necessary to perpetuate dogma itself, *which is the essence of religions*" (*DA*, 447, emphasis added). A bit later, he claims that "when *any religion* has taken deep root in a democracy, be very careful not to shake it. . . . If it were absolutely necessary for a democracy to make the choice between one [religion of metempsychosis] or [materialism], I should not hesitate, and should think the citizens run less danger of reducing themselves to the level of brutes by thinking that their soul would pass into a pig's body than by believing that it is nothing" (*DA*, 544). The abundance of such sentiments in *Democracy in America* shows that the three factors determining the structure of social relations would more properly be referred to as law, mores, and dogma. Religion, understood as theology, is for Tocqueville simply part of mores or common opinion. This is precisely why he claims that "if one looks very closely into the matter, one finds that religion is strong less as a revealed doctrine than as part of common opinion" (*DA*, 436). Hence, three main points can be stated: first, sociologically speaking Tocqueville is unconcerned with theology; second, *religion* and *dogma* are nearly synonymous; and third, as will be explained presently, the sovereignty of the people is the primary and necessary dogma underlying American democratic society (*DA*, 433).[60]

So, why can the European not imitate American manly courage in industry? We now have a simple answer: they do not share the same dogma. America and Europe may share the same basic theological principles, but they do not share the same dogma. In America the fundamental and, we might even say, universal dogma is what Tocqueville calls "the dogma of the sovereignty of the people." On this point he is very direct: "In the United States the dogma of the sovereignty of the people is not an isolated doctrine, bearing no relation to the people's habits and prevailing ideas; on the contrary, one should see it as the last link in a chain of opinions which binds around the whole Anglo-American world" (*DA*, 397).[61] This doctrine penetrates deeply "into the ideas, the opinions, and all the habits of the Americans at the same time that it becomes established in their laws; and in order to change their laws, they would in a sense have to change the whole of themselves" (*DA*, 397). Thus to understand America, and, by the same token, to understand Europe in her relation to America, one must grasp this most basic factor lying at the bottom of the democratic heart. Nothing informs American mores and laws more than the dogma, the universally shared opinion, that all people are equal. The most basic belief is that no man or class of men has any natural right to preside over the affairs of other men. Tocqueville explicitly refers to this as "the dogma of equality."[62] When Tocqueville visited America, this dogma had not yet come to hold sway in Europe. Given what follows, it is safe to say that it still has not come to hold sway in the manifold honor cultures that persevere in the modern age.

For Tocqueville the dogma of the sovereignty of the people obtrudes not only in American political life but in American domestic life as well (*DA*, 291). The belief that no man or class of men has a natural right to preside over others politically shapes household affairs and the relations between the sexes, between husband and wife (*DA*, 12). Tocqueville even goes so far as to state that the dogma of equality "reigns supreme in the souls of the women" (*DA*, 291). Given the history of inequality endured by women, this is hardly surprising. Further, because this dogma of equality reigns supreme in the souls of women, Tocqueville is quite sure that in America "it is women who shape mores."

The centrality of this point for understanding Tocqueville's project cannot be overstated. It was the guiding principle for the first volume of *Democracy in America* and remained with him throughout the second: "There have never been free societies without mores, and as I observed in the first part of this book, it is woman who shapes these mores. Therefore everything which has a bearing on the status of women, their habits, and their thoughts is, in my view, of great political importance" (*DA*, 590).[63] The logic is clear: (1) dogma reigns supreme in women; (2) mores are derived from dogma; and (3) women are therefore responsible for mores.[64] Thus, if like Tocqueville we regard the predominant mores of American men as best characterized by an agitated and relentless quest for economic well-being, then we can draw a particular conclusion—these mores originate with women. And because women are responsible for the mores in America, it is not by coincidence that household management, or as the Greeks called it, *oikonomika*, replaces the *bios politikos*. In the Greek polis, to participate in political life meant to distinguish oneself through conspicuous speech and deeds. Pericles' funeral oration, for example, is a quintessential political act. Leonidas leading the Spartan Three Hundred at Thermopylae is another quintessential political act. In the same vein, Aristophanes' comedies and Plato's dialogues are quintessential political acts. In America, Tocqueville observes, men do not strive to distinguish themselves with conspicuous speech and deed. Instead, they feverishly throw themselves into "the important business of pinmaking," as Adam Smith puts it in his *Wealth of Nations*. The successful democratic man is no Achilles or Euripides; he is, instead, Christopher Newman, a manufacturer of washtubs, as so painfully described by Henry James in *The American*. In short, pursuing things pertaining to the household in the public sphere is what "makes" the democratic man. Politics becomes economics on a grand scale.[65]

In the eyes of an ancient Greek, or a typical French aristocrat, there is little to praise in this way of being. For Tocqueville, however, American men pursue their economic aims heroically, and this economic courage is the great strength of American mores. And because it is the women in America who determine social mores, their women must also be courageous. Save for a few historic anomalies, like Joan of Arc or Aisha, there are few instances in any time or place of feminine *andreia*, if I may be so bold to use such an oxymoron. We must go all the way back to Herodotus's marveling at the manly courage of Artemisia, or to Aristophanes' effort to include women as part of manly courage, to see similar efforts to create a vision of courage and courageous citizenship that includes women. For Tocqueville, there is little doubt that although women had not yet achieved legal equality with men in America, in terms of mores and dogma they certainly had. Hence Tocqueville's general claim about the virtues of American women: "If anyone asks me what I think the chief cause of the extraordinary prosperity and growing power of this nation, I should answer that it is due to the superiority of their women" (*DA*, 603).

The Limits of Economic Courage

What we find in the American context, then, is courage with a feminine character. It is an unmanned courage but not an unmanly courage. Because economic courage reveals a fundamental care for well-being, because it reveals contract and exchange as the predominant mode of articulation, and because this courage is available to women, it follows that the general social fabric will have something of a feminine character. Can we speak intelligently about the consequences of a feminine social fabric? There are many consequences of this development, some positive and some not so. First, and most obviously, women's sharing in the creation of the social fabric opens the way for their greater participation in society. This pertains not only to legal and political matters but also to moral matters. Let us recall for a moment what was stated earlier: because human beings find themselves most illustratively articulated (i.e., jointed together) in situations colored by courage, social relations with a feminine character will make it possible for women to enter the milieu in which courage appears. In the case of the American woman, as Tocqueville puts it, "the vices and dangers of society are soon plain to her, and seeing them clearly, she judges them without illusion and faces them without fear, for she is full of confidence in her own powers, and it seems that this feeling is shared by all around her" (*DA*, 590). In other words, courage ceases to be the exclusive domain of men. Women can not only participate in the social articulation but also partake of the existentially revelatory character of courage.

To be sure, some object to Tocqueville's claims about American women.[66] How, for example, can he claim that women are equal when they clearly do not participate in the political sphere in the same capacity and to the same extent as the men? How can a feminine democracy and unmanned courage be reconciled with Tocqueville's own admission that "in America inexorable public opinion carefully keeps woman within the little sphere of domestic interests and duties and will not let her go beyond them" (*DA*, 592)? Tocqueville's answer to this is plain: there is little, if any, difference between the public and the private realms. Economics is merely household management on a grand scale.

Generally speaking, however, Tocqueville's interpreters argue the opposite. According to Allan Bloom, for instance, Tocqueville considers the household to be quite separate from the public domain.[67] The function of women and the private realm is to attenuate the passions and the corrosive, self-interested quality of men's activities in the public realm. Bloom is correct, but it is also true that in the private realm of the household American women, through the regularity of their habits and morals, play the role of tempering and legitimating the democratic passions. The business inside the house and outside the house is the same, and in both realms the aim is the expedient and efficacious accumulation of wealth. Like Bloom, Delba Winthrop considers the private and public realms to be distinct from each other in Tocqueville's thought. American public society, she claims, is portrayed as inauthentic in comparison to the private, so that "women have little or nothing to gain from coming out into it" and, "because they take no part in public life . . . are more likely to embody democracy's finer aspirations."[68] Here again, however, if it were true that the public and private realms mirrored each other and were founded on the same principles, then both realms would be inauthentic or neither.

Tocqueville's position on the authenticity of the public and private realms is somewhat difficult to determine. But given that for Tocqueville "the dogma of equality reigns supreme in women," and given that "no novelty in the United States struck [Tocqueville] more vividly . . . than the equality of conditions" (*DA*, 9), there must be a closer kinship between the public and private than commentators like Bloom and Winthrop recognize. This is the position taken by Jean Bethke Elshtain, who argues that "Tocqueville's most interesting contribution to an understanding of the public and private resides not so much in his gloss on the virtues of American womanhood, but in his insight that domestic institutions, in some way, mesh with or reflect the higher political order."[69] The more pressing question, however, is whether, for Tocqueville, public institutions determine domestic order, or domestic institutions determine public order. While Elshtain is right to argue that no great disjuncture separates the public and private, she mistakenly argues that for Tocqueville public order flows into the private realm. In fact, he suggests the reverse: that the nature of the public order is shaped by the ordering principle of the household.

Tocqueville never explicitly states this in *Democracy in America*, but he does employ a metaphor that supports this claim. At the outset, in what might be called his discussion of political geography, Tocqueville envisions the continent before the arrival of the Europeans. He regards America at that time as an "empty cradle of a great nation" (*DA*, 30). He means that, although the natives already occupied the land, it was empty of ideology: in other words, it was not yet determined whether the dogma of equality or the dogma of inequality would be nursed in the cradle. We already know Tocqueville's story. The dogma of equality was put into the cradle, and it now pervades American society. The question of whether the household influences the public realm or vice versa is answered in Tocqueville's second use of the cradle metaphor: "Go back; look at the baby in his mother's arms; see how the outside world is first reflected in the still hazy mirror of his mind; consider the first examples that strike his attention; listen to the first words which awaken his dormant powers of thought; and finally take notice of the first struggles he has to endure. Only then will you understand the origin of the prejudices, habits, and passions which are to dominate his life. *The whole man is there, if one may put it so, in the cradle*" (*DA*, 31). In short, the mother inculcates the child with the prevailing mores in the household. In America then, the mother, in whose soul the dogma of equality reigns supreme, makes the man and consequently the larger structure of social relations.[70]

Thus Tocqueville rightly saw the door open for women to participate in the American way of life. Because the dogma of equality had so thoroughly suffused the soul of the American woman, it is not too far-fetched to state, not only that she opened the door herself, but also that she built it. That she chose not to walk through it had more to do with the ethos of economic efficacy than with male oppression. Tocqueville thinks that the American woman, through the exercise of her reason, recognizes that although she is morally equal to men, intrinsic differences make her more suited to certain roles in the pursuit of wealth.[71] In other words, she courageously sacrifices herself for the greater good. The interest of the economy (properly understood) and of the family (properly understood) is better served if women engage in domestic tasks of the household while men engage in domestic tasks writ large. Thus Tocqueville argues that "the Americans do not think that man and woman have the duty or the right to do the same things, but they show an equal regard for the part played by both and think of them as beings of equal worth, though their fates are different. They do not expect courage of the same sort or for the same purposes from woman as from man, *but they never question her courage*" (*DA*, 603; emphasis added). Were the relations of American society articulated by martial courage, this could never be said. But because American society has a feminine character, and because the women have determined its mores, all of society is open to whosoever possesses economic courage.

The second main consequence of Tocqueville's feminine democracy is also positive. When a community is articulated by economic courage, the prospect for peace is greatly increased. Relations between men and women, and between all people, for that matter, are established not by the demands of violence but by contract and exchange: "The ever increasing number of men of property devoted to peace, the growth of personal property which war so rapidly devours, mildness of mores, gentleness of heart, that inclination to pity which equality inspires, that cold and calculating spirit which leave little room for sensitivity to the poetic and violent emotions of wartime—all these causes act together to damp down the warlike fervor" (*DA*, 646).[72] Put otherwise, the threat to self-interest that we find in a community articulated by violence is attenuated in a community articulated by contract and exchange. Economic courage serves material interest, whereas martial courage destroys it. As Tocqueville eloquently puts it, "Trade is the natural enemy of all violent passion. Trade loves moderation, delights in compromise, and is most careful to avoid danger" (*DA*, 637). He does not, of course, mean that trade avoids all risk to life and limb. We have already seen Tocqueville's portrayal of the intrepid commercial spirit in America. But trade avoids dangers to material well-being. In effect, danger is acceptable insofar as it is confined to the individual and is unacceptable if it threatens the social fabric that permits the orderly and constant pursuit of wealth. This is why Tocqueville explicitly claims that "violent political passions have little hold on men whose whole thoughts are bent on the pursuit of well-being. Their excitement about small matters makes them calm about great ones" (*DA*, 638). Thus democratic man, with his economic courage, is inclined to love peace, and this is a great benefit to America that fits very well with Tocqueville's view of human community: "In this fortunate country, nothing attracts the restlessness of the human spirit toward political passions. . . . Nothing is easier than becoming rich in America; naturally, the human spirit, which needs a dominant passion, in the end turns all its thoughts toward gain."[73]

There is a hint of irony in this statement. Democracy is inclined to peace, but for the sake of "little undertakings." Tocqueville does not regard this as an altogether good thing because "war is a hazard to which all nations are subject, democracies as well as the rest. No matter how greatly such nations may be devoted to peace, they must be ready to defend themselves if attacked, or in other words, they must have an army" (*DA*, 646). Even a peaceful democratic regime must maintain an army, and men are needed to fulfill this role. Yet in democracies, where people desire wealth above all else, it is difficult to recruit the best men into the army. As Tocqueville says, "In democracies the richest, best-educated, and ablest citizens hardly ever adopt a military career" (*DA*, 648). Those who readily join are often those "with a lower standard of intelligence and rougher habits than the nation at large" (*DA*, 648). Thus the army becomes a "little uncivilized nation [that] holds the weapons and it alone knows how to use them" (*DA*, 649). As violence declines in the larger culture, so does the knowledge of how to control and limit violence. In other words, the army, inadequately restrained, poses a threat to the larger society whose interests it is supposed to protect:

> The danger from the turbulent and warlike spirit of the army is actually increased in democracies by the pacific temper of the citizens. There is nothing more dangerous than an army amid an unwarlike

> nation. The citizens' excessive love of quiet puts the constitution every day at the mercy of the soldiers.
>
> One can therefore make this generalization, that although their interests and inclinations naturally incline democracies to peace, their armies exercise a constant pull toward war and revolution.
>
> Military revolutions, which are hardly ever a serious threat in aristocracies, are always to be feared in democracies. They should be reckoned among the most threatening of the perils which face their future existence. Statesmen must never relax their efforts to find a remedy for this evil. (*DA*, 649)

In short, when violence is not practiced in the public realm, there is no education or practical experience for limiting it.[74]

When forced into war, however, a democratic people, armed with their economic courage, will fight like no other. As Tocqueville writes, "War, having destroyed every industry, in the end becomes itself the one great industry, and every eager and ambitious desire sprung from equality is focused on it. For that reason those same democratic nations which are so hard to drag on to the battlefield sometimes perform prodigious feats once one has succeeded in putting arms in their hands" (*DA*, 646). It is unclear here if "prodigious" means prodigious in honor or in scope. Certainly such a nation will be capable of mustering great effort against the injustices of other great foes, but at the same time there will be little to limit the excessive use of force against weaker foes. The problem here, then, is not necessarily the army (although their monopoly on arms is problematic), but the instincts of the people who compose it. Tocqueville suggests that the same desires will exist in the military as in the larger democratic society: the less intelligent and coarser people composing the army will desire reputation, power, and above all, wealth. "The same restless spirit which prevails in the civil life of a democracy is seen in the army too; what men want is not a certain rank, but constant promotion" (*DA*, 650). In civilian life this desire leads to a desire for peace, but in army life it inspires the desire for war, since in war promotions are more readily obtained. Thus Tocqueville strangely concludes that "of all armies those which long for war most ardently are the democratic ones, but that of all peoples those most deeply attached to peace are the democratic nations. And the most extraordinary thing about the whole matter is that it is equality which is responsible for both these contradictory results" (*DA*, 647).

Finally, it must be asked: Does the unmanning of courage present a threat to the long-term strength and stability of democratic regimes? Tocqueville thinks it may, but not because of a lack of virtue or an inordinate desire for power among the officer class, as Hobbes or Nietzsche might argue. Instead, the threat comes from a different source. War, Tocqueville says, does not inevitably lead democratic governments in the direction of military regimes, "but it must invariably and immeasurably increase the powers of civil government; it must almost automatically concentrate the direction of all men and the control of all things in the hands of the government. If that does not lead to despotism by sudden violence, it leads men gently in that direction by their habits. All those who seek to destroy the freedom of the democratic nations must know that war is the surest and shortest means to accomplish this" (*DA*, 650). In other words, war necessarily causes power to be focused in the central government, much to the detriment of local bodies of power. As a result, the courage and the mode of articulation—economic courage and exchange—that Tocqueville sees as essential to the successful American democratic experiment may undermine itself.[75]

SIX

The Aftermath

The ancients had heroes and put men on their stages; we, on the contrary, put only heroes on the stage and hardly have any men.

—Jean-Jacques Rousseau, *Politics and the Arts: Letter to M. d'Alembert on the Theatre*

Taking Measure

In the beginning, it was said that man is nothing other than what he makes of himself and that nothing is more difficult to make than a courageous man. We have now marched through nearly two and a half millennia of human beings doing precisely this—making themselves courageous. The standard was set by the heroes of the ancient world. The Spartans made courageous men through the most arduous physical and psychological training imaginable. They transmogrified and incorporated the audacity of the singular Homeric hero into their own self-sacrificing Spartan knight. As a result, manly courage came to be bound up with the willingness to set aside self-interest for the sake of Sparta. This "for the sake of Sparta," however, was not without limits. Self-interest was set aside, not for the sake of Spartan wealth or liberty, but for Spartan honor. This was the great Spartan accomplishment. Courage, manliness, and good citizenship came to be associated with Spartan honor. The individual's capacity to subordinate his own love of honor and victory to the honor of the community became the measure of courage: not fighting skill and fearlessness but the willingness to hold one's place in the phalanx. The courageous man was he who could, and would, risk life and limb for the sake of the man fighting to his left, regardless of his blood relation. Courage was, at bottom, measured by one's concern for others.

To this day we speak of soldiers making the "ultimate sacrifice." A certain awe and respect is still afforded to the courageous soldier and to martial courage in general. It matters little whether the soldier survives the battle. Courage elevates the soldier above the general run of mankind. He accomplishes the most difficult of tasks—willingly risking life and limb for the sake of something transcending his own immediate self-interest. In the final measure, then, there is something about this way of being that is deeply attractive. Whether it is the ability to transcend the intense desire for self-preservation or the emergence of the deep bonds of friendship and social solidarity, martial courage is axiomatically good and worth emulation. When all is said and done, to be courageous and unselfish is a good thing.

As it happens, courage is bound up with manliness. Thus when we regard the soldier and the difficult trials he has navigated, we often wonder how we would stand in such circumstances. Would we have the heart to disregard our desire for self-preservation? Could we risk life and limb unselfishly? Could we make ourselves courageous? Because martial courage is axiomatically good, we may ask ourselves how we might measure up to the soldier's courage and manliness. Forgoing self-preservation, however, is not the exclusive domain of men. To measure courage by the dichotomous categories of manly and unmanly, male and female, is therefore problematic. There is no good reason to think men and women alike cannot risk life and limb for the sake of something transcending themselves. In other words, while courage may be bound up with manliness, it is not inseparable from men. Measuring ourselves, then, is not an exact science. Courage is a good, but the good of courage must be obtained outside precise measure, dichotomous or otherwise. This immeasurability of courage, of course, does not stop us from pursuing the question. In fact, that it has an enduring appeal, and that it is persistently held up as the mark of a good citizen, forces certain questions on us. Courage impels us to ask not only "What is a good man?" but an even more rudimentary question: "What does it mean to be human?"

The question yields this answer: to be human is to find oneself amid a community of care. To be a courageous human being is to participate selflessly in a community of care. Put otherwise, questioning the immeasurable reveals what we make of ourselves in our comportment with other human beings and the world in which we find ourselves. Courage reveals the ground of our collective lives. Yet just as questioning courage is an inquiry into political life, it also brings to light deeply divergent communities of care. These divergent cares are precisely what this book pursues. We have found that although courage is almost always considered an abiding human good, and that although humans almost always endeavor to be courageous, the martially courageous man is not always considered the paragon of courage. The politically courageous, the morally courageous, or the economically courageous person may also exemplify the quintessence of courage. Because martial courage and honor are not without problems, there is no reason to regard justice, freedom, or well-being as inherently inferior to honor as the measure of good human community. If, however, the pursuit of any care can be axiomatically good, then to be human is to participate in any community of care. If one care is as good as another, cares cease to be fundamental cares; if they cease to be fundamental cares, then it is no longer helpful to talk about courage. People risk life and limb for fundamental cares, not just any care; and courage reveals these fundamental cares.

The Limits of Courage

Is it not possible, then, to have more than one fundamental care? Can one not muster one's courage for a plurality of cares? On the surface, it would seem so. Tocqueville's cares are certainly manifold, and it is difficult to think of Rousseau as wholly unconcerned with justice. Similarly, while the Spartans fought for honor, the possibility of being enslaved has always been a strong impetus to courage. Homer's heroes, while pursuing everlasting glory, rarely missed a chance to accumulate the material spoils of war. Even today, American Marines fight for liberty while holding firmly to their "Death before dishonor" creed. But while it is surely possible to have diverse cares, I would argue that it is not possible to hold, simultaneously, diverse fundamental cares.

For example, while Tocqueville's cares are manifold, his fundamental care is not. In March of 1837, just a couple years after the publication of the second volume of *Democracy in America*, Tocqueville wrote to Henry Reeve: "I have only one passion, the love of liberty and human dignity. All forms of government are in my eyes only more or less perfect ways of satisfying this holy and legitimate passion of man."[1] Tocqueville is revealing that as a young man his *ne plus ultra* good was liberty. This fundamental care, however, was no fleeting fancy. To Madame Swetchine nearly twenty years later he wrote: "As always, I consider freedom to be the greatest of goods. I still see freedom as one of the most fertile sources of manly virtues and great actions."[2] So, it appears that liberty is his abiding fundamental care. However, we have seen that Tocqueville was at least willing to tip his hat to economic courage and the heroic pursuit of wealth. His partiality for martial courage and honor is also evident, and he obviously cares about justice. For example, he says that in the modern age there are those "whose object is to make men materialists, to find out what is useful without concern for justice, to have science quite without belief and prosperity without virtue. Such men are called champions of modern civilization, and they insolently put themselves at its head, usurping a place which has been abandoned to them, though they are utterly unworthy of it."[3] Examples like this are numerous in Tocqueville's work and they indicate that we ought to care about justice. His references to justice, however, do not typically portray it as a *ne plus ultra* good. He refers to the good of justice either in the abstract, as when he mentions "offenses which human justice can neither define nor judge,"[4] or in the context of its use in the pursuit of liberty: "The great object of justice is to substitute the idea of right for that of violence, to put intermediaries between the government and the use of its physical force."[5] In short, Tocqueville cares for justice because, as few would deny, it is good. Justice, however, does not elicit the language of courage from Tocqueville. It is an important care but not his fundamental one.

Much the same can be said about honor. As the preceding chapter made clear, honor has an important place in Tocqueville's view of the world, but it is not his fundamental care. While honor can be a good thing, the violence bound up with honor cultures gives Tocqueville serious pause. In Appendix I of *Democracy in America* Tocqueville describes a culture based on honor, the Iroquois nation, and invokes the story of Champlain's experience with these honorable people: Champlain, he writes, "lived alone for a whole winter with these barbarians without a moment's risk to his person or to his property."[6] Iroquois honor is remarkable because it respects the ancient laws of hospitality. However, Tocqueville also describes the Iroquois as "barbarians" and quotes Charlevoix's description of their practice of scalping captured enemies: "As soon as they saw their village's huts, they cut long poles and fixed the scalps they had shared as booty to them, carrying them in triumph. At sight of this the women came running up, jumped into the water, and swam to the canoes; they then took the bleeding scalps from their husbands' hands and hung them around their necks."[7] While honor is a good thing when it secures the liberty of one's person and property, the barbarity of its attendant violence rules it out as Tocqueville's fundamental care.

There is little doubt, then, that Tocqueville's fundamental care is singular: liberty. It was his singular passion while writing *Democracy in America*, and it remained his *ne plus ultra* good right to the end of his life. That it was not merely one care among others is evidenced by Tocqueville's language describing liberty. In a letter to Eugène Stoffels (July 24, 1836) he says, "I have always loved freedom instinctively, and all my reflections lead me to believe that no moral and political greatness is possible for long without it. I am therefore as strongly attached to freedom as to morality, and I am ready to lose some of my tranquility to achieve it."[8] For Tocqueville, "peace and tranquility" are synonymous and stand in contrast to "war and agitation." For the sake of liberty, then, he is willing to lose some of his tranquility; he is willing to stand courageously. For Tocqueville, it is the care toward which "manly virtues and great action" should be directed. It is the care for which he is willing to risk life and limb.

To claim that Tocqueville's fundamental care is singular, however, does not yet establish that it is universally impossible to be, say, politically courageous *and* martially courageous. Socrates, for instance, was known for both his martial and political courage. The "evidence" for his courage is that during the rout at Delium he did not retreat too quickly, that he could endure the privations of a campaign better than others, and that at Potidaea he walked barefoot on the frost after a particularly cold night.[9] Even if we accept these stories as evidence of courage, there is still no compelling reason to conclude that Socrates showed courage at either Delium or Potidaea for the sake of honor. If the laws of one's city demand that one go to war, one might just as well hold one's place in the line for the sake of justice as for the sake of honor. This is the argument Socrates proffers in *Crito* for not fleeing his death sentence. The immutable justice of the laws trumps the opinion of the many, which is the basis of honor. As fundamental cares, then, justice and honor cannot be held simultaneously.

And this is not merely a problem of logic. It may well be too much to ask of the human mind to risk life and limb for two fundamental cares simultaneously. It is possible, however, to imagine a young man loving victory and honor but, when mature, developing a new care. The thirty-year-old Socrates in Aristophanes' *Clouds* is certainly different from the sixty-nine-year-old Socrates in Plato's *Crito* and *Phaedo.* Granted, Aristophanes and Plato employ a different Socrates for different dramatic purposes, but even the most ardent defender of Socrates can agree that while the young Socrates may have been Aristophanic, he matured. In Platonic terms, Socrates' transformation from Sophist to philosopher is like the prisoner's emergence from the cave. In other words, fundamental cares can change. One can be both martially courageous and politically courageous, but not at the same time.

If one can be martially courageous in one's youth and, say, politically courageous in maturity, can one have different fundamental cares closer in time? For example, can one be martially courageous in the morning, economically courageous in the afternoon, and politically courageous in the evening? Plato presents such a scenario with his description of the democratic man in *The Republic*, book 8. This man, Plato writes, "lives his life day by day, indulging each appetite as it makes itself felt. . . . Sometimes he seems to want to be the philosopher. More frequently, he goes in for politics, rising to say or do whatever comes into his head. If he develops an enthusiasm for military men, he rushes to join them; if for businessmen, then he is off in that direction."[10] Plato's point, however, is that this sort of person has no fundamental cares. Courage, we will recall, involves a certain steadfastness of the soul. It involves a resoluteness and orderliness in one's life. The type of person he describes here is just the opposite. As Plato puts it, "His life lacks all discipline and order, yet he calls it a life of pleasure, freedom, and happiness and is resolved to stay the course."[11] He is not standing courageously for a care that cuts to the heart of his existence, nor is he standing for that which defines his community. The existentially revelatory character of courage is missing precisely because his cares come and go arbitrarily.

What this might reveal, however, is the possibility of caring fundamentally about holding multiple fundamental cares. As Plato puts it, this is the sort of "man who insists on subjecting everything to the rule of equality," including the cares that give shape to community.[12] What might invoke bellicose language is not a particular fundamental care but a way of life that regards every care as fundamental, should one so choose. Thus the good citizen is not measured by his or her capacity to stand courageously for honor, justice, autonomy, or wealth; rather, he is "the one who displays the greatest diversity in personal qualities and lifestyles."[13] While it seems that this democratic soul loves liberty, the reality is that he loves choice. The freedom to choose requires that he not be inhibited in pursuing his own lifestyle by another standing courageously for her own fundamental care. All cares, after all, are fundamental. Thus when we speak of caring fundamentally about having multiple fundamental cares we are ultimately talking about a way of being that abhors the need to stand courageously for the sake of any care. In other words, caring fundamentally about having multiple fundamental cares is really a desire to be free of all threats to one's own cares, no matter how arbitrary they might be. The desire to live free of all threats, of course, is a pithy description of cowardice.

If there were nothing to fear in the world, there would be no need to make courageous men and women of ourselves. Without conflict, the difficult task of making ourselves courageous can be replaced with making whatever we want of ourselves. This mirrors the utopian view of history and the world given by Karl Marx and Friedrich Engels. For Marx, the "history of all mankind hitherto is a history of class conflict."[14] In the age of capitalism the conflict is between the workers and the owners of the means of production. If these nodes of conflict are generalized, then one can reinterpret Marx's philosophy of history: the history of all mankind hitherto is a conflict between the owners of the means of violence and those unable, or unwilling, to make themselves into mechanics of violence. Therefore, to overcome a history of conflict, it is necessary to allow everyone a portion of the means of violence and either (1) hope for a détente based on some sort of philosophical-psychological program of Mutually Assured Destruction or (2) hope that everyone's portion will be too small to enable them to pursue a fundamental care. In other words, the equal distribution of the means of violence also means the equal distribution of honor, justice, freedom, and wealth. If these are equally distributed, there will be no need to make courageous men of ourselves.

This utopian vision also characterizes Marx and Engels' view of the end of history. At the end of history, when communism flowers, a man will no longer have "exclusive spheres of activity" forced on him "from which he cannot escape." One will not need to commit oneself to any particular care, and one will certainly not need to risk life and limb for any "exclusive sphere." In fact, in a communist system, where radical egalitarianism pertains not only to classes but also to "lifestyles," it is "possible for me to do one thing today and another tomorrow, to hunt in the morning, fish in the afternoon, rear cattle in the evening, criticise after dinner, just as I have a mind, without ever becoming hunter, fisherman, shepherd, or critic."[15] In other words, one can do what honor lovers do (hunt) and do what justice lovers do (philosophize), but not have these spheres of activity intrude on one's own identity-crafting project. Fundamental cares thus come to be called "preferences," and certain "ways of being" become whimsical lifestyles. In this utopian vision, we can all live carefree lifestyles.

Having No Measure

What does it mean to be carefree? It means to care about nothing enough to risk life and limb for its sake. This is not the same as being unable to risk life and limb. If one cares about something but is unable to muster the courage to stand firm for it, then one is a coward. But to care about nothing, to have nothing in one's life that might inspire one to risk life and limb, is something different. To have no fundamental care is nihilism. Nihilism itself has a long history, but its story is told most vividly by Nietzsche.[16] For Nietzsche, there are actually two kinds of nihilism: passive and active. Active nihilism is "a sign of increased power of the spirit."[17] With this disposition, the "spirit may have grown so strong that previous goals ('convictions,' articles of faith) have become incommensurate."[18] One might even say that previous fundamental cares are overturned by active nihilism, and this is why active nihilism "reaches its maximum of relative strength as a violent force of destruction."[19] For Nietzsche at least, this is a healthy disposition. Passive nihilism, on the other hand, is pathological. It is a "decline and recession of the power of the spirit." The passive nihilist, like the coward, is "hindered from moving forward."[20] Fundamental cares simply have no value for this nihilist. There are no *ne plus ultra* aims and, in general,

> a feeling of valuelessness [is] reached from the realization that the overall character of existence may not be interpreted by means of the concept of "aim," the concept of "unity," or the concept of "truth." Existence has no goal or end; any comprehensive unity in the plurality of events is lacking: the character of existence is not "true," is false. One simply lacks any reason for convincing oneself that there is a true world. Briefly: the categories of "aim," "unity," "being" which we used to project some value into the world—we pull out again; so the world looks valueless.[21]

In short, for the passive nihilist nothing is worthy of risking life and limb. The three categories that encapsulate the good of courage seem to have no worth. The aim of one's fighting unit, for example, seems to be without worth. The unity, camaraderie, and sense of belonging are absent, and the good of participating in a mode of existence that transcends the finitude of one's personal being is not evident. Courage illuminates the shared aim of one's community, opens the way to feelings of solidarity and meaningful friendships transcending the individual, and, in the end, tells us who we are. Aim, unity, and being are deeply appealing and call out to us. The passive nihilist, however, fails to hear this call. Or better, the passive nihilist lacks the wherewithal to hear this call because it takes courage to respond to the demands of aim, unity, and being.

Missing Courage

This study has considered various ways humans make themselves courageous, but an important question remains: Are types of courage missing from it? Can we imagine a courage aiming at a fundamental care distinct from honor, justice, freedom, or wealth? The answer to this is obvious. Many people have risked life and limb for cares that fall outside one of these descriptions. After all, these interpretations of courage and fundamental cares are taken exclusively from Western texts. The non-Western canon is replete with stories of courage, martial exploits, and philosophical discussions of man and war. Take, for example, the *Bhagavad Gita.* The *Gita* is a sacred Hindu scripture that tells the story of a conversation between the divine Lord Krishna and Prince Arjuna on the eve of the Kurukshetra War. Krishna is advising Arjuna about his duties as a prince, a warrior, and a man. On the surface, the *Gita* can be understood in terms of martial courage and honor, but this interpretation would becloud an unfamiliar fundamental care.[22] Gandhi, for instance, read the *Gita* as an allegory of the battle between good and evil in the human soul and concluded that the truly courageous man should aspire, not to physical honor and victory, but to *karmayoga*, the full realization of the self.[23] In this view it is possible to parallel courage with nonviolence (ahimsa)—a courage that has truth as its *ne plus ultra* good.[24] What is meant by *karmayoga* and *ahimsa* is beyond the scope of this discussion; however, it is clear that invoking courage as an interpretive lens in non-Western traditions can reveal hitherto unfamiliar fundamental cares.

Have types of courage and fundamental cares within the West been omitted from this study? One might pursue such a question empirically and simply ask people for what they might be willing to risk life and limb. If one asked young college students today, one might first be met with stares of incomprehension; few students have heard the call of courage. This is a generation, after all, that has been car-seated, seat-belted, bike-helmeted, padded, and protected from their earliest days. This is not to say that the youth today are nihilists and cowards, but that they are products of their time.[25] Some, however, have a ready answer. A few Spartan souls, often ROTC students, will flatly state their willingness to die for their country. When they are pressed, it becomes obvious that for them "country" is the symbolic marker for a love of liberty. In the abstract, they profess a fundamental care for liberty, but their warrior instincts are little, if any, different from those of the Spartan—*Kriegsbruderlichkeit* and honor will keep them in the line in the heat of battle.

That American students, ROTC or not, love freedom is not surprising, nor is it surprising when many more profess a willingness to risk life and limb for the sake of a boyfriend, a girlfriend, a best friend, or a family member. This kind of courage, after all, is no more American than Spartan but part of the universal human experience. When we think of our willingness to risk life and limb for our children, for example, we are talking about this kind of courage. We will risk life and limb for no other reason than the love we have for our children. We will risk life and limb for boyfriends or girlfriends because we love them. In some ways this courage parallels martial courage. In the heat of battle, it is the love a warrior has for his brothers in arms that keeps him in the line. There is, however, an important distinction. The love between soldiers is forged; it is learned in basic training and plays itself out in battle. This love is predicated on what soldiers *do* together. They train together, march together, fight together, and sometimes die together. Of course, in this milieu friendships characterized by other kinds of love develop, but the relationship between soldiers *qua* soldiers is replaceable. The whole point of the phalanx, for example, was to transform the basis of the warriors' relationships from who one *is* to what one *does*. It is not one's brother next to whom one fights in the line, but one's brother in arms. Should he fall and be replaced by the man behind him in the ranks, one's commitment to the replacement remains the same. We love our daughter, however, for who she *is*. If she dies, another child cannot step forward to replace her. Even a perfect genetic clone does not replace what has been lost. With the loss of the child, the central element eliciting both our love and our courage is also lost. Courage is mustered because we love another simply for being who he or she is. This courage for the sake of love is therefore existential.

Existential courage has two general variants: religious and nonreligious. For the religious variant, Christianity and Christian love is a good example. For Christians, God is love (1 John 4:8). In fact, one can go so far as to say that for Christians all existence is love.[26] Religious existential courage is therefore risking life and limb for the sake of God. Some might point to the early martyrs as good examples of this courage. Martyrdom, whether exemplified by a Christian roasting in a brazen bull or by a zealous suicide bomber, is by definition not courage. If one is certain that one is going to die, then one's actions cannot be characterized as risking life and limb and are thus not courageous. They may be inspiring, but they are not courageous. There are, of course, good examples of melding manly courage with Christian principles. A vivid example can be found with the Crusaders. Bernard of Clairvaux's description of the Knights Templar illustrates this type of courage:

> The knight of Christ, I say, may strike with confidence and die yet more confidently, for he serves Christ when he strikes, and serves himself when he falls. Neither does he bear the sword in vain, for he is God's minister, for the punishment of evildoers and for the praise of the good. If he kills an evildoer, he is not a mankiller, but, if I may so put it, a killer of evil. He is evidently the avenger of Christ towards evildoers and he is rightly considered a defender of Christians. Should he be killed himself, we know that he has not perished, but has come safely into port. When he inflicts death it is to Christ's profit, and when he suffers death, it is for his own gain. The Christian glories in the death of the pagan, because Christ is glorified.[27]

Like martial courage, this type of courage is often couched in terms of honor and glory, but it is for the honor or glory of God. The Christian variant of existential courage can thus be understood as a subordination of the individual's will to a higher cause. We saw a similar phenomenon with martial courage in Sparta: the individual's desire for honor was subordinated to the collective Spartan honor. In both cases, courage allows the individual to transcend his own finite being by risking life and limb for a greater good. In the Christian case it is for God or, in Augustine's language, the City of God.[28]

Existential courage can also be regarded in a nonreligious way. Paul Tillich says this courage "is the self-affirmation of being in spite of the fact of nonbeing."[29] This stands in contrast to the Christian view of the world in which God is the cause of all being. Insofar as God causes all being, all being is good. The evil in the world is not a consequence of God's creation. Instead, evil is the absence of being, or the absence of good. Nonbeing simply does not have an ontological status in the same way as being, or good; it is not merely the opposite of being.[30] To give it this status would be Manichaeism, against which Augustine so valiantly fought. But in the nonreligious form of existential courage, nonbeing obtains a radically different status. Regarding this form for existential courage, Paul Tillich suggests that "nonbeing is not a concept like others. It is the negation of every concept; but as such it is an inescapable content of thought and, as the history of thought has shown, the most important one after being-itself."[31] Whereas religious existential courage takes its bearings from Being, the concept of nonbeing lies at the heart of nonreligious existential courage.

One can point to Nietzsche as the father of this neo-Manichaeism. In his first book, *The Birth of Tragedy*, Nietzsche likens nonbeing to an abyss. For Nietzsche, the world in which we exist, the world of human life, is full of suffering. The usual response to suffering in the world is to retreat to another world, a higher world, for meaning. In other words, the response to "the abyss of being [dem Abgrunde des Seins]" is to imbue it with meaning by positing God, heaven, and the afterlife.[32] For Nietzsche, this is existential cowardice and is pathological. Human beings ought to live courageously in the face of what he calls the "horror or absurdity of existence."[33] They ought to look into "the deepest abyss of being" and affirm life.[34] Existential courage is thus saying yes to existence despite the horror and absurdity. The existentially courageous person stands firm in the face of the abyss and professes his love for all being, including the meaninglessness, the suffering, and the abyss. As Nietzsche puts it in *Thus Spoke Zarathustra*, "Courage also destroys giddiness at abysses: and where does man not stand at an abyss? Is seeing itself not—seeing abysses?"[35] Existential courage allows one to love existence and to create meaning without recurring to some God, or some divine ground. It allows joy and laughter in this life without depending on an afterlife. It allows one to look directly into the abyss and say joyfully, "Was *that* life? Well then! Once more!"[36]

Another variant of existential courage can be seen in the work of Martin Heidegger. What Nietzsche calls the abyss Heidegger more pointedly calls *das Nicht* (the nothing). Heidegger, however, uses different language for the relationship humans have toward *das Nicht.* Like the courage that Nietzsche envisions, but unlike the courage we have already discussed, existential courage is not about overcoming fear of physical harm but about overcoming "existential fear." Heidegger calls this existential fear "anxiety" (Angst).[37] Whereas with, say, martial courage, one risks one's life and limb for the sake of honor, existential courage is overcoming the anxiety one has in the face of the Nothing that stands at the heart of all existence. In other words, while the types of courage discussed above are almost always bound up with some vision of God and an afterlife, nonreligious existential courage demands a way of life where, besides living in the world among other beings, one must accept that there is Nothing. As Heidegger explains, our world consists of "beings only, and besides that nothing; being alone, and further—nothing; solely beings, and beyond that—nothing."[38] Neither God nor immortality stands as the basis of courage. This is precisely why anxiety should not be confused with fear, which always has an entity as its object, an entity that can be identified, that one can put one's finger on, so to speak.[39] Thus, whereas fear is determinate, anxiety is indeterminate. It is impossible to determine the object of anxiety because the Nothing is not an object. Instead, "one feels ill at ease [es ist einem unheimlich]."[40] One feels not-at-home. One is anxious about something on which one can get no hold. As Heidegger puts it, "Anxiety reveals the nothing. We 'hover' in anxiety."[41]

For Heidegger, existential courage is a healthy reaction to this anxiety. Courage is not what we do in the face of an enemy physically threatening us but how we react to the groundlessness of our existence. Like the Spartan warrior, we have two options: standing resolutely or fleeing. In this case, fleeing (Flucht) is not physically running away but recoiling into a way of life that refuses to confront the hard fact that besides beings there is nothing. It is falling back into the average everyday way of a being in relation to the Nothing. This way of being is, for the most part, characterized by willfully refusing to confront this difficult fact. As Heidegger puts it, existential cowardice is "falling into the 'they' and the 'world' of its concern, [and] is what we have called 'fleeing' [Flucht] in the face of itself."[42] Existential courage, in contrast, he calls resoluteness (Entschlossenheit). "Resoluteness," Heidegger writes, "signifies letting oneself be summoned out of one's lostness in the 'they.'"[43]

Resoluteness permits one to distinguish oneself from undifferentiated existence. In this sense, existential courage, just like other kinds of courage, is bound up with self-overcoming; it opens the way to transcending one's own being without reference to an otherworldly realm of existence. As Heidegger argues, "anxiety individualizes," and "this individualization brings Dasein back from its falling, and makes manifest to it that authenticity and inauthenticity [Eigentlichkeit und Uneigentlichkeit] are possibilities of its Being."[44] Existential courage is thus the healthy way of being because it paves the way to a fundamental care hitherto unnoticed: authenticity. In short, for Heidegger, one musters existential courage for the sake of authentic existence.

The Virtue of Courage

This overview of existential courage is, of course, preliminary. It does, however, bring to light not only that courage can take forms not explored in this book but that there may be types of courage that escape our imagination altogether. Even this sketch of existential courage reveals several seemingly diverse fundamental cares. There seems to be, after all, little in common between Christian love, Nietzschean joy, and Heideggerian authenticity. However, the references to being and nonbeing fix them in close relation to one another. Moreover, their relationship is deepened by a consideration of their close ties to the idea of transcendence. In particular, existential courage is bound up with overcoming the "mereness" of human existence for the sake of a higher form of existence. Whether it be overcoming the natural love of self (amor sui) in favor of the love of God (amor Dei), overcoming the natural hatred of the self in order to become the Overman (Übermensch), or remembering and embracing Being (Sein), existential courage aims to elevate the individual to a higher way of being. It lifts the individual out of the isolation and givenness of finite biological life. Like all the kinds of courage explored in this book, existential courage allows the individual to make something more of himself, and *this* is the great virtue of courage.

The virtue of courage, then, is paradoxical. On the one hand, it opens the way for the individual to assert himself in the larger play of human existence. Courage allows the individual to participate meaningfully in the larger community of which is he is part. On the other hand, the self-affirming insertion of one's self into the larger play of being is an act of self-overcoming. In his study of existential courage, Paul Tillich sees precisely this paradox. Courage, he says, "is an expression of the essential act of everything that participates in being, namely self-affirmation."[45] In other words, one affirms and overcomes oneself at the same time. With courage—and perhaps only with courage—one can make whatever one chooses to make of oneself; but courage perforce reminds us that making more of ourselves requires participation in a collective way of being. It reminds us that overcoming requires participation in a way of being that transcends ourselves. As Tocqueville might put it, courage whispers a reminder that "everyone belongs much more to this collective Being than he does to himself, that towards this Being no one ought to be indifferent, much less by treating such indifference as a sort of languid virtue, to enervate many of our noblest instincts; that every one is responsible for the fortunes of this collective Being; that every one is bound to work out its prosperity, and to watch that it be not governed except by respectable, beneficent and legitimate authorities."[46]

The virtue of courage, then, is twofold. Much of this book has invoked courage as a social scientific virtue. As a social scientific virtue, courage allows a better understanding of deeply divergent views of good community. This book's lengthy exploration of the nexus between courage and honor is meant, not simply as a paean to Spartan virtue, but as a sympathetic interpretation of an "honor culture" that can shed much light on contemporary politics, both local and global. Honor, after all, still stands at the heart of many communities today. From a modern, liberal democratic vantage point, however, the tendency is to regard honor as a moribund fundamental care and the willingness to risk life and limb for its sake as barbaric, unreasonable, and anachronistic. But because reports of the death of honor have been greatly exaggerated, it behooves us to understand honor as a lover of honor might understand it herself.[47]

This, of course, requires an openness and sympathy outside the usual comportment of the social scientist or a community informed by the social scientific approach. With courage, the social scientific approach might overcome this obstacle. As Tillich reminds us, "The experience of courage proves to be an outstanding key for the ontological approach to reality," and it is outstanding precisely because of its inherent appeal.[48]

The presentation of an honor culture through a narrative of courage thus affords an opportunity to look at honor without an interpretive lens clouded by our own fundamental cares and preferred modes of articulation. Similarly, the identification of political, moral, and economic courage in contradistinction to martial courage uncovers further ways of understanding our own communities vis-à-vis the courage and fundamental cares of others. By imbuing our social science with courage, we find ourselves holding a candle, however dim or bright it may be, up to the framework of collective human life in general. In short, courage provides an interpretive tool with which we can begin to understand radically different political orders stemming from different fundamental cares.

This interpretive tool, it should be added, is not meant to supplant the social scientific reliance on reason for explaining collective human existence. In fact, the aim of the ontological approach is not really explanation at all. Instead, the aim is somewhat deeper, or lower, as it were. The appeal of courage is not to the mind and reason, but to the gut, which is the home of courage. We must, for example, feel in our gut what it takes to risk life and limb for the sake of honor. If we can muster this sense, we may find a way into political life otherwise closed to the assumptions we employ in our rational actor models. We may, paradoxically, find understanding that resides beneath the liminality of our reason.

Just as courage opens the way to an understanding that resides beneath the liminality of reason, it also provides a means for connecting to our fellow human beings. While we may never fully understand what another human being is saying, especially if she speaks a foreign language, and while we may never be able to follow another person's logic or understand fully why a person would risk life and limb for something, we can most certainly recognize a courageous act. Courage is thus a language without language, a language that closes the gap between people. However, in closing the gap between people, courage can also disclose antithetical fundamental cares. While economic courage and a community based on the pursuit of "well-being," for instance, might be considered a debasement of all that is good about our human condition, recognizing courage in its pursuit invokes a universal experience that may somehow reveal an otherwise undisclosed value. The same can be said for the stalwart and courageous pursuit of justice. While one may not agree with, say, Socrates' politics, it is difficult not to recognize and respect him for making a courageous man of himself. The same can be said about the courageous pursuit of any fundamental care. While we may not agree, we may recognize, in its courageous pursuit a common thread of humanity—and this is the social scientific virtue of courage.

And this brings us to the second aspect of the virtue of courage. Courage is a virtue in an unsocial scientific way as well. Alongside temperance, prudence, and justice, it is part of a long tradition regarding human virtue. We have seen this already in the thought of many figures in the Western tradition, all of whom consider each virtue an excellence that lends itself to one's overall good character. In this view, a just, courageous, prudent, and temperate human being is better than an unjust, imprudent, immoderate coward. And this holds even when one is not fighting in the line with one's battle brothers. In the Christian tradition, courage, justice, temperance, and prudence are cardinal virtues upon which the theological virtues (faith, hope, and love) and the moral life hinge. Today, in both the religious and secular worlds, there are throwbacks to bygone times who still cling to courage as a human virtue, not because it buttresses any particular view of the world, but because the world itself would be a better place if it were filled with virtuous individuals. In other words, no matter what we care about fundamentally, no matter how our community is articulated, the good life cannot be achieved in a world populated by vicious people. And this is the unsocial scientific virtue of courage: goodness requires virtue.

The human virtue of courage thus lies precisely in its unscientific character. Whereas the social sciences adhere to the basic principle of objectivity—that it is out of bounds to make value claims regarding good and bad—courage is always good because it stands at the heart of good community. Courage is a human virtue because it need not depend on reason. Courage, we will recall, is mustered. It is the power upon which one draws when there is no time for reason, or when reason fails altogether. Courage is what allows us to stand unquestioningly in defense of our friends and family. It is what permits us to step up immediately to protect our children without first reasoning through the cause and effect of our actions. Courage, like all virtue, is a prerational well from which we can draw in our pursuit of the good life.[49] In this unscientific way, courage is a firewall that protects us when our empirical selves fail.

I will conclude this book by invoking Jean-Jacques Rousseau a final time. It is Rousseau, after all, who steadily calls our attention to the need for strength and virtue to counter the weakness of our empirical selves. In his *Letter to M. d'Alembert on the Theatre*, Rousseau retells a story told by Plutarch. The story is meant to contrast a people who rely on reason for their virtue and a people whose first lessons in good citizenship are bound up with courage. The story, drawn from Plutarch's *Sayings of Unknown Spartans*, is transcribed as follows:

> An old Athenian was looking for a seat at the theatre and could not find one. Some youngsters, seeing him in difficulty, waved to him from afar. He came, but they pushed close together and made fun of him. The good man made his way around the theatre in this fashion, not knowing what to do with himself and constantly jeered by the fair youth. The ambassadors of Sparta noticed it and, standing up immediately, gave the old man an honorable place in their midst. The action was observed by the whole audience and universally applauded. "Woe is me," cried out the old man in a pained tone, "the Athenians know what is decent, but the Lacedaemonians practice it."[50]

For Rousseau, the Spartans are a model of virtue worthy of emulation. While they are able to attend the theater and most likely enjoy the performance, they do not depend on the theater for training in general decency, nor do they fear that the theater will corrupt them. Their habitual virtue spills over into the average everyday life of a good community. And no matter how eloquent we may be, or how sophisticated our philosophical training, when life demands that we act decently in the here and now, there is no substitute for the selfless habits of courageous action. Let this be our resolute stand and the first lesson in courage.

Notes

ONE. (Re)Introducing Courage

1. Not all modern theorists leave courage entirely out of their considerations. William Galston, for example, includes it, along with law-abidingness and loyalty, as a generic virtue of citizenship (William Galston, *Liberal Purposes* [Cambridge: Cambridge University Press, 1991], 221). For Galston, the entire gamut of virtues for liberal society, for economics, and for politics includes independence, tolerance, the work ethic, delay of gratification, adaptability, discernment, moderation, patience, empathy, resolve, and practical wisdom (224–27).

2. Mark E. Warren, "What Should We Expect from More Democracy? Radically Democratic Responses to Politics," *Political Theory* 24, no. 2 (1996): 244.

3. Ibid., 264.

4. Galston, *Liberal Purposes*, 123.

5. Immanuel Kant, "Perpetual Peace," in *Kant's Political Writings*, ed. Hans Reiss (Cambridge: Cambridge University Press, 1970), 112.

6. John Rawls, *A Theory of Justice* (Cambridge, MA: Harvard University Press, 1971), 327. In *Political Liberalism*, Rawls is even more emphatic on this point. Here he claims that political philosophy should not pursue moral truths or metaphysical foundations; given the plurality of

"reasonable yet incompatible" moral, religious, and philosophical systems in constitutional democracies, political philosophy should aim at "a shared public basis of the justification of political and social institutions" rather than comprehensive doctrines, which include "ideals of personal virtue and character." John Rawls, *Political Liberalism* (New York: Columbia University Press, 1993), 134, 75. For Rawls, these comprehensive doctrines and moral theories are much too contested to function safely as the common thread of justification in a pluralistic society.

7. Jon Elster, "Rationality and the Emotions," *Economic Journal* 106, no. 438 (1996): 1386.

8. Ibid.

9. Ibid.

10. Thomas Hobbes, *Leviathan*, ed. C. B. Macpherson (New York: Penguin Books, 1968), 189.

11. John Finnis, *Natural Law and Natural Rights* (Oxford: Oxford University Press, 1980), 86. Finnis holds play, knowledge, aesthetic experience, friendship, practical reasonableness, and religion to be equally fundamental (86–90).

12. A parallel can be drawn here with Bernard Williams's "ground projects" (Bernard Williams, *Moral Luck: Philosophical Papers, 1973–1980* [Cambridge: Cambridge University Press, 1981]). For Williams, "An individual person has a set of desires, concerns or, as I shall call them, projects which help to constitute a character" (5). Ground projects, he writes, provide "the motive force which propels [a man] into the future and gives him a reason for living" (12). While fundamental cares also help constitute a character, more importantly, as will soon become evident, they help constitute community.

13. Thus for Jason Scorza courage can be "stripped of any special normative content or context" and can be defined empirically as "a capacity to carry on in spite of fear or in the face of danger," or, in agreement with Hemingway, as "grace under pressure." Jason A. Scorza, "The Ambivalence of Political Courage," *Review of Politics* 63, no. 4 (2001): 640.

14. William Galston, "Liberal Virtues," *American Political Science Review* 82, no. 4 (1988): 1282.

15. Michael Sandel, "Liberalism and Republicanism: Friends or Foes? A Response to Richard Dagger," *Review of Politics* 61, no. 2 (1999): 212. But see also Michael Sandel, *Democracy's Discontent* (Cambridge, MA: Harvard University Press, 1996), and Michael Sandel, "The Procedural Republic and the Unencumbered Self," *Political Theory* 12, no. 1 (1984): 81–96.

16. One may recall Jean-Paul Sartre here: "The phenomenologist will interrogate emotion about consciousness or about man. He will ask it not only what it is but what it has to teach us about a being, one of whose characteristics is exactly that he is capable of being moved. . . . Every human fact is, in essence, significative. If you remove its signification, you remove its nature as a human fact. . . . To signify is to indicate another thing; and to indicate it in such a way that in developing signification one will find precisely the thing signified." Jean-Paul Sartre, *The Philosophy of Existentialism,* trans. W. Baskin (New York: Philosophical Library, 1965), 198–99.

17. Martin Heidegger, *Being and Time,* trans. J. Macquarrie (New York: Harper, 1962), 227.

18. Ibid.

19. Ibid., 323. For more on care (Sorge) in Heidegger's thought, see Theodore Kisiel, *Heidegger's Way of Thought: Critical and Interpretive Signposts* (New York: Continuum, 2002), 68–69; Thomas R. Flynn, "*Angst* and Care in the Early Heidegger: The Ontic/Ontologic Aporia," *International Studies in Philosophy* 12, no. 1 (1980): 61–76; Will McNeill, "Care for the Self: Originary Ethics in Heidegger and Foucault," *Philosophy Today* 42, no. 1 (1998): 53–64; Lisa D. Campolo, "Derrida and Heidegger: The Critique of Technology and the Call to Care," *Journal of the American Academy of Religion* 53, no. 3 (1985): 431–48; John Paley, "Heidegger and the Ethics of Care," *Nursing Philosophy* 1, no. 1 (2000): 64–75; Eva Picardi, "Rorty, Sorge, and Truth," *International Journal of Philosophical Studies* 9, no. 3 (2001): 431–39; John D. Caputo, "*Sorge* and *Kardia:* The Hermeneutics of Facticity and the Categories of the Heart," in *Reading Heidegger from the Start: Essays in His Earliest Thought,* ed. Theodore J. Kisiel (Albany: State University of New York Press, 1994), 327–43; J. L. Mehta, *The Philosophy of Martin Heidegger* (Varanasi: Banaras Hindu University Press, 1967), esp. 192–221; Thomas Langan, *The Meaning of Heidegger: A Critical Study of an Existentialist Phenomenology* (New York: Columbia University Press, 1959), esp. 41–50; Michael E. Zimmerman, *Eclipse of the Self: The Development of Heidegger's Concept of Authenticity* (Athens: Ohio University Press, 1981), esp. 53–68.

20. Heidegger, *Being and Time,* 242. The story is #220 from the Fables of Hyginus.

21. Ibid., 243.

22. Carol Gilligan, *In a Different Voice: Psychological Theory and Women's Development* (Cambridge, MA: Harvard University Press, 1982), 17.

23. Ibid.

24. Ibid., 30. While the term *ethics of care* is not Gilligan's own, it has given birth to a prodigious scholarship. See, for example, Nel Noddings, *Caring: A Feminine Approach to Ethics and Moral Education* (Berkeley: University of California Press, 1984); Virginia Held, *The Ethics of Care: Personal, Political, and Global* (Oxford: Oxford University Press, 2006); Selma Sevenhuijsen, *Citizenship and the Ethics of Care: Feminist Considerations on Justice, Morality, and Politics* (New York: Routledge, 1998); Fiona Robinson, *Globalizing Care* (Boulder, CO: Westview Press, 1999). Yet, as argued here, the claim that the ethics of care is decidedly the domain of women is controversial. Joan Tronto, for instance, argues that "the equation of 'care' with 'female' is questionable because the evidence to support the link between gender difference and different moral perspectives is inadequate" (Joan Tronto, "Beyond Gender Difference to a Theory of Care," *Signs* 12, no. 4 [1987]: 646). See also John M. Broughton, "Women's Rationality and Men's Virtues: A Critique of Gender Dualism in Gilligan's Theory of Moral Development," *Social Research* 50, no. 3 (1983): 597–624; Catherine G. Greeno and Eleanor E. Maccoby, "How Different Is the 'Different Voice'?" *Signs* 11, no. 2 (1986): 310–16; and Linda K. Kerber, "Some Cautionary Words for Historians," *Signs* 11, no. 2 (1986): 304–10.

25. Gilligan, *In a Different Voice*, 30–31.

26. Rawls, *Theory of Justice*, 12, 136–42.

27. Gilligan, *In a Different Voice*, 31.

28. Ibid., 30.

29. See Noddings, *Caring*, 51.

30. Gilligan, *In a Different Voice*, 35.

31. Ibid., 17.

32. Ibid.

33. Harvey C. Mansfield, *Manliness* (New Haven: Yale University Press, 2006), 23. See also Harvey C. Mansfield, "Is Manliness a Virtue?" paper presented in the Bradley Lecture Series, American Enterprise Institute for Public Policy Research, Washington, DC, 1997.

34. See especially Michel Foucault, *Discipline and Punish: The Birth of the Prison*, trans. Alan Sheridan (New York: Vintage Books, 1977).

TWO. Martial Courage and Honor

The saying of the first epigraph is invoked in Julian A. Pitt-Rivers, "Honour and Social Status," in *Honour and Shame: The Values of the Mediterra-*

nean, ed. Jean G. Peristiany (Chicago: University of Chicago Press, 1966), 25. The second epigraph is from Herodotus, *The Histories,* ed. John M. Marincola, trans. Aubrey de Sélincourt (New York: Penguin Books, 1996); all citations to this work are from this edition and are given parenthetically in the text. Where necessary, I have modified the translations of passages from this work for the purposes of terminological consistency and precision.

1. The battle at Marathon, Herodotus reports, yielded 6,400 dead Persians and only 192 Athenian casualties (*Histories* 6.117). In addition to the rout, it was after this battle that Eucles made the famous 26.2 mile run to Athens to announce the victory (νίκη). As Victor Davis Hanson reports, Eucles is often confused with Pheidippides, who had earlier run 150 miles from Athens to Sparta in less than two days to warn of the Persian landing at Marathon. Victor Davis Hanson, *The Wars of the Ancient Greeks and Their Invention of Western Military Culture* (London: Cassell, 1999), 93.

2. Pausanius reports only about three million. Herodotus's precision as a historian is often questioned. Paul Keyser, for instance, demonstrates basic arithmetic problems; see his "Errors of Calculation in Herodotus," *Classical Journal* 81, no. 3 (1986): 230–42. Detlev Fehling goes further, suggesting that where numbers are lacking, Herodotus simply makes them up. His numbers, however, are not arbitrary inventions. Instead, he makes use of "typical numbers"—"numbers of the kind habitually chosen when a number has to be invented for a story. The criterion for inclusion in this category is a large enough collection of parallels; and by that criterion the role of typical numbers in Herodotus is considerable and self-evident." Detlev Fehling, *Herodotus and His "Sources": Citation, Invention, and Narrative Art,* trans. J. G. Howie (Leeds: Francis Cairns, 1989), 217. For more on the historical problems in Herodotus, see J. L. Moles, "Truth and Untruth in Herodotus and Thucydides," in *Lies and Fiction in the Ancient World,* ed. Christopher Gill and T. P. Wiseman (Exeter: University of Exeter Press, 1993); and W. Kendrick Pritchett, *The Liar School of Herodotos* (Amsterdam: J. C. Gieben, 1993). This said, for Herodotus the veracity of facts is less important than the meaning they convey. He merely wants "to say what is said, without committing himself in any way to believing everything he tells" (7.152; but cf. John Marincola, *The Greek Historians* [Oxford: Oxford University Press, 2001], 32). His point is clear: a people expresses and understands itself in certain ways, and these expressions are not undermined by the "factuality" of the facts. More tolerant versions of Herodotus's historical imprecision can be found in the work of

Norman Austin, who claims that "Herodotus' primary purpose, then, was to do for a contemporary event what Homer did for the Trojan War," and Charles W. Fornara, who claims that "Herodotus' method is artistic, not historical. He has created a drama to which the audience, as the 'dramatist' well knows, and indeed demands, will bring a level of comprehension that altogether changes its point. What appear to be mere anecdotes without direction are in reality magnificent and richly allusive passages." Norman Austin, introduction to *The Greek Historians*, ed. Norman Austin (New York: D. van Nostrand, 1969), 35; Charles W. Fornara, *Herodotus: An Interpretive Essay* (Oxford: Clarendon Press, 1971), 65. Others claim that Herodotus knows more than he is given credit for. Arther Ferrill, for instance, argues that historical and tactical errors in Herodotus are exaggerated; see his "Herodotus and the Strategy and Tactics of the Invasion of Xerxes," *American Historical Review* 72, no. 1 (1966): 102–15, but see also William Kelly Prentice, "Thermopylae and Artemisium," *Transactions and Proceedings of the American Philological Association* 51 (1920): 5–18.

3. The enormity of the battle still resonates in modern popular culture. Steven Pressfield, for example, romanticized the battle in a commercially successful fictional account (*Gates of Fire: An Epic Novel of the Battle of Thermopylae* (Thorndike, ME: G. K. Hall, 1999). In 1962 the battle was relived in a movie, *The Spartan 300*, directed by Rudolph Maté. More recently, Frank Miller and Lynn Varley's graphic novel *300* (Dark Horse, 1999) was remade into a Zach Snyder–directed epic Hollywood movie.

4. The Greek habit of quarreling among themselves did not go unnoticed in the ancient world. Herodotus reports Mardonius—Xerxes' cousin and trusted advisor—as saying that "the Greeks are pugnacious enough, and start fights on the spur of the moment without sense of judgment to justify them. . . . Even the victors never get off without heavy losses, and as for the losers—well, they're wiped out. Now surely, as they all speak the same language, they ought to be able to find a better way of settling their difference: by negotiation, for instance, or an interchange of views—indeed by anything rather than fighting" (*Histories* 7.9b).

5. For more on ancient Greek passes and roads, see W. Kendrick Pritchett, *Studies in Ancient Greek Topography* (Berkeley: University of California Press, 1965), vols. 3 and 4.

6. Not retreating from Thermopylae raises the question of suicide missions. Insofar as we hold fast to our definition of courage—risking life and limb for the sake of something—suicide missions are not courageous. One is not *risking* life and limb if there is no hope of survival. Risk implies

hope, and with suicide missions there is no hope. But because part of the decision to stand at Thermopylae was based on the appeal for reinforcements, it is clear that the contingent harbored hopes of surviving. That they would all perish was not certain; Spartan courage and experience was such that losing in battle was almost inconceivable, even against overwhelming odds. For example, of Dieneces, who is specifically remembered for his courage and for being one of the best men in the contingent, Herodotus says: "Of all the Spartans and Thespians who fought so valiantly the most signal proof of courage [ἀνὴρ ἄριστος] was given by the Spartan Dieneces. It is said that before the battle he was told by a native of Trachis that, when the Persians shot their arrows, there were so many of them that they hid the sun. Dieneces, unmoved, merely remarked: 'This is pleasant news that the stranger from Trachis brings us: if the Persians hide the sun, we shall have our battle in the shade'" (Herodotus *Histories* 7.226). Simply put, the mission, even by the individual warriors, was not regarded as suicidal. This position also applies to contemporary suicide bombers—these are not courageous acts.

7. In ancient Sparta there were three castes—the Spartiates, the Perioeci, and the Helots. As Tigerstedt reports, there were "the Spartiates, who alone possessed full citizenship, living in Sparta but possessing the best land in Laconia (and Messenia); the Perioeci, as their name 'the ones which live in the surroundings' implies, inhabiting the frontier districts with a certain measure of self-government, free but without full political rights, not professional soldiers but land-owners, like the Spartiates themselves; and the unfree serfs, the 'Helots,' who cultivated the land of the Spartiates—and perhaps also that of the Perioeci." E. N. Tigerstedt, *The Legend of Sparta in Classical Antiquity* (Stockholm: Almqvist and Wiksell, 1965), 38. Much is written about the relationship between Spartan military strength and her number of full citizens. Though the actual number of Spartiates available for call-up varies from estimation to estimation, it is generally agreed that during the fifth century Sparta was in a constant struggle against a declining population. If, as Aristotle reports, the number of Spartiates remaining at his time had dwindled to about one thousand, sending three hundred full citizens to Thermopylae a hundred years earlier was no small sacrifice (Aristotle *Politics* 1270a40). For more, see K. M. T. Chrimes Atkinson, *Ancient Sparta: A Re-examination of the Evidence* (Manchester: Manchester University Press, 1949), 348, and Tigerstedt, *Legend of Sparta*, 108.

8. William Ian Miller, *The Mystery of Courage* (Cambridge, MA: Harvard University Press, 2000).

9. Cf. Hannah Arendt, *The Human Condition* (Chicago: University of Chicago Press, 1958).

10. Lendon, for example, refers to Sparta as "perhaps the most perfectly totalitarian culture the West has known." J. E. Lendon, "Spartan Honor," in *Polis and Polemos: Essays on Politics, War, and History in Ancient Greece*, ed. Charles D. Hamilton and Peter Krentz (Claremont, CA: Regina Books, 1997), 107. See also Victor Ehrenberg, "A Totalitarian State," in *Aspects of the Ancient World*, ed. Victor Ehrenberg (New York: W. Salloch, 1946).

11. In Herodotus's *Histories*, φιλοτιμία appears only once, at 3.53.4. Here, interestingly, the daughter of Periander, the tyrant of Corinth, invokes the word when exhorting her brother to return to Corinth. That a woman uses the word to chastise a young man's obstinacy is probably not a coincidence. Cf. Thucydides *Peloponnesian War* 2.65.7, 3.82.8, 8.89.3. See also Aristotle *Nicomachean Ethics* 1107b, 1117b, 1125b, 1159a, *Politics* 1267b, 1271a, 1312a, 1318b, and *Rhetoric* 1389a; Plutarch *Nicias* 3.2, 4.1, 9.2, 12.1, 12.3, 20.4, *Lysander* 5.4, 19.1, 21.3, 23.5, *Cimon* 8.8, 17.6, *Alcibiades* 6.3, 11.1, 12.1, 16.3, 34.2, *Themistocles* 3.3, 5.2, 5.4, 6.1, 6.1, *Aristides* 1.5, 10.4, 11.9, 14.2, and *Pericles* 11.3; Xenophon *Memorabilia* 3.3.13 and *Hellenica* 4.1.37.

12. Plato *Republic* 545a, my translation. See also *Republic* 347b and 475a and *Phaedrus* 256c.

13. Lendon, "Spartan Honor," 106.

14. Ethnographers report that even in modern-day village life the idea of *filotimia* still resonates and remains bound up with self-restraint, truth to one's "word," chastity, and the subordination of self-interest to the collective good. Michael Herzfeld, for instance, reports that as late as the 1970s in a rural Greek village during a water shortage it was both natural and easily understood when the mayor, over the public-address system, enjoined the entire community "to 'show *filotimo* [verb]' by subordinating selfish to collective interests." Michael Herzfeld, "Honour and Shame: Problems in the Comparative Analysis in Moral Systems," *Man* 15, no. 2 (1980): 343.

15. Xenophon *Constitution of the Lacedaemonians* 9.4; translation from *Scripta minora*, trans. E. C. Marchant (Cambridge, MA: Harvard University Press, 1925).

16. Notable recent exceptions are Frank Henderson Stewart, *Honor* (Chicago: University of Chicago Press, 1994); Sharon R. Krause, *Liberalism with Honor* (Cambridge, MA: Harvard University Press, 2002); and James Bowman, *Honor: A History* (New York: Encounter Books, 2006).

17. Peristiany, *Honour and Shame*, 9.

18. Stanley Brandes, "Reflections on Honor and Shame in the Mediterranean," in *Honor and Shame and the Unity of the Mediterranean*, ed. David D. Gilmore (Washington, DC: American Anthropological Association, 1987), 121.

19. Edward Westermark, *The Origin and Development of Moral Ideas* (London: Macmillan, 1912–17), 137.

20. Pitt-Rivers, "Honour and Social Status," 22.

21. Ibid.

22. The commingling of honor and recognition derives its modern theoretical depth from the work of G. W. F. Hegel, especially his description of the slave-master dialectic in his *Phenomenology of Spirit*. For more, see Alexandre Kojève, *Introduction to the Reading of Hegel: Lectures on the Phenomenology of Spirit* (Ithaca: Cornell University Press, 1980), and the particularly modern interpretations of Charles Taylor, "The Politics of Recognition," in *New Contexts of Canadian Criticism*, ed. Ajay Heble, Donna Palmateer, and J. R. T. Struthers (Peterborough: Broadview Press, 1997), and *Sources of the Self: the Making of the Modern Identity* (Cambridge, MA: Harvard University Press, 1989).

23. Peristiany, *Honour and Shame*, 11. Sharon Krause echoes this, arguing that the "reason for the relative weakness of honor in democracy is the obscurity of individuals in mass society. . . . The obscurity of individuals in democratic societies keeps them from obeying honor's rules closely, because obscurity interferes with the public regulation of praise and blame" (*Liberalism with Honor*, 73, 74). While this captures nicely the essence of honor cultures, it is at odds with a major component of Krause's definition of honor. Whereas honor certainly is inextricably bound up with public praise and blame, Krause repeatedly argues that honor is "a quality of character" that is an "internal phenomenon" (3). This internal phenomenon, Krause suggests, is "the personal desire for self-respect" (5, but cf. 29, 95, 147, 177, 184). An honorable student, for example, "adheres to the honor code out of respect, not from fear of reprisals or the promise of public approval. She owes it to herself to live up to the code; to do otherwise would be to let herself down. Her reward is personal gratification, the

pleasure of having resisted the allures of the ring of Gyges" (3). This, as will become clearer, is not an altogether accurate description of honor. Instead, it is a conflation of honor and guilt. The very reason Plato invokes the Gyges myth is to move away from virtue based on external opinion (i.e., honor) to virtue based on an internal awareness of right and wrong (i.e., justice). The difference between an honor culture and guilt culture lies in precisely the difference between "respect" and "self-respect." Hence, when Krause argues that "the honorable person does not wish to save the world but only to be able to face himself in the mirror and look his fellows in the eye without shame or regret," she is only half correct (62). Mirrors pertain to self-knowledge and guilt, not honor. They pertain to honor if and only if they are accompanied by the concept of sincerity and authenticity, which, as Lionel Trilling so eloquently tells us in *Sincerity and Authenticity* (Cambridge, MA: Harvard University Press, 1971), is a modern, Western, liberal, and Christian phenomenon. In this light, one might also be tempted to reinterpret Banfield's classic study of life in a small Mediterranean town as one that neglects, either willfully or perforce, the centrality of honor. Edward C. Banfield, *The Moral Basis of a Backward Society* (Glencoe, IL: Free Press; Chicago: Research Center in Economic Development and Cultural Change, 1958).

24. Plutarch *Lycurgus.*

25. Hans van Wees, *Status Warriors: War, Violence, and Society in Homer and History* (Amsterdam: J. C. Gieben, 1992), 72.

26. Pitt-Rivers, "Honour and Social Status," 26.

27. Ibid.

28. According to Paul Cartledge, "The history of Sparta, it is not too much to say, is fundamentally the history of the class struggle between the Spartans and the Helots." Paul Cartledge, *Agesilaos and the Crisis of Sparta* (Baltimore: Johns Hopkins University Press, 1987), 13. This sentiment also appears in Thucydides' claim that "at all times most of the Lacadaemonians' relations with the helots were based mainly on security" (*Peloponnesian War* 6.30; translation from *The Peloponnesian War*, trans. Steven Lattimore [Indianapolis: Hackett, 1998]) and in Aristotle's statement, in the *Politics* (1269a39), that "the helots attacked the Spartans, always on the look-out for any mischance that may befall their masters" (translation from Aristotle, *The Politics*, trans. T. A. Sinclair [New York: Penguin Books, 1951]). See also Richard J. A. Talbert, "The Role of the Helots in the Class Struggle at Sparta," *Historia* 38, no. 1 (1989): 22–40; and G. E. M. de Ste Croix,

"The Helot Threat," in *Sparta*, ed. Michael Whitby (New York: Routledge, 2002).

29. Peristiany, *Honour and Shame*, 10.

30. Xenophon *Spartan Society* 9.1; translation from appendix to Plutarch, *Plutarch on Sparta*, ed. and trans. Richard Talbert (London: Penguin Books, 1988).

31. Ibid.

32. Theodor Fontane, *Effi Briest* (New York: Penguin Books, 1967), 215–16. For more on this vision of dishonor, and dishonor in general, see Stewart, *Honor*, 114–16.

33. Not all modern commentators would agree that this sort of justice is brutish and unwarranted. Peter French, for instance, argues that revenge is a fundamental aspect of morality that has "fallen into disrepute without being seriously examined." Peter A. French, *The Virtues of Vengeance* (Lawrence: University Press of Kansas, 2001), x. Moreover, "in our so-called civilized time, we have removed the personal recognition and response obligations from the shoulders of individuals and created institutional mechanisms as substitutes. And we call it justice. In large measure, what we have done, however, is to strip morality of its most effective and involved element: individual action provoked by the recognition of evil, the resentment drive to set things right" (80–81).

34. J. K. Campbell, "Honour and the Devil," in Peristiany, *Honour and Shame*, 145.

35. Fontane, *Effi Briest*, 215.

36. Campbell, "Honour and the Devil," 145.

37. Such a view of battle still resonates. Mark Bowden, in his account of the battle of Mogadishu (October 3–4, 1993), recounts the thoughts of an Army Ranger at the outset of the battle. The Ranger had injured his elbow playing volleyball in the hangar a few days earlier. He was diagnosed with bursitis and cellulitis, had the wound drained, was fitted with a cast, and slated for return to the United States. The battle began and, as Bowden reports, "The Ranger had been going nuts listening to the radio. These were his brothers, his Ranger buddies out there pinned down, and they were getting hammered. He heard screams of pain and fear in the voices of hardened men. This was the big fight they'd all been preparing for all these years, and here he was, pacing around the radio with a fucking cast on his arm!" Mark Bowden, *Black Hawk Down: A Story of Modern War* (New York: Atlantic Monthly Press, 1999), 149. Later, in an act

reminiscent of Eurytus, the Ranger cut the cast off and headed into the battle (159). He "couldn't wait to find the guys on his chalk. He desperately wanted them to know that he hadn't sat out the fight back at the hangar, but had fought in after them, twice. It was important that they know he had come after them" (297).

38. There may be, however, more to this story. There have been, throughout the history of warfare, malingerers. Malingerers have been known to fake all sorts of maladies to get themselves out of the line of fire, including amnesia, deafness, mutism, paralysis, and blindness. It might very well be that the two were malingering and were, in point of fact, cowards. However, that Eurytus returned to the battle and perished suggests that the two actually were suffering from ophthalmia, as Herodotus reports. Herodotus relates another story of warriors going blind, this one emerging from the battle at Marathon. There, he writes, "Epizelus, the son of Cuphagoras, an Athenian soldier, was fighting bravely [ἀγαθός] when suddenly he lost the sight of both eyes, though nothing had touched him anywhere—neither sword, spear, nor missile. From that moment he continued blind as long as he lived" (Herodotus *Histories* 6.117). In this example, Herodotus gives no hint that the warrior's honor suffered. On the contrary, he is described as brave (ἀγαθός). He went blind in battle, yet thanks to some marvel was able to survive. Presumably he was a very lucky man, or he made a beeline for the rear echelons. Whichever is the case, Epizelus—the Athenian—suffered no shame for the incident, and his honor remained intact.

39. Joseph M. Bryant, *Moral Codes and Social Structure in Ancient Greece: A Sociology of Greek Ethics from Homer to the Epicureans and Stoics* (Albany: State University of New York Press, 1996), 158.

40. Similarly, a person in exile is a φυγάς.

41. Bryant, *Moral Codes*, 103.

42. William James, *The Principles of Psychology* (New York: H. Holt, 1890), 293–94, quoted in Kipling D. Williams, *Ostracism: The Power of Silence* (New York: Guilford Press, 2001), 2.

43. K. Williams, *Ostracism*, 6–8.

44. Roger D. Masters, "Ostracism, Voice, and Exit: The Biology of Social Participation," in *Ostracism: A Social and Biological Phenomenon*, ed. Margaret Gruter and Roger D. Masters (New York: Elsevier, 1986), 239, 237.

45. Miller, *Mystery of Courage*, 17.

46. Ibid., 18.

47. One is here reminded of Plutarch's report of the words of an unknown Spartan woman: "A woman, when she saw her son approaching, asked how their country was doing. When he said, 'All the men are dead,' she picked up a tile, threw it at him and killed him, saying: 'Then did they send you to bring us the bad news?'" Plutarch *Sayings of Spartan Women* 241b; translation from Plutarch, *Plutarch on Sparta*, 160.

48. A. W. H. Adkins, *Merit and Responsibility: A Study in Greek Values* (Oxford: Clarendon Press, 1960), 154.

49. Ibid., 155. For these examples, Adkins points to Theognis 1033; Hesiod *Works and Days* 701; Sophocles *Ajax* 367 and *Electra* 1152; and Euripides *Heracles* 281.

50. Adkins, *Merit and Responsibility*, 49.

51. Ruth Benedict, *The Chrysanthemum and the Sword: Patterns of Japanese Culture* (Cleveland, OH: Meridian Books, 1967), 223. For more on the "mechanisms of shame and guilt," see Bernard Williams, *Shame and Necessity* (Berkeley: University of California Press, 1993), 219–23.

52. B. Williams, *Shame and Necessity*, 89–90.

53. E. R. Dodds, *The Greeks and the Irrational* (Berkeley: University of California Press, 1951), 18. James Bowman provides an excellent account of the "tyranny of face" in honor cultures. In Bowman's account, Saddam Hussein "lied repeatedly [about weapons of mass destruction in Iraq] because he was part of an honor culture that demanded he lie" (*Honor*, 28). To deny having them would be to lose face, but "but to have yielded to American or United Nations pressure would have been seen as dishonoring in his own eyes and in those of the Arab world, where such things remain supremely important" (30).

54. In some circles, cowardice is regarded as a genetic flaw that can be avoided with proper breeding. It can therefore be discussed in terms of husbandry or natural selection. A vivid, if not unschooled, representation of this can be found in George Patton's "Speech to the Third Army" on June 5, 1944, the eve of the Allied invasion of France: "Each man must not think only of himself, but also of his buddy fighting beside him. We don't want yellow cowards in this Army. They should be killed off like rats. If not, they will go home after this war and breed more cowards. The brave men will breed more brave men. Kill off the Goddamned cowards and we will have a nation of brave men!"

55. Douglas L. Cairns, *Aidos: The Psychology and Ethics of Honour and Shame in Ancient Greek Literature* (Oxford: Clarendon Press, 1993), 2–3.

56. Ibid., 2.

57. See Homer *Iliad* 2.224, 5.764, 8.198, 10.218, 13.81, 15.53, 15.113, 15.478, 15.559, 15.653, 16.394, 17.319, 22.38, 24.22, 24.93.

58. Homer *Iliad* 2.258–64; here and subsequently, translated passages from this work are from *The Iliad*, ed. and trans. Richard Lattimore (Chicago: University of Chicago Press, 1951), and are given parenthetically in the text.

59. B. Williams, *Shame and Necessity*, 78.

60. This sense of shame occurs once more in the *Iliad* when Thetis is called to speak with Zeus. There, because of her inferior rank, Thetis expresses her deference and respect by asking, "What does he, the great god, want with me? I feel shamefast [αἰδέομαι] to mingle with immortals" (24.90–91). A bit later, Zeus acknowledges her respect (αἰδῶ) for him (24.111) and advises her to go tell her son, Achilles, in whom there is no shame (αἰδώς) (24.45), to stop dragging Hektor around and to give his body back (24.116). Evidently, even the gods are supposed to feel this shame—Athena chastises Ares for a similar rage-inspired ugly scene: "Madman, mazed of your wits, this is ruin! Your ears can listen still to reality, but your mind is gone and your discipline [αἰδώς]" (15.129).

61. Cairns, *Aidos*, 68.

62. But see also 13.95.

63. As in the U.S. Army Regulations, Regulation 600-8-22 (Military Awards), February 1995.

64. From a Royal Warrant, given by Queen Victoria "at Our Court at Buckingham Palace, this twenty-ninth day of January, in the nineteenth year of Our reign, and in the Year of Our Lord, 1856." According to the Ministry of Veterans Affairs of Canada, "as part of the British Empire and later Commonwealth, Canada relied on the British honours system to recognize service members for gallantry in battle." In typical Canadian fashion, "since the Second World War, Canada developed its own honour system, and expanded it considerably in the late 1960's and early 1970's." Of course, there have been no wars in which Canadian military personnel have had a chance to distinguish themselves since World War II, so, contrary to the very purpose of military awards for gallantry, "Canada developed its own decoration for *bravery in peacetime*" (emphasis added). Ministry of Veterans Affairs of Canada, "Modern Honours of Canada (1972)—Victoria Cross (VC) Canadian Version," January 23, 2001, www.vac-acc.gc.ca/remembers/sub.cfm?source=collections/cmdp/mainmenu/group02/canvc.

65. What is most conspicuous is that little British addendum: "in the presence of the enemy."

66. For more on the charge in battle, see especially ch. 12, "The Charge," in Victor Davis Hanson, *The Western Way of War: Infantry Battle in Classical Greece* (New York: Knopf, 1989). Interestingly, Tim O'Brien, who understands well the problem of modern Western individualism and isolation, nevertheless suggests that most of his comrades in Vietnam considered the charge to be the epitome of courage. Tim O'Brien, *If I Die in a Combat Zone; Box Me Up and Ship Me Home* (New York: Delacorte Press, 1973). As he writes: "It's the charge, the light brigade with only one man, that is the first thing to think about when thinking about courage. People who do it are remembered as brave, win or lose. They are heroes forever. It seems like courage, the charge" (134). Though his comrades regard the solitary charge as the quintessence of courage, O'Brien himself is not so sure. He later admits that "courage is more than the charge" (141) but maintains that the shotgun is the ultimate weapon of courage. The bearer of the shotgun, after all, must possess "an exact blend of courage and skill and self-confidence. The weapon is neither accurate nor lethal at much over fifty yards. So it shows the skill of the carrier, a man who must work his way close enough to the prey to make a shot, close enough to see the enemy's eyes and the tone of his skin. To get that close requires courage and confidence" (81–82).

67. But see also 6.130. For a good history of the hoplite and phalanx fighting, see Paul Cartledge, *Spartan Reflections* (Berkeley: University of California Press, 2001), 153–66. See also J. F. Lazenby, *The Spartan Army* (Warminster: Aris Phillips, 1985), and Atkinson, *Ancient Sparta*, esp. 348–96.

68. H. Michell, *Sparta* (Cambridge: Cambridge University Press, 1964), 252. For more on Spartan weapons and armor, see J. K. Anderson, "Hoplite Weapons and Offensive Arms," in *Hoplites: The Classical Greek Battle Experience*, ed. Victor Davis Hanson (London: Routledge, 1991); Michael M. Sage, *Warfare in Ancient Greece: A Sourcebook* (New York: Routledge, 1996); Hanson, *Western Way of War;* and John Rich and Graham Shipley, *War and Society in the Greek World* (London: Routledge, 1993).

69. Xenophon *Constitution of the Lacedaemonians* 13.5, my translation.

70. Lazenby, *Spartan Army*, 37.

71. Xenophon *Hellenica* 4.3.19; translation from *Xenophon's Hellenica*, trans. C. L. Brownson, O. J. Todd, and E. C. Marchant, vol. 1 (New York: G. P. Putnam's Sons, 1918).

72. For an excellent account of the experience of fighting close in, see John Lazenby, "The Killing Zone," in Hanson, *Hoplites.*

73. Cartledge, *Spartan Reflections,* 162.

74. Aristotle goes so far as to say that suicide is cowardly: "To seek death [ἀποθνήσκειν] in order to escape [φεύγοντα] from poverty, or the pangs of love, or from pain or sorrow, is not the act of a courageous man, but rather of a coward [μᾶλλον δειλοῦ]; for it is weakness to fly from troubles [φεύγων κακόν], and the suicide does not endure death because it is noble [καλὸν] to do so, but to escape evil." *Nicomachean Ethics* 1116a17; translation from *Nicomachean Ethics,* trans. H. Rackham (Cambridge, MA: Harvard University Press, 1975).

75. W. Miller, *Mystery of Courage,* 20.

76. Ibid., 21.

77. Pressfield, *Gates of Fire,* 267–69.

78. Plutarch *Lycurgus* 16; translation, as "Life of Lycurgus," from Plutarch, *Plutarch on Sparta.*

79. Plutarch *Moralia* 240f, my translation.

80. Plutarch *Moralia* 241a.

81. Plutarch *Moralia* 240.

82. For an excellent and thorough account of the "upbringing," see Nigel M. Kennell, *The Gymnasium of Virtue: Education and Culture in Ancient Sparta* (Chapel Hill: University of North Carolina Press, 1995).

83. Xenophon *Spartan Society* 11; translation from appendix to Plutarch, *Plutarch on Sparta.*

84. The difficulty in reconciling the desire for personal glory and serving the public interest is lucidly discussed by Jean-Pierre Vernant, who claims that "Sparta has the reputation of being a city where the sense of honor is systematically developed, from the earliest age, by the constant practice, public and institutionalized, of blame and praise, of sarcasm and glorification, but where, on the other hand, the individual is trained from childhood to submit himself entirely and in all things to the interests of the state." Jean-Pierre Vernant, "Between Shame and Glory: The Identity of the Young Spartan Warrior," in *Mortals and Immortals: Collected Essays,* ed. Froma I. Zeitlin (Princeton: Princeton University Press, 1991), 221.

85. Dodds, *Greeks and the Irrational,* 29.

86. Horace *Odes* 3.2.13–21; translation from *Odes and Carmen Saeculare of Horace,* 3rd ed., ed. and trans. John Conington (London: Bell and Daldy, 1863) .

87. Alasdair MacIntyre, *After Virtue* (Notre Dame: University of Notre Dame Press, 1981), 123.

88. Gray's soldierly experience is of especial interest because it came after his philosophical training, a rather rare occurrence, historically speaking. As Gray reports, he received his draft orders—his "greetings from the President . . . in the same mail that brought word from Columbia University that [his] doctorate in philosophy was conferred." J. Glenn Gray, *The Warriors: Reflections on Men in Battle* (Lincoln: University of Nebraska Press, 1959), xxiii; all subsequent citations to this work are given parenthetically in the text.

89. Chris Hedges, *War Is a Force That Gives Us Meaning* (New York: PublicAffairs, 2002), 3.

90. Ibid., 5.

91. One is here further reminded of General George Patton's "Speech to the Third Army" on June 5th, 1944. He said to the crowd of mostly untested soldiers: "There is one great thing that you men will all be able to say after this war is over and you are home once again. You may be thankful that twenty years from now when you are sitting by the fireplace with your grandson on your knee and he asks you what you did in the great World War II, you WON'T have to cough, shift him to the other knee and say, "Well, your Granddaddy shoveled shit in Louisiana." No, Sir, you can look him straight in the eye and say, "Son, your Granddaddy rode with the Great Third Army and a Son-of-a-Goddamned-Bitch named Georgie Patton!"

92. See Ernst Jünger, *Storm of Steel*, trans. M. Hoffman (New York: Penguin Books, 2004).

93. Max Weber, *Gesammelte Aufsätze sur Religionsssoziologie*, vol. 1 (Tübingen: J. C. B. Mohr, 1947), 549, my translation.

94. Michael Gelven, *War and Existence: A Philosophical Inquiry* (University Park: Pennsylvania State University Press, 1994), 63.

95. Ibid., 65.

96. Ibid., 68.

97. Hedges, *War Is a Force*, 40.

98. One is here reminded of René Char's poetry inspired by his participation in the French Resistance in World War II. René Char, *Leaves of Hypnos* (New York: Grossman, 1973).

99. Richard Holmes, *Acts of War: The Behavior of Men in Battle* (New York: Free Press, 1986), 36.

100. Ibid., 32.

101. One is here reminded of the U.S. Marine Corps Rifleman's Creed: "This is my rifle. There are many like it, but this one is mine. It is my life. I must master it as I must master my life. Without me my rifle is useless. Without my rifle, I am useless. I must fire my rifle true. I must shoot straighter than the enemy who is trying to kill me. I must shoot him before he shoots me. I will. My rifle and I know that what counts in war is not the rounds we fire, the noise of our burst, or the smoke we make. We know that it is the hits that count. We will hit. My rifle is human, even as I am human, because it is my life. Thus, I will learn it as a brother. I will learn its weaknesses, its strengths, its parts, its accessories, its sights and its barrel. I will keep my rifle clean and ready, even as I am clean and ready. We will become part of each other. Before God I swear this creed. My rifle and I are the defenders of my country. We are the masters of our enemy. We are the saviors of my life. So be it, until victory is America's and there is no enemy."

102. Holmes, *Acts of War*, 34.

103. Ibid., 38–39.

104. Ibid., 42–43.

105. There is no textual evidence that Mardonius was responsible for the outrage at Thermopylae. Blame appears to fall directly on Xerxes, who, it should be noted here, by this point in the war had already fled back to Persia. If there is any implication of Mardonius's involvement in the mistreatment of Leonidas's body, it comes from the tainted implication of Xerxes at 8.114.

106. Gerald F. Linderman, *Embattled Courage: The Experience of Combat in the American Civil War* (New York: Free Press, 1987), 66.

107. Ibid.

108. Ibid.

109. Ibid., 68.

110. Ibid., 69.

111. William James, "The Moral Equivalent of War," in *Writings, 1902–1910*, ed. Bruce Kuklick (New York: Literary Classics of the United States, 1987), 1287.

112. Ibid., 1290–91.

113. Ibid., 1290.

114. Ibid.

115. Tom Brokaw, *The Greatest Generation* (New York: Random House, 1998), xx.

116. Ibid.

117. Dave Grossman, *On Killing: The Psychological Cost of Learning to Kill in War and Society* (Boston: Little, Brown, 1995), 287.

118. T. O'Brien, *If I Die*, 88.

119. Ibid., 124.

120. Grossman, *On Killing*, 288.

121. Ibid., 286.

122. Ibid., 286–87.

123. Ibid., 286.

124. Suzanne Mettler, "Bringing the State Back into Civic Engagement: Policy Feedback Effects of the G.I. Bill for World War II Veterans," *American Political Science Review* 96, no. 2 (2002): 351–65, esp. 359–62.

THREE. Political Courage and Justice

1. Peristiany, *Honour and Shame*, 10.

2. Johan Huizinga, *Homo Ludens: A Study of the Play-Element in Culture* (Boston: Beacon Press, 1955). For more on the relationship between blood and sacrality, see Barbara Ehrenreich, *Blood Rites: Origins and History of the Passions of War* (New York: Metropolitan Books, 1997); Gelven, *War and Existence*, 63–75; Wees, *Status Warriors;* and J. Ginat, *Blood Revenge: Family Honor, Mediation, and Outcasting*, 2nd ed. (Portland, OR: Sussex Academic Press, 1997).

3. Pitt-Rivers, "Honour and Social Status," 26.

4. Ibid., 29.

5. Karen Bassi, "The Semantics of Manliness in Ancient Greece," in *Andreia: Studies in Manliness and Courage in Classical Antiquity*, ed. Ralph Mark Rosen and Ineke Sluiter (Boston: Brill, 2003), 33. Cf. Ryan Balot, "Courage in the Democratic Polis," *Classical Quarterly* 54, no. 2 (2004): 406, and Joseph Roisman, "The Rhetoric of Courage in the Athenian Orators," in Rosen and Sluiter, *Andreia*.

6. Bassi, "Semantics of Manliness," 34.

7. Sarah E. Harrell, "Marvelous Andreia: Politics, Geography, and Ethnicity in Herodotus' *Histories*," in Rosen and Sluiter, *Andreia*, 77.

8. Ibid., 89.

9. Ibid., 91.

10. Bassi, "Semantics of Manliness," 38.

11. As an adjective, *agênôr*, like *andreia*, means "manly" or "heroic." However, unlike *andreia*, *agênôr* almost always has a bestial connotation. For example, in the *Iliad* the mad Achilles is compared to a lion's "savage anger" (agênori thumôi) (24.42). Achilles is said to be *agênôr*, which is variously translated as haughty, proud, headstrong, or arrogant (9.699). Often in the *Odyssey* the same word is used to describe the arrogant suitors (mnêstêras agênoras) (1.104, 144, 298, 17.65). While this word appears often in Homer, Aeschylus, Pausanius, Apollodorus, and Pindar, it never appears in Plato's work.

12. Bassi, "Semantics of Manliness," 39–40.

13. Ibid., 42.

14. Balot, "Courage," 410.

15. For more on the place of free speech in aristocracies in the ancient world, see Kurt A. Raaflaub, "Aristocracy and Freedom of Speech," in *Free Speech in Classical Antiquity*, ed. Ineke Sluiter and Ralph Rosen (Leiden: Brill, 2004), esp. 51–54. Raaflaub argues that although free speech was not a value in and of itself in Sparta, "the famous 'rhetra,' a set of rules for communal decision making that dates to the late seventh century and is complemented by a slightly later 'rider,' receives due attention: attributed to the mythical lawgiver, Lycurgus, it endowed the assembly of the damos with power and decision (kratos and nikê) but the council (gerousia) with initiative and control" (52). As for discussing policy and "doing politics" before going to battle, the Spartans were certainly not apolitical. For example, see Donald Kagan's discussion of why the Spartans chose Nicomedes to lead the expeditionary force to Doris rather than Pleistoanax or Archidamus (*The Outbreak of the Peloponnesian War* [Ithaca: Cornell University Press, 1969], 87).

16. Balot, "Courage," 417.

17. Not to mention Nicias, as discussed below. That the Athenians were deeply ensconced in a shame culture is not lost on Balot, who admits that "Pericles also mobilized attitudes of shame centered on living up to the ideals of one's ancestors" (Balot, "Courage," 417). That the shame is "appropriate" (418) adds little to the distinction. Aristotle, in the *Nicomachean Ethics*, also recognizes the relationship between courage and compulsion (1116a20).

18. Clifford Orwin, *The Humanity of Thucydides* (Princeton: Princeton University Press, 1994), 16.

19. Ibid.

20. Thucydides *Peloponnesian War* 2.39; translation from *The Peloponnesian War*, trans. Steven Lattimore (Indianapolis: Hackett, 1998). All subsequent citations to this work are from this edition (hereafter cited as *PW*) and are given parenthetically in the text.

21. Plato *Philebus* 89d. Cf. *Republic* 335e, 565e, 582e, 583e, and 603e, and *Symposium* 195e.

22. Xenophon *Memorabilia* 3.5.1.

23. For a different view on Pericles' contrast of *rhathumia* and *ponos*, see Victoria Wohl, *Love among the Ruins: The Erotics of Democracy in Classical Athens* (Princeton: Princeton University Press, 2002), 51.

24. The word appears forty times in Thucydides, four times in book 2 alone: 2.22, 2.73, 2.93, 2.100.

25. Helen North, *Sophrosyne: Self-Knowledge and Self-Restraint in Greek Literature* (Ithaca: Cornell University Press, 1966), 100.

26. Ibid.

27. According to Gregory Vlastos, however, *hêsychia* was not unknown in Athens. Evidence of its use goes back as far as Solon, who employs it to describe the sea as peaceful, in contrast to *krasis* (disturbed) (frag. 13.61, as cited by Vlastos). Similarly, political life in Athens can be peaceful or disturbed: "That *hêsychia* has the same sense in politics is clear from Solon's exhortation to the nobles: 'Still [ἡσυχάσαντες] the strong heart within your breast/You who have forced your way to good things in excess [ἐς κόρον]/Put your proud [literally, "great"] mind within the measure.'" Gregory Vlastos, "Solonian Justice," *Classical Philology* 41, no. 2 (1946): 68.

28. Josiah Ober, *Political Dissent in Democratic Athens: Intellectual Critics of Popular Rule* (Princeton: Princeton University Press, 1998), 86.

29. Pindar *Pythian Odes* 8: "Hesykhia (Tranquility), goddess of friendly intent, daughter of Dike (Justice), you who make cities great, holding the supreme keys of counsel and of wars"; translation from Pindar, *The Odes of Pindar*, trans. G. S. Conway (London: Dent, 1972).

30. The word used here—ἐμαλακίσθη—is used by Herodotus (μαλακώτερος) with regard to Telines' womanliness (*Histories* 7.153.3–4).

31. For more on Pericles' vacillation between aristocracy and democracy, see Nicole Loraux, *The Invention of Athens: The Funeral Oration in the Classical City*, trans. Alan Sheridan (Cambridge, MA: Harvard University Press, 1986), esp. 180–87.

32. For more on the use of funeral orations and free speech in the democratic city, see ibid. and Ryan Balot, "Free Speech, Courage, and Democratic Deliberation," in Sluiter and Rosen, *Free Speech.*

33. It might well be that acquiring honor and victory in the war against Sparta, while at the same time living a generally rhathumic life, is in itself victory. It is almost as if Pericles is taunting the Spartans: "We are just as good as you at war and battle, if not better—and we don't even have to work at it!"

34. Simon Hornblower, *A Commentary on Thucydides: Volume 1, Books I–III* (Oxford: Clarendon Press, 1991), 316, 317.

35. Ineke Sluiter and Ralph Mark Rosen, "General Introduction," in Rosen and Sluiter, *Andreia,* 13, 14.

36. Aristophanes *Frogs* 477–85, my translation.

37. Aristophanes *Frogs* 487–91, my translation.

38. For more on the relationship between *andreia* and "guts" (ἀφοβόσπλαγχνοσ), see Bassi, "Semantics of Manliness," 45 n. 54: "The primary visceral meaning of the term is established in the first occurrence where Aeacus tells Dionysus that Echidna will 'rend your innards' (ἢ τὰ σπλάγχνα σου διασπαράξει, 473). The other two refer to the anger of Aeschylus, which—given his martial disposition in the play—may erupt into physical violence. Dionysus' challenge to Xanthias at 494–96 helps to contextualize the two later references to the σπλάγχνα of Aeschylus; having 'guts' is no guarantee of 'real' martial prowess."

39. Aristophanes *Frogs* 895–900, my translation.

40. Aristophanes *Frogs* 948–75, my translation.

41. Aristophanes *Assemblywomen* 105–9, in Aristophanes, *The Knights; Peace; The Birds; The Assemblywomen; Wealth,* trans. David Barrett and Alan H. Sommerstein (New York: Penguin Books, 1978); all subsequent quotations from this work are to this edition.

42. Aristophanes *Assemblywomen* 622.

43. Aristophanes *Assemblywomen* 626.

44. Aristophanes *Assemblywomen* 628.

45. Sluiter and Rosen, "General Introduction," 14.

46. Aristophanes *Knights* 508–13, in Aristophanes, *Knights; Peace; The Birds;* all subsequent quotations from this work are to this edition. Similar claims can be found in *The Acharnians,* where the Chorus says: "So far, so wide has news of his great courage spread already that the Persian King himself, when testing out the Spartan embassy, first asked them which combatant was the stronger in her naval force, then asked them which

combatant was the target of this poet's abuse; 'for these,' he said, 'are people who've been turned into much better men, and they will be decisive victors, having him to give advice'" (665–77); and in *The Wasps*, the Chorus actually compares the poet's service to the city as "courage worthy of Heracles" (1030, but see 1017–42; translation from *The Complete Plays of Aristophanes*, ed. Moses Hadas [New York: Bantam Books, 1962]).

47. See Thucydides *PW* 4.1–41. The charge also appears explicitly in *The Knights* when the sausage seller proves to be even more effective at theft.

48. Aristophanes *Knights* 45–48.

49. Aristophanes *Knights* 388–89.

50. Adriaan Rademaker, "'Most citizens are *Euryproktoi* now': (Un) manliness in Aristophanes," in Rosen and Sluiter, *Andreia*, 115. For more on the role of comedy on political critique, see the essay "Aristophanes in America," in J. Peter Euben, *Platonic Noise* (Princeton: Princeton University Press, 2003).

51. Aristophanes *Assemblywomen* 519. Rademaker notes that the only characters in Aristophanes' works called *andreia* without sarcasm "are, paradoxically, women: Lysistrata in *Lys.* 549, 1108, and the women at the assembly in *Eccl.* 519. Theirs is not the standard 'martial' *andreia* of course, but rather the successful management of the affairs of the polis when men have made a mess of them." Rademaker, "Most citizens are *Euryproktoi* now," 115 n. 1.

52. Roisman, "Rhetoric of Courage," 128.

53. Rademaker, "Most citizens are *Euryproktoi* now," 119.

54. Aristophanes *Knights* 1239 (on his theft and lying) and 1242, 1247 (on his engaging in prostitution); see also 876, 878.

55. Rademaker, "Most citizens are *Euryproktoi* now," 120. For more on male prostitution and the law, see K. J. Dover, *Greek Homosexuality* (Cambridge, MA: Harvard University Press, 1978), 19–38; Clifford Hindley, "Law, Society and Homosexuality in Classical Athens," *Past and Present* 133 (1991): 167–83; J. J. Winkler, "Laying Down the Law: The Oversight of Men's Sexual Behavior in Classical Athens," in *Before Sexuality: The Construction of Erotic Experience in the Ancient Greek World*, ed. D. M. Halperin, J. J. Winkler, and F. I. Zeitlin (Princeton: Princeton University Press, 1990); and David Cohen, *Law, Sexuality, and Society: The Enforcement of Morals in Classical Athens* (Cambridge: Cambridge University Press, 1991).

56. Rademaker, in "Most citizens are *Euryproktoi* now" (123), provides good evidence for this in a passage from Aeschines' *Against Timarchus*

(1.29). For more on the distinction between active (erastes) and passive (eromenōs) participation, see Dover, *Greek Homosexuality*, 16, 42–54. Also helpful are David Halperin, "Plato on Erotic Reciprocity," *Classical Antiquity* 5 (1986): 60–80; Radcliffe G. Edmons, "Socrates the Beautiful: Role Reversal and Midwifery in Plato's *Symposium*," *Transactions and Proceedings of the American Philological Association* 130 (2000): 261–85; Kenneth Moore, "Eros, Hybris and Mania: Love and Desire in Plato's *Laws* and Beyond," *Polis: The Journal of the Society for Greek Political Thought* 24, no. 1 (2007): 112–33; Mark Golden, "Slavery and Homosexuality at Athens," *Phoenix* 38, no. 4 (1984): 308–24; Robert J. Littman, "The Loves of Alcibiades," *Transactions and Proceedings of the American Philological Association* 101 (1970): 1877–1902; Page DuBois, "The Homoerotics of the 'Phaedrus,'" *Pacific Coast Philology* 17, nos. 1/2 (1982): 9–15, David Halperin, "Platonic Eros and What Men Call Love," *Ancient Philosophy* 5 (1985): 161–204; T. K. Hubbard, "Popular Perceptions of Elite Homosexuality in Classical Athens," *Arion* 6, no. 1 (1998): 48–78; Thomas F. Scanlon, "The Dispersion of Pederasty and the Athletic Revolution in Sixth-Century BC Greece," *Journal of Homosexuality* 39, nos. 3/4 (2005): 63–85.

57. Aristotle *Nicomachean Ethics* 1103a16; translation from *The Nicomachean Ethics*, ed. and trans. David Ross (Oxford: Oxford University Press, 1980), hereafter cited parenthetically in the text as *NE;* see also 1115a5. All subsequent quotations are from this edition unless otherwise noted. The other moral virtues are temperance (σοφπρσύνη), liberality (ἐλευθεριότης), magnificence (μεγαλοπρέπεια), magnanimity (μεγαλοψυχία), gentleness (πραότης), friendliness (φιλία), truthfulness (ἀληθευτικός), wit (εὐτράπελοι), shame (αἰδώς), justice (δικαιοσύνη), and an unnamed virtue that lies between ambition and unambitiousness (1125a39).

58. The five types of pseudocourage are civic courage; courage based on experience; courage stemming from blind emotions, such as pain; courage from optimism; and courage from ignorance.

59. Aristotle *Politics* 1271a17; translation from *The Complete Works of Aristotle*, trans. Benjamin Jowett (Princeton: Princeton University Press, 1991), with my modifications when it falls short. Subsequent quotations from this work are to this edition, with my modifications, and citations are given parenthetically in the text.

60. That Aristotle is fond of the word is beyond question, as it appears over six hundred times in his oeuvre.

61. Susan Collins recognizes this distinction well, suggesting that the moral motivation to courage is a "longing for the noble." Susan D. Col-

lins, *Aristotle and the Rediscovery of Citizenship* (New York: Cambridge University Press, 2006), 47–66. Cf. Steven B. Smith, "Goodness, Nobility and Virtue in Aristotle's Political Science," *Polity* 19, no. 1 (1986): 5–26. Mark Lutz points to similar language in Plato's thought, suggesting that philosophy is an erotic pursuit of the noble; see Mark J. Lutz, *Socrates' Education to Virtue: Learning the Love of the Noble* (Albany: State University of New York Press, 1998), 83–110.

62. *NE* 1179b5, but see also 1125b10 for Aristotle's only other use of φιλόκαλος. The only other ancient writer of note who uses φιλόκαλος with any frequency is Xenophon (*Memorabilia* 3.11.9, *Symposium* 4.15, *Cyropaedia* 1.3.3, 2.1.22, 8.3.5). Plato uses is it at *Critias* 111e and *Phaedrus* 248c.

63. Collins, *Aristotle,* 53.

64. Ibid., 50.

65. For more on the centrality and usefulness of Aristotle's considerations on justice, see Judith A. Swanson, "Aristotle on Liberality: Its Relation to Justice and Its Public and Private Practice," *Polity* 27, no. 1 (1994): 3–23; and W. von Leyden, *Aristotle on Equality and Justice: His Political Argument* (New York: St. Martin's Press, 1985). Less convinced of the centrality of justice are, for example, Fred Dycus Miller, *Nature, Justice, and Rights in Aristotle's Politics* (Oxford: Clarendon Press, 1995); Delba Winthrop, "Aristotle and Theories of Justice," *American Political Science Review* 72, no. 4 (1978): 1201–16; and Bernard Yack, "Natural Right and Aristotle's Understanding of Justice," *Political Theory* 18, no. 2 (1990): 216–37.

66. Stephen G. Salkever, *Finding the Mean: Theory and Practice in Aristotelian Political Philosophy* (Princeton: Princeton University Press, 1990), 174.

67. Collins, *Aristotle,* 50 n. 6. Aristotle's position on women is much debated. Harold Levy, for instance, claims that most interpreters of Aristotle are too categorical in accusing him of denying women their rightful place in political life. As Levy puts it, "Scholars have overlooked Aristotle's indirection and ambiguity on this question, and have prematurely foreclosed counterinterpretation of the text." Harold Levy, "Does Aristotle Exclude Women from Politics?" *Review of Politics* 52, no. 3 (1990): 397. But see also Darrell Dobbs, "Family Matters: Aristotle's Appreciation of Women and the Plural Structure of Society," *American Political Science Review* 90, no. 1 (1996): 74–89; Jean Bethke Elshtain, *Public Man, Private Woman: Women in Social and Political Thought* (Princeton: Princeton University Press, 1981); and Judith Swanson, "Aristotle on Nature, Human

Nature, and Justice: A Consideration of the Natural Functions of Men and Women in the City," in *Action and Contemplation: Studies in the Moral and Political Thought of Aristotle*, ed. Robert C. Bartlett and Susan D. Collins (Albany: State University of New York Press, 1999).

68. As Steven Smith puts it, "When we put the statement that moral action is performed for the love of the noble together with the statement that all actions aim at some good, we are led to the conclusion that the end to be attained must be noble [kalon] and the one who attains it must be both noble and good, that is, high-minded and gentlemanly [kalokagathon]" ("Goodness, Nobility," 18). For more on the great-souled man in Aristotle's thought, see Jacob Howland, "Aristotle's Great-Souled Man," *Review of Politics* 64, no. 1 (2002): 27–56; Ryan Patrick Hanley, "Aristotle on the Greatness of the Greatness of Soul," *History of Political Thought* 23, no. 1 (2002): 1–20; W. F. R. Hardie, "'Magnanimity' in Aristotle's *Ethics*," *Phronesis* 23 (1978): 63–79; John von Heyking, "*Ab virilitate ad perseverantiae gloriae:* Comparing Aristotle's and Thomas Aquinas's Pedagogy on Manliness," paper presented at the annual meeting of the American Political Science Association, Boston, September 2002; Harry V. Jaffa, *Thomism and Aristotelianism: A Study of the Commentary by Thomas Aquinas of the Nicomachean Ethics* (Chicago: University of Chicago Press, 1952); Stephen A. White, *Sovereign Virtue: Aristotle on the Relation between Happiness and Prosperity* (Stanford: Stanford University Press, 1992), 250–71; and Nancy Sherman, "Common Sense and Uncommon Virtue," *Midwest Studies in Philosophy* 13 (1988): 97–114. For a discussion of magnanimity from Aristotle to Churchill, see Carson Holloway, *Magnanimity and Statesmanship* (Lanham, MD: Lexington Books, 2008).

69. Howland, "Aristotle's Great-Souled Man," 32.

70. Angela Hobbs, *Plato and the Hero: Courage, Manliness and the Impersonal Good* (Cambridge: Cambridge University Press, 2000), 137. See also Ober, *Political Dissent*, esp. 197–206; James C. Haden, "Two Types of Power in Plato's 'Gorgias,'" *Classical Journal* 87 (1992): 313–26; George Klosko, "The Insufficiency of Reason in Plato's Gorgias," *Western Political Quarterly* 36 (1983): 579–95; Devin Stauffer, "Socrates and Callicles: A Reading of Plato's 'Gorgias,'" *Review of Politics* 64 (2002): 627–57; Eric Voegelin, "The Philosophy of Existence: Plato's 'Gorgias,'" *Review of Politics* 11 (1949): 477–98; James L. Wiser, "Philosophy as Political Action: A Reading of the Gorgias," *American Journal of Political Science* 19 (1975): 313–22.

71. Plato *Apology* 18b. For more on the argument and action of Plato's *Apology*, see Alister Cameron, *Plato's Affair with Tragedy* (Cincinnati: University of Cincinnati Press, 1978); Theodore de Laguna, "The Interpretation of the Apology," *Philosophical Review* 18, no. 1 (1909): 23–37; Shinro Kato, "The Apology: The Beginning of Plato's Own Philosophy," *Classical Quarterly* 41, no. 2 (1991): 356–64; Ernst Moritz Manesse, "A Thematic Interpretation of Plato's *Apology* and *Crito*," *Philosophy and Phenomenological Research* 40, no. 3 (1980): 393–400; Michael Zuckert, "Rationalism and Political Responsibility: Just Speech and Just Deed in the 'Clouds' and the 'Apology' of Socrates," *Polity* 17, no. 2 (1984): 271–97; Thomas L. Pangle, "The Political Defense of Socratic Philosophy: A Study of Xenophon's 'Apology of Socrates to the Jury,'" *Polity* 18, no. 1 (1985): 98–114; Gerald M. Mara, *Socrates' Discursive Democracy: Logos and Ergon in Platonic Political Philosophy* (Albany: State University of New York Press, 1997), esp. 31–61; and Leo Strauss, *Studies in Platonic Political Philosophy* (Chicago: University of Chicago Press, 1983), 38–54.

72. As Thucydides puts it, "One of the chief features in his organization of the country was to abolish the council chambers and magistrates of the petty cities, and to merge them in the single council-chamber [bouleutêrion] and town-hall [prutaneion] of the present capital. Individuals might still enjoy their private property just as before, but they were henceforth compelled to have only one political center, viz. Athens, which thus counted all the inhabitants of Attica among her citizens" (*PW* 2.15).

73. Eric Voegelin, *Plato* (Baton Rouge: Louisiana State University Press, 1966), 24. As part of this "soul care" in Plato's thought, Oona Eisenstat suggests that a central tactic of Socrates is to "awaken shame" in his interlocutors. Oona Eisenstadt, "Shame in the *Apology*," in *Politics, Philosophy, Writing: Plato's Art of Caring for Souls*, ed. Zdravko Planinc (Columbia: University of Missouri Press, 2001), 42. Such a tactic is consistent with the presentation of Socrates in the mold of the traditional hero, but it seems more likely that rather than "awakening" it, Socrates is attempting to associate an already deep sense of shame with another issue—injustice, rather than unmanliness.

74. Allan Bloom, "Interpretive Essay," in *The Republic of Plato*, ed. and trans. Allan Bloom (New York: Basic Books, 1991), 354. See also Lawrence A. Tritle, *From Melos to My Lai: War and Survival* (New York: Routledge, 2000), esp. 34–54.

75. Bloom, "Interpretive Essay," 354.

76. Ibid.

77. For a thorough account of Achilles' place in *Republic* 3 and 4, see Hobbs, *Plato and the Hero,* 199–219.

78. Plato *Republic* 390d; translation from *The Republic of Plato,* 2nd ed., ed. and trans. Allan Bloom (New York: Basic Books, 1991); subsequent citations to this work in this chapter are to this edition and are given parenthetically in the text.

79. The relationship between Plato and the poets has a long scholarly history. For example, see Carleton L. Brownson, "Reasons for Plato's Hostility to the Poets," *Transactions and Proceedings of the American Philological Association* 28 (1897); 5–41; William Chase Greene, "Plato's View of Poetry," *Harvard Studies in Classical Philology* 29 (1918): 1–75; George Ainslie Hight, "Plato and the Poets," *Mind* 31, no. 122 (1922): 195–99; Thomas Shearer Duncan, "Plato and Poetry," *Classical Review* 40, no. 8 (1945): 481–94; Darnell Rucker, "Plato and the Poets," *Journal of Aesthetics and Art Criticism* 25, no. 2 (1966): 167–70; Morriss Henry Partee, "Plato's Banishment of Poetry," *Journal of Aesthetics and Art Criticism* 29, no. 2 (1970): 209–22; Norman Gulley, "Plato on Poetry," *Greece and Rome* 24, no. 2 (1977): 154–69; and Mary P. Nichols, "Socrates' Contest with the Poets in Plato's Symposium," *Political Theory* 32, no. 2 (2004): 186–206.

80. Bloom, "Interpretive Essay," 360.

81. Ibid., 359.

82. Discussion of courage in Plato's major texts is ample and important. See, for example, *Republic* 430c, 503e, and 535a–c, *Statesman* 306a–b, and *Laws* 631c, 696b, 963e, and 964b.

83. See Stewart Umphrey, "On the Theme of Plato's *Laches,*" *Interpretation* 6, no. 1 (1977): 1–11; and Daniel T. Devereux, "Courage and Wisdom in Plato's *Laches,*" *Journal of the History of Philosophy* 15, no. 1 (1977): 129–41. An interesting debate in contemporary scholarship has revolved around an analysis of the nature of virtue. See, for example, Daniel T. Devereux, "The Unity of the Virtues in Plato's *Protagoras* and *Laches,*" *Philosophical Review* 101, no. 4 (1992): 765–89; Terry Penner, "What Laches and Nicias Miss—and Whether Socrates Thinks Courage Merely a Part of Virtue," *Ancient Philosophy* 12, no. 1 (1992): 1–27; Kenneth W. Cooley, "Unity and Diversity of the Virtues in the *Charmides, Laches,* and *Protagoras,*" *Kinesis* 1 (1969): 100–106; and Carol S. Gould, "Socratic Intellectualism and the Problem of Courage: An Interpretation of Plato's *Laches,*" *History of Philosophy Quarterly* 4, no. 3 (1987): 265–79.

84. Lysimachus is the son of Aristeides "the Just," who, along with Themistocles, was the champion of the people after the Persian Wars. Themistocles and Aristeides were co-responsible for the reconstruction of the vaunted Athenian walls and, as Aristotle indicates in the *Athenian Constitution*, "Aristeides was skilled in the political arts and was outstanding among his contemporaries for his uprightness." Aristotle *Athenian Constitution* 23.3; translation from *The Athenian Constitution*, trans. P. J. Rhodes (New York: Penguin Books, 1984). He was also largely responsible for the creation of the Delian League and later for convincing the Athenians to assert their leadership there (24.1). Melesias, on the other hand, was the son of Thucydides, who was the champion of the wealthy at the same time Pericles was championing the people. This Thucydides (not the historian), is reputed to be the brother-in-law of Cimon, and in Aristotle's reckoning it was widely agreed that he and the very Nicias of this dialogue "were not only gentlemen but were public-spirited and behaved like fathers towards the whole city" (28.5). Incidentally, Thucydides was ostracized in 443. In short, both Lysimachus's and Melesias's fathers were preeminent men in Athenian political life who garnered considerable fame for their virtue and good citizenship.

85. Plato *Laches* 179d; translation from *The Roots of Political Philosophy: Ten Forgotten Socratic Dialogues*, ed. Thomas L. Pangle (Ithaca: Cornell University Press, 1987). All subsequent citations to this work in this chapter will be given parenthetically in the text and will be based on this translation, unless otherwise indicated.

86. Walter Schmid, *On Manly Courage: A Study of Plato's Laches* (Carbondale: Southern Illinois University Press, 1992), 6. As for a precise dramatic date, I defer to Hoerber, who considers 421 to be as good a guess as any; Robert G. Hoerber, "Plato's *Laches*," *Classical Philology* 63 (1968): 95. Less precisely, the dialogue must be situated between the battle at Delium (424) and the death of Laches (418).

87. Thucydides is not alone in this assessment of Nicias. Plutarch says Nicias was afraid of the people and that, "timid as he was by nature, and distrustful of success, in war he managed to succeed in hiding his cowardice under a cloak of good fortune" (Plutarch *Nicias* 2.4; translation from *Lives*, ed. Charles W. Eliot [Cambridge, MA: Harvard University Press, 1997], but cf. 4.3, 8.1, and 14.2). For a more sympathetic assessment of Nicias, see Gerasimos Santas, who claims, "If any men should know about courage—at least the courage of the battlefield—[Nicias and Laches]

should." Gerasimos Santas, "Socrates at Work on Virtue and Knowledge in Plato's *Laches*," *Review of Metaphysics* 22 (1969): 435.

88. This same question is pursued by Mark Blitz, "Introduction to the Reading of Plato's *Laches*," *Interpretation* 5, no. 2 (1975): 185–225; and James H. Nichols Jr., "Introduction to the *Laches*," in Pangle, *Roots of Political Philosophy.*

89. Schmid, *On Manly Courage*, 8.

90. For a fuller discussion of the relationship between fear of the unknown and Nicias's understanding of courage, see Darrell Dobbs, "For Lack of Wisdom: Courage and Inquiry in Plato's *Laches*," *Journal of Politics* 48, no. 4 (1986): 825–49.

91. Schmid, *On Manly Courage*, 9.

92. Cf. Plato *Symposium* 220e–221c.

93. Laches did not entirely escape public notoriety. In his *Wasps*, Aristophanes mocks Laches for the withdrawal from Sicily in 427. Aristophanes portrays a housedog named Labes stealing a whole Sicilian cheese. The dog is put on trial and eventually convicted on the evidence of a Sicilian cheese–flavored belch. Laches is being accused of shamelessly embezzling part of the sailors' pay and for taking bribes from the Sicilians to retreat. For an explanation of the joke, see David Braund, "Aristophanes at Acanthus, *Wasps* 968–969," *Classical Quarterly* 49, no. 1 (1995): 321–24. Cf. D. M. MacDowell, *Aristophanes and Athens* (Oxford: Oxford University Press, 1995).

94. Darrell Dobbs argues that Laches is certainly superior to Nicias because of "his willingness to acknowledge his own perplexity and to attempt a genuine inquiry to resolve it" ("For Lack of Wisdom," 829). Most commentators have, mistakenly I argue, held Nicias up as superior to Laches either because he is a more able discursive partner (for example, Paul Friedlander, *"Laches,"* in *Plato* [New York: Pantheon Books, 1964], 42) or because Laches "lacks steadfastness on the unfamiliar terrain of philosophical discussion" (Michael O'Brien, "The Unity of *Laches*," *Yale Classical Studies* 18 [1963]: 138).

95. Cf. Plato *Symposium* 221a–b, where Alcibiades claims to have witnessed Socrates outstrip Laches in collectedness in the retreat at Delium.

96. In the *Laws*, Plato's Athenian asserts that the core of education is to engage the soul of the child at play. The parallel to the argument being made here is striking: education in virtue for children is to "make one desire and love to become a good citizen who knows how to rule and be ruled

with justice" (*Laws* 643d); translations of this and subsequent passages from this work are taken from *The Laws of Plato*, trans. T. L. Pangle (Chicago: University of Chicago Press, 1988). For more on the theme of education in the *Laches* and in Plato in general, see Charles L. Griswold, "Philosophy, Education, and Courage in Plato's *Laches*," *Interpretation* 14, no. 2 (1986): 177–93; Thomas O. Buford, "Plato on the Educational Consultant: An Interpretation of the *Laches*," *Idealistic Studies* 7, no. 2 (1977): 151–93; Lutz, *Socrates' Education to Virtue*; J. Peter Euben, *Corrupting Youth: Political Education, Democratic Culture, and Political Theory* (Princeton: Princeton University Press, 1997); and especially Waller R. Newell, *Ruling Passion: The Erotics of Statecraft in Platonic Political Philosophy* (Lanham, MD: Rowman and Littlefield, 2000), 103–42.

97. For more on this, see Plato *Laws* 677b, where the Athenian mentions "the contrivances that city dwellers use against one another, motivated by the desire to have more [pleonexia], the love of victory [φιλονικία], and all the mischief they think up against each other." The description is quite appropriate for Nicias and is echoed in the *Republic* (586c), where Socrates describes poor citizenship and the violence of the lover of victory.

98. Schmid claims there are three Sophists involved in the dialogue: Stesilaus, Damon, and Prodicus. As for Stesilaus, Schmid argues that he is "the symbol, as it were, of sophistry in military things, the little professor of military science, the man who claims to teach virtue through the study of the arts of war" (*On Manly Courage*, 20).

99. In *Euthydemus* 271d, Socrates explicitly refers to ὁπλομαχία as an area of sophistic instruction. Moreover, in his *Memorabilia* (3.1.1–15), Xenophon has Socrates take Diodorus to task for learning the art of generalship from the Sophist Dionysodorus.

100. Aristide Tessitore's interpretation is even more critical. He claims that Laches displays a "weakness of character" because, while he can hold steadfast to his deeds in battle, he is not steadfast in argument. Aristide Tessitore, "Courage and Comedy in Plato's *Laches*," *Journal of Politics* 56, no. 1 (1994): 125.

101. There has been a flourishing of recent scholarship concerning the relationship between Plato's Socrates and democratic politics. See, for example, J. Euben, *Corrupting Youth;* Mara, *Socrates' Discursive Democracy;* Paul Stern, "The Philosophic Importance of Political Life: On the 'Digression' in Plato's *Theatetus*," *American Political Science Review* 96, no. 2 (2002):

275–89; and John R. Wallach, *The Platonic Political Art: A Study of Critical Reason and Democracy* (University Park: Pennsylvania State University Press, 2001).

102. In book 4 of the *Republic,* Socrates offers a partial definition of courage that departs from the strictly martial understanding: "Courage is a preservative. Strengthened by education, it preserves convictions about the things that are legitimately to be feared and those that are not. Courage makes a man hold fast to these convictions no matter whether he is threatened by danger or lured by desire" (429c).

103. In the *Republic,* Socrates invokes the same metaphor. In the search for justice, he says, "we must be like hunters who surround a thicket to make sure that the quarry doesn't escape" (432b). In *The Sophist* Plato explicitly invokes the metaphor of hunting. First he says that "the Sophist [is] a very troublesome creature to hunt down" (218d). A bit later (223b), having elaborated the metaphor, he claims that the Sophist is himself a sort of hunter, but of a rather ignoble variety: he is an appropriative and acquisitive sort who "hunts man, privately, for hire, taking money in exchange, having the semblance of education—and this is termed Sophistry, and is a hunt after young men of wealth and rank—such is the conclusion." Translation from Plato, *The Collected Dialogues of Plato,* trans. E. Hamilton and H. Cairns (New York: Pantheon Books, 1961). Cf. *Euthydemus* 290b–d and *Laws* 824a. For more on hunting in the ancient world, see J. K. Anderson, *Hunting in the Ancient World* (Berkeley: University of California Press, 1985), and Denison Bingham Hull, *Hounds and Hunting in Ancient Greece* (Chicago: University of Chicago Press, 1964).

104. Nietzsche's language for this is very illustrative. He calls it "philosophizing with a hammer." Friedrich Nietzsche, *Twilight of the Idols,* in *Twilight of the Idols; and The Anti-Christ* (Baltimore: Penguin Books, 1968).

105. Cf. Plato *Protagoras* 313c, where Socrates derides the wares of the Sophists as "doctrine" and "rehearsed phrases" (μάθηματα) that are fed to the souls of the young.

106. Recall Nicias's speech after the naval defeat at Syracuse. At a most inappropriate time, all he can muster is more rehearsed phrases and platitudes (*PW* 7.64).

107. For an interesting discussion of forethought in the *Laches,* see Michael Nass, "Philosophy Bound: The Fate of the Promethean Socrates," in *Research in Phenomenology* (Pittsburgh: Duquesne University Press, 1995).

FOUR. Moral Courage and Autonomy

The chapter epigraph is from *Emile: or, On Education* (New York: Basic Books, 1979), 445.

1. Herodotus *Histories* 7.228, my translation.

2. Plato *Crito* 53b, but see also 53c. Translation here and subsequently is from *Four Texts on Socrates: Plato's Euthyphro, Apology, and Crito, and Aristophanes' Clouds*, ed. and trans. Thomas G. West and Grace Starry West (Ithaca: Cornell University Press, 1984). Subsequent citations refer to this translation unless otherwise noted. More detailed accounts of Socrates' relationship with the city, the laws, and his friends can be found in Strauss, *Studies*, 54–66; Ann Congleton, "Two Kinds of Lawlessness: Plato's Crito," *Political Theory* 2, no. 4 (1974): 432–46; M. Dyson, "The Structure of the Laws' Speech in Plato's Crito," *Classical Quarterly* 28, no. 2 (1978): 427–36; J. Peter Euben, "Philosophy and Politics in Plato's Crito," *Political Theory* 6, no. 2 (1978): 149–72; Frederick Rosen, "Obligation and Friendship in Plato's Crito," *Political Theory* 1, no. 3 (1973): 307–16; Daniel M. Farrell, "Illegal Actions, Universal Maxims, and the Duty to Obey the Law: The Case for Civil Authority in the Crito," *Political Theory* 6, no. 2 (1978): 173–89; Michael J. Rosano, "Citizenship and Socrates in Plato's 'Crito,'" *Review of Politics* 62, no. 3 (2000): 451–77; and Steven M. DeLue, "Plato's Crito as a Defense of Critical Inquiry," *Journal of Politics* 39, no. 2 (1977): 472–79.

3. See also Plato *Apology* 28e, where Socrates also compares his actions to the warrior staying in line: "When the rulers you elected to rule me stationed me in Potidaea and Amphipolis and at Delium, I stayed then where they stationed me and ran the risk of dying like anyone else, but when the god stationed me, as I supposed and assumed, ordering me to live philosophizing and examining myself and others, I had then left my station because I feared death or any other matter whatever." The translation here is from Plato, *Four Texts on Socrates.*

4. One is here reminded of later thinkers, such as Augustine and Aquinas, who both claim that an unjust law is no law at all.

5. See, for example, Nathan Tarcov, "Rousseau and the Discovery of Political Compassion," in *The Legacy of Rousseau*, ed. Clifford Orwin and Nathan Tarcov (Chicago: University of Chicago Press, 1997); Richard

Boyd, "Pity's Pathologies Portrayed: Rousseau and the Limits of Democratic Compassion," *Political Theory* 32, no. 4 (2004): 519–46; and Jonathan Marks, "Rousseau's Discriminating Defense of Compassion," *American Political Science Review* 101, no. 4 (2007): 727–39.

6. Jean-Jacques Rousseau, *The First and Second Discourses* (New York: St. Martin's Press, 1964), 33. All subsequent citations to the First *(FD)* and Second Discourses (*SD*) will be to this edition and will be given parenthetically in text.

7. Laurence Cooper suggests that the "desire to maintain and extend our being" is foundational to Rousseau's thought; Laurence D. Cooper, "Between Eros and Will to Power: Rousseau and 'the Desire to Extend Our Being,'" *American Political Science Review* 98, no. 1 (2004): 106. For more on the idea of immortality in Rousseau, see Ann McArdle, "Rousseau on Rousseau: The Individual and Society," *Review of Politics* 39, no. 2 (1977): 250–79; and Ronald Grimsley, *Rousseau and the Religious Quest* (Oxford: Clarendon Press, 1968), esp. 87–129.

8. For more detailed descriptions of virtue in Rousseau, see Joseph R. Reisert, *Jean-Jacques Rousseau: A Friend of Virtue* (Ithaca: Cornell University Press, 2003), who emphatically claims that "Rousseau advances one consistent, critical theme: he complains that his contemporaries lack virtue" (10). Also worthwhile are Carol Blum, *Rousseau and the Republic of Virtue: The Language of Politics in the French Revolution* (Ithaca: Cornell University Press, 1986); Arthur M. Melzer, *The Natural Goodness of Man: On the System of Rousseau's Thought* (Chicago: University of Chicago Press, 1990); Peter Emberley, "Rousseau and the Domestication of Virtue," *Canadian Journal of Political Science / Revue canadienne de science politique* 17, no. 4 (1984): 731–53; Judith Nisse Shklar, *Men and Citizens: A Study of Rousseau's Social Theory* (London: Cambridge University Press, 1969); Joseph R. Reisert, "Authenticity, Justice, and Virtue in Taylor and Rousseau," *Polity* 33, no. 2 (2000): 305–30; and Jeffrey A. Smith, "Nationalism, Virtue, and the Spirit of Liberty in Rousseau's 'Government of Poland,'" *Review of Politics* 65, no. 3 (2003): 409–37. Rousseau's complaint is echoed later by Nietzsche in his *Genealogy of Morals*, but it is precisely against the virtues advocated by Rousseau that Nietzsche rails. For more, see Keith Ansell-Pearson, *Nietzsche contra Rousseau: A Study of Nietzsche's Moral and Political Thought* (Cambridge: Cambridge University Press, 1991).

9. See Joshua Mitchell, *Not by Reason Alone: Religion, History, and Identity in Early Modern Political Thought* (Chicago: University of Chicago Press, 1993), for a good account of the exterior/interior division in Rous-

seau's thought. For an eloquent account of the history of authenticity, see Trilling, *Sincerity and Authenticity*, and especially his discussion of Rousseau (58–67). Also helpful are Stephen Ellenburg, *Rousseau's Political Philosophy: An Interpretation from Within* (Ithaca: Cornell University Press, 1976), esp. 167–200; Arthur M. Melzer, "The Origin of the Counter-Enlightenment: Rousseau and the New Religion of Sincerity," *American Political Science Review* 90, no. 2 (1996): 344–60, and "Rousseau and the Modern Cult of Sincerity," in Orwin and Tarcov, *Legacy of Rousseau;* Margaret Ogrodnick, *Instinct and Intimacy: Political Philosophy and Autobiography in Rousseau* (Toronto: University of Toronto Press, 1999), esp. 20–29; Reisert, "Authenticity, Justice"; Elizabeth Rose Wingrove, "Interpretive Practices and Political Designs: Reading Authenticity, Integrity, and Reform in Jean-Jacques Rousseau," *Political Theory* 29, no. 1 (2001): 91–111; Jonathan Marks, "Jean-Jacques Rousseau, Michael Sandel and the Politics of Transparency," *Polity* 33, no. 4 (2001): 619–42; and Greg Hill, *Rousseau's Theory of Human Association: Transparent and Opaque Communities* (New York: Palgrave Macmillan, 2006).

10. Reisert, *Jean-Jacques Rousseau*, 95–96. In his otherwise good account of the idea of friendship in Rousseau, Reisert overstates a problem in Bloom's essay, "Rousseau and the Romantic Project" (in Bloom's *Love and Friendship* [New York: Simon and Schuster, 1993], 39–156). He claims that because Bloom understands Rousseau as holding "a fundamentally materialist conception of man" he is "forced to treat friendship as nothing more than a 'secondary offshoot' of the sexual passion" (78). For Bloom, it only "appears" this way. This view of friendship in Rousseau's thought is not universal. Mira Morgenstern, for example, asks why, in *La nouvelle Héloïse*, "friendship, which seems by nature a pure and mature emotion, cannot succeed in actually establishing a society of authenticity and happiness at Clarens? The answer may be found in the nature of friendship itself. . . . Friendship in and of itself does not guarantee the purity of its intentions . . . and is not always an adequate substitute for the love it is supposed to replace." Mira Morgenstern, *Rousseau and the Politics of Ambiguity: Self, Culture, and Society* (University Park: Pennsylvania State University Press, 1996), 103; but see also Lisa Disch, "Claire Loves Julie: Reading the Story of Women's Friendship in *La nouvelle Heloise*," *Hypatia* 9, no. 3 (1994): 19–45. For more on the relationship between friendship and politics, see Richard Avramenko and John von Heyking, *Friendship and Politics: Essays in Political Thought* (Notre Dame: University of Notre Dame Press, 2008); Eduardo A. Velásquez, *Love and Friendship: Rethinking Politics*

and Affection in Modern Times (Lanham, MD: Lexington Books, 2002); Jacques Derrida, *Politics of Friendship* (London: Verso, 1997); Preston King and Heather Devere, eds., *The Challenge to Friendship in Modernity* (London: Frank Cass, 2000); Neera Kapur Badhwar, ed., *Friendship: A Philosophical Reader* (Ithaca: Cornell University Press, 1993); Judith Nisse Shklar, "Politics and Friendship," *Proceedings of the American Philosophical Society* 137, no. 2 (1993): 207–12; and Jason A. Scorza, "Liberal Citizenship and Civic Friendship," *Political Theory* 32, no. 1 (2004): 85–108.

11. Cf. Carl Schmitt, *The Concept of the Political*, trans. G. Schwab (Chicago: University of Chicago Press, 1996), where a similar claim is made about friends, enemies, and emergency situations. Cf. John Caputo, who, reading Heidegger, writes: "Danger is a gift of destiny, and the lack of danger is dangerous, the highest and deepest and most perilous danger of all." John D. Caputo, "Spirit and Danger," in *Ethics and Danger: Essays on Heidegger and Continental Thought*, ed. Arleen B. Dallery, Charles E. Scott, and P. Holley Roberts (Albany: State University Press of New York, 1992). Cf. Robert Dostal, "Friendship and Politics: Heidegger's Failing," *Political Theory* 20, no. 3 (1992): 399–423; and Dean Cocking and Jeanette Kennett, "Friendship and Moral Danger," *Journal of Philosophy* 97, no. 5 (2000): 278–96.

12. He is here, of course, referring to the Persian invasions.

13. Judith Nisse Shklar, "Rousseau's Two Models: Sparta and the Age of Gold," *Political Science Quarterly* 81, no. 1 (1966): 33. For Shklar, Sparta is central to Rousseau's work, especially the *Social Contract.* As she puts it, "While Rousseau eventually claimed that the principles of the Social Contract were drawn from Genevan practice, there is little reason to accept this, especially as the remark was made in order to defend the book against the attacks of the Genevan authorities. . . . Thus, though a flowery dedication to Geneva opens the *Social Contract*, its institutions and history are scarcely ever mentioned again. Sparta and Rome are the models" (37). Cf. Paul Cartledge, "The Socratics' Sparta and Rousseau's," in *Sparta: New Perspectives*, ed. Stephen Hodkinson and Anton Powell (London: Classical Press of Wales, 1999).

14. For a complication of Rousseau's relationship to Socrates, see Clifford Orwin, "Rousseau's Socratism," *Journal of Politics* 60, no. 1 (1998): 174–87. For elaboration on Socrates and Cato as "exemplary lives," see Christopher Kelly, *Rousseau's Exemplary Life: The Confessions as Political Philosophy* (Ithaca: Cornell University Press, 1987), 48–57.

15. As Rousseau says, "All examples teach us that in such military regulations, and in all regulations that resemble them, study of the sciences is much more apt to soften and enervate courage than to strengthen and animate it" (*FD*, 55).

16. Jean-Jacques Rousseau, "Discourse on This Question: Which Is the Virtue Most Necessary for a Hero and Which Are the Heroes Who Lacked This Virtue?" in *Social Contract; Discourse on the Virtue Most Necessary for a Hero; Political Fragments; and, Geneva Manuscript*, ed. Roger D. Masters and Christopher Kelly (Hanover, NH: University Press of New England, 1994). All subsequent citations to this work (*DH*) will be to this edition and will be given parenthetically in the text. Scholarship on this discourse is sparse, but helpful are David R. Cameron, "The Hero in Rousseau's Political Thought," *Journal of the History of Ideas* 45, no. 3 (1984): 397–419; M. W. Jackson, "Rousseau's Discourse on Heroes and Heroism," *Proceedings of the American Philosophical Society* 133, no. 3 (1989): 434–46; and Christopher Kelly, "Rousseau's Case for and against Heroes," *Polity* 30, no. 2 (1997): 446–66.

17. Stephen G. Salkever, "Rousseau and the Concept of Happiness," *Polity* 11, no. 1 (1978): 34. Another teleological interpretation can be found in Jeffrey A. Smith, "Natural Happiness, Sensation, and Infancy in Rousseau's 'Emile,'" *Polity* 35, no. 1 (2002): 93–120. Less broad is the understanding of Gerald Mara, who argues that "Rousseau endorses political obligation as a means through which human beings can become virtuous and happy." Gerald M. Mara, "Rousseau's Two Models of Political Obligation," *Western Political Quarterly* 33, no. 4 (1980): 537. For more on happiness in Rousseau's work, see Z. M. Trachtenberg, "Frail Happiness: An Essay on Rousseau," *Ethics* 112, no. 4 (2002): 870–72; and Denise Schaeffer, "Reconsidering the Role of Sophie in Rousseau's Emile," *Polity* 30, no. 4 (1998): 607–26.

18. Andrew Levine, *The Politics of Autonomy: A Kantian Reading of Rousseau's Social Contract* (Amherst: University of Massachusetts Press, 1976), 5–43. As Rousseau puts it in the *Social Contract*, his main task is "to find a form of association which will defend the person and goods of each member with the collective force of all, and under which each individual, while uniting himself with the others, obeys no one but himself, and remains as free as before." Jean-Jacques Rousseau, *The Social Contract*, trans. M. Cranston (New York: Penguin Books, 1968), 60. For more on Rousseau and autonomy (moral freedom), see D. J. Allan, "Nature, Education and

Freedom According to Jean-Jacques Rousseau," *Philosophy* 12, no. 46 (1937): 191–207; H. D. Lewis, "Freedom and Authority in Rousseau," *Philosophy* 53, no. 205 (1978): 353–62; William T. Bluhm, "Freedom in 'The Social Contract': Rousseau's 'Legitimate Chains,'" *Polity* 16, no. 3 (1984): 359–83; Joshua Cohen, "Reflections on Rousseau: Autonomy and Democracy," *Philosophy and Public Affairs* 15 (Summer 1986): 275–88; Penny A. Weiss, "Sex, Freedom and Equality in Rousseau's Emile," *Polity* 22, no. 4 (1990): 603–25; Alexander Kaufman, "Reason, Self-Legislation and Legitimacy: Conceptions of Freedom in the Political Thought of Rousseau and Kant," *Review of Politics* 59, no. 1 (1997): 25–52; John T. Scott, "Rousseau and the Melodious Language of Freedom," *Journal of Politics* 59, no. 3 (1997): 803–29; Steven G. Affeldt, "The Force of Freedom: Rousseau on Forcing to be Free," *Political Theory* 27, no. 3 (1999): 299–333; and Richard L. Velkley, *Freedom and the Human Person* (Washington, DC: Catholic University of America Press, 2007). Less convinced about Rousseau's championing of freedom is, of course, Isaiah Berlin, *Freedom and Its Betrayal: Six Enemies of Human Liberty*, ed. H. Hardy (Princeton: Princeton University Press, 2002).

19. Melissa A. Butler, "Rousseau and the Politics of Care," in *Feminist Interpretations of Jean-Jacques Rousseau*, ed. Lynda Lange (University Park: Pennsylvania State University Press, 2002), 213, 217.

20. Kelly, "Rousseau's Case," 351. Kelly also argues that the "other-directedness" of the hero's intentions is a facade: "Rousseau's clear position is that pursuit of the public good is a means to the end of the heroes," and "while heroes may be useful to 'public felicity' in certain circumstances, they are always dangerous" (351, but see also Christopher Kelly, *Rousseau as Author: Consecrating One's Life to the Truth* (Chicago: University of Chicago Press, 2003), esp. 82–115, for the argument in its fuller context). More sympathetic and closer to Rousseau's meaning is Jackson, who argues that the danger from heroes lies not in their intention to fleece the general public of their goods and freedoms but in their tendency, although they "are supposed to be dedicated to the common good, [to] destroy that common good in their own rivalries. This happens because the end of the hero is not the good of others but the glory derived from serving the good of others" ("Rousseau's Discourse," 437).

21. One is here reminded of Machiavelli's Prince, who is neither virtuous in the conventional way nor explicitly selfless, as is characteristic of the martially courageous. For a more detailed account comparing Machiavelli and Rousseau, see Ruth Weissbourd Grant, "Integrity and Politics:

An Alternative Reading of Rousseau," *Political Theory* 22, no. 3 (1994): 414–43. Grant's full argument can be found in Ruth Weissbourd Grant, *Hypocrisy and Integrity: Machiavelli, Rousseau, and the Ethics of Politics* (Chicago: University of Chicago Press, 1997). Rousseau's republicanism has been explored at greater length by James Conniff, "On the Obsolescence of the General Will: Rousseau, Madison, and the Evolution of Republican Political Thought," *Western Political Quarterly* 28, no. 1 (1975): 32–58; Ellenburg, *Rousseau's Political Philosophy*, esp. pt. 4; Maurizio Viroli, *Jean-Jacques Rousseau and the "Well-Ordered Society,"* trans. Derek Hanson (Cambridge: Cambridge University Press, 1988); Antony Black, "Christianity and Republicanism: From St. Cyprian to Rousseau," *American Political Science Review* 91, no. 3 (1997): 647–56; and Elizabeth Rose Wingrove, *Rousseau's Republican Romance* (Princeton: Princeton University Press, 2000).

22. Whether Rousseau was rejecting the Enlightenment is a matter of debate. Graeme Garrard argues persuasively that Rousseau "was an enemy rather than a critic of the Enlightenment" and provides a nice summary of this debate (Graeme Garrard, *Rousseau's Counter-Enlightenment: A Republican Critique of the Philosophes* [Albany: State University of New York Press, 2003], 3). Similarly, Ernst Cassirer claims that the "spiritual leaders of the French Enlightenment . . . saw [in Rousseau] a *daemonic* force at work; a man possessed, driven about restlessly, whose tortured restlessness threatened to rob them of their intellectual property, on which they had believed themselves planted securely and firmly." Ernst Cassirer, *The Question of Jean-Jacques Rousseau*, trans. Peter Gay (Bloomington: Indiana University Press, 1954), 91. Others hold that Rousseau, while a critic of the Enlightenment, was very much part of it: see especially Melzer, "Origin of the Counter-Enlightenment," and Mark Hulliung, *The Autocritique of Enlightenment: Rousseau and the Philosophes* (Cambridge, MA: Harvard University Press, 1994). Cf. Nannerl O. Keohane, "'The Masterpiece of Policy in Our Century': Rousseau on the Morality of the Enlightenment," *Political Theory* 6, no. 4 (1978): 457–84; Terence E. Marshall, "Rousseau and Enlightenment," *Political Theory* 6, no. 4 (1978): 421–55; Lori J. Marso, "The Stories of Citizens: Rousseau, Montesquieu, and de Stael Challenge Enlightenment Reason," *Polity* 30, no. 3 (1998): 435–63; and Julia Simon-Ingram, "Alienation, Individuation, and Enlightenment in Rousseau's Social Theory," *Eighteenth-Century Studies* 24, no. 3 (1991): 315–35.

23. See also Jean-Jacques Rousseau, *Emile: or, On Education* (New York: Basic Books, 1979), 282–83: Primitive man "lives almost without

diseases as well as passions and neither foresees nor senses death. When he senses it, his miseries make it desirable to him. . . . Foresight of death makes it horrible and accelerates it." Subsequent citations to this work (hereafter abbreviated as *E*) refer to this translation and are given parenthetically in the text. Cf. Augustine, *Concerning the City of God against the Pagans,* trans. H. S. Bettenson (London: Penguin Books, 1972), 13.10, and Heidegger, *Being and Time,* 2.1.51.

24. Augustine, *The Happy Life,* trans. L. Schopp (St. Louis: B. Herder Book, 1939), 81.

25. John 3:16.

26. The idea of time in Augustine's thought has been explored at greater length in Richard Avramenko, "The Wound and Salve of Time: Augustine's Politics of Human Happiness," *Review of Metaphysics* 60 (2007): 779–811. For more, see Sigurd Böhm, *La temporalité dans l'anthropologie augustinienne* (Paris: Editions du Cerf, 1984); Jean Guitton, *Le temps et l'éternité chez Plotin et Saint Augustin* (Paris: Boivin et Cie, 1933); Robert Jordan, "Time and Contingency in St. Augustine," *Review of Metaphysics* 8 (1955): 394–417; M. B. Pranger, "Time and Narrative in Augustine's 'Confessions,'" *Journal of Religion* 81, no. 3 (2001): 377–93; K. A. Rogers, "Augustine on Time and Eternity," *American Catholic Philosophical Quarterly* 70, no. 2 (1996): 207–23; J. Schneider and H. J. Schneider, "Time and Temporality: Modern Understanding of Augustine's Concept of Time," *Philosophisches Jahrbuch* 109, no. 1 (2002): 17–43; Roland J. Teske, *Paradoxes of Time in Saint Augustine* (Milwaukee: Marquette University Press, 1996); Calvin L. Troup, *Temporality, Eternity, and Wisdom: The Rhetoric of Augustine's Confessions* (Columbia: University of South Carolina Press, 1999); and James Wetzel, "Time after Augustine," *Religious Studies* 31, no. 3 (1995): 341–57.

27. Mark J. Temmer, *Time in Rousseau and Kant* (Geneva: E. Droz, 1958), 13.

28. Cf. Avramenko, "Wound and Salve," 801.

29. Temmer, *Time in Rousseau,* 9.

30. Along these lines, Mary Nichols argues that the educative goal of *Emile* is to teach moral autonomy—"to connect Emile to other human beings while maintaining his self-dependence and freedom." Mary P. Nichols, "Rousseau's Novel Education in the *Emile,*" *Political Theory* 13, no. 4 (1985): 536. For more on the educative project in *Emile,* see Henry J. Perkinson, "Rousseau's Emile: Political Theory and Education," *History of Education Quarterly* 5, no. 2 (1965): 81–96; Patrick Coleman, "Characterizing Rous-

seau's Emile," *MLN* 92, no. 4 (1977): 761–78; Josué V. Harari, "Therapeutic Pedagogy: Rousseau's Emile," *MLN* 97, no. 4 (1982): 787–809; Janie Vanpée, "Reading Lessons in Rousseau's 'Emile ou de l'Education,'" *Modern Language Studies* 20, no. 3 (1990): 40–49; F. W. Dame, "Jean-Jacques Rousseau's Views on Adult Education," *International Review of Education* 42, nos. 1–3 (1996): 205–26; Scott Walter, "The 'Flawed Parent': A Reconsideration of Rousseau's *Emile* and Its Significance for Radical Education in the United States," *British Journal of Educational Studies* 44, no. 3 (1996): 260–74; and Mabel Lewis Sahakian and William S. Sahakian, *Rousseau as Educator* (New York: Twayne, 1974).

31. Laurence D. Cooper, "Human Nature and the Love of Wisdom: Rousseau's Hidden (and Modified) Platonism," *Journal of Politics* 64, no. 1 (2002): 109. Roger Masters suggests that while *Emile* is certainly about education for the natural man, the first task is even more fundamental to Rousseau's project: "Since Rousseau considered man's natural goodness to be the central thesis of his works, the *Emile* appears to be the most philosophical analysis of Rousseau's fundamental principle." Roger D. Masters, *The Political Philosophy of Rousseau* (Princeton: Princeton University Press, 1968), 3.

32. In Maurizio Viroli's reading of Rousseau, order, not autonomy, emerges as the grand theme: "Virtue," he writes, "is the love of order" (*Jean-Jacques Rousseau*, 17–24). Cf. Lester G. Crocker, "Order and Disorder in Rousseau's Social Thought," *PMLA* 94, no. 2 (1979): 247–60.

33. As Rousseau puts it, pity will not make one weak and susceptible to servitude because it aims not at particular individuals but at mankind in general: "To prevent pity from degenerating into weakness, it must, therefore, be generalized and extended to the whole of mankind" (*E*, 253).

34. One is here reminded of what Plato calls "lingering death" (*Republic* 406b).

35. As Rousseau puts it: "Let another in my stead take charge of this invalid. I am not able to teach living to one who thinks of nothing but how to keep himself from dying" (*E*, 53).

36. The role of language in Rousseau's thought is explored in greater depth by Christopher Kelly, "To Persuade without Convincing: The Language of Rousseau's Legislator," *American Journal of Political Science* 31, no. 1 (1987): 321–35; Scott, "Rousseau"; J. Patrick Dobel, "The Role of Language in Rousseau's Political Thought," *Polity* 18, no. 4 (1986): 638–58; and Robert L. Politzer, "A Detail in Rousseau's Thought: Language and Perfectibility," *Modern Language Notes* 72, no. 1 (1957): 42–47.

37. See also Nietzsche's "Uses and Disadvantages of History for Life," in *Untimely Meditations* (Cambridge: Cambridge University Press, 1983), 62, where he makes the claim that without intestinal fortitude one might bleed to death from a scratch.

38. That Rousseau continues to use *strength* in the same way is quite certain: "My child, there is no happiness [bonheur] without courage [courage] nor virtue [vertu] without struggle [combat]. The word virtue comes from strength [force]. Strength is the foundation of all virtue" (*E*, 444).

39. "Moral freedom," Rousseau says, "alone makes man the master of himself; for to be governed by appetite alone is slavery, while obedience to a law one prescribes to oneself is freedom" (*Social Contract*, 65).

40. Matthew William Maguire, *The Conversion of Imagination: From Pascal through Rousseau to Tocqueville* (Cambridge, MA: Harvard University Press, 2006), 12. Cf. Kelly, *Rousseau as Author*, esp. 76–115; and Margery Sabin, "Imagination in Rousseau and Wordsworth," *Comparative Literature* 22, no. 4 (1970): 328–45.

41. Maguire, *Conversion of Imagination*, 81.

42. The place of women in Rousseau's work is the topic of considerable scholarship. Linda Zerilli, for instance, argues that women signify disorder and chaos for Rousseau and are thus excluded from the social contract and "are a scapegoat precipitated by the disorder in men." Linda M. G. Zerilli, *Signifying Woman: Culture and Chaos in Rousseau, Burke, and Mill* (Ithaca: Cornell University Press, 1994), 19. More sympathetic is Nicole Fermon, who argues that a central task of Rousseau is to transform passions into less dangerous "sentiments": "The urgency of denaturing passions into sentiments and woman's role in the process thus attain paramount importance." Nicole Fermon, *Domesticating Passions: Rousseau, Woman, and Nation* (Hanover: Wesleyan University Press, 1997), 9. For more, see Madelyn Gutwirth, "Madame de Stael, Rousseau, and the Woman Question," *PMLA* 86, no. 1 (1971): 100–109; Susan Moller Okin, "Rousseau's Natural Woman," *Journal of Politics* 41, no. 2 (1979): 393–416; Penny A. Weiss, "Rousseau, Antifeminism, and Woman's Nature," *Political Theory* 15, no. 1 (1987): 81–98; Penny A. Weiss and Anne Harper, "Rousseau's Political Defense of the Sex-Roled Family," *Hypatia* 5, no. 3 (1990): 90–109; Disch, "Claire Loves Julie"; Morgenstern, *Rousseau*; Rita C. Manning, "Rousseau's Other Woman: Collette in 'Le devin du village,'" *Hypatia* 16, no. 2 (2001): 27–42; Lynda Lange, *Feminist Interpretations of Jean-Jacques*

Rousseau (University Park: Pennsylvania State University Press, 2002); Paul Thomas, "Jean-Jacques Rousseau, Sexist?" *Feminist Studies* 17, no. 2 (1991): 195–217; and Victor G. Wexler, "'Made for Man's Delight': Rousseau as Antifeminist," *American Historical Review* 81, no. 2 (1976): 266–91.

43. This is not to say that Rousseau was an atheist or antireligious. The proclamation of his deistic "faith" in the well-known "Profession of Faith of the Savoyard Vicar" speaks loudly enough to this (*E*, 266–313). For a thorough account of religion in Rousseau's thought, see Pierre-Maurice Masson, *La religion de J. J. Rousseau*, 2nd ed. (Paris: Hachette et Cie, 1916); and Grimsley, *Rousseau*. Also of interest are Kelly, *Rousseau's Exemplary Life*, which argues that of Socrates, Cato, and Jesus, Rousseau believed that Jesus lived the most exemplary life (64); Gilbert F. LaFreniere, "Rousseau and the European Roots of Environmentalism," *Environmental History Review* 14, no. 4 (1990): 41–72, who points to Rousseau's deism as the origin of modern environmentalism; Joshua Mitchell, "The Equality of All under the One in Luther and Rousseau: Thoughts on Christianity and Political Theory," *Journal of Religion* 72, no. 3 (1992): 351–65, and *Not by Reason Alone;* Harvey Mitchell, "Reclaiming the Self: The Pascal-Rousseau Connection," *Journal of the History of Ideas* 54, no. 4 (1993): 637–58; Mark S. Cladis, "Tragedy and Theodicy: A Meditation on Rousseau and Moral Evil," *Journal of Religion* 75 (1995): 181–99; John Darling, "Understanding and Religion in Rousseau's 'Emile,'" *British Journal of Educational Studies* 33, no. 1 (1985): 20–34; Morris Dickstein, "The Faith of a Vicar: Reason and Morality in Rousseau's Religion," *Yale French Studies*, no. 28 (1961): 48–54; Victor Gourevitch, "The Religious Thought," in *The Cambridge Companion to Rousseau*, ed. Patrick Riley (Cambridge: Cambridge University Press, 2001). For more on Rousseau's account of civil religion in *Social Contract* 4.8, see Ronald Beiner, "Machiavelli, Hobbes, and Rousseau on Civil Religion," *Review of Politics* 55, no. 4 (1993): 617–38; Diane Fourny, "Rousseau's Civil Religion Reconsidered," *French Review* 60, no. 4 (1987): 485–96; and Fred H. Willhoite Jr., "Rousseau's Political Religion," *Review of Politics* 27, no. 4 (1965): 501–15.

44. Vanpée, "Reading Lessons," 41.

45. Ibid.

46. As Rousseau puts it: "I hate books. Then only teach one to talk about what one does not know" (*E*, 184). Later, he reiterates this: "I do not tire of repeating it: put all the lessons of young people in actions rather

than in speeches. Let them learn nothing in books which experience can teach them" (*E*, 251).

47. The proscription of reading for children certainly rings strange to the twenty-first-century ear, but, as one scholar points out, there simply was no children's literature at the time: "Before *Emile* many of the books were merely children's versions of adult books, such as *Pilgrim's Progress*, *Gulliver's Travels*, and *Robinson Crusoe*. After *Emile*, the trend changed, and the movement of writing expressly for children gained impetus." Sylvia W. Patterson, *Rousseau's Emile and Early Children's Literature* (Metuchen, NJ: Scarecrow Press, 1971), 7.

48. Denise Schaeffer, "The Utility of Ink: Rousseau and *Robinson Crusoe*," *Review of Politics* 64, no. 1 (2001): 122. Cf. Todd R. Flanders, "Rousseau's Adventure with Robinson Crusoe," *Interpretation: A Journal of Political Philosophy* 24, no. 3 (1997): 319–38; Vanpée, "Reading Lessons," 41.

49. Despite his seeming adoration of the isolated natural man, Rousseau is certain that man cannot live in complete isolation: "A man who wanted to regard himself an isolated being, not depending at all on others and sufficient unto himself, could only be miserable" (*E*, 193).

50. Martha Nussbaum, "Compassion: The Basic Social Emotion," *Social Philosophy and Policy* 13 (1996): 27–58. It might be suggested that Nussbaum would disagree with my argument that compassion resides beneath reason. As she puts it, "Those who look to compassion for an intuitive or nonreasoned alternative to judgments based on principle—and, in general, for an alternative to Enlightenment conceptions of the basis of morality—are looking in the wrong place. I shall argue that all compassion is 'rational' in the descriptive sense in which that term is frequently used—that is, not merely impulsive, but involving thought or belief" (31). Her ensnarement of "reason," however, suggests that we are instead in agreement—one does not, on impulse, become a lover of honor or freedom. Such a love is, instead, part of a long-standing, well-considered view of one's world.

51. Clifford Orwin, "Rousseau and the Discovery of Political Compassion," in Orwin and Tarcov, *Legacy of Rousseau*, 297.

52. Mira Morgenstern, for example, suggests that pity is "the first step of Émile's socialization. It allows Émile to become more human by giving him, though his newly acquired imagination, an expanded awareness of the species to which he belongs." Morgenstern, *Rousseau*, 64, but see especially the whole of her second chapter, "Pity, Imagination, and

Love." Richard Boyd also provides a fine interpretation of the relationship between compassion and the imagination in Rousseau's work but is skeptical about the appropriateness of compassion as the moral foundation of democracy: "Although it is founded on the apprehension of the identity of our nature as fellow-creatures [semblables], even in Rousseau's account pity is inevitably bound up with relational differences that are the very antithesis of natural equality. Trying to make compassion central to democratic theory reifies the very distinctions it aims to overcome" ("Pity's Pathologies Portrayed," 521). Jonathan Marks regards these same shortcomings of compassion as its strength: "Compassion need not be stronger than it is because it has allies among the social passions, namely gratitude and friendship, that may motivate action on behalf of others where compassion fails" ("Rousseau's Discriminating Defense," 730). For more on the concept of pity in Rousseau's thought, see Orwin, "Rousseau and the Discovery," 302, Masters, *Political Philosophy of Rousseau*, 45–53; Ogrodnick, *Instinct and Intimacy*, 130–61; N. J. H. Dent, *Rousseau: An Introduction to His Psychological, Social, and Political Theory* (New York: Blackwell, 1989), 126–45; and Leo Strauss, *Natural Right and History* (Chicago: University of Chicago Press, 1953), 270.

53. For more on the extension and distension of time, see Augustine's *Confessions*, book 11, which I have explored in some depth in "The Wound and Salve of Time," especially 797–801.

54. Kant makes a similar claim, which he calls the "unsocial sociability of man." Immanuel Kant, "Idea for a Universal History with a Cosmopolitan Purpose," in *Kant's Political Writings*, ed. Hans Reiss (Cambridge: Cambridge University Press, 1970), 44. This passage also serves as the basis of Tzvetan Todorov's insightful book *Frail Happiness: An Essay on Rousseau* (University Park: Pennsylvania State University Press, 2001).

55. Rousseau invokes these words at the outset of book 5 of *Emile* with regard to female companionship. Cf. Genesis 2:18.

56. Boyd, because of the *Schadenfreude* character of compassion in this sense, points to this passage as a further argument against compassion as the basis of democracy ("Pity's Pathologies Portrayed," 525).

57. "Attachment can exist without being returned, but friendship never can. It is an exchange, a contract like others, but it is the most sacred of all. The word *friend* has no correlative other than itself. Any man who is not his friend's friend is most assuredly a cheat, for it is only in returning or feigning to return friendship that one can obtain it" (*E*, 233).

FIVE. Economic Courage and Wealth

1. And as Melissa Butler points out, for Rousseau "the state itself became a kind of maternal state" ("Rousseau," 222).

2. Clifford Orwin, "Moist Eyes—from Rousseau to Clinton," *Public Interest*, no. 128 (Summer 1997): 3.

3. Ibid., 5.

4. Ibid., 21.

5. Berlin, *Freedom and Its Betrayal*, 31.

6. Ibid., 37.

7. Ibid., 47. For more sympathetic accounts, see Affeldt, "Force of Freedom," 299–333; H. Lewis, "Freedom and Authority"; James I. McAdam, "Rousseau and the Friends of Despotism," *Ethics* 74, no. 1 (1963): 34–43; and Judith Nisse Shklar, "Rousseau's Images of Authority," *American Political Science Review* 58, no. 4 (1964): 919–32.

8. Berlin, *Freedom and Its Betrayal*, 49.

9. C. S. Lewis, *The Abolition of Man, or, Reflections on Education with Special Reference to the Teaching of English in the Upper Forms of Schools* (San Francisco: HarperSanFrancisco, 2001), 24.

10. Ibid., 26.

11. Ibid., 24.

12. Friedrich Nietzsche, *On the Genealogy of Morals*, trans. Walter Kaufmann (New York: Vintage Books, 1967), 54, and *Thus Spoke Zarathustra: A Book for Everyone and No One*, trans. R. J. Hollingdale (New York: Penguin Books, 1969), 45.

13. José Ortega y Gasset, *The Revolt of the Masses* (New York: W. W. Norton, 1993); Schmitt, *Concept of the Political;* Martin Heidegger, *Introduction to Metaphysics*, trans. G. Fried (New Haven: Yale University Press, 2000); Kojève, *Introduction.*

14. For full biographical accounts of Tocqueville, see J. P. Mayer, *Alexis de Tocqueville* (New York: Arno Press, 1979); Xavier de La Fournière, *Alexis de Tocqueville: Un monarchiste indépendant* (Paris: Perrin, 1981); Andre Jardin, *Tocqueville: A Biography* (New York: Farrar Straus Giroux, 1988); and Hugh Brogan, *Alexis de Tocqueville: A Life* (New Haven: Yale University Press, 2007).

15. Alexis de Tocqueville, *Democracy in America*, ed. J. P. Mayer, trans. George Lawrence (New York: Harper and Row, 1969), 9; in this chapter, subsequent citations to this work (hereafter *DA*) are given parenthetically

in the text and refer to this edition. The claim is made numerous times in his writings, usually with this same matter-of-fact frankness: "The particular and predominating fact peculiar to [democratic ages] is equality of conditions, and the chief passion which stirs men at such times is the love of this same equality" (*DA*, 504); "Humanity is driven by an unknown force which we can hope to moderate, but not to defeat, which sometimes gently urges and sometimes shoves us towards the destruction of aristocracy" (Alexis de Tocqueville, *The Old Regime and the French Revolution*, trans. A. S. Kahan [Chicago: University of Chicago Press, 1998], 87). For more, see Pierre Manent, *Tocqueville and the Nature of Democracy*, trans. J. Waggoner (Lanham, MD: Rowman and Littlefield, 1996), 29–45.

16. Marvin Zetterbaum, "Tocqueville: Neutrality and the Use of History," *American Political Science Review* 58, no. 3 (1964): 613.

17. Tocqueville asserts that he aspires to "a political science for a world itself quite new" (*DA*, 12). According to Larry Siedentop, "The originality of Tocqueville's method has seldom been noticed. Yet it represented a breakthrough in social thought. . . . Indeed, by joining empiricist and introspective forms of explanation, Tocqueville's method suggests that relying merely on one or the other creates a false dilemma for social thought—confining it either to an 'external' or an 'internal' vantage-point, when the real need is to explore the interaction of social conditions and personal intentions. They must be examined side by side. For they are two sides of the same coin." Larry Siedentop, *Tocqueville* (Oxford: Oxford University Press, 1994), 70, 71. This new political science is discussed in depth by Saguiv A. Hadari, *Theory in Practice: Tocqueville's New Science of Politics* (Stanford: Stanford University Press, 1989); but see also C. B. Welch, *De Tocqueville* (Oxford: Oxford University Press, 2001), 13–23; Marvin Zetterbaum, *Tocqueville and the Problem of Democracy* (Stanford: Stanford University Press, 1967), 143–44; Joshua Mitchell, *The Fragility of Freedom: Tocqueville on Religion, Democracy, and the American Future* (Chicago: University of Chicago Press, 1995), 215–22; John C. Koritansky, "Decentralization and Civic Virtue in Tocqueville's 'New Science of Politics,'" *Publius* 5, no. 3 (1975): 63–81, and *Alexis de Tocqueville and the New Science of Politics: An Interpretation of Democracy in America* (Durham, NC: Carolina Academic Press, 1986); Stephen Frantzich, "Teaching through Tocqueville," *PS: Political Science and Politics* 32, no. 2 (1999): 203–5; and M. R. R. Ossewaarde, *Tocqueville's Moral and Political Thought: New Liberalism* (London: Routledge, 2004), 52–79.

18. Zetterbaum, *Tocqueville*, 21. For immanentist interpretations of the "providentiality" of equality, see E. T. Gargan, "Tocqueville and the Problem of Historical Prognosis," *American Historical Review* 68, no. 2 (1963): 332; and Jack Lively, *The Social and Political Thought of Alexis de Tocqueville* (Oxford: Clarendon Press, 1962), esp. 10.

19. As Tocqueville puts it, "Running through the pages of our history, there is hardly an important event in the last seven hundred years which has not turned out to be advantageous for equality. . . . All peoples have been driven pell-mell along the same road, and have worked together, some against their will and some unconsciously, blind instruments in the hand of God" (*DA*, 11–12).

20. Tocqueville's intention in writing *Democracy in America* as a lesson for his French brethren is clear; as he writes in a November 15, 1839, letter to J. S. Mill, "You must not forget that [*DA*, vol. 2] was written in a country, and for a country, where equality having achieved a complete triumph, and aristocracy having been beaten entirely out of the field, the object is not to create or to prevent a system, but, finding it there, to correct its faults." Alexis de Tocqueville, *Memoir, Letters, and Remains of Alexis de Tocqueville*, vol. 2 (Whitefish, MT: Kessinger, 2007), 57–58. Tocqueville puts the thesis directly to Kergolay: "We ourselves are moving, my dear friend, toward a democracy without limits. . . . We are being pushed toward it by an irresistible force. All the efforts that will be made to stop this movement will only provide pauses. . . . Riches will tend more and more to be equalized." Tocqueville to Kergolay, June 29, 1831, in Alexis de Tocqueville, *Alexis de Tocqueville: Selected Letters on Politics and Society*, trans. J. Toupin and R. Boesche (Berkeley: University of California Press, 1985), 55. The same lesson concludes *Democracy in America:* "The nations of our day cannot prevent conditions of equality from spreading in their midst. But it depends upon themselves whether equality is to lead to servitude or freedom, knowledge or barbarism, prosperity or wretchedness" (*DA*, 705).

21. Nietzsche, *On the Genealogy*, 44.

22. Krause, *Liberalism with Honor*, 19.

23. This is not to say that it was wholly absent. Though rare, remnants of the love of honor, and violence as the basis human articulation, occasionally obtruded. As Tocqueville says, "The surface of American society is covered with a layer of democratic paint, but from time to time one can see the old aristocratic colors breaking through" (*DA*, 49).

24. As Tocqueville puts it, "Thus, to conclude, compressing my essential thought into a single sentence, it is the dissimilarities and inequalities among men which give rise to the notion of honor; as such differences become less, it grows feeble; and when they disappear, it will vanish too" (*DA*, 627). For more on this "close and necessary" relationship between inequality and honor, see Lively, *Social and Political Thought*, 38–39.

25. One will recall the relationship between self-interest and cowardice in the Homeric world and especially in the Spartan case. Moreover, one would do well to recall the central thrust of Plato's *Republic*—Socrates' rebuttal of Thrasymachus's claim that justice is the interest of the stronger.

26. Zetterbaum takes this point farther, suggesting that for Tocqueville "the democratic revolution, accompanied as it is by the gradual disappearance of aristocratic forms, is thus the agency by which man's nature is revealed. Inquiry into the nature of democratic man is inquiry into the nature of man per se. . . . He believed he had perceived man's nature directly, through his examination of men and mores in America, as well as indirectly, through his reconstruction of the genesis of morality" (*Tocqueville*, 35).

27. Tocqueville's assessment of this democratic predilection is mixed: "One usually finds that love of money [l'amour des richesses] is either the chief or a secondary motive at the bottom of everything Americans do. This gives a family likeness to all their passions and soon makes them wearisome to contemplate" (*DA*, 615).

28. See also *DA*, 615: "In aristocratic nations money is the key to the satisfaction of but few of the vast array of possible desires; in democracies it is the key to them all."

29. This claim that human beings are not inherently violent has more recently been made empirically. In *On Killing*, Dave Grossman attempts to show that human beings have an inherent aversion to killing other human beings and thus must be "taught." Soldiers, throughout the modern era at least, have almost inexplicable rates of failing to pull the trigger in battle, shooting over the heads of the enemy, and firing into the ground. The phenomenon was discovered by the military establishment, and actions were taken to desensitize soldiers to killing; thus kill rates have risen steadily since the beginning of the Vietnam War. This natural aversion, however, is present in only 95 percent of soldiers, which means 5 percent are "natural-born killers."

30. Hobbes, *Leviathan*, 186.

31. Tocqueville does mention that in the Indian peoples of North America the sociological predisposition to violence and savagery could be found. In a footnote to his description of the natives, he describes the difficulties the Americans had in eradicating the natives' natural impulses toward violence (see *DA*, 318–19). This apparent contradiction in Tocqueville's thought—that honor and violence are not natural or essential characteristics of human beings, yet that Indians are "naturally" violent—is quite interesting.

32. Zetterbaum claims that for Tocqueville not only are honor codes relative, but they stand in contradistinction to natural law as a source of moral judgment (*Tocqueville*, 36–37). Cf. Lively, *Social and Political Thought*, 63; Hadari, *Theory in Practice*, 112; Bruce Frohnen, *Virtue and the Promise of Conservatism: The Legacy of Burke and Tocqueville* (Lawrence: University Press of Kansas, 1993), 122; and Peter Augustine Lawler, *The Restless Mind: Alexis de Tocqueville on the Origin and Perpetuation of Human Liberty* (Lanham, MD: Rowman and Littlefield, 1993), 137.

33. One is reminded here of the most violent contest in the ancient Greek Olympics, the *pankration*. In this form of fighting, no holds were barred, no mode of striking one's opponent was prohibited. In fact, there were only two rules, and these pertained to what was dishonorable: a fighter was not permitted to put his fingers in an opponent's orifices, and, more importantly, he could not kill his opponent. If a fighter killed his opponent, the dead man would be declared victor and be conferred all the honors and prizes just as if he were still alive! See, for example, the famous *pankration* match of the Fifty-fourth Olympiad between Arrhichion of Phigalia and his unnamed competitor in Philostratus *Imagines* 2.6.

34. Hence the persistence of duels in aristocratic cultures. For more, see chapter 2's section "The Fate of the Coward: Dishonor" and chapter 3's section "Political Courage and the Problem of Violence." While Tocqueville recognizes the place of duels in aristocracies (*DA*, 616), he also sees their irrationality: "In the new states of the Southwest the citizens almost always take justice into their own hands, and murders are of frequent occurrence. That is because the people's habits are too rough and because enlightenment is not sufficiently widespread in that wilderness for people to see the advantage of giving strength to the law; duels are still preferred to lawsuits" (*DA*, 225). For more on the duel, see Robert Baldick, *The Duel: A History of Duelling* (New York: C. N. Potter, 1965); Robert A. Nye, "Fencing, the Duel and Republican Manhood in the Third Republic," *Journal of Contemporary History* 25, nos. 2/3 (1990): 365–77; W. J. Rorabaugh, "The

Political Duel in the Early Republic: Burr v. Hamilton," *Journal of the Early Republic* 15, no. 1 (1995): 1–23; Joanne B. Freeman, "Dueling as Politics: Reinterpreting the Burr-Hamilton Duel," *William and Mary Quarterly* 53, no. 2 (1996): 289–318; and Barbara Holland, *Gentlemen's Blood: A History of Dueling from Swords at Dawn to Pistols at Dusk* (New York: Bloomsbury, 2003).

35. Eliot A. Cohen, "Tocqueville on War," in *Tocqueville's Political Science: Classic Essays,* ed. Peter Augustine Lawler (New York: Garland, 1992), 316.

36. Ibid., 317.

37. The failure to understand the habits and ideas of honor cultures may itself lead to war. Bowman, for instance, argues that the Western misunderstanding of (or obliviousness to) the demands that honor culture made of Saddam Hussein with regard to weapons of mass destruction was a major factor precipitating the Second Gulf War (Bowman, *Honor,* 28–33).

38. Tocqueville is very clear on this point in a June 9, 1831, letter to Chabrol: "One must not look here either for that family spirit, or for those ancient traditions of honor and virtue, that distinguish so eminently several of our old societies of Europe. A people that seems to live only to enrich itself could not be a virtuous people in the strict meaning of the word; but it is well ordered." Tocqueville, *Selected Letters,* 40.

39. Krause, *Liberalism with Honor,* 67.

40. Ibid. Krause continues, to the detriment of her argument, by providing a long list of qualities that supposedly describe the essence of old-regime honor. While it is true that "courage, pride, high and principled ambition, the desires for distinction" are defining characteristics of this way of being, "self-respect" is at best secondary if not entirely out of place. In addition, "the sense of duty to oneself" runs contrary to the other-interestedness at the core of the courageous self, and the "love of liberty as an end in itself" describes an altogether different fundamental care—one that may in fact be Tocqueville's fundamental care (see Alan S. Kahan, *Aristocratic Liberalism: The Social and Political Thought of Jacob Burckhardt, John Stuart Mill, and Alexis de Tocqueville* [New York: Oxford University Press, 1992]) but is not a defining characteristic of honor lovers properly understood.

41. This is not to say that Tocqueville himself viewed industrialism in America with unreserved admiration. In a July 28, 1831, letter to Eugène Stoffels, he says, "The unfavorable is an immoderate desire to grow rich, and to do so rapidly; perpetual instability of purpose, and a continual

longing for change; a total absence of established customs and traditions; a trading and manufacturing spirit which is carried into everything, even where it is least appropriate." Alexis de Tocqueville, *Memoir, Letters, and Remains* (Boston: Ticknor and Fields, 1862), 370.

42. Albert O. Hirschman, *The Passions and the Interests: Political Arguments for Capitalism before Its Triumph* (Princeton: Princeton University Press, 1977), 11; subsequent citations to this work (abbreviated as *PI*) are given parenthetically in the text. For an excellent account of this worldview, see Johan Huizinga, *The Waning of the Middle Ages: A Study of the Forms of Life, Thought, and Art in France and the Netherlands in the XIVth and XVth Centuries* (1924; repr., Garden City, NY: Doubleday Anchor, 1954). The distinction between fame and glory, it can be argued, is lost in the modern world, as evidenced by Leo Braudy, *The Frenzy of Renown: Fame and Its History* (1986; repr., New York: Vintage Books, 1997).

43. On this point there is a certain kinship between Tocqueville and Plato. For Plato, democratic man "lives his life day by day, indulging each appetite as it makes itself felt. One day he is drinking heavily and listening to the flute; on the next he is dieting and drinks only water. Then he tries some exercise, only to lapse into idleness and lethargy. Sometimes he seems to want to be the philosopher. More frequently, he goes in for politics, rising to say or do whatever comes into his head. If he develops an enthusiasm for military men, he rushes to join them; if for businessmen, then he is off in that direction. His life lacks all discipline and order, yet he calls it a life a pleasure, freedom, and happiness and is resolved to stay the course." Plato *Republic* 561c–d; translation from *The Republic*, trans. R. W. Sterling and W. C. Scott (New York: W. W. Norton, 1985).

44. See Plato *Republic* 440a. For an interesting account of Tocqueville's sympathies being divided between aristocracy and democracy, see Alan Macfarlane, *The Riddle of the Modern World* (New York: St. Martin's Press, 2000), 154–58.

45. Tocqueville, *Selected Letters*, 143. Again, we are reminded of Nietzsche's description of the Last Man in the Prologue to *Thus Spoke Zarathustra*.

46. Alexis de Tocqueville, *The European Revolution and Correspondence with Gobineau* (Gloucester, MA: P. Smith, 1968), 84. For more on the long history of knightly-aristocratic honor among the French nobility, see Brian Sandberg, *Warrior Pursuits: Noble Culture and Civil Conflict in Early Modern France* (Baltimore: Johns Hopkins University Press, 2010).

47. For more on this sense of powerlessness, see Roger Boesche, *The Strange Liberalism of Alexis de Tocqueville* (Ithaca: Cornell University Press, 1987), 69.

48. According to Laura Janara, this exaggerated display of manly courage would be corrosive of social bonds in more contexts than the Spartan phalanx; individualism as described by Tocqueville is similarly a form of "excessive, self-deceptive masculinism." This "textually male individualism is too much," and thus Tocqueville "recommends the integration of lessons from his textually maternal aristocracy—lessons in textually female political liberty and religion." Laura Janara, *Democracy Growing Up: Authority, Autonomy, and Passion in Tocqueville's Democracy in America* (Albany: State University of New York Press, 2002), 152.

49. Arthur Schlesinger Jr., "Individualism and Apathy in Tocqueville's *Democracy*," in *Reconsidering Tocqueville's Democracy in America*, ed. Abraham S. Eisenstadt (New Brunswick: Rutgers University Press, 1988), 98. Schlesinger also refers to individualism as "a 'crude' interpretation of self-interest" that "upsets the balance between virtue and interest" (98). In Bruce Frohnen's understanding, "the search for money" causes those "'kind of men' to let their guard down against tyranny because they "have fallen under the spell of *individualism*" (Frohnen, *Virtue and the Promise*, 133, 134). For more on Tocqueville and individualism, see W. H. George, "Montesquieu and de Tocqueville and Corporative Individualism," *American Political Science Review* 16, no. 1 (1922): 10–21; Lively, *Social and Political Thought*, 71–85; Zetterbaum, *Tocqueville*, 60–66; Jean-Claude Lamberti, *La notion d'individualisme chez Tocqueville* (Paris: Presses Universitaires de France, 1970); Boesche, *Strange Liberalism*, 42–53; Jean-Claude Lamberti, *Tocqueville and the Two Democracies* (Cambridge, MA: Harvard University Press, 1989), 168–83; Robert N. Bellah, "The Quest for the Self: Individualism, Morality, Politics," in *Interpreting Tocqueville's Democracy in America*, ed. Ken Masugi (Savage, MD: Rowman and Littlefield, 1991); Siedentop, *Tocqueville*, 86–92; Jean-Michel Heimonet, *Tocqueville et le devenir de la démocratie: La perversion de l'idéal* (Paris: L'Harmattan, 1999), 35–44; James T. Schleifer, *The Making of Tocqueville's Democracy in America* (Indianapolis: Liberty Fund, 2000), 305–22; Schlesinger, "Individualism and Apathy"; D. Villa, "Hegel, Tocqueville, and Individualism," *Review of Politics* 67, no. 4 (2005): 659–86; L. J. Hebert, "Individualism and Intellectual Liberty in Tocqueville and Descartes," *Journal of Politics* 69, no. 2 (2007): 525–37; Jack Turner, "American Individualism and Structural Injustice: Tocqueville, Gender, and Race," *Polity* 40 (2008): 197–215.

50. J. Mitchell, *Fragility of Freedom*, 3.

51. Scant research has been done on the concepts of time and history in Tocqueville's thought. Exceptions include Delba Winthrop, "Tocqueville's 'Old Regime': Political History," *Review of Politics* 43, no. 1 (1981): 88–111; A. S. Levy, *America Discovered a Second Time: French Perceptions of American Notions of Time from Tocqueville to Laboulaye* (New Haven: Yale University Press, 1996); Janara, *Democracy Growing Up*, 17–18; Welch, *De Tocqueville*, 57–58; and Leonard J. Hochberg, "Reconciling History with Sociology?" *Journal of Classical Sociology* 7, no. 1 (2007): 23–54.

52. Cf. Andrew Sabl, "Community Organizing as Tocquevillean Politics: The Art, Practices, and Ethos of Association," *American Journal of Political Science* 46, no. 1 (2002): 1–19.

53. For more on Tocqueville's view on federalism, see Delba Winthrop, "Tocqueville on Federalism," *Publius: The Journal of Federalism* 6, no. 3 (1976): 93–115; Ralph C. Hancock, "Tocqueville on the Good of American Federalism," *Publius: The Journal of Federalism* 20, no. 2 (1990) 89–108; and P. C. Kissam, "Alexis de Tocqueville and American Constitutional Law: On Democracy, the Majority Will, Individual Rights, Federalism, Religion, Civic Associations, and Originalist Constitutional Theory," *Maine Law Review* 59, no. 1 (2007): 35.

54. The point is stated even more clearly in his *Journey to America:* "If a man gets the idea of any social improvement whatsoever, a school, a hospital, a road, he does not think of turning to the authorities. He announces his plan, offers to carry it out, calls for the strength of other individuals to aid his efforts, and fights hand to hand against each obstacle." Alexis de Tocqueville, *Journey to America*, ed. J. P. Mayer, trans. George Lawrence (Garden City, NY: Anchor Books, 1971), 39.

55. In a June 9, 1831, letter to Ernest de Chabrol, Tocqueville writes, "Imagine, my dear friend, if you can, a society formed of all the nations of the world: English, French, Germans . . . people having different languages, beliefs, opinions: in a word, a society without roots, without memories, without prejudices, without routines, without common ideas, without a national character, yet a hundred times happier than our own; more virtuous? I doubt it. That is the starting point: *What serves as the link among such diverse elements? What makes all of this into one people? Interest. That is the secret. The private interest that breaks through at each moment, the interest that, moreover, appears openly and even proclaims itself as a social theory*" (Tocqueville, *Selected Letters*, 38).

56. In a June 29, 1831, letter to Kergolay, he calls them "common opinions" and mentions two: the belief that republican government is the best form, and "a faith in human wisdom and good sense, faith in the doctrine of human perfectibility" (Tocqueville, *Selected Letters*, 46–47).

57. In a footnote in *Journey to America*, Tocqueville states this definitively with regard to juries. He "values [juries] in civil cases" because "laws are always unsteady as long as they are not based for support on morals. Mores are the only tough and durable power among a people. . . . It is in grappling with these suits that the institution of the jury truly penetrates into habits, fashions the human mind to its forms, and finally comes to be merged into the whole conception of justice. Once it has entered in this way into mores, it cannot be removed from the laws in criminal matters" (304–5 n.). Tocqueville held firm to this view of laws and institutions vis-à-vis mores and religion throughout his life. In a September 17, 1853, letter to Claude-François de Corcelle he writes, "I accord institutions only a secondary influence on the destiny of men. Would to God I believed more in the omnipotence of institutions! I would have more hope for our future, because by chance we might, someday, stumble onto the precious piece of paper that would contain the recipe for all wrongs. . . . I am quite convinced that political societies are not what their laws make them, but what sentiments, beliefs, ideas, habits of the heart, and the spirit of the men who form them, prepare them in advance to be, as well as what nature and education have made them" (Tocqueville, *Selected Letters*, 294).

58. In trying to make sense of religion in America, Tocqueville recognizes a key difference from the European aristocratic mind. As he writes to Kergolay on June 29, 1831, "As for what we generally understand by beliefs, ancient mores, ancient traditions, the power of memories, I have not seen any trace of these up to now. I even doubt that religious opinions have as great a power as one thinks at first sight." Later, in the same letter, he writes, "It is evident that here, generally speaking, religion does not move people deeply," but also states, "I do not doubt that this disposition of minds still has influence on the political regime. It gives a moral and regular shape to ideas; it stops the deviations of the spirit of innovation" (Tocqueville, *Selected Letters*, 47, 49, 52–53). This distinction between the democratic coloring of religion and the aristocratic is, I believe, the basis of Tocqueville's indifference to the particular religion that recurs in *Democracy in America* (528–30, 546, 669). Insofar as one's approach to religion is democratic, just about any religion will do, sociologically speaking—as

long as it preaches the economy of salvation through an expansion of temporal horizons. Lawler argues, correctly I believe, that "Tocqueville understood himself not to be fortunate enough to have religious faith" (Lawler, *Restless Mind*, 157). For more on religion, or, as I will call it hereafter, theology, in Tocqueville's thought, see Ralph C. Hancock, "The Uses and Hazards of Christianity in Tocqueville's Attempt to Save Democratic Souls," in Masugi, *Interpreting Tocqueville's Democracy;* Cynthia Hinckley, "Tocqueville on Religion and Modernity: Making Catholicism Safe for Liberal Democracy," in Lawler, *Tocqueville's Political Science;* and especially J. Mitchell, *Fragility of Freedom.*

59. For more on this functionalist view of religion and American democracy, see Lively, *Social and Political Thought*, 197; Zetterbaum, *Tocqueville*, 7, 18–19, 147; Sanford Kessler, "Tocqueville on Civil Religion and Liberal Democracy," *Journal of Politics* 39, no. 1 (1977): 119–46; William Galston, "Tocqueville on Liberalism and Religion," *Social Research* 54, no. 3 (1987): 500–501; Cynthia J. Hinckley, "Tocqueville on Religious Truth and Political Necessity," *Polity* 23, no. 1 (1990): 39–52; Lawler, *Restless Mind;* Sanford Kessler, *Tocqueville's Civil Religion: American Christianity and the Prospects for Freedom* (Albany: State University of New York Press, 1994).

60. See also Manent, *Tocqueville*, 38–39.

61. But see also 58, 59, 67, 85, 181, 183, 433–36, 693.

62. Alexis de Tocqueville, *Recollections* (New York: Meridian Books, 1959), 78.

63. His view of this holds for France as well. As he writes in an October 20, 1856, letter to Mme Swetchine, "During my experience, now long, of public life, nothing has struck me more than the influence of women on this matter—an influence all the greater, because it is indirect. I do not hesitate to say that they give to every nation a moral temperament, which shows itself in its politics. I could illustrate this by many examples. A hundred times I have seen weak men show real public virtue, because they had by their sides women who supported them." This, of course, depends on women having good habits in this regard. Women can also be the source of vice. In the same letter, he writes, "I have observed the domestic influence gradually transforming a man, naturally generous, noble, and unselfish, into a cowardly, commonplace, place-hunting self-seeker, thinking of public business only as a means of making himself comfortable;—and this simply by daily contact with a well-conducted woman, a faithful wife, an excellent mother, but from whose mind the grand notion of public duty was entirely absent." Tocqueville, *Memoir, Letters* [2007], 334.

64. We must also add, then, that women are responsible for the moral content of the laws. Since laws take their shape from mores and mores from dogma, "Any discussion of the political laws of the United States must [also] always begin with the dogma of the sovereignty of the people" (*DA*, 58).

65. In *The Human Condition*, Hannah Arendt argues that this is characteristic not merely of democracy but of modernity in general. She describes it in terms of a blurring of the once clear boundary between the private and public realms and a reordering of the values of the *bios theoretikos* and the *vita activa*.

66. See, for example, Margaret A. Brabant, "Alexis de Tocqueville's Eternal Feminine," *Southeastern Political Review* 23, no. 1 (1995): 83–99. More sympathetic interpretations can be found in Jean Bethke Elshtain, "Women, Equality, and the Family," *Journal of Democracy* 11, no. 1 (2000): 157–63; and Dorothea Israel Wolfson, "Tocqueville on Liberalism's Liberation of Women," *Perspectives on Political Science* 25, no. 4 (1996): 203–7.

67. Allan Bloom, "The Relation of the Sexes: Rousseauian Reflections on the Crisis of Our Times," in Lawler, *Tocqueville's Political Science.*

68. Delba Winthrop, "Tocqueville's American Woman and 'the True Conception of Democratic Progress,'" *Political Theory* 14, no. 2 (1986): 240. See also Peter Augustine Lawler, "Alexis de Tocqueville and the Public/Private Dichotomy: Implications for Public Service Today," *Public Integrity* 3 (Spring 2001): 131–41; William Mathie, "God, Woman, and Morality: The Democratic Family in the New Political Science of Alexis de Tocqueville," *Review of Politics* 57, no. 1 (1995): 29–30; F. L. Morton, "Sexual Equality and the Family in Tocqueville's *Democracy in America*," *Canadian Journal of Political Science* 17, no. 2 (1984): 309–24; Susan Moller Okin, *Justice, Gender and the Family* (New York: Basic Books, 1989), 19; and Manent, *Tocqueville.*

69. Elshtain, *Public Man, Private Woman*, 130. Supporters of this position include Siedentop, *Tocqueville*, 78, and especially Janara, who argues that it is an error to "project onto Tocqueville's analysis an exaggerated separation of family and public as discrete realms, not only spatially but psychologically." Laura Janara, "Democracy's Family Values: Alexis de Tocqueville on Anxiety, Fear, and Desire," *Canadian Journal of Political Science* 34, no. 3 (2001): 553.

70. For more on the family in Tocqueville's thought, see Sanford Kessler, "Tocqueville on Sexual Morality," in Lawler, *Tocqueville's Political Science;* Reiji Matsumoto, "Tocqueville on the Family," *Tocqueville Review* 8 (1986/87): 127–52; and Bloom, *Love and Friendship.*

71. Tocqueville contrasts this belief to the idea of some Europeans that men and women should be not only equal but the same, with the same duties and rights, an arrangement that "degrades them both, and . . . could produce nothing but feeble men and unseemly women" (*DA*, 601).

72. For more on the problem of race in *Democracy in America*, see Delba Winthrop, "Race and Freedom in Tocqueville," in Lawler, *Tocqueville's Political Science.*

73. Tocqueville, *Selected Letters*, 39. Here, however, we must bear in mind Tocqueville's statement that in America "ambition for power gives place to love of well-being, a more vulgar but less dangerous passion" (*DA*, 161).

74. Elsewhere, Tocqueville claims that when "the taste for physical pleasure has grown more rapidly than either education or experience of free institutions, the time comes when men are carried away and lose control of themselves at sight of the new good things they are ready to snatch. Intent only on getting rich, they do not notice that close connection between private fortunes and general prosperity. There is no need to drag their rights away from citizens of this type; they themselves voluntarily let them go. They find it a tiresome inconvenience to exercise political rights which distract them from industry. . . . They cannot waste their precious time in unrewarding work. Such things are all right for idlers to play at, but they do not become men of weight occupied with the serious business of life" (*DA*, 540).

75. For more on the problem of abundance in democracy, see Roger Boesche, "Why Did Tocqueville Fear Abundance? or The Tension between Commerce and Citizenship," *History of European Ideas* 9, no. 1 (1988): 25–48; Joao Carlos Espada, "The Perils of Prosperity," *Journal of Democracy* 11, no. 1 (2000): 135–41; Laura Janara, "Commercial Capitalism and the Democratic Psyche: The Threat to Tocquevillean Citizenship," *History of Political Thought* 12, no. 2 (2001): 317–50; and Stephen Macedo, "Capitalism, Citizenship and Community," *Social Philosophy and Policy* 6, no. 1 (1988): 113–39.

SIX. The Aftermath

The epigraph from Jean-Jacques Rousseau's *Politics and the Arts: Letter to M. d'Alembert on the Theatre* is taken from the translation by Allen D. Bloom (Ithaca: Cornell University Press, 1960), 32.

1. Tocqueville, *Selected Letters*, 115.

2. Alexis de Tocqueville, *The Tocqueville Reader: A Life in Letters and Politics* (Oxford: Blackwell, 2002), 272.

3. Alexis de Tocqueville, *Democracy in America* (Garden City, NY: Doubleday, 1969), 17.

4. Ibid., 78, but see also 95 and 250.

5. Ibid., 139.

6. Ibid., 712.

7. Ibid., 711. Elsewhere Tocqueville describes the taking of these honor trophies as a "horrible practice" (311). And in another passage, the charge of barbarity is leveled at those of European descent: "In the new states of the Southwest the citizens almost always take justice into their own hands and murders are of frequent occurrence. That is because the people's habit are too rough and because enlightenment is not sufficiently widespread in that wilderness for people to see the advantage of giving strength to the law; duels are still preferred to lawsuits there" (225).

8. Tocqueville, *Tocqueville Reader*, 153.

9. Plato *Laches* 181b and *Symposium* 220b.

10. Plato *Republic* 561d–e; translation from *The Republic*, trans. R. W. Sterling and W. C. Scott (New York: W. W. Norton, 1985). All further quotations from the *Republic* in this chapter are taken from this edition.

11. Plato *Republic* 561d–e.

12. Plato *Republic* 561d–e.

13. Plato *Republic* 562a.

14. Karl Marx and Friedrich Engels, "Manifesto of the Communist Party," in *The Marx-Engels Reader*, ed. Robert C. Tucker (New York: W. W. Norton, 1978) 469–500.

15. Karl Marx and Friedrich Engels, *The German Ideology: Part One*, ed. C. J. Arthur (New York: International Publishers, 1970), 53.

16. See, for instance, Michael Allen Gillespie, *Nihilism before Nietzsche* (Chicago: University of Chicago Press, 1995). In his *Manliness*, Harvey Mansfield suggests that Nietzsche's dictum that "man would rather will nothingness than not will" is bound up with the "unmanning" of man. Because "human" is no longer privileged in the expression "human nature," man no longer has signposts directing and ennobling his manly assertions. Consequently, humans are free to make whatsoever they choose of themselves: men can makes brutes of themselves, which is "manly nihilism," and women can make men of themselves, which is womanly nihilism. Thus, whereas Nietzsche is suggesting that the will to power *qua* the will to

power must be vented, if not at something or someone, then in a destructive and pathological direction, Mansfield interprets Nietzsche's statement to mean the absence of immutable patterns to emulate for proper manliness and womanliness.

17. Friedrich Nietzsche, *The Will to Power*, trans. W. A. Kaufmann and R. J. Hollingdale (New York: Random House, 1967), #22.

18. Ibid., #23.

19. Ibid.

20. Ibid., #657. In this same aphorism, Nietzsche asks, "'What is active?'—reaching out for power."

21. Ibid., #12A. Elsewhere, he says, passive nihilism is a "weary nihilism that no longer attacks. . . . The strength of the spirit may be worn out, exhausted, so that previous goals and values have become incommensurate and no longer are believed; so that the synthesis of values and goals (on which every strong culture rests) dissolves and the individual values war against each other: disintegration—and whatever refreshes, heals, calms, numbs emerges into the foreground in various disguises, religious or moral, or political, or aesthetic, etc." (#23).

22. For just this reason, the comparative study of non-Western texts requires special methodological attention. See, for instance, the approaches outlined by Anthony Parel and Ronald C. Keith, *Comparative Political Philosophy: Studies under the Upas Tree* (Newbury Park, CA: Sage Publications, 1992); Fred R. Dallmayr, *Beyond Orientalism: Essays on Cross-cultural Encounter* (Albany: State University of New York Press, 1996), and *Border Crossings: Toward a Comparative Political Theory* (Lanham, MD: Lexington Books, 1999); and, more recently, Roxanne Euben, "Traveling Theorists and Translating Practices," in *What Is Political Theory?* ed. Stephen K. White and J. Donald Moon (Thousand Oaks, CA: Sage Publications, 2004); Lee Jenco, "'What Does Heaven Ever Say?' A Methods-Centered Approach to Cross-cultural Engagement," *American Political Science Review* 101, no. 4 (2007): 741–55; Farah Godrej, "Toward a Cosmopolitan Political Thought: The Hermeneutics of Interpreting the 'Other,'" *Polity* 41 (2009); 135–65; and Fred R. Dallmayr and Abbas Manoochehri, *Civilizational Dialogue and Political Thought: Tehran Papers* (Lanham, MD: Lexington Books, 2007).

23. Makhadev Haribhai Desai and Gandhi, *The Gospel of Selfless Action or the Gita According to Gandhi* (Ahmedabad: Navajivan Publishing House, 1948). As Gandhi puts it in his introduction to his translation of the *Gita*, "When I first became acquainted with the *Gita*, I felt that it was

not a historical work but that, under the guise of physical warfare, it described the duel that perpetually went on in the hearts of mankind, and that physical warfare was brought in merely to make the description of the internal duel more alluring. This preliminary intuition became more confirmed on a closer study of religion and the *Gita*. A study of the *Mahabharata* gave it added confirmation" (127).

24. See Farah Godrej, "Non-violence and Gandhi's Truth: A Method for Moral and Political Arbitration," *Review of Politics* 68, no. 2 (2006): 287–317. As Gandhi puts it, "*Ahimsa* is the means and Truth is the end. Means to be means must always be within our reach, and so *ahimsa* becomes our supreme duty and Truth becomes God for us. If we take care of the means, we are bound to reach the end sooner or later." Gandhi and Raghavan Narasimhan Iyer, *The Moral and Political Writings of Mahatma Gandhi* (Oxford: Oxford University Press, 1986), 2:230–31.

25. As Nietzsche says, it "is the conscience of the present-day" to "abolish all danger," which is "the cause of fear," and in doing so, fulfill the "imperative of herd timidity: 'we wish that there will one day *no longer be anything to fear!*'" Friedrich Nietzsche, *Beyond Good and Evil: Prelude to a Philosophy of the Future* (New York: Penguin Books, 1990), #201.

26. Cf. Augustine: "There are three things: he that loves, and that which is loved, and love." Augustine *On the Trinity* 8.10, in *Basic Writings of Saint Augustine* (New York: Random House, 1948).

27. Bernard, *In Praise of the New Knighthood: A Treatise on the Knights Templar and the Holy Places of Jerusalem* (Kalamazoo, MI: Cistercian Publications, 2000).

28. Augustine's *City of God*, it should keep in mind, is a polemic against the pagans. For more on faith and courage, see the chapter called "Courage and Transcendence" in Paul Tillich, *The Courage to Be* (New Haven: Yale University Press, 1980), esp. 171–78.

29. Tillich, *Courage to Be*, 155.

30. See Augustine, *The Writings against the Manicheans and against the Donatists*, ed. P. Schaff (New York: Christian Literature, 1887), for an exhaustive collection of his writings on Manichaeism. For the status of evil, see Augustine, *Confessions*, trans. H. Chadwick (Oxford: Oxford University Press, 1991), 113–15.

31. Tillich, *Courage to Be*, 34.

32. Friedrich Nietzsche, *The Birth of Tragedy, and The Case of Wagner*, trans. Walter Kaufmann (New York: Vintage Books, 1967), 129.

33. Ibid., 60.

34. Ibid., 95.

35. Nietzsche, *Thus Spoke Zarathustra,* 177.

36. Ibid., 178. Cf. 298: "Do you possess courage [Muth], O my brothers? Are you stout-hearted? *Not* courage in the presence of witnesses, but hermits' and eagles' courage, which not even a god observes any more? I do not call cold-spirited mulish, blind, or intoxicated men stout-hearted. He possesses heart who knows fear but *masters* fear; who sees the abyss, but sees it with *pride.*"

37. In a similar way, Sartre uses *le néant* (the nothing) and "anguish" (l'angoisse). Jean-Paul Sartre, *Being and Nothingness* (New York: Citadel Press, 2001).

38. Martin Heidegger, "What Is Metaphysics?" in *Basic Writings,* ed. David Farrell Krell (San Francisco: Harper, 1993), 95.

39. Cf. Heidegger, *Being and Time,* 231.

40. Heidegger, "What Is Metaphysics?" 101.

41. Ibid.

42. Heidegger, *Being and Time,* 230. Nietzsche refers to the groundlessness of all being as a "fact" that we must face. How we face this fact determines our character. Thucydides, he claims, exemplifies the proper way of facing this reality, while Plato does not. As he puts it, "*Courage* in face of reality ultimately distinguishes such natures as Thucydides and Plato: Plato is a coward in face of reality—consequently he flees into the ideal." Nietzsche, *Twilight of the Idols,* 118.

43. Heidegger, *Being and Time,* 230.

44. Ibid.

45. Tillich, *Courage to Be,* 20.

46. Tocqueville, *Memoir, Letters* [2007], 333.

47. Cf. Peter Berger, "On the Obsolescence of the Concept of Honor," in *Revisions: Changing Perspectives in Moral Philosophy,* ed. Stanley Hauerwas and Alasdair MacIntyre (Notre Dame: University of Notre Dame Press, 1983).

48. Tillich, *Courage to Be,* 31.

49. Cf. Charles McMoran Wilson [Lord Moran], *The Anatomy of Courage* (Boston: Houghton Mifflin, 1967), who holds this view of courage, which he often calls "will power." In his study of courage at the Battle of the Somme, Moran says that "in the trenches a man's will power [courage] was his capital and he was always spending, so that wise and thrifty company officers watched the expenditure of every penny lest their men went bankrupt" (63–64). The hell of World War I lay not only in the ab-

surd loss of life, but in the lack of any respite from the battle where soldiers could replenish their courage: "The real difference between the war of 1914 and the wars of history lay in the absence of a close period, when men safe for the moment could rest and build up a reserve. It ended inevitably in the breaking of men who would have passed the test of any single day's fighting with credit; many too were broken for good, they could not come again" (69).

50. Jean-Jacques Rousseau, *Politics and the Arts: Letter to M. d'Alembert on the Theatre* (Ithaca: Cornell University Press, 1960), 32. For the original story, see Plutarch *Moralia* 235d.

Bibliography

Adkins, A. W. H. *Merit and Responsibility: A Study in Greek Values.* Oxford: Clarendon Press, 1960.

Affeldt, Steven G. "The Force of Freedom: Rousseau on Forcing to Be Free." *Political Theory* 27, no. 3 (1999): 299–333.

Allan, D. J. "Nature, Education and Freedom According to Jean-Jacques Rousseau." *Philosophy* 12, no. 46 (1937): 191–207.

Anderson, J. K. "Hoplite Weapons and Offensive Arms." In *Hoplites: The Classical Greek Battle Experience,* edited by V. D. Hanson. London: Routledge, 1991.

———. *Hunting in the Ancient World.* Berkeley: University of California Press, 1985.

Ansell-Pearson, Keith. *Nietzsche contra Rousseau: A Study of Nietzsche's Moral and Political Thought.* Cambridge: Cambridge University Press, 1991.

Arendt, Hannah. *The Human Condition.* Charles R. Walgreen Foundation Lectures. Chicago: University of Chicago Press, 1958.

Aristophanes. *The Knights; Peace; The Birds; The Assemblywomen; Wealth.* Translated by David Barrett and Alan H. Sommerstein. New York: Penguin Books, 1978.

———. *Wasps.* In *The Complete Plays of Aristophanes,* edited by Moses Hadas. New York: Bantam Books, 1962.

Aristotle. *The Athenian Constitution.* Translated by P. J. Rhodes. New York: Penguin Books, 1984.

———. *Nicomachean Ethics.* Translated by H. Rackham. Cambridge, MA: Harvard University Press, 1975.

———. *The Nicomachean Ethics.* Translated by W. D. Ross. Oxford: Oxford University Press, 1980.

———. *The Politics.* Translated by T. A. Sinclair. New York: Penguin Books, 1951.

———. *Politics.* In *The Complete Works of Aristotle,* translated by Benjamin Jowett. Princeton: Princeton University Press, 1991.

Atkinson, K. M. T. Chrimes. *Ancient Sparta: A Re-examination of the Evidence.* Manchester: Manchester University Press, 1949.

Augustine. *Concerning the City of God against the Pagans.* Translated by H. S. Bettenson. London: Penguin Books, 1972.

———. *Confessions.* Translated by H. Chadwick. Oxford: Oxford University Press, 1991.

———. *The Happy Life.* Translated by L. Schopp. St. Louis: B. Herder, 1939.

———. *On the Trinity.* In *Basic Writings of Saint Augustine.* New York: Random House, 1948.

———. *The Writings against the Manicheans and against the Donatists.* Edited by P. Schaff. Nicene and Post-Nicene Fathers of the Christian Church. New York: Christian Literature Company, 1887.

Austin, Norman. Introduction to *The Greek Historians,* edited by Norman Austin. New York: D. van Nostrand, 1969.

Avramenko, Richard. "The Wound and Salve of Time: Augustine's Politics of Human Happiness." *Review of Metaphysics* 60 (2007): 779–811.

Avramenko, Richard, and John von Heyking. *Friendship and Politics: Essays in Political Thought.* Notre Dame: University of Notre Dame Press, 2008.

Badhwar, Neera Kapur, ed. *Friendship: A Philosophical Reader.* Ithaca: Cornell University Press, 1993.

Baldick, Robert. *The Duel: A History of Duelling.* New York: C. N. Potter, 1965.

Balot, Ryan. "Courage in the Democratic Polis." *Classical Quarterly* 54, no. 2 (2004): 406–23.

———. "Free Speech, Courage, and Democratic Deliberation." In *Free Speech in Classical Antiquity,* edited by Ineke Sluiter and Ralph Rosen. Leiden: Brill, 2004.

Banfield, Edward C. *The Moral Basis of a Backward Society.* Glencoe, IL: Free Press; Chicago: Research Center in Economic Development and Cultural Change, 1958.

Bassi, Karen. "The Semantics of Manliness in Ancient Greece." In *Andreia: Studies in Manliness and Courage in Classical Antiquity,* edited by Ralph Mark Rosen and Ineke Sluiter. Boston: Brill, 2003.

Beiner, Ronald. "Machiavelli, Hobbes, and Rousseau on Civil Religion." *Review of Politics* 55, no. 4 (1993): 617–38.

Bellah, Robert N. "The Quest for the Self: Individualism, Morality, Politics." In *Interpreting Tocqueville's Democracy in America,* edited by Ken Masugi. Savage, MD: Rowman and Littlefield, 1991.

Benedict, Ruth. *The Chrysanthemum and the Sword: Patterns of Japanese Culture.* Cleveland, OH: Meridian Books, 1967.

Berger, Peter. "On the Obsolescence of the Concept of Honor." In *Revisions: Changing Perspectives in Moral Philosophy,* edited by Stanley Hauerwas and Alasdair MacIntyre. Notre Dame: University of Notre Dame Press, 1983.

Berlin, Isaiah. *Freedom and Its Betrayal: Six Enemies of Human Liberty.* Edited by H. Hardy. Princeton: Princeton University Press, 2002.

Bernard. *In Praise of the New Knighthood: A Treatise on the Knights Templar and the Holy Places of Jerusalem.* Cistercian Fathers Series. Kalamazoo, MI: Cistercian Publications, 2000.

Black, Antony. "Christianity and Republicanism: From St. Cyprian to Rousseau." *American Political Science Review* 91, no. 3 (1997): 647–56.

Blitz, Mark. "Introduction to the Reading of Plato's *Laches.*" *Interpretation* 5, no. 2 (1975): 185–225.

Bloom, Allan. "Interpretive Essay." In *The Republic of Plato,* edited and translated by Allan Bloom. New York: Basic Books, 1991.

———. *Love and Friendship.* New York: Simon and Schuster, 1993.

———. "The Relation of the Sexes: Rousseauian Reflections on the Crisis of Our Times." In *Tocqueville's Political Science: Classic Essays,* edited by Peter Augustine Lawler. New York: Garland, 1992.

Bluhm, William T. "Freedom in 'The Social Contract': Rousseau's 'Legitimate Chains.'" *Polity* 16, no. 3 (1984): 359–83.

Blum, Carol. *Rousseau and the Republic of Virtue: The Language of Politics in the French Revolution.* Ithaca: Cornell University Press, 1986.

Boesche, Roger. *The Strange Liberalism of Alexis de Tocqueville.* Ithaca: Cornell University Press, 1987.

———. "Why Did Tocqueville Fear Abundance? or The Tension between Commerce and Citizenship." *History of European Ideas* 9, no. 1 (1988): 25–45.

Böhm, Sigurd. *La temporalité dans l'anthropologie augustinienne.* Paris: Editions du Cerf, 1984.

Bowden, Mark. *Black Hawk Down: A Story of Modern War.* New York: Atlantic Monthly Press, 1999.

Bowman, James. *Honor: A History.* New York: Encounter Books, 2006.

Boyd, Richard. "Pity's Pathologies Portrayed: Rousseau and the Limits of Democratic Compassion." *Political Theory* 32, no. 4 (2004): 519–46.

Brabant, Margaret A. "Alexis de Tocqueville's Eternal Feminine." *Southeastern Political Review* 23, no. 1 (1995): 83–99.

Brandes, Stanley. "Reflections on Honor and Shame in the Mediterranean." In *Honor and Shame and the Unity of the Mediterranean,* edited by D. D. Gilmore. Washington, DC: American Anthropological Association, 1987.

Braudy, Leo. *The Frenzy of Renown: Fame and Its History.* 1986. Reprint, New York: Vintage Books, 1997.

Braund, David. "Aristophanes at Acanthus, *Wasps* 968–969." *Classical Quarterly* 49, no. 1 (1995): 321–24.

Brogan, Hugh. *Alexis de Tocqueville: A Life.* New Haven: Yale University Press, 2007.

Brokaw, Tom. *The Greatest Generation.* New York: Random House, 1998.

Broughton, John M. "Women's Rationality and Men's Virtues: A Critique of Gender Dualism in Gilligan's Theory of Moral Development." *Social Research* 50, no. 3 (1983): 597–642.

Brownson, Carleton L. "Reasons for Plato's Hostility to the Poets." *Transactions and Proceedings of the American Philological Association* 28 (1897): 5–41.

Bryant, Joseph M. *Moral Codes and Social Structure in Ancient Greece: A Sociology of Greek Ethics from Homer to the Epicureans and Stoics.* SUNY Series in the Sociology of Culture. Albany: State University of New York Press, 1996.

Buford, Thomas O. "Plato on the Educational Consultant: An Interpretation of the *Laches.*" *Idealistic Studies* 7, no. 2 (1977): 151–93.

Butler, Melissa A. "Rousseau and the Politics of Care." In *Feminist Interpretations of Jean-Jacques Rousseau,* edited by Lynda Lange. University Park: Pennsylvania State University Press, 2002.

Cairns, Douglas L. *Aidos: The Psychology and Ethics of Honour and Shame in Ancient Greek Literature.* Oxford: Clarendon Press, 1993.

Cameron, Alister. *Plato's Affair with Tragedy.* Cincinnati: University of Cincinnati Press, 1978.

Cameron, David R. "The Hero in Rousseau's Political Thought." *Journal of the History of Ideas* 45, no. 3 (1984): 397–419.

Campbell, J. K. "Honour and the Devil." In *Honour and Shame: The Values of Mediterranean Society,* edited by Jean G. Peristiany. Chicago: University of Chicago Press, 1966.

Campolo, Lisa D. "Derrida and Heidegger: The Critique of Technology and the Call to Care." *Journal of the American Academy of Religion* 53, no. 3 (1985): 431–48.

Caputo, John D. "*Sorge* and *Kardia:* The Hermeneutics of Facticity and the Categories of the Heart." In *Reading Heidegger from the Start: Essays in His Earliest Thought,* edited by Theodore J. Kisiel. Albany: State University of New York Press, 1994.

———. "Spirit and Danger." In *Ethics and Danger: Essays on Heidegger and Continental Thought,* edited by Arleen B. Dallery, Charles E. Scott, and P. Holley Roberts. Albany: State University Press of New York, 1992.

Cartledge, Paul. *Agesilaos and the Crisis of Sparta.* Baltimore: Johns Hopkins University Press, 1987.

———. "The Socratics' Sparta and Rousseau's." In *Sparta: New Perspectives,* edited by Stephen Hodkinson and Anton Powell. London: Classical Press of Wales, 1999.

———. *Spartan Reflections.* Berkeley: University of California Press, 2001.

Cassirer, Ernst. *The Question of Jean-Jacques Rousseau.* Translated by Peter Gay. Bloomington: Indiana University Press, 1954.

Char, René. *Leaves of Hypnos.* New York: Grossman, 1973.

Cladis, Mark S. "Tragedy and Theodicy: A Meditation on Rousseau and Moral Evil." *Journal of Religion* 75 (1995): 181–99.

Cocking, Dean, and Jeanette Kennett. "Friendship and Moral Danger." *Journal of Philosophy* 97, no. 5 (2000): 278–96.

Cohen, David. *Law, Sexuality, and Society: The Enforcement of Morals in Classical Athens.* Cambridge: Cambridge University Press, 1991.

Cohen, Eliot A. "Tocqueville on War." In *Tocqueville's Political Science: Classic Essays,* edited by Peter Augustine Lawler. New York: Garland, 1992.

Cohen, Joshua. "Reflections on Rousseau: Autonomy and Democracy." *Philosophy and Public Affairs* 15 (Summer 1986): 275–88.

Coleman, Patrick. "Characterizing Rousseau's Emile." *MLN* 92, no. 4 (1977): 761–78.

Collins, Susan D. *Aristotle and the Rediscovery of Citizenship.* New York: Cambridge University Press, 2006.

Congleton, Ann. "Two Kinds of Lawlessness: Plato's Crito." *Political Theory* 2, no. 4 (1974): 432–46.

Conniff, James. "On the Obsolescence of the General Will: Rousseau, Madison, and the Evolution of Republican Political Thought." *Western Political Quarterly* 28, no. 1 (1975): 32–58.

Cooley, Kenneth W. "Unity and Diversity of the Virtues in the *Charmides, Laches,* and *Protagoras.*" *Kinesis* 1 (1969): 100–106.

Cooper, Laurence D. "Between Eros and Will to Power: Rousseau and 'The Desire to Extend Our Being.'" *American Political Science Review* 98, no. 1 (2004): 105–19.

———. "Human Nature and the Love of Wisdom: Rousseau's Hidden (and Modified) Platonism." *Journal of Politics* 64, no. 1 (2002): 108–25.

Crocker, Lester G. "Order and Disorder in Rousseau's Social Thought." *PMLA* 94, no. 2 (1979): 247–60.

Dallmayr, Fred R. *Beyond Orientalism: Essays on Cross-cultural Encounter.* Albany: State University of New York Press, 1996.

———. *Border Crossings: Toward a Comparative Political Theory.* Global Encounters. Lanham, MD: Lexington Books, 1999.

Dallmayr, Fred R., and Abbas Manoochehri. *Civilizational Dialogue and Political Thought: Tehran Papers.* Global Encounters. Lanham, MD: Lexington Books, 2007.

Dame, F. W. "Jean-Jacques Rousseau's Views on Adult Education." *International Review of Education* 42, nos. 1–3 (1996): 205–26.

Darling, John. "Understanding and Religion in Rousseau's 'Emile.'" *British Journal of Educational Studies* 33, no. 1 (1985): 20–34.

DeLue, Steven M. "Plato's Crito as a Defense of Critical Inquiry." *Journal of Politics* 39, no. 2 (1977): 472–79.

Dent, N. J. H. *Rousseau: An Introduction to His Psychological, Social, and Political Theory.* New York: Blackwell, 1989.

Derrida, Jacques. *Politics of Friendship.* London: Verso, 1997.

Desai, Makhadev Haribhai, and Gandhi. *The Gospel of Selfless Action or the Gita According to Gandhi.* Ahmedabad: Navajivan Publishing House, 1948.

de Ste Croix, G. E. M. "The Helot Threat." In *Sparta,* edited by Michael Whitby. New York: Routledge, 2002.

Devereux, Daniel T. "Courage and Wisdom in Plato's *Laches*." *Journal of the History of Philosophy* 15, no. 1 (1977): 129–41.

———. "The Unity of the Virtues in Plato's *Protagoras* and *Laches*." *Philosophical Review* 101, no. 4 (1992): 765–89.

Dickstein, Morris. "The Faith of a Vicar: Reason and Morality in Rousseau's Religion." *Yale French Studies*, no. 28 (1961): 48–54.

Disch, Lisa. "Claire Loves Julie: Reading the Story of Women's Friendship in *La nouvelle Heloise*." *Hypatia* 9, no. 3 (1994): 19–45.

Dobbs, Darrell. "Family Matters: Aristotle's Appreciation of Women and the Plural Structure of Society." *American Political Science Review* 90, no. 1 (1996): 74–89.

———. "For Lack of Wisdom: Courage and Inquiry in Plato's *Laches*." *Journal of Politics* 48, no. 4 (1986): 825–49.

Dobel, J. Patrick. "The Role of Language in Rousseau's Political Thought." *Polity* 18, no. 4 (1986): 638–58.

Dodds, E. R. *The Greeks and the Irrational.* Sather Classical Lectures 25. Berkeley: University of California Press, 1951.

Dostal, Robert. "Friendship and Politics: Heidegger's Failing." *Political Theory* 20, no. 3 (1992): 399–423.

Dover, K. J. *Greek Homosexuality.* Cambridge, MA: Harvard University Press, 1978.

DuBois, Page. "The Homoerotics of the 'Phaedrus.'" *Pacific Coast Philology* 17, nos. 1/2 (1982): 9–15.

Duncan, Thomas Shearer. "Plato and Poetry." *Classical Review* 40, no. 8 (1945): 481–94.

Dyson, M. "The Structure of the Laws' Speech in Plato's Crito." *Classical Quarterly* 28, no. 2 (1978): 427–36.

Edmons, Radcliffe G. "Socrates the Beautiful: Role Reversal and Midwifery in Plato's *Symposium*." *Transactions and Proceedings of the American Philological Association* 130 (2000): 261–85.

Ehrenberg, Victor. "A Totalitarian State." In *Aspects of the Ancient World*, edited by Victor Ehrenberg. New York: W. Salloch, 1946.

Ehrenreich, Barbara. *Blood Rites: Origins and History of the Passions of War.* New York: Metropolitan Books, 1997.

Eisenstadt, Oona. "Shame in the *Apology*." In *Politics, Philosophy, Writing: Plato's Art of Caring for Souls*, edited by Zdravko Planinc. Columbia: University of Missouri Press, 2001.

Ellenburg, Stephen. *Rousseau's Political Philosophy: An Interpretation from Within.* Ithaca: Cornell University Press, 1976.

Elshtain, Jean Bethke. *Public Man, Private Woman: Women in Social and Political Thought.* Princeton: Princeton University Press, 1981.

———. "Women, Equality, and the Family." *Journal of Democracy* 11, no. 1 (2000): 157–63.

Elster, Jon. "Rationality and the Emotions." *Economic Journal* 106, no. 438 (1996): 1386–97.

Emberley, Peter. "Rousseau and the Domestication of Virtue." *Canadian Journal of Political Science / Revue canadienne de science politique* 17, no. 4 (1984): 731–53.

Espada, Joao Carlos. "The Perils of Prosperity." *Journal of Democracy* 11, no. 1 (2000): 135–41.

Euben, J. Peter. *Corrupting Youth: Political Education, Democratic Culture, and Political Theory.* Princeton: Princeton University Press, 1997.

———. "Philosophy and Politics in Plato's *Crito.*" *Political Theory* 6, no. 2 (1978): 149–72.

———. *Platonic Noise.* Princeton: Princeton University Press, 2003.

Euben, Roxanne. "Traveling Theorists and Translating Practices." In *What Is Political Theory?*, edited by Stephen K. White and J. Donald Moon. Thousand Oaks, CA: Sage Publications, 2004.

Farrell, Daniel M. "Illegal Actions, Universal Maxims, and the Duty to Obey the Law: The Case for Civil Authority in the Crito." *Political Theory* 6, no. 2 (1978): 173–89.

Fehling, Detlev. *Herodotus and His "Sources": Citation, Invention, and Narrative Art.* Translated by J. G. Howie. Leeds: Francis Cairns, 1989.

Fermon, Nicole. *Domesticating Passions: Rousseau, Woman, and Nation.* Hanover: Wesleyan University Press, 1997.

Ferrill, Arther. "Herodotus and the Strategy and Tactics of the Invasion of Xerxes." *American Historical Review* 72, no. 1 (1966): 102–15.

Finnis, John. *Natural Law and Natural Rights.* Oxford: Oxford University Press, 1980.

Flanders, Todd R. "Rousseau's Adventure with Robinson Crusoe." *Interpretation: A Journal of Political Philosophy* 24, no. 3 (1997): 319–38.

Flynn, Thomas R. "*Angst* and Care in the Early Heidegger: The Ontic/Ontologic Aporia." *International Studies in Philosophy* 12, no. 1 (1980): 61–76.

Fontane, Theodor. *Effi Briest.* Penguin Classics L190. New York: Penguin Books, 1967.

Fornara, Charles W. *Herodotus: An Interpretive Essay.* Oxford: Clarendon Press, 1971.

Foucault, Michel. *Discipline and Punish: The Birth of the Prison.* Translated by Alan Sheridan. New York: Vintage Books, 1977.

Fourny, Diane. "Rousseau's Civil Religion Reconsidered." *French Review* 60, no. 4 (1987): 485–96.

Frantzich, Stephen. "Teaching through Tocqueville." *PS: Political Science and Politics* 32, no. 2 (1999): 203–5.

Freeman, Joanne B. "Dueling as Politics: Reinterpreting the Burr-Hamilton Duel." *William and Mary Quarterly* 53, no. 2 (1996): 289–318.

French, Peter A. *The Virtues of Vengeance.* Lawrence: University Press of Kansas, 2001.

Friedlander, Paul. "Laches." In *Plato.* New York: Pantheon Books, 1964.

Frohnen, Bruce. *Virtue and the Promise of Conservatism: The Legacy of Burke and Tocqueville.* Lawrence: University Press of Kansas, 1993.

Galston, William. *Liberal Purposes.* Cambridge: Cambridge University Press, 1991.

———. "Liberal Virtues." *American Political Science Review* 82, no. 4 (1988): 1277–90.

———. "Tocqueville on Liberalism and Religion." *Social Research* 54, no. 3 (1987): 500–501.

Gandhi and Raghavan Narasimhan Iyer. *The Moral and Political Writings of Mahatma Gandhi.* Oxford: Oxford University Press, 1986.

Gargan, E. T. "Tocqueville and the Problem of Historical Prognosis." *American Historical Review* 68, no. 2 (1963): 332.

Garrard, Graeme. *Rousseau's Counter-Enlightenment: A Republican Critique of the Philosophes.* SUNY Series in Social and Political Thought. Albany: State University of New York Press, 2003.

Gelven, Michael. *War and Existence: A Philosophical Inquiry.* University Park: Pennsylvania State University Press, 1994.

George, W. H. "Montesquieu and de Tocqueville and Corporative Individualism." *American Political Science Review* 16, no. 1 (1922): 10–21.

Gillespie, Michael Allen. *Nihilism before Nietzsche.* Chicago: University of Chicago Press, 1995.

Gilligan, Carol. *In a Different Voice: Psychological Theory and Women's Development.* Cambridge, MA: Harvard University Press, 1982.

Ginat, J. *Blood Revenge: Family Honor, Mediation, and Outcasting.* 2nd ed. Portland, OR: Sussex Academic Press, 1997.

Godrej, Farah. "Non-violence and Gandhi's Truth: A Method for Moral and Political Arbitration." *Review of Politics* 68, no. 2 (2006): 287–317.

———. "Toward a Cosmopolitan Political Thought: The Hermeneutics of Interpreting the 'Other.'" *Polity* 41 (2009): 135–65.

Golden, Mark. "Slavery and Homosexuality at Athens." *Phoenix* 38, no. 4 (1984): 308–24.

Gould, Carol S. "Socratic Intellectualism and the Problem of Courage: An Interpretation of Plato's *Laches*." *History of Philosophy Quarterly* 4, no. 3 (1987): 265–79.

Gourevitch, Victor. "The Religious Thought." In *The Cambridge Companion to Rousseau*, edited by Patrick Riley. Cambridge: Cambridge University Press, 2001.

Grant, Ruth Weissbourd. *Hypocrisy and Integrity: Machiavelli, Rousseau, and the Ethics of Politics.* Chicago: University of Chicago Press, 1997.

———. "Integrity and Politics: An Alternative Reading of Rousseau." *Political Theory* 22, no. 3 (1994): 414–43.

Gray, J. Glenn. *The Warriors: Reflections on Men in Battle.* Lincoln: University of Nebraska Press, 1959.

Greene, William Chase. "Plato's View of Poetry." *Harvard Studies in Classical Philology* 29 (1918): 1–75.

Greeno, Catherine G., and Eleanor E. Maccoby. "How Different Is the 'Different Voice'?" *Signs* 11, no. 2 (1986): 310–16.

Grimsley, Ronald. *Rousseau and the Religious Quest.* Oxford: Clarendon Press, 1968.

Griswold, Charles L. "Philosophy, Education, and Courage in Plato's *Laches*." *Interpretation* 14, no. 2 (1986): 177–93.

Grossman, Dave. *On Killing: The Psychological Cost of Learning to Kill in War and Society.* Boston: Little, Brown, 1995.

Guitton, Jean. *Le temps et l'éternité chez Plotin et Saint Augustin.* Paris: Boivin et Cie, 1933.

Gulley, Norman. "Plato on Poetry." *Greece and Rome* 24, no. 2 (1977): 154–69.

Gutwirth, Madelyn. "Madame de Stael, Rousseau, and the Woman Question." *PMLA* 86, no. 1 (1971): 100–109.

Hadari, Saguiv A. *Theory in Practice: Tocqueville's New Science of Politics.* Stanford: Stanford University Press, 1989.

Haden, James C. "Two Types of Power in Plato's 'Gorgias.'" *Classical Journal* 87 (1992): 313–26.

Halperin, David. "Plato on Erotic Reciprocity." *Classical Antiquity* 5 (1986): 60–80.

———. "Platonic Eros and What Men Call Love." *Ancient Philosophy* 5 (1985): 161–204.

Hancock, Ralph C. "Tocqueville on the Good of American Federalism." *Publius: The Journal of Federalism* 20, no. 2 (1990): 89–108.

———. "The Uses and Hazards of Christianity in Tocqueville's Attempt to Save Democratic Souls." In *Interpreting Tocqueville's Democracy in America*, edited by Ken Masugi. Savage, MD: Rowman and Littlefield, 1991.

Hanley, Ryan Patrick. "Aristotle on the Greatness of the Greatness of Soul." *History of Political Thought* 23, no. 1 (2002): 1–20.

Hanson, Victor Davis. *The Wars of the Ancient Greeks: And Their Invention of Western Military Culture.* The Cassell History of Warfare. London: Cassell, 1999.

———. *The Western Way of War: Infantry Battle in Classical Greece.* New York: Knopf, 1989.

Harari, Josué V. "Therapeutic Pedagogy: Rousseau's Emile." *MLN* 97, no. 4 (1982): 787–809.

Hardie, W. F. R. "'Magnanimity' in Aristotle's *Ethics*." *Phronesis* 23 (1978): 63–79.

Harrell, Sarah E. "Marvelous *Andreia:* Politics, Geography, and Ethnicity in Herodotus' *Histories*." In *Andreia: Studies in Manliness and Courage in Classical Antiquity*, edited by Ralph Mark Rosen and Ineke Sluiter. Boston: Brill, 2003.

Hebert, L. J. "Individualism and Intellectual Liberty in Tocqueville and Descartes." *Journal of Politics* 69, no. 2 (2007): 525–37.

Hedges, Chris. *War Is a Force That Gives Us Meaning.* New York: PublicAffairs, 2002.

Heidegger, Martin. *Being and Time.* Translated by J. Macquarrie. New York: Harper, 1962.

———. *Introduction to Metaphysics.* Translated by G. Fried. New Haven: Yale University Press, 2000.

———. "What Is Metaphysics?" In *Basic Writings*, edited by David Farrell Krell. San Francisco: Harper, 1993.

Heimonet, Jean-Michel. *Tocqueville et le devenir de la démocratie: La perversion de l'idéal.* Paris: L'Harmattan, 1999.

Held, Virginia. *The Ethics of Care: Personal, Political, and Global.* Oxford: Oxford University Press, 2006.

Herodotus. *The Histories.* Translated by Aubrey de Sélincourt. Penguin Classics. New York: Penguin Books, 1996.

Herzfeld, Michael. "Honour and Shame: Problems in the Comparative Analysis in Moral Systems." *Man* 15, no. 2 (1980): 339–51.

Heyking, John von. "*Ab virilitate ad perseverantiae gloriae:* Comparing Aristotle's and Thomas Aquinas's Pedagogy on Manliness." Paper presented at the annual meeting of the American Political Science Association, Boston, September 2002.

Hight, George Ainslie. "Plato and the Poets." *Mind* 31, no. 122 (1922): 195–99.

Hill, Greg. *Rousseau's Theory of Human Association: Transparent and Opaque Communities.* New York: Palgrave Macmillan, 2006.

Hinckley, Cynthia. "Tocqueville on Religion and Modernity: Making Catholicism Safe for Liberal Democracy." In *Tocqueville's Political Science: Classic Essays,* edited by Peter Augustine Lawler. New York: Garland, 1992.

———. "Tocqueville on Religious Truth and Political Necessity." *Polity* 23, no. 1 (1990): 39–52.

Hindley, Clifford. "Law, Society and Homosexuality in Classical Athens." *Past and Present* 133 (1991): 167–83.

Hirschman, Albert O. *The Passions and the Interests: Political Arguments for Capitalism before Its Triumph.* Princeton: Princeton University Press, 1977.

Hobbes, Thomas. *Leviathan.* Edited by C. B. Macpherson. New York: Penguin Books, 1968.

Hobbs, Angela. *Plato and the Hero: Courage, Manliness and the Impersonal Good.* Cambridge: Cambridge University Press, 2000.

Hochberg, Leonard J. "Reconciling History with Sociology?" *Journal of Classical Sociology* 7, no. 1 (2007): 23–54.

Hoerber, Robert G. "Plato's *Laches.*" *Classical Philology* 63, no. 2 (1968): 95–105.

Holland, Barbara. *Gentlemen's Blood: A History of Dueling from Swords at Dawn to Pistols at Dusk.* New York: Bloomsbury, 2003.

Holloway, Carson. *Magnanimity and Statesmanship.* Lanham, MD: Lexington Books, 2008.

Holmes, Richard. *Acts of War: The Behavior of Men in Battle.* New York: Free Press, 1986.

Homer. *Iliad.* Translated by Richard Lattimore. Chicago: University of Chicago Press, 1951.

Horace. *Odes and Carmen Saeculare of Horace.* Ed. and trans. John Conington. 3rd ed. London: Bell and Daldy, 1863.

Hornblower, Simon. *A Commentary on Thucydides: Volume 1, Books I–III.* 2 vols. Oxford: Clarendon Press, 1991.

Howland, Jacob. "Aristotle's Great-Souled Man." *Review of Politics* 64, no. 1 (2002): 27–56.

Hubbard, T. K. "Popular Perceptions of Elite Homosexuality in Classical Athens." *Arion* 6, no. 1 (1998): 48–78.

Huizinga, Johan. *Homo Ludens: A Study of the Play-Element in Culture.* Boston: Beacon Press, 1955.

———. *The Waning of the Middle Ages: A Study of the Forms of Life, Thought, and Art in France and the Netherlands in the XIVth and XVth Centuries.* 1924. Reprint, Garden City, NY: Doubleday Anchor, 1954.

Hull, Denison Bingham. *Hounds and Hunting in Ancient Greece.* Chicago: University of Chicago Press, 1964.

Hulliung, Mark. *The Autocritique of Enlightenment: Rousseau and the Philosophes.* Cambridge, MA: Harvard University Press, 1994.

Jackson, M. W. "Rousseau's Discourse on Heroes and Heroism." *Proceedings of the American Philosophical Society* 133, no. 3 (1989): 434–46.

Jaffa, Harry V. *Thomism and Aristotelianism: A Study of the Commentary by Thomas Aquinas of the Nicomachean Ethics.* Chicago: University of Chicago Press, 1952.

James, William. "The Moral Equivalent of War." In *Writings, 1902–1910,* edited by Bruce Kuklick. New York: Literary Classics of the United States, 1987.

———. *The Principles of Psychology.* New York: H. Holt, 1890.

Janara, Laura. "Commercial Capitalism and the Democratic Psyche: The Threat to Tocquevillean Citizenship." *History of Political Thought* 12, no. 2 (2001a): 317–50.

———. *Democracy Growing Up: Authority, Autonomy, and Passion in Tocqueville's Democracy in America.* SUNY Series in Political Theory. Contemporary Issues. Albany: State University of New York Press, 2002.

———. "Democracy's Family Values: Alexis de Tocqueville on Anxiety, Fear, and Desire." *Canadian Journal of Political Science* 34, no. 3 (2001): 551–78.

Jardin, Andre. *Tocqueville: A Biography.* New York: Farrar Straus Giroux, 1988.

Jenco, Lee. "'What Does Heaven Ever Say?' A Methods-Centered Approach to Cross-cultural Engagement." *American Political Science Review* 101, no. 4 (2007): 741–55.

Jordan, Robert. "Time and Contingency in St. Augustine." *Review of Metaphysics* 8 (1955): 394–417.

Jünger, Ernst. *Storm of Steel.* Translated by M. Hofmann. New York: Penguin Books, 2004.

Kagan, Donald. *The Outbreak of the Peloponnesian War.* Ithaca: Cornell University Press, 1969.

Kahan, Alan S. *Aristocratic Liberalism: The Social and Political Thought of Jacob Burckhardt, John Stuart Mill, and Alexis de Tocqueville.* New York: Oxford University Press, 1992.

Kant, Immanuel. "Idea for a Universal History with a Cosmopolitan Purpose." In *Kant's Political Writings*, edited by Hans Reiss. Cambridge: Cambridge University Press, 1970.

———. "Perpetual Peace." In *Kant's Political Writings*, edited by Hans Reiss. Cambridge: Cambridge University Press, 1970.

Kato, Shinro. "The Apology: The Beginning of Plato's Own Philosophy." *Classical Quarterly* 41, no. 2 (1991): 356–64.

Kaufman, Alexander. "Reason, Self-Legislation and Legitimacy: Conceptions of Freedom in the Political Thought of Rousseau and Kant." *Review of Politics* 59, no. 1 (1997): 25–52.

Kelly, Christopher. *Rousseau as Author: Consecrating One's Life to the Truth.* Chicago: University of Chicago Press, 2003.

———. "Rousseau's Case for and against Heroes." *Polity* 30, no. 2 (1997): 447–66.

———. *Rousseau's Exemplary Life: The Confessions as Political Philosophy.* Ithaca: Cornell University Press, 1987.

———. "To Persuade without Convincing: The Language of Rousseau's Legislator." *American Journal of Political Science* 31, no. 1 (1987): 321–35.

Kennell, Nigel M. *The Gymnasium of Virtue: Education and Culture in Ancient Sparta.* Studies in the History of Greece and Rome. Chapel Hill: University of North Carolina Press, 1995.

Keohane, Nannerl O. "'The Masterpiece of Policy in Our Century': Rousseau on the Morality of the Enlightenment." *Political Theory* 6, no. 4 (1978): 457–84.

Kerber, Linda K. "Some Cautionary Words for Historians." *Signs* 11, no. 2 (1986): 304–10.

Kessler, Sanford. "Tocqueville on Civil Religion and Liberal Democracy." *Journal of Politics* 39, no. 1 (1977): 119–46.

———. "Tocqueville on Sexual Morality." In *Tocqueville's Political Science: Classic Essays*, edited by Peter Augustine Lawler. New York: Garland, 1992.

———. *Tocqueville's Civil Religion: American Christianity and the Prospects for Freedom.* Albany: State University of New York Press, 1994.

Keyser, Paul. "Errors of Calculation in Herodotus." *Classical Journal* 81, no. 3 (1986): 230–42.

King, Preston, and Heather Devere, eds. *The Challenge to Friendship in Modernity.* London: Frank Cass, 2000.

Kisiel, Theodore. *Heidegger's Way of Thought: Critical and Interpretive Signposts.* New York: Continuum, 2002.

Kissam, P. C. "Alexis de Tocqueville and American Constitutional Law: On Democracy, the Majority Will, Individual Rights, Federalism, Religion, Civic Associations, and Originalist Constitutional Theory." *Maine Law Review* 59, no. 1 (2007): 35.

Klosko, George. "The Insufficiency of Reason in Plato's Gorgias." *Western Political Quarterly* 36 (1983): 579–95.

Kojève, Alexandre. *Introduction to the Reading of Hegel: Lectures on the Phenomenology of Spirit.* Translated by R. Queneau. Ithaca: Cornell University Press, 1980.

Koritansky, John C. *Alexis de Tocqueville and the New Science of Politics: An Interpretation of Democracy in America.* Durham, NC: Carolina Academic Press, 1986.

———. "Decentralization and Civic Virtue in Tocqueville's 'New Science of Politics.'" *Publius* 5, no. 3 (1975): 63–81.

Krause, Sharon R. *Liberalism with Honor.* Cambridge, MA: Harvard University Press, 2002.

La Fournière, Xavier de. *Alexis de Tocqueville: Un monarchiste indépendant.* Paris: Perrin, 1981.

LaFreniere, Gilbert F. "Rousseau and the European Roots of Environmentalism." *Environmental History Review* 14, no. 4 (1990): 41–72.

Laguna, Theodore de. "The Interpretation of the Apology." *Philosophical Review* 18, no. 1 (1909): 23–37.

Lamberti, Jean-Claude. *La notion d'individualisme chez Tocqueville.* Paris: Presses Universitaires de France, 1970.

———. *Tocqueville and the Two Democracies.* Cambridge, MA: Harvard University Press, 1989.

Langan, Thomas. *The Meaning of Heidegger: A Critical Study of an Existentialist Phenomenology.* New York: Columbia University Press, 1959.

Lange, Lynda. *Feminist Interpretations of Jean-Jacques Rousseau.* Re-reading the Canon. University Park: Pennsylvania State University Press, 2002.

Lawler, Peter Augustine. "Alexis de Tocqueville and the Public/Private Dichotomy: Implications for Public Service Today." *Public Integrity* 3 (Spring 2001): 131–41.

———. *The Restless Mind: Alexis de Tocqueville on the Origin and Perpetuation of Human Liberty.* Lanham, MD: Rowman and Littlefield, 1993.

———, ed. *Tocqueville's Political Science: Classic Essays.* New York: Garland, 1992.

Lazenby, John F. "The Killing Zone." In *Hoplites: The Classical Greek Battle Experience,* edited by V. D. Hanson. London: Routledge, 1991.

———. *The Spartan Army.* Warminster: Aris and Phillips, 1985.

Lendon, J. E. "Spartan Honor." In *Polis and Polemos: Essays on Politics, War, and History in Ancient Greece,* edited by Charles D. Hamilton and Peter Krentz. Claremont, CA: Regina Books, 1997.

Levine, Andrew. *The Politics of Autonomy: A Kantian Reading of Rousseau's Social Contract.* Amherst: University of Massachusetts Press, 1976.

Levy, A. S. *America Discovered a Second Time: French Perceptions of American Notions of Time from Tocqueville to Laboulaye.* New Haven: Yale University Press, 1996.

Levy, Harold. "Does Aristotle Exclude Women from Politics?" *Review of Politics* 52, no. 3 (1990): 397–416.

Lewis, C. S. *The Abolition of Man, or, Reflections on Education with Special Reference to the Teaching of English in the Upper Forms of Schools.* San Francisco: HarperSanFrancisco, 2001.

Lewis, H. D. "Freedom and Authority in Rousseau." *Philosophy* 53, no. 205 (1978): 353–62.

Leyden, W. von. *Aristotle on Equality and Justice: His Political Argument.* New York: St. Martin's Press, 1985.

Linderman, Gerald F. *Embattled Courage: The Experience of Combat in the American Civil War.* New York: Free Press, 1987.

Littman, Robert J. "The Loves of Alcibiades." *Transactions and Proceedings of the American Philological Association* 101 (1970): 1877–1902.

Lively, Jack. *The Social and Political Thought of Alexis de Tocqueville.* Oxford: Clarendon Press, 1962.

Loraux, Nicole. *The Invention of Athens: The Funeral Oration in the Classical City.* Translated by Alan Sheridan. Cambridge, MA: Harvard University Press, 1986.

Lutz, Mark J. *Socrates' Education to Virtue: Learning the Love of the Noble.* Albany: State University of New York Press, 1998.

MacDowell, D. M. *Aristophanes and Athens.* Oxford: Oxford University Press, 1995.

Macedo, Stephen. "Capitalism, Citizenship and Community." *Social Philosophy and Policy* 6, no. 1 (1988): 113–39.

Macfarlane, Alan. *The Riddle of the Modern World.* New York: St. Martin's Press, 2000.

MacIntyre, Alasdair. *After Virtue.* Notre Dame: University of Notre Dame Press, 1981.

Maguire, Matthew William. *The Conversion of Imagination: From Pascal through Rousseau to Tocqueville.* Cambridge, MA: Harvard University Press, 2006.

Manent, Pierre. *Tocqueville and the Nature of Democracy.* Translated by J. Waggoner. Lanham, MD: Rowman and Littlefield, 1996.

Manesse, Ernst Moritz. "A Thematic Interpretation of Plato's *Apology* and *Crito.*" *Philosophy and Phenomenological Research* 40, no. 3 (1980): 393–400.

Manning, Rita C. "Rousseau's Other Woman: Collette in 'Le devin du village.'" *Hypatia* 16, no. 2 (2001): 27–42.

Mansfield, Harvey C. "Is Manliness a Virtue?" Paper presented in the Bradley Lecture Series, American Enterprise Institute for Public Policy Research, Washington, DC, 1997.

———. *Manliness.* New Haven: Yale University Press, 2006.

Mara, Gerald M. "Rousseau's Two Models of Political Obligation." *Western Political Quarterly* 33, no. 4 (1980): 536–49.

———. *Socrates' Discursive Democracy: Logos and Ergon in Platonic Political Philosophy.* Albany: State University of New York Press, 1997.

Marincola, John. *The Greek Historians.* Oxford: Oxford University Press, 2001.

Marks, Jonathan. "Jean-Jacques Rousseau, Michael Sandel and the Politics of Transparency." *Polity* 33, no. 4 (2001): 619–42.

———. "Rousseau's Discriminating Defense of Compassion." *American Political Science Review* 101, no. 4 (2007): 727–39.

Marshall, Terence E. "Rousseau and Enlightenment." *Political Theory* 6, no. 4 (1978): 421–55.

Marso, Lori J. "The Stories of Citizens: Rousseau, Montesquieu, and de Stael Challenge Enlightenment Reason." *Polity* 30, no. 3 (1998): 435–63.

Marx, Karl, and Friedrich Engels. *The German Ideology: Part One.* Edited by C. J. Arthur. New York: International Publishers, 1970.

———. "Manifesto of the Communist Party." In *The Marx-Engels Reader,* edited by Robert C. Tucker. New York: W. W. Norton, 1978.

Masson, Pierre-Maurice. *La religion de J. J. Rousseau.* 2nd ed. Paris: Hachette et Cie, 1916.

Masters, Roger D. "Ostracism, Voice, and Exit: The Biology of Social Participation." In *Ostracism: A Social and Biological Phenomenon,* edited by Margaret Gruter and Roger D. Masters. New York: Elsevier, 1986.

———. *The Political Philosophy of Rousseau.* Princeton: Princeton University Press, 1968.

Masugi, Ken, ed. *Interpreting Tocqueville's Democracy in America.* Savage, MD: Rowman and Littlefield, 1991.

Mathie, William. "God, Woman, and Morality: The Democratic Family in the New Political Science of Alexis de Tocqueville." *Review of Politics* 57, no. 1 (1995): 7–30.

Matsumoto, Reiji. "Tocqueville on the Family." *Tocqueville Review* 8 (1986/87): 127–52.

Mayer, J. P. *Alexis de Tocqueville.* European Political Thought. New York: Arno Press, 1979.

McAdam, James I. "Rousseau and the Friends of Despotism." *Ethics* 74, no. 1 (1963): 34–43.

McArdle, Ann. "Rousseau on Rousseau: The Individual and Society." *Review of Politics* 39, no. 2 (1977): 250–79.

McNeill, Will. "Care for the Self: Originary Ethics in Heidegger and Foucault." *Philosophy Today* 42, no. 1 (1998): 53–64.

Mehta, J. L. *The Philosophy of Martin Heidegger.* Varanasi: Banaras Hindu University Press, 1967.

Melzer, Arthur M. *The Natural Goodness of Man: On the System of Rousseau's Thought.* Chicago: University of Chicago Press, 1990.

———. "The Origin of the Counter-Enlightenment: Rousseau and the New Religion of Sincerity." *American Political Science Review* 90, no. 2 (1996): 344–60.

———. "Rousseau and the Modern Cult of Sincerity." In *The Legacy of Rousseau,* edited by Clifford Orwin and Nathan Tarcov. Chicago: University of Chicago Press, 1997.

Mettler, Suzanne. "Bringing the State Back into Civic Engagement: Policy Feedback Effects of the G.I. Bill for World War II Veterans." *American Political Science Review* 96, no. 2 (2002): 351–65.

Michell, H. *Sparta.* Cambridge: Cambridge University Press, 1964.

Miller, Fred Dycus. *Nature, Justice, and Rights in Aristotle's Politics.* Oxford: Clarendon Press, 1995.

Miller, William Ian. *The Mystery of Courage.* Cambridge, MA: Harvard University Press, 2000.

Mitchell, Harvey. "Reclaiming the Self: The Pascal-Rousseau Connection." *Journal of the History of Ideas* 54, no. 4 (1993): 637–58.

Mitchell, Joshua. "The Equality of All under the One in Luther and Rousseau: Thoughts on Christianity and Political Theory." *Journal of Religion* 72, no. 3 (1992): 351–65.

———. *The Fragility of Freedom: Tocqueville on Religion, Democracy, and the American Future.* Chicago: University of Chicago Press, 1995.

———. *Not by Reason Alone: Religion, History, and Identity in Early Modern Political Thought.* Chicago: University of Chicago Press, 1993.

Moles, J. L. "Truth and Untruth in Herodotus and Thucydides." In *Lies and Fiction in the Ancient World,* edited by C. Gill and T. P. Wiseman. Exeter: University of Exeter Press, 1993.

Moore, Kenneth. "Eros, Hybris and Mania: Love and Desire in Plato's *Laws* and Beyond." *Polis: The Journal of the Society for Greek Political Thought* 24, no. 1 (2007): 112–33.

Morgenstern, Mira. *Rousseau and the Politics of Ambiguity: Self, Culture, and Society.* University Park: Pennsylvania State University Press, 1996.

Morton, F. L. "Sexual Equality and the Family in Tocqueville's *Democracy in America.*" *Canadian Journal of Political Science* 17, no. 2 (1984): 309–24.

Nass, Michael. "Philosophy Bound: The Fate of the Promethean Socrates." In *Research in Phenomenology.* Pittsburgh: Duquesne University Press, 1995.

Newell, Waller R. *Ruling Passion: The Erotics of Statecraft in Platonic Political Philosophy.* Lanham, MD: Rowman and Littlefield, 2000.

Nichols, James H., Jr. "Introduction to the *Laches.*" In *The Roots of Political Philosophy: Ten Forgotten Socratic Dialogues,* edited by T. L. Pangle. Ithaca: Cornell University Press, 1987.

Nichols, Mary P. "Rousseau's Novel Education in the *Emile.*" *Political Theory* 13, no. 4 (1985): 535–58.

———. "Socrates' Contest with the Poets in Plato's Symposium." *Political Theory* 32, no. 2 (2004): 186–206.

Nietzsche, Friedrich. *Beyond Good and Evil: Prelude to a Philosophy of the Future.* Penguin Classics. New York: Penguin Books, 1990.

———. *The Birth of Tragedy, and The Case of Wagner.* Translated by Walter Kaufmann. New York: Vintage Books, 1967.

———. *On the Genealogy of Morals.* Translated by Walter Kaufmann. New York: Vintage Books, 1967.

———. "On the Uses and Disadvantages of History for Life." In *Untimely Meditations.* Cambridge: Cambridge University Press, 1983.

———. *Thus Spoke Zarathustra: A Book for Everyone and No One.* Translated by R. J. Hollingdale. New York: Penguin Books, 1969.

———. *Twilight of the Idols; and The Anti-Christ.* Baltimore: Penguin Books, 1968.

———. *The Will to Power.* Translated by W. A. Kaufmann and R. J. Hollingdale. New York: Random House, 1967.

Noddings, Nel. *Caring: A Feminine Approach to Ethics and Moral Education.* Berkeley: University of California Press, 1984.

North, Helen. *Sophrosyne: Self-Knowledge and Self-Restraint in Greek Literature.* Ithaca: Cornell University Press, 1966.

Nussbaum, Martha. "Compassion: The Basic Social Emotion." *Social Philosophy and Policy* 13 (1996): 27–58.

Nye, Robert A. "Fencing, the Duel and Republican Manhood in the Third Republic." *Journal of Contemporary History* 25, nos. 2/3 (1990): 365–77.

O'Brien, Michael. "The Unity of *Laches.*" *Yale Classical Studies* 18 (1963): 133–47.

O'Brien, Tim. *If I Die in a Combat Zone, Box Me Up and Ship Me Home.* New York: Delacorte Press, 1973.

Ober, Josiah. *Political Dissent in Democratic Athens: Intellectual Critics of Popular Rule.* Princeton: Princeton University Press, 1998.

Ogrodnick, Margaret. *Instinct and Intimacy: Political Philosophy and Autobiography in Rousseau.* Toronto: University of Toronto Press, 1999.

Okin, Susan Moller. *Justice, Gender and the Family.* New York: Basic Books, 1989.

———. "Rousseau's Natural Woman." *Journal of Politics* 41, no. 2 (1979): 393–416.

Ortega y Gasset, José. *The Revolt of the Masses.* New York: W. W. Norton, 1993.

Orwin, Clifford. *The Humanity of Thucydides.* Princeton: Princeton University Press, 1994.

———. "Moist Eyes—from Rousseau to Clinton." *Public Interest,* no. 128 (Summer 1997): 3–21.

———. "Rousseau and the Discovery of Political Compassion." In *The Legacy of Rousseau*, edited by Clifford Orwin and Nathan Tarcov. Chicago: University of Chicago Press, 1997.

———. "Rousseau's Socratism." *Journal of Politics* 60, no. 1 (1998): 174–87.

Orwin, Clifford, and Nathan Tarcov, eds. *The Legacy of Rousseau*. Chicago: University of Chicago Press, 1997.

Ossewaarde, M. R. R. *Tocqueville's Moral and Political Thought: New Liberalism*. Routledge Studies in Social and Political Thought 41. London: Routledge, 2004.

Paley, John. "Heidegger and the Ethics of Care." *Nursing Philosophy* 1, no. 1 (2000): 64–75.

Pangle, Thomas L. "The Political Defense of Socratic Philosophy: A Study of Xenophon's 'Apology of Socrates to the Jury.'" *Polity* 18, no. 1 (1985): 98–114.

———, ed. *The Roots of Political Philosophy: Ten Forgotten Socratic Dialogues*. Ithaca: Cornell University Press, 1987.

Parel, Anthony, and Ronald C. Keith. *Comparative Political Philosophy: Studies under the Upas Tree*. Newbury Park, CA: Sage Publications, 1992.

Partee, Morriss Henry. "Plato's Banishment of Poetry." *Journal of Aesthetics and Art Criticism* 29, no. 2 (1970): 209–22.

Patterson, Sylvia W. *Rousseau's Emile and Early Children's Literature*. Metuchen, NJ: Scarecrow Press, 1971.

Penner, Terry. "What Laches and Nicias Miss—and Whether Socrates Thinks Courage Merely a Part of Virtue." *Ancient Philosophy* 12, no. 1 (1992): 1–27.

Peristiany, Jean G. *Honour and Shame: The Values of Mediterranean Society*. The Nature of Human Society Series. Chicago: University of Chicago Press, 1966.

Perkinson, Henry J. "Rousseau's Emile: Political Theory and Education." *History of Education Quarterly* 5, no. 2 (1965): 81–96.

Philostratus. *Imagines*. Translated by A. Fairbanks. Loeb Classical Library. London: G. P. Putnam's Sons, 1931.

Picardi, Eva. "Rorty, Sorge, and Truth." *International Journal of Philosophical Studies* 9, no. 3 (2001): 431–39.

Pindar. *The Odes of Pindar*. Translated by G. S. Conway. London: Dent, 1972.

Pitt-Rivers, Julian A. "Honour and Social Status." In *Honour and Shame: The Values of Mediterranean Society*, edited by Jean G. Peristiany. Chicago: University of Chicago Press, 1966.

Plato. *Apology*. In *Four Texts on Socrates: Plato's Euthyphro, Apology, and Crito, and Aristophanes' Clouds*, edited and translated by Thomas G. West and Grace Starry West. Ithaca: Cornell University Press, 1984.

———. *The Collected Dialogues of Plato*. Translated by E. Hamilton and H. Cairns. Bollingen Series, 71. New York: Pantheon Books, 1961.

———. *Crito*. In *Four Texts on Socrates: Plato's Euthyphro, Apology, and Crito, and Aristophanes' Clouds*. Edited and translated by Thomas G. West and Grace Starry West. Ithaca: Cornell University Press, 1984.

———. *Laches*. In *The Roots of Political Philosophy: Ten Forgotten Socratic Dialogues*, edited by T. L. Pangle. Ithaca: Cornell University Press, 1987.

———. *The Laws of Plato*. Translated by T. L. Pangle. Chicago: University of Chicago Press, 1988.

———. *The Republic*. Translated by R. W. Sterling and W. C. Scott. New York: W. W. Norton, 1985.

———. *The Republic, I–V*. Translated by P. Shorey. Loeb Classical Library 5. Cambridge, MA: Harvard University Press, 1930.

———. *The Republic, VI–X*. Translated by P. Shorey. 2 vols. Loeb Classical Library. Cambridge, MA: Harvard University Press, 1935.

———. *The Republic of Plato*. Translated by Allen D. Bloom. 2nd ed. New York: Basic Books, 1991.

Plutarch. *Nicias*. In Plutarch's *Lives*, ed. Charles W. Eliot. Cambridge, MA: Harvard University Press, 1997.

———. *Plutarch on Sparta*. Edited and translated by Richard J. A. Talbert. London: Penguin Books, 1988.

———. *Plutarch's Moralia*. Translated by F. C. Babbitt. 14 vols. Vol. 3. New York: G. P. Putnam's Sons, 1927.

Politzer, Robert L. "A Detail in Rousseau's Thought: Language and Perfectibility." *Modern Language Notes* 72, no. 1 (1957): 42–47.

Pranger, M. B. "Time and Narrative in Augustine's 'Confessions.'" *Journal of Religion* 81, no. 3 (2001): 377–93.

Prentice, William Kelly. "Thermopylae and Artemisium." *Transactions and Proceedings of the American Philological Association* 51 (1920): 5–18.

Pressfield, Steven. *Gates of Fire: An Epic Novel of the Battle of Thermopylae*. Thorndike, ME: G. K. Hall, 1999.

Pritchett, W. Kendrick. *The Liar School of Herodotos*. Amsterdam: J. C. Gieben, 1993.

———. *Studies in Ancient Greek Topography*. Berkeley: University of California Press, 1965.

Raaflaub, Kurt A. "Aristocracy and Freedom of Speech." In *Free Speech in Classical Antiquity*, edited by Ineke Sluiter and Ralph Rosen. Leiden: Brill, 2004.

Rademaker, Adriaan. "'Most citizens are *Euryproktoi* now': (Un)manliness in Aristophanes." In *Andreia: Studies in Manliness and Courage in Classical Antiquity*, edited by Ralph Mark Rosen and Ineke Sluiter. Boston: Brill, 2003.

Rawls, John. *Political Liberalism*. New York: Columbia University Press, 1993.

———. *A Theory of Justice*. Cambridge, MA: Harvard University Press, 1971.

Reisert, Joseph R. "Authenticity, Justice, and Virtue in Taylor and Rousseau." *Polity* 33, no. 2 (2000): 305–30.

———. *Jean-Jacques Rousseau: A Friend of Virtue*. Ithaca: Cornell University Press, 2003.

Rich, John, and Graham Shipley. *War and Society in the Greek World*. London: Routledge, 1993.

Robinson, Fiona. *Globalizing Care*. Boulder, CO: Westview Press, 1999.

Rogers, K. A. "Augustine on Time and Eternity." *American Catholic Philosophical Quarterly* 70, no. 2 (1996): 207–23.

Roisman, Joseph. "The Rhetoric of Courage in the Athenian Orators." In *Andreia: Studies in Manliness and Courage in Classical Antiquity*, edited by Ralph Mark Rosen and Ineke Sluiter. Boston: Brill, 2003.

Rorabaugh, W. J. "The Political Duel in the Early Republic: Burr v. Hamilton." *Journal of the Early Republic* 15, no. 1 (1995): 1–23.

Rosano, Michael J. "Citizenship and Socrates in Plato's 'Crito.'" *Review of Politics* 62, no. 3 (2000): 451–77.

Rosen, Frederick. "Obligation and Friendship in Plato's Crito." *Political Theory* 1, no. 3 (1973): 307–16.

Rosen, Ralph Mark, and Ineke Sluiter, eds. *Andreia: Studies in Manliness and Courage in Classical Antiquity*. Boston: Brill, 2003.

Rousseau, Jean-Jacques. "Discourse on This Question: Which Is the Virtue Most Necessary for a Hero and Which Are the Heroes Who Lacked This Virtue?" In *Social Contract; Discourse on the Virtue Most Necessary for a Hero; Political Fragments; and, Geneva Manuscript*, edited by Roger D. Masters and Christopher Kelly. Hanover, NH: University Press of New England, 1994.

———. *Emile: or, On Education*. New York: Basic Books, 1979.

———. *The First and Second Discourses.* Edited by R. D. Masters and J. R. Masters. New York: St. Martin's Press, 1964.

———. *Politics and the Arts: Letter to M. d'Alembert on the Theatre.* Translated by Allen D. Bloom. Agora Editions. Ithaca: Cornell University Press, 1960.

———. *The Social Contract.* Translated by M. Cranston. New York: Penguin Books, 1968.

Rucker, Darnell. "Plato and the Poets." *Journal of Aesthetics and Art Criticism* 25, no. 2 (1966): 167–70.

Sabin, Margery. "Imagination in Rousseau and Wordsworth." *Comparative Literature* 22, no. 4 (1970): 328–45.

Sabl, Andrew. "Community Organizing as Tocquevillean Politics: The Art, Practices, and Ethos of Association." *American Journal of Political Science* 46, no. 1 (2002): 1–19.

Sage, Michael M. *Warfare in Ancient Greece: A Sourcebook.* New York: Routledge, 1996.

Sahakian, Mabel Lewis, and William S. Sahakian. *Rousseau as Educator.* New York: Twayne, 1974.

Salkever, Stephen G. *Finding the Mean: Theory and Practice in Aristotelian Political Philosophy, Studies in Moral, Political, and Legal Philosophy.* Princeton: Princeton University Press, 1990.

———. "Rousseau and the Concept of Happiness." *Polity* 11, no. 1 (1978): 27–45.

Sandberg, Brian. *Warrior Pursuits: Noble Culture and Civil Conflict in Early Modern France.* Baltimore: Johns Hopkins University Press, 2010.

Sandel, Michael. *Democracy's Discontent.* Cambridge, MA: Harvard University Press, 1996.

———. "Liberalism and Republicanism: Friends or Foes? A Response to Richard Dagger." *Review of Politics* 61, no. 2 (1999): 209–14.

———. "The Procedural Republic and the Unencumbered Self." *Political Theory* 12, no. 1 (1984): 81–96.

Santas, Gerasimos. "Socrates at Work on Virtue and Knowledge in Plato's *Laches.*" *Review of Metaphysics* 22, no. 3 (1969): 433–60.

Sartre, Jean-Paul. *Being and Nothingness.* New York: Citadel Press, 2001.

———. *The Philosophy of Existentialism.* Translated by W. Baskin. New York: Philosophical Library, 1965.

Scanlon, Thomas F. "The Dispersion of Pederasty and the Athletic Revolution in Sixth-Century BC Greece." *Journal of Homosexuality* 39, nos. 3/4 (2005): 63–85.

Schaeffer, Denise. "Reconsidering the Role of Sophie in Rousseau's *Emile.*" *Polity* 30, no. 4 (1998): 607–26.

———. "The Utility of Ink: Rousseau and *Robinson Crusoe.*" *Review of Politics* 64, no. 1 (2001): 121–48.

Schleifer, James T. *The Making of Tocqueville's Democracy in America.* Indianapolis: Liberty Fund, 2000.

Schlesinger, Arthur, Jr. "Individualism and Apathy in Tocqueville's *Democracy.*" In *Reconsidering Tocqueville's Democracy in America*, edited by Abraham S. Eisenstadt. New Brunswick: Rutgers University Press, 1988.

Schmid, Walter. *On Manly Courage: A Study of Plato's Laches.* Carbondale: Southern Illinois University Press, 1992.

Schmitt, Carl. *The Concept of the Political.* Translated by G. Schwab. Chicago: University of Chicago Press, 1996.

Schneider, J., and H. J. Schneider. "Time and Temporality: Modern Understanding of Augustine's Concept of Time." *Philosophisches Jahrbuch* 109, no. 1 (2002): 17–43.

Scorza, Jason A. "The Ambivalence of Political Courage." *Review of Politics* 63, no. 4 (2001): 637–61.

———. "Liberal Citizenship and Civic Friendship." *Political Theory* 32, no. 1 (2004): 85–108.

Scott, John T. "Rousseau and the Melodious Language of Freedom." *Journal of Politics* 59, no. 3 (1997): 803–29.

Sevenhuijsen, Selma. *Citizenship and the Ethics of Care: Feminist Considerations on Justice, Morality, and Politics.* New York: Routledge, 1998.

Sherman, Nancy. "Common Sense and Uncommon Virtue." *Midwest Studies in Philosophy* 13 (1988): 97–114.

Shklar, Judith Nisse. *Men and Citizens: A Study of Rousseau's Social Theory.* London: Cambridge University Press, 1969.

———. "Politics and Friendship." *Proceedings of the American Philosophical Society* 137, no. 2 (1993): 207–12.

———. "Rousseau's Images of Authority." *American Political Science Review* 58, no. 4 (1964): 919–32.

———. "Rousseau's Two Models: Sparta and the Age of Gold." *Political Science Quarterly* 81, no. 1 (1966): 25–51.

Siedentop, Larry. *Tocqueville.* Oxford: Oxford University Press, 1994.

Simon-Ingram, Julia. "Alienation, Individuation, and Enlightenment in Rousseau's Social Theory." *Eighteenth-Century Studies* 24, no. 3 (1991): 315–35.

Sluiter, Ineke, and Ralph Mark Rosen. "General Introduction." In *Andreia: Studies in Manliness and Courage in Classical Antiquity*, edited by Ralph Mark Rosen and Ineke Sluiter. Boston: Brill, 2003.

Smith, Jeffrey A. "Nationalism, Virtue, and the Spirit of Liberty in Rousseau's "'Government of Poland.'" *Review of Politics* 65, no. 3 (2003): 409–37.

———. "Natural Happiness, Sensation, and Infancy in Rousseau's 'Emile.'" *Polity* 35, no. 1 (2002): 93–120.

Smith, Steven B. "Goodness, Nobility and Virtue in Aristotle's Political Science." *Polity* 19, no. 1 (1986): 5–26.

Stauffer, Devin. "Socrates and Callicles: A Reading of Plato's 'Gorgias.'" *Review of Politics* 64 (2002): 627–57.

Stern, Paul. "The Philosophic Importance of Political Life: On the 'Digression' in Plato's *Theatetus*." *American Political Science Review* 96, no. 2 (2002): 275–89.

Stewart, Frank Henderson. *Honor*. Chicago: University of Chicago Press, 1994.

Strauss, Leo. *Natural Right and History*. Charles R. Walgreen Foundation Lectures. Chicago: University of Chicago Press, 1953.

———. *Studies in Platonic Political Philosophy*. Chicago: University of Chicago Press, 1983.

Swanson, Judith A. "Aristotle on Liberality: Its Relation to Justice and Its Public and Private Practice." *Polity* 27, no. 1 (1994): 3–23.

———. "Aristotle on Nature, Human Nature, and Justice: A Consideration of the Natural Functions of Men and Women in the City." In *Action and Contemplation: Studies in the Moral and Political Thought of Aristotle*, edited by Robert C. Bartlett and Susan D. Collins. Albany: State University of New York Press, 1999.

Talbert, Richard J. A. "The Role of the Helots in the Class Struggle at Sparta." *Historia* 38, no. 1 (1989): 22–40.

Tarcov, Nathan. "Rousseau and the Discovery of Political Compassion." In *The Legacy of Rousseau*, edited by Clifford Orwin and Nathan Tarcov. Chicago: University of Chicago Press, 1997.

Taylor, Charles. "The Politics of Recognition." In *New Contexts of Canadian Criticism*, edited by A. J. Heble, Donna Palmateer, and J. R. T. Struthers. Peterborough: Broadview Press, 1997.

———. *Sources of the Self: The Making of the Modern Identity*. Cambridge, MA: Harvard University Press, 1989.

Temmer, Mark J. *Time in Rousseau and Kant.* Geneva: E. Droz, 1958.

Teske, Roland J. *Paradoxes of Time in Saint Augustine.* Aquinas Lecture, 1996. Milwaukee: Marquette University Press, 1996.

Tessitore, Aristide. "Courage and Comedy in Plato's *Laches.*" *Journal of Politics* 56, no. 1 (1994): 115–33.

Thomas, Paul. "Jean-Jacques Rousseau, Sexist?" *Feminist Studies* 17, no. 2 (1991): 195–217.

Thucydides. *The Peloponnesian War.* Translated by Steven Lattimore. Indianapolis: Hackett, 1998.

Tigerstedt, E. N. *The Legend of Sparta in Classical Antiquity.* Stockholm Studies in History of Literature 9, 15, 21. Stockholm: Almqvist and Wiksell, 1965.

Tillich, Paul. *The Courage to Be.* New Haven: Yale University Press, 1980.

Tocqueville, Alexis de. *Democracy in America.* Edited by J. P. Mayer. Translated by George Lawrence. New York: Harper and Row, 1969.

———. *The European Revolution and Correspondence with Gobineau.* Gloucester, MA: P. Smith, 1968.

———. *Journey to America.* Edited by J. P. Mayer. Translated by George Lawrence. Garden City, NY: Anchor Books, 1971.

———. *Memoir, Letters, and Remains.* Boston: Ticknor and Fields, 1862.

———. *Memoir, Letters, and Remains of Alexis de Tocqueville.* Vol. 2. Whitefish, MT: Kessinger, 2007.

———. *The Old Regime and the French Revolution.* Translated by A. S. Kahan. Vol. 1. Chicago: University of Chicago Press, 1998.

———. *Recollections.* New York: Meridian Books, 1959.

———. *Selected Letters on Politics and Society.* Translated by J. Toupin and R. Boesche. Edited by R. Boesche. Berkeley: University of California Press, 1985.

———. *The Tocqueville Reader: A Life in Letters and Politics.* Edited by O. Zunz and A. S. Kahan. Oxford: Blackwell, 2002.

Todorov, Tzvetan. *Frail Happiness: An Essay on Rousseau.* University Park: Pennsylvania State University Press, 2001.

Trachtenberg, Z. M. "Frail Happiness: An Essay on Rousseau." *Ethics* 112, no. 4 (2002): 870–72.

Trilling, Lionel. *Sincerity and Authenticity.* Cambridge, MA: Harvard University Press, 1971.

Tritle, Lawrence A. *From Melos to My Lai: War and Survival.* New York: Routledge, 2000.

Tronto, Joan. "Beyond Gender Difference to a Theory of Care." *Signs* 12, no. 4 (1987): 644–63.

Troup, Calvin L. *Temporality, Eternity, and Wisdom: The Rhetoric of Augustine's Confessions.* Studies in Rhetoric/Communication. Columbia: University of South Carolina Press, 1999.

Turner, Jack. "American Individualism and Structural Injustice: Tocqueville, Gender, and Race." *Polity* 40, no. 2 (2008): 197–215.

Umphrey, Stewart. "On the Theme of Plato's *Laches.*" *Interpretation* 6, no. 1 (1977): 1–11.

Vanpée, Janie. "Reading Lessons in Rousseau's 'Emile ou De l'education.'" *Modern Language Studies* 20, no. 3 (1990): 40–49.

Velásquez, Eduardo A. *Love and Friendship: Rethinking Politics and Affection in Modern Times.* Lanham, MD: Lexington Books, 2002.

Velkley, Richard L. *Freedom and the Human Person.* Washington, DC: Catholic University of America Press, 2007.

Vernant, Jean-Pierre. "Between Shame and Glory: The Identity of the Young Spartan Warrior." In *Mortals and Immortals: Collected Essays,* edited by Froma I. Zeitlin. Princeton: Princeton University Press, 1991.

Villa, D. "Hegel, Tocqueville, and Individualism." *Review of Politics* 67, no. 4 (2005): 659–86.

Viroli, Maurizio. *Jean-Jacques Rousseau and the 'Well-Ordered Society.'* Translated by Derek Hanson. Cambridge: Cambridge University Press, 1988.

Vlastos, Gregory. "Solonian Justice." *Classical Philology* 41, no. 2 (1946): 65–83.

Voegelin, Eric. "The Philosophy of Existence: Plato's 'Gorgias.'" *Review of Politics* 11 (1949): 477–98.

———. *Plato.* Baton Rouge: Louisiana State University Press, 1966.

Wallach, John R. *The Platonic Political Art: A Study of Critical Reason and Democracy.* University Park: Pennsylvania State University Press, 2001.

Walter, Scott. "The 'Flawed Parent': A Reconsideration of Rousseau's *Emile* and Its Significance for Radical Education in the United States." *British Journal of Educational Studies* 44, no. 3 (1996): 260–74.

Warren, Mark E. "What Should We Expect from More Democracy? Radically Democratic Responses to Politics." *Political Theory* 24, no. 2 (1996): 241–70.

Weber, Max. *Gesammelte Aufsätze sur Religionsssoziologie.* Vol. 1. Tübingen: J. C. B. Mohr, 1947.

Wees, Hans van. *Status Warriors: War, Violence, and Society in Homer and History.* Dutch Monographs on Ancient History and Archaeology 9. Amsterdam: J. C. Gieben, 1992.

Weiss, Penny A. "Rousseau, Antifeminism, and Woman's Nature." *Political Theory* 15, no. 1 (1987): 81–98.

———. "Sex, Freedom and Equality in Rousseau's *Emile.*" *Polity* 22, no. 4 (1990): 603–25.

Weiss, Penny, and Anne Harper. "Rousseau's Political Defense of the Sex-Roled Family." *Hypatia* 5, no. 3 (1990): 90–109.

Welch, C. B. *De Tocqueville.* Oxford: Oxford University Press, 2001.

Westermark, Edward. *The Origin and Development of Moral Ideas.* 2nd ed. 2 vols. London: Macmillan, 1912–17.

Wetzel, James. "Time after Augustine." *Religious Studies* 31, no. 3 (1995): 341–57.

Wexler, Victor G. "'Made for Man's Delight': Rousseau as Antifeminist." *American Historical Review* 81, no. 2 (1976): 266–91.

White, Stephen A. *Sovereign Virtue: Aristotle on the Relation between Happiness and Prosperity.* Stanford Series in Philosophy. Stanford: Stanford University Press, 1992.

Willhoite, Fred H., Jr. "Rousseau's Political Religion." *Review of Politics* 27, no. 4 (1965): 501–15.

Williams, Bernard. *Moral Luck: Philosophical Papers, 1973–1980.* Cambridge: Cambridge University Press, 1981.

———. *Shame and Necessity.* Berkeley: University of California Press, 1993.

Williams, Kipling D. *Ostracism: The Power of Silence.* Emotions and Social Behavior. New York: Guilford Press, 2001.

Wilson, Charles McMoran [Lord Moran]. *The Anatomy of Courage.* Boston: Houghton Mifflin, 1967.

Wingrove, Elizabeth Rose. "Interpretive Practices and Political Designs: Reading Authenticity, Integrity, and Reform in Jean-Jacques Rousseau." *Political Theory* 29, no. 1 (2001): 91–111.

———. *Rousseau's Republican Romance.* Princeton: Princeton University Press, 2000.

Winkler, J. J. "Laying Down the Law: The Oversight of Men's Sexual Behavior in Classical Athens." In *Before Sexuality: The Construction of Erotic Experience in the Ancient Greek World,* edited by D. M. Halperin,

J. J. Winkler, and F. I. Zeitlin. Princeton: Princeton University Press, 1990.

Winthrop, Delba. "Aristotle and Theories of Justice." *American Political Science Review* 72, no. 4 (1978): 1201–16.

———. "Race and Freedom in Tocqueville." In *Tocqueville's Political Science: Classic Essays,* edited by Peter Augustine. Lawler. New York: Garland, 1992.

———. "Tocqueville on Federalism." *Publius: The Journal of Federalism* 6, no. 3 (1976): 93–115.

———. "Tocqueville's American Woman and 'the True Conception of Democratic Progress.'" *Political Theory* 14, no. 2 (1986): 239–61.

———. "Tocqueville's 'Old Regime': Political History." *Review of Politics* 43, no. 1 (1981): 88–111.

Wiser, James L. "Philosophy as Political Action: A Reading of the Gorgias." *American Journal of Political Science* 19 (1975): 313–22.

Wohl, Victoria. *Love among the Ruins: The Erotics of Democracy in Classical Athens.* Princeton: Princeton University Press, 2002.

Wolfson, Dorothea Israel. "The Superiority of the American Woman: Tocqueville's Teaching on Women, Marriage and the Family." PhD diss., Cornell University, Ithaca, 1995.

———. "Tocqueville on Liberalism's Liberation of Women." *Perspectives on Political Science* 25, no. 4 (1996): 203–7.

Xenophon. *"Constitution of the Lacedaemonians."* In *Scripta minora,* translated by E. C. Marchant. Cambridge, MA: Harvard University Press, 1925.

———. *Memorabilia.* In *Xenophon,* translated by C. L. Brownson, O. J. Todd, and E. C. Marchant. Loeb Llassical Library. New York: G. P. Putnam's Sons, 1918.

———. *Spartan Society.* In *Plutarch on Sparta.* London: Penguin Books, 1988.

———. *Xenophon's Hellenica.* Translated by C. L. Brownson, O. J. Todd, and E. C. Marchant. 7 vols. Vol. 1. Loeb Classical Library. New York: G. P. Putnam's Sons, 1918.

Yack, Bernard. "Natural Right and Aristotle's Understanding of Justice." *Political Theory* 18, no. 2 (1990): 216–37.

Zerilli, Linda M. G. *Signifying Woman: Culture and Chaos in Rousseau, Burke, and Mill, Contestations.* Ithaca: Cornell University Press, 1994.

Zetterbaum, Marvin. "Tocqueville: Neutrality and the Use of History." *American Political Science Review* 58, no. 3 (1964): 611–21.

———. *Tocqueville and the Problem of Democracy.* Stanford: Stanford University Press, 1967.

Zimmerman, Michael E. *Eclipse of the Self: The Development of Heidegger's Concept of Authenticity.* Athens: Ohio University Press, 1981.

Zuckert, Michael. "Rationalism and Political Responsibility: Just Speech and Just Deed in the 'Clouds' and the 'Apology' of Socrates." *Polity* 17, no. 2 (1984): 271–97.

Index

RICHARD AVRAMENKO

is assistant professor of political science at the University of Wisconsin, Madison. He is the co-editor, with Jon von Heyking, of *Friendship and Politics: Essays in Political Thought* (University of Notre Dame Press, 2008).